Music

Reference Sources in the Humanities Series
James Rettig, Series Editor

Music: A Guide to the Reference Literature. By William S. Brockman.

On the Screen: A Film, Television, and Video Research Guide. By Kim N. Fisher.

Philosophy: A Guide to the Reference Literature. By Hans E. Bynagle.

MUSIC

A GUIDE TO THE REFERENCE LITERATURE

William S. Brockman

LIBRARIES UNLIMITED, INC.
Littleton, Colorado
1987

LIBRARIES UNLIMITED, INC.
P.O. Box 263
Littleton, Colorado 80160-0263

Library of Congress Cataloging-in-Publication Data

Brockman, William S.
Music : a guide to the reference literature / William S. Brockman.
xv, 254 p. 17x25 cm. -- (Reference sources in the humanities series)
Includes indexes.
ISBN 0-87287-526-1
1. Music--Bibliography. 2. Reference books--Music--Bibliography.
I. Title. II. Series.
ML113.B85 1987
016.78--dc19 87-26462
CIP
MN

Libraries Unlimited books are bound with Type II nonwoven material that meets and exceeds National Association of State Textbook Administrators' Type II nonwoven material specifications Class A through E.

Contents

Part 3
BIBLIOGRAPHIES OF MUSIC LITERATURE

Part 4
BIBLIOGRAPHIES OF MUSIC

Part 5
DISCOGRAPHIES

Part 6
SUPPLEMENTAL SOURCES

Abbreviations

annot., annotated or annotation
assoc., associate, associated, or association
Aufl., Auflage (edition)
CD, compact disc
col., color
coll., collected or collection
comp(s)., compiler(s)
corr., corrected
discog., discography or discographies
ed(s)., editor(s), editorial, or edition
enl., enlarged
EP, extended-play record
LP, long-playing record
n.d., no date
n.p., no place; no publisher
n.s., new series
pa., paper
prelim., preliminary
repr., reprint, reprints, or reprinted
rev., revised or revision
rpm, revolutions per minute
supp., supplement
trans., translated or translator

Preface

Every discipline continuously renews its reference literature to record new theories, revised theses, discoveries, deaths, and developments in the application of theory. New editions of standard works and new titles appear from time to time, while serials bibliographies index each year's outpouring of journal articles, monographs, and festschriften. This series, Reference Sources in the Humanities, takes as its purpose the identification, description, and organization of the reference literature of the humanities disciplines. The volumes in this series, emphasizing the Anglo-American reference literature of recent decades, are intended to serve the needs of undergraduates, graduate students, professors exploring adjunct disciplines, librarians building and using reference collections, and intellectually curious adults interested in systematic, self-guided study of the humanities.

Like bibliographic guides to the literature of any discipline, guides in this series are intended to serve various users in various ways. Students being initiated into the ways of a discipline can use these guides to learn the structure of the discipline's secondary literature, to find sources which will enable them to find definitions of specialized terms, to identify significant historical figures, to gain an overview of a topic, etc. Specialists may use them to refresh their memories about once familiar sources and to advise their students on approaches to problems. Librarians will use them to build and evaluate reference collections, and to answer patron questions.

The volumes in the Reference Sources in the Humanities series are designed to serve all of these users and purposes. Each volume in the series is organized principally by reference genre, including types specific to each discipline. This will facilitate their efficient use by reference librarians, a group trained to think in terms of reference genre (e.g., encyclopedias, dictionaries, indexes and abstracts, biographical directories, bibliographies, etc.) within subject categories, when they seek a particular type of reference work in one of the humanities disciplines. Because no discipline's reference literature can completely convey its most recent discoveries, each volume also includes information on key journals and associations and research centers, the sources from which much of any discipline's new knowledge emanates and by means of which that knowledge is disseminated. While each of these guides describes the reference literature of its discipline as that literature presently exists, each also contributes to that literature's renewal and growth.

James Rettig
Series Editor

Introduction

The literature of music reflects the multifarious and ephemeral nature of music itself. Music is an art, a business, an occupation, a field of study, an inspiration to worship, and a psychological tool. Its essence can be recorded in staff notation, in other forms of notation, on a piano roll, in tablature for specific instruments, in magnetic form to be read by a computer, or as a sound recording in the form of a tape, LP, or CD. These written and aural records of music are its primary literature. The secondary literature of music responds to live music and to its primary literature in the form of reviews, fan magazines, scholarly articles, program notes, pedagogical works, dissertations, biographies, and histories.

The reference literature of music is notably diverse because it must address fundamentally dissimilar aspects of music: performance and performers, written music, recordings, and secondary literature. Like other disciplines, music has its own dictionaries, encyclopedias, indexes, and bibliographies of its written literature, but it also requires unique forms of reference tools—discographies, bibliographies of music, indexes to thematic incipits—which meet its own particular demands. Reference works in music, as in other disciplines, compile and digest current knowledge; their point of view is essentially retrospective. Yet, by defining the nature of the field, they establish a foundation and a direction for future scholarship. Such monumental reference works as Eitner's *Biographische-bibliographisches Quellen-Lexikon* (see entry 414) and *Die Musik in Geschichte und Gegenwart* (see entry 19) have not only established themselves as indispensable, but have also encouraged a conception of the primacy of European art music that has predominated through the nineteenth and twentieth centuries.

The New Grove Dictionary of Music and Musicians (see entry 20) and newer kinds of reference works, notably discographies, exemplify a broadened scholarly conception of music, and reflect a growing interest in the study and performance of a variety of musics. Musicology has embraced sociology in the study of popular music as a telling barometer of popular culture. The Library of Congress regularly sponsors concerts of folk and ethnic music. The sitar and instruments of the gamelan orchestra are featured in performances of traditional non-Western music and employed in contemporary compositions. Works composed with the aid of a computer are questioning our assumptions about the relationship between composer and performer.

Concurrent with a broadened interest in all forms of music has been an increased scholarly focus on early (pre-1800) music. *Early Music* (see entry 591) and *Early Music History* (see entry 592), two fine journals which began publication in 1973 and 1981, respectively, exemplify this interest. The most important bibliographical development for early music has been the Répertoire international des sources musicales, or International Inventory of Musical Sources, commonly referred to as RISM. The project began in the 1950s as a joint venture of the International Association of Music Libraries and the International Musicological Society. Its purpose is to identify the locations in libraries throughout the world of early printed and manuscript sources of music and of early writings about music. A number of alphanumerically designated series and subseries of bibliographies and directories have been published under the auspices of RISM.

A growing appreciation for American music has been a particularly important factor in the development of new reference works. In looking to the past, Sonneck's *Bibliography of Early Secular American Music* of 1905 (see entry 433) foreshadowed the publication, beginning in 1983, of the periodical *American Music* (see entry 562), and of the publication in 1986 of *The New Grove Dictionary of American Music* (see entry 65). These and other new resources have given a scholarly validity to the hymns, spirituals, blues, rags, musicals, folk songs, jazz compositions, and rock tunes which have been the fruits of our culture and in which so many Americans have participated.

The development of new reference works in music in the last fifteen years demands an up-to-date survey. The last single-volume comprehensive survey of the reference literature of music was the 1974 edition of Duckles's *Music Reference and Research Materials* (see entry 5). The first volume of Marco's *Information on Music*, published in 1975 (see entry 9), is more restricted in scope, and volumes 2 and 3 are devoted to particular geographical regions. The bibliography of reference works in Pruett and Slavens's 1985 work, *Research Guide to Musicology* (see entry 12), is highly selective.

The present guide does not attempt to compete with the international and retrospective scopes of Duckles and Marco. It is offered as a summary guide to the important current and retrospective sources of information on music, and it emphasizes, but is not restricted to, works in English. It is directed to an audience of college and graduate students, researchers, and librarians. It includes works published not only in the United States but also Canada, Great Britain, West Germany, France, Italy, Denmark, Austria, Switzerland, the Netherlands, and Australia.

The guide is necessarily selective, yet it gives an overview of the most important materials for research. It includes those reference works of national or international significance which are most useful and successful in their own design and in comparison with similar works. Reference works chosen for inclusion gather factual data about music or musicians; provide significant historical overviews; or bibliographically point the way to other resources. Greater attention has been paid to works published during the last fifteen years which were unavailable to Duckles or to Marco, but similar criteria have been applied to the selection of older works. In areas in which the quantity of reference works outruns the quality, such as collective biographies of rock musicians or guides to Broadway show tunes, the guide has omitted works which take an adulatory fan's-eye-view in favor of those few which offer critical perspective.

Language dictionaries, general encyclopedias, and national bibliographies are critical to research in music. However, the breadth of the field of music has necessitated the guide's strict omission of any works which extend beyond the field. Mixter's *General Bibliography for Music Research* (see entry 10) and Marco's *Information on Music* examine some of these more general works.

In addition to reference works, the guide includes current periodicals and national and international associations and research institutions. Current periodicals and organizations are sources of information for ongoing research and for developments which are too recent to be found in reference works. Periodicals, particularly *Notes* (see entry 639), include as articles and regular features such reference tools as directories, definitions of terms, and bibliographies. These have not been included as fully annotated entries, but are selectively cited in annotations and chapter introductions.

Thematic catalogs and bibliographies devoted to individual composers or performers retain their value (unless superseded) long after publication. However, there are simply too many of these to be included comprehensively. As the intention of the guide is to present an overview of the literature, a representative selection of such works which are numbers within series or which were published within the last few years has been included. Other bibliographies of reference works devoted to individuals have been mentioned in appropriate annotations and chapter introductions.

The cutoff date for entries cannot be defined precisely. Relevant titles were collected through April 1987, but some works known to have been published since late 1986 were not available. All items, except those identified as forthcoming, have been examined by the author. Facsimile reprints, mentioned in order to establish the availability of works otherwise out of print, were not always examined.

The arrangement of the guide parallels an approach to research which proceeds from the general to the specific and from the retrospective to the current. Chapters gather reference works by function. Periodicals and organizations are listed in separate chapters. By means of the table of contents and introductions to chapters, users can survey works which have a similar purpose.

The indexes offer access by entry number to specific works. Titles of works given full annotations, works or series cited within entries, and distinctive titles (other than simply bulletin or newsletter) of publications of organizations all appear in the index. Names of authors, editors, translators, and compilers are all indexed, whether or not they appear as main entries. The subject index covers all entries.

Part 1 covers general reference sources. Chapter 1 examines the broadest of information sources, guides to the literature. By mapping research strategies, these works serve a didactic as well as a bibliographic purpose.

In chapters 2 through 8 are the kinds of works which Marco's *Information on Music* terms "direct information sources"—works which in themselves are compendia of information. These chapters proceed from a survey of comprehensive encyclopedias and general information sources in chapter 2 to more specialized works in succeeding chapters and finally to the directories in chapter 8 which geographically locate individuals and institutions.

One step removed from direct information sources are bibliographies, which enumerate works in a particular subject area, of a particular character, or within a particular library collection. Bibliographies in music can be broadly grouped into three types: lists of music, of music literature, and of both. Part 2 covers general bibliographic sources. Chapters 9, 10, and 11 examine varieties of bibliographies which include, for the most part, both music and music literature. These are sources (or series, in the case of works listed in chapter 10) which are likely to be of use to most researchers. Part 3 presents bibliographies of music literature. Chapters 12, 13, and 14 separate bibliographies of music literature into three groups: those devoted to specific forms of music literature, those that identify information resources pertaining to individuals, and those that, for the most part, emphasize a particular subject. Part 4—chapters 15, 16, and 17—examines bibliographies of music: sources that cover primarily eighteenth-century and older works, those that list more current vocal works, and those that list newer music and performing editions.

In their form of presentation, discographies are allied to bibliographies. Part 5—chapters 18 and 19—examines works that list recordings on a retrospective and ongoing basis. Part 6 supplements the chapters covering reference works. Chapters 20 and 21 are devoted to periodicals and organizations; the organizations in chapter 21 are subdivided by function into six groups.

Within chapters, entries are generally listed in alphabetical order by author or title (or, in the final chapter, by title of organization). In some instances the alphabetical sequence has been modified to accommodate a numbered series or another more meaningful arrangement.

Works in nonprint formats discussed in the guide include several indexes and bibliographies in microfiche, a database for recorded works (MUSICAT, entry 554), and *RILM Abstracts* (see entry 327), which is available both in printed and online versions. RILM is the only widely available database devoted to music. The *Directory of Computer Assisted Research in Musicology* (see entry 162) lists many more specialized projects of this nature. Entries for nonprint titles have been assigned to chapters according to function and integrated with other entries for titles in printed form.

Entries for monographic titles cite the most recent editions in preference to the first edition, although the date of the first edition is generally mentioned in the annotation. Multiple publishers given in the citations are copublishers, not distributors. The form of the bibliographic citation provides additional information about the character of each work by mentioning special features such as bibliographies, discographies, illustrations, indexes, and notated music. Library of Congress card numbers (including those for foreign publications if the Library of Congress has assigned them), International Standard Book Numbers, International Standard Serial Numbers, and citations to facsimile reprints have been included when available. Pagination has been included solely to give an idea of the size of a work. Only numbered pages have been indicated; unnumbered pages, unless they form a substantial portion of a work, have not been included. The introduction to chapter 20, which features current periodicals, explains particular points brought out in the bibliographic citations within that section.

Annotations are descriptive, evaluative, and comparative. They indicate what the work offers a researcher and how it is organized. Evaluative comments note exceptionally well-presented or useful features, or warn users of possible pitfalls. References to other works are given in order to suggest alternate or more effective sources for similar information, or to illustrate a point by comparison.

The guide could not have been compiled without the assistance of many individuals and institutions. Drew University provided me with time for research during a sabbatical leave and during many other odd hours; with technical assistance through the loan of a microcomputer; with administrative support in the form of postage, telephone use, and online searching of the DIALOG and OCLC databases; and of course, with a rich collection which has continually offered surprises. Research was performed primarily at the Blanche and Irving Laurie Music Library at the Douglass Library of Rutgers University, and at the Music Division and the Rodgers and Hammerstein Archives of Recorded Sound of the New York Public Library. Other libraries whose collections were valuable to my research were the Talbott Library of Westminster Choir College, the Firestone Library of Princeton University, the Institute of Jazz Studies of Rutgers University, the Sprague Library of Montclair State College, and the Morris County Free Library. I thank the staffs of these libraries for their assistance.

Lydia Ledeen, Professor of Music at Drew University, read parts of the manuscript and provided helpful comments. For specific advice and suggestions I would like to thank Alice Copeland, Lessie Culmer-Nier, Bob Kenselaar, Evelyn Meyer, Phil Schaap, Greg Strong, Roger Tarman, and Nancy Wicklund. Josie Cook, Julia Craven, Stacey Mosesman, and Audrey Rigsbee were particularly helpful in getting things done. My thanks extend also to the publishers and organizations who so willingly responded to my requests for information and publications. I owe my editor, Jim Rettig, special appreciation for his continued encouragement and always valuable and clear-headed suggestions. Finally, I thank Annie Copeland for her own encouragement, help in verifying a multitude of facts, diligent proofreading, and tolerance of my sometimes obsessive devotion to the writing of this work.

Part 1
GENERAL REFERENCE SOURCES

1

Guides to the Literature

These works introduce researchers to the literature of music by means of an overview or interpretation of resources. They are distinguished from subject bibliographies by their breadth of scope and their inclusion of various forms of literature, particularly of reference works. Some, such as Duckles's *Music Reference and Research Materials* (see entry 5), are primarily enumerative in format; others, such as Watanabe's *Introduction to Music Research* (see entry 14), are more instructional. In addition to general works, the chapter includes works of this nature which cover specific types of music.

1. **A Basic Music Library: Essential Scores and Books**. 2d ed. Compiled by the Music Library Association Committee on Basic Music Collection under the direction of Pauline S. Bayne. Edited by Robert Michael Fling. Chicago: American Library Association, 1983. xii, 357p. LC 83-2768. ISBN 0-8389-0375-4pa.

This selection guide for small and medium-sized libraries aims to suggest the best, least expensive, and most useful score anthologies, study scores, performing editions, vocal scores, instrumental methods and studies, and works of music literature. The well-organized chapters and extensive indexing offer a variety of approaches to students as well as to librarians. The evaluations of published music are particularly valuable to a user who lacks the background to choose one edition over another. The selection of music literature covers not only reference works but individual biographies, periodical titles, and works on theory and history. Each of the 2,262 numbered entries gives full bibliographical information including ISBN, ISSN, or publisher's number for scores, and the price.

2. Booth, Mark W. **American Popular Music: A Reference Guide**. Westport, Conn.: Greenwood Press, 1983. xvi, 212p. bibliog. index. (American Popular Culture Series). LC 82-21062. ISBN 0-313-21305-4.

This is a particularly literate and informed guide to the literature of all facets of American popular music from its eighteenth-century origins to twentieth-century dance band music, tin pan alley songs, blues, ragtime, jazz, country, folk, and rock. Booth devotes a substantial bibliographic essay to each of these forms, discussing and comparing bibliographies and discographies, general reference works, collective and individual biographies, and history and commentary. A bibliography with complete citations follows each chapter. Appendixes list significant dates in American popular music and addresses of selected prominent music reference collections. This updates and provides an alternate approach to David Horn's *Literature of American Music* (see entry 342).

3. Davies, J. H. **Musicalia: Sources of Information in Music**. 2d ed., rev. and enl. Oxford, England: Pergamon Press, 1969. 184p. LC 76-77013.

Davies's guide stands out for its attention to the details other guides ignore—gypsy music, national anthems, and spurious compositions, for instance—and for its mingling of significant periodical articles with its discussions of books. Each chapter addresses a specific audience: the orchestral and band conductor, the singer, the music librarian, and others. A user could profitably choose an appropriate chapter to survey the literature from a particular viewpoint, or use the index to locate specific titles, authors, or subjects. Appendixes, which should be used with an eye to the date of their compilation, list locations of named music collections in Britain, music publishers and publishers' organizations, and performing rights organizations.

4. Druesedow, John E., Jr. **Library Research Guide to Music: Illustrated Search Strategy and Sources**. Ann Arbor, Mich.: Pierian Press, 1982. x, 86p. illus. bibliog. index. (Library Research Guides Series, No. 6). LC 81-86634. ISBN 0-87650-138-2pa.

Using a sample topic—"Debussy and Stravinsky: Relationship and Influences"—this guide for undergraduates follows the several stages of research from choosing and refining a topic, to using a variety of resources, to evaluating works. Druesedow writes in an informal and inviting manner, attempting to instill confidence in using foreign languages while demonstrating the use of particular reference works. Text alternates with reproductions of sample entries from several dozen works. The author cites general sources and sources specific to music. An appendix gives a brief quiz on basic library skills essential to library research. The guide concludes with a classified outline of "Basic Reference Sources for Courses in Music."

5. Duckles, Vincent. **Music Reference and Research Materials: An Annotated Bibliography**. 3d ed. New York: Free Press; London: Collier Macmillan, 1974. xvi, 526p. index. LC 73-10697. ISBN 0-02-907700-1.

Extensive international coverage of the literature (despite the author's modest claims to the contrary) combined with a well-organized arrangement, cogent annotations, and informed introductory material make this a most essential guide for librarians and graduate students. Duckles's bibliographical seine includes current works and historical works (published as far back as the eighteenth century) in English and a number of European languages, and extends to the literatures of national and ethnic musical forms throughout the world. The 1,922 entries cover not only reference works, but also periodical articles, histories, and surveys, making this a true guide to the literature. Duckles features listings by country of national biographical dictionaries and catalogs of music libraries; listings by composer's name of bibliographies of music and music literature; citations to book reviews for many entries; detailed bibliographic information, including citations to reprints, for entries; and author, subject, and title indexes.

6. Floyd, Samuel A., Jr., and Marsha J. Reisser. **Black Music in the United States: An Annotated Bibliography of Selected Reference and Research Materials**. Millwood, N.Y.: Kraus International, 1983. xv, 234p. index. LC 82-49044. ISBN 0-527-30164-7.

This selective guide for researchers lists 388 books, repositories, and archives that are resources for the study of black music in the United States. An appendix includes twenty-three general reference works which are "indispensable to basic research." The bibliography is organized by form into eighteen sections. Its apt selection of titles, all in English, is not confined to reference works, but includes histories, pedagogical works, and iconographies. Annotations extend to between one and two hundred words and cite reviews. A listing by state of libraries and private collections throughout the United States describes the holdings of each, and notes publications, access, and names of staff in addition to addresses and telephone numbers. Indexes list titles, personal names, and subjects.

7. Kennington, Donald, and Danny L. Read. **The Literature of Jazz: A Critical Guide**. 2d ed., rev. Chicago: American Library Association, 1980. xi, 236p. bibliog. index. LC 80-19837. ISBN 0-8389-0313-4pa.

Publication of this second edition following the first edition of 1971 demonstrates both the growth of the literature of jazz and the need for such a guide. Although it purports to cover "all significant material published in English up to the end of 1979," including books, theses and dissertations, and periodical titles, some citations obviously have not been updated since the first edition. Chapters organize works by topic. Each chapter opens with an essay comparing individual works. A bibliography, including brief annotations for works not discussed in the essay, follows. A name index covers both authors and others listed in the bibliographies or mentioned in the text. The guide is important to any level of research in jazz: it points out key works for those new to the field, and suggests alternate titles to researchers needing a more thorough approach.

8. Marco, Guy A. **Opera: A Research and Information Guide**. New York: Garland, 1984. xvii, 373p. index. (Garland Reference Library of the Humanities, Vol. 468). LC 83-49312. ISBN 0-8240-8999-5.

In chapters organizing citations by type of reference work or by subject, this annotated bibliography presents a knowledgeable overview of the literature. Marco uses the term "information" broadly to justify the inclusion of general reference works as well as works specifically dealing with opera. The guide includes citations in twelve or more European languages to articles as well as to books. Marco's focus is narrow enough to allow him to delve into details such as the literature of opera houses and into studies of individual composers and countries. Annotations are substantial: Marco thoroughly evaluates the items he includes, but tends to allot too much space to his own opinions. The 704 numbered citations contain references to many other works; the author/title and subject indexes include all. The guide includes a checklist of opera composers with 1,051 of their major works, together with a title index to the checklist. Farkas's *Opera and Concert Singers* (see entry 379) is a companion volume.

9. Marco, Guy A. **Information on Music: A Handbook of Reference Sources in European Languages**. Littleton, Colo.: Libraries Unlimited, 1975-84. 3v. LC 74-32132.

Volume I: Basic and Universal Sources. Guy A. Marco, with Sharon Paugh Ferris. 1975. xvi, 164p. index. ISBN 0-87287-096-0.

Volume II: The Americas. Guy A. Marco, Ann M. Garfield, and Sharon Paugh Ferris. 1977. 296p. index. ISBN 0-87287-141-X.

Volume III: Europe. Guy A. Marco, with Sharon Paugh Ferris and Ann G. Olszewski. 1984. xviii, 519p. index. ISBN 0-87287-401-X.

Originally projected for six volumes, then for eight, Marco's handbook now has been wrapped up in three volumes (though he writes, "we hope to issue supplements"). His criteria of "excellence, convenience, and uniqueness" translate into an annotated listing of some thirty-seven hundred books, articles, journals, dissertations, and a handful of unpublished works, about twice the number Duckles (see entry 5) includes. Marco's coverage transcends that of Duckles with the inclusion of general reference works, such as encyclopedias and language dictionaries, and many more works relating to specific countries. Sequential publishing of the volumes has complicated their arrangement. Volume 2 updates volume 1 in a prefatory section and lists revisions to volume 1 in an appendix. Volume 3 updates volume 2 in a prefatory section and lists revisions to volumes 1 and 2 in an appendix. Volume 2 provides author/title and subject indexes to itself and to volume 1; volume 3 indexes only itself. The subject indexes use Library of Congress terminology with all its limitations—for instance, pages of headings needlessly subdivide the word "music." Duckles's work, with its careful organization, selection, and annotation, is preferable to volume 1. Volumes 2 and 3, which include about 85 percent of the entries in the three volumes and offer more concise annotations and a better sense of scope than does volume 1, are detailed and useful guides to the literature of music of individual countries in North and South America, Europe, and the Soviet republics.

10. Mixter, Keith E. **General Bibliography for Music Research**. 2d ed. Detroit: Information Coordinators, 1975. 135p. (Detroit Studies in Music Bibliography, No. 33). LC 72-174731. ISBN 0-911772-75-8.

This is not a guide to books about music; it is a guide to general bibliographies, dictionaries, encyclopedias, indexes, union lists, and catalogs which a thorough researcher will need to consult in addition to reference works specific to music. The author's bibliographic essays try to extract features of these general works that would be of particular interest to musicians. A chapter on indexes and editions of vocal texts lists collections and bibliographies of lyrics, ballads, verses, and works for the theater in Latin, English, German, French, Italian, and Spanish.

11. Nettl, Bruno. **Reference Materials in Ethnomusicology: A Bibliographic Essay**. 2d ed., rev. Detroit: Information Coordinators, 1967. xv, 40p. (Detroit Studies in Music Bibliography, No. 1). LC 68-481. ISBN 0-911772-21-9pa.

Nettl restricts his definition of ethnomusicology to "the music of non-literate or primitive cultures and of the oriental high cultures." The text discusses surveys and compendia covering specific techniques of research, musical elements, and the variety of approaches to ethnomusicology. A list of cited publications follows the text. Though dated, the volume sets out basic definitions and identifies important standard works.

12. Pruett, James W., and Thomas P. Slavens. **Research Guide to Musicology**. Chicago: American Library Association, 1985. ix, 175p. bibliog. index. (Sources of Information in the Humanities, No. 4). LC 84-24379. ISBN 0-8389-0331-2.

Pruett, past president of the Music Library Association and former editor of *Notes* (see entry 639), is responsible for the first half's "Introduction to Research in Music." His fourteen chapters on the approaches of musicology and the scholarship of the periods of music history are sophisticated and informative essays with references in the text to substantial bibliographies following each chapter. Slavens, the series editor, is responsible for the less useful annotated bibliography of about 150 reference works and scholarly music periodicals. Users should be cautious of omissions and incomplete information in this section, which cites Gold's *Jazz Lexicon* rather than his newer *Jazz Talk*, cites the second two volumes of Feather's *Encyclopedias of Jazz* without mentioning the first, and cites a single year of the *Bibliographic Guide to Music* with no indication that it is published annually. The subject index belies its computer origin with the isolated entry for "1970s" (why not 1980s or 320 B.C.?) preceding the alphabetical sequence.

13. Taylor, Paul. **Popular Music since 1955: A Critical Guide to the Literature**. New York: Mansell, 1985. xvi, 533p. bibliog. indexes. LC 84-17080. ISBN 0-7201-1727-5.

Through citations to sixteen hundred monographs and two hundred periodicals published in English between 1955 and 1982, Taylor documents and makes sense out of a literature which is largely ephemeral. His implied definition of "popular" is "rock," and he intends that this guide complement *The Literature of Jazz: A Critical Guide* (see entry 7).

An introductory essay precedes each chapter's citations. Citations themselves give full bibliographic descriptions, including enumerating successive editions. A descriptive and evaluative annotation accompanies each entry. The longest chapter (about half the length of the book) lists works on individual artists and groups, including eighty books on Elvis Presley alone. A glossary defining the argot of rock, and author, title, and well-detailed subject indexes help to make this a versatile source of information.

14. Watanabe, Ruth T. **Introduction to Music Research**. Englewood Cliffs, N.J.: Prentice-Hall, 1967. viii, 237p. index. LC 67-20360. ISBN 0-13-489641-6.

This has been a prominent guide to music research for years; publication of the *Research Guide to Musicology* (see entry 12) does not diminish its usefulness in introducing graduate students to the practical aspects of research. The author presents the research process in three discrete sections. "Library Orientation" explains the mechanics of library catalogs and music collections, though the development of online catalogs and bibliographic utilities over the last twenty years has outdated the chapter on catalog card format. "The Research Paper" guides a student from selection of a topic through the bibliography of books, periodicals, and music into organization of the paper itself. The author suggests means of evaluating sources, and cites a wide range of research tools in the text and in the bibliographies appended to each chapter. The "Survey of Research Materials" explains the variety and use of forms of reference works and describes a number of contemporary music periodicals. Indexes of names, titles, and subjects speak for the book's versatility. The forte of this introduction is its conceptual approach, which complements the bibliographical approach.

2

Comprehensive Encyclopedias and General Information Sources

This chapter surveys works whose intention is to encompass broadly the field of music. It includes a multivolume set which calls itself a dictionary (*The New Grove Dictionary of Music and Musicians*, entry 20) and a single-volume work which calls itself an encyclopedia (*The New College Encyclopedia of Music*, entry 26). These works have in common the attempt to be encyclopedic—to summarize knowledge about music and musicians. Both the concise and the expansive forms have a value which depends on a researcher's needs. All include subject and biographical entries. Included in this chapter are the most prominent works in English and two German works (*MGG*, entry 19 and *Riemann*, entry 24) whose scope is worldwide.

15. Ammer, Christine. **The Harper Dictionary of Music**. 2d ed. New York: Harper & Row, 1986. 480p. illus. music. LC 85-45612. ISBN 0-06-181020-7.

This is a relatively nontechnical but reliable source distinguished by a good number of black-and-white illustrations and musical examples. It includes entries for terms, musical forms, instruments, and composers. Lists of important operas, operettas, Renaissance composers, concertos, and other items give the student unfamiliar with music a sense of scope. The second edition (1st ed. 1972) compares favorably with *The New College Encyclopedia of Music* (see entry 26), but is more up-to-date.

16. Blom, Eric, comp. **Everyman's Dictionary of Music**. 5th ed. Revised by Sir Jack Westrup with the collaboration of John Caldwell, Edward Olleson, and R. J. Beck. London: J. M. Dent & Sons, 1974. xiii, 793p. music. LC 77-360883. ISBN 0-460-02151-6.

Of the single volume reference works in music, this takes the most abbreviated form, yet the quantity and range of its entries recommend it as an important work. It differs from *The Oxford Dictionary* (see entry 18), for instance, not only in its shorter entries, but also in its inclusion of more musical examples and of birth and death dates, rather than merely years, for entries for persons. Such entries include composers, performers, and writers on music, and restrict themselves to biographical facts but include selected work lists. Other entries cover theoretical terms, individual works, or bring together lists such as "National Anthems," and "Quotations," listing works which have taken passages from other works.

17. Isaacs, Alan, and Elizabeth Martin, ed. **Dictionary of Music**. New York: Facts on File, 1983. 425p. illus. music. LC 82-12067. ISBN 0-87196-752-9.

"This volume is designed as a personal handbook for the musician, music student, and music lover: it will not provide critical opinion or detailed analysis of composers and their works," warns the preface. The dictionary's entries cover composers, performers, works, instruments, orchestras, and terms in brief but reliable form. It includes more biographies of contemporary figures than does *The New College Encyclopedia* (see entry 26), but devotes less space to terminology, and uses fewer notated examples in its definitions. The appendix shows, in notated form, names of notes and rests in English and American usage, clefs, keys and key signatures, and time signatures.

18. Kennedy, Michael. **The Oxford Dictionary of Music**. rev. and enl. ed. New York: Oxford University Press, 1985. xiv, 810p. music. LC 84-22803. ISBN 0-19-311333-3.

The dictionary, a revised edition of *The Concise Oxford Dictionary of Music* (3d ed. 1980), is a versatile single volume source which offers much more than its title implies. Entries (the dust jacket claims a total of eleven thousand) include composers, performers, writers, librettists, choreographers, instruments, schools, concert halls, compositions, songs (even "Beer Barrel Polka"), and terms. Biographical entries give factual summations of the subject's life and work, generally in one or two paragraphs. In the case of major composers, these extend to a page or two and include an evaluation of their principal achievements along with substantial (though not complete) work lists giving dates of composition and first performance. Entries for individual works include those with distinctive titles, usually with the title in the original language, and give a brief description and the circumstances of the first performance. A star before a term signifies a cross-reference. Kennedy livens his compressed and abbreviated style with occasional anecdotes. The dictionary's breadth, particulary in the area of non-English terminology, makes it a first choice for short factual information.

19. **Die Musik in Geschichte und Gegenwart: allgemeine Enzyklopädie der Musik**. Unter Mitarbeit zahlreicher Musikforscher des In- und Auslandes herausgegeben von Friedrich Blume; **Register**, zusammengestelt und bearbeitet von Elisabeth und Harald Heckmann unter Mitwirkung von Thomas Zimmer. Kassel, West Germany: Bärenreiter-Verlag, 1949-86. 17v. illus. music. bibliog. index. LC 50-3662. ISBN 3-7618-0641-8.

MGG initiated a truly encyclopedic view of music in its transcendence of the national emphases of previous encyclopedias. Its publication, from the initial volume in 1949 to the completion of the *Register* (index) in 1986, paralleled the development of postwar Germany. Its worldwide outlook, which resulted in part from the signed contributions of over thirteen hundred authors from more than forty countries, was a necessary precursor to that of *The New Grove* (see entry 20).

While the latter work was published more recently and its language is more amenable to the needs of English-speaking researchers, it by no means supercedes *MGG*. Styles and overall appearance differ greatly; the nonbiographical articles in *The New Grove* tend to be short and specific, while *MGG* gives extended entries covering broad concepts. The full-page color and black-and-white plates in *MGG* offer a unique enough resource to have inspired at least one separately published index (Terence Ford, "Index to the Facsimiles of Polyphonic Music before 1600 Published in *Die Musik in Geschichte und Gegenwart*," *Notes* 39 [December 1982]: 283-315). *MGG* distinguishes itself with the bibliographies appended to articles, although the plethora of abbreviations and the cramped typeface in these can be frustrating.

Composers comprise half the entries. These follow a standard format: a biography, followed by a work list, an interpretive essay on the subject's work, and a list of references. The work lists are, in many cases, exhaustive, and note publishers and first performances. Other entries cover cities, countries, and geographical areas throughout the world; musical terminology; genres and periods (including four substantial surveys by the editor, Friedrich Blume: "Renaissance," "Barock," "Klassik," and "Romantik"); individuals, including writers and performers; organizations; and acoustics. Each of the first fourteen volumes includes a list of articles and their authors, a list of authors and their articles, and lists of illustrations and plates.

Volumes 15 and 16 form an alphabetical supplement to the previous fourteen volumes, and include errata (also in volumes 3, 7, and 10); the closings of entries for subjects who have died; entries for contemporary persons who had not been included originally (notably, Duke Ellington and Louis Armstrong); entries for persons who had been omitted from the *A* to *D* sections of the initial volumes due to previous editorial choices; and new subjects. Volume 17, completed seven years after the publication of volume 16, indexes names and subjects in all previous volumes, and highlights with graphic symbols primary entries, illustrations, musical examples, and errata in the text.

20. **The New Grove Dictionary of Music and Musicians.** Stanley Sadie, ed. London: Macmillan; Washington, D.C.: Grove's Dictionaries of Music; Hong Kong: Peninsula Publishers, 1980. 20v. illus. music. bibliog. index. LC 79-26207. ISBN 0-333-23111-2.

Both Sir George Grove in his preface to the 1879-89 first edition and Stanley Sadie in his preface to the present edition have expressed an intention to be all-inclusive. Grove covered "all the points ... on which those interested in the Art, and alive to its many and far-reaching associations, can desire to be informed." *The New Grove* "seeks to discuss everything that can be reckoned to bear on music in history and on present-day musical life." The world has changed, conceptions of music have changed, and the initial four volumes, expanded to nine by the fifth edition (1954), have now expanded to twenty. Only 3 percent of the new edition's text comes from previous editions.

As a work of joint authorship which employed almost twenty-five hundred writers, many of whom are premier scholars in their fields, *The New Grove* reflects a variety of styles and approaches. Though the editors have sought factual accuracy, the preface emphasizes "it is a part of a dictionary's role to present a variety of standpoints." Thus the work is an amalgam and collective expression of the current state of musical scholarship.

The most significant of the dictionary's developments over previous editions is the broadening of its concept of music to a worldwide viewpoint. It includes hundreds of terminological and survey articles on non-Western music. Though it certainly has not reduced its concern for the European tradition (the article on J. S. Bach extends to fifty-five pages, for instance), it brings into the mainstream topics which were formerly categorized as the domain of ethnomusicology (for example, the "Australia" article devotes three pages to "art music" and seventeen pages to folk and aboriginal forms).

More than half of the entries are on composers. Particularly for major composers, these give both biographical data and musical analysis and extensive work lists. Other persons given individual entries include performers, scholars, writers, librettists, dancers, patrons, printers, instrument makers, and others significant in the history of music. Numerous entries cover a variety of geographical areas – cities, countries, and regions of the world. As a dictionary, *The New Grove* gives definitions for musical terminology. As a history, it covers genres and forms. As an encyclopedia, it includes a range of survey articles such as "Analysis" and "Performing Practice." Its features are too numerous to be capsulized, but four – the lists of dictionaries and encyclopedias, editions, libraries, and periodicals – are of particular use to librarians. Most entries include bibliographies of books and articles; many are quite extensive. The abbreviated and sometimes irritating citation style identifies authors by last name and initial letter of their first name, gives place of publication but not publisher, and supplies only the initial page number for most journal articles.

There is no index in the usual sense, but an "Index of Terms Used in Articles on Non-Western Music, Folk Music and Kindred Topics" at the end of the last volume gives brief definitions for such terms and locates them within articles. Cross-references appear in the body of the work from unused terms and from terms within the texts of articles. A list of contributors in the last volume gives, for those living, the last known place of work or residence. Though it does not list contributors' entries, the entries themselves are signed.

The New Grove is the most inclusive reference source for music in the English language, and one of the most important in any language. Though its roots remain in Britain (as shown in the preference for British terminology such as "crotchet" rather than "quarter note"), it is the primary resource for the world's music.

21. **The New Oxford Companion to Music**. Denis Arnold, general ed. New York: Oxford University Press, 1983. 2v. illus. music. LC 83-233314. ISBN 0-19-311316-3.

Percy Scholes flavored the first ten editions of *The Oxford Companion* with the opinions and orientation of a midcentury Englishman. The *New Oxford Companion* is a work of joint authorship which compensates for the loss of an individual's idiosyncracies with the individual styles of signed articles and a greater appreciation for twentieth-century music and for non-Western forms of music. It has dropped some handy compilations such as "Nicknamed Compositions" and "Misattributed Compositions." The typeface is larger, the illustrations clearer and more plentiful – the drawings detailing the workings of instruments are especially good. Like the Scholes editions, the *New Oxford Companion*'s strength lies in extended entries for composers, instruments, theoretical topics, and individual countries, and for broad surveys such as "History of Music" or "Opera." Many entries include brief bibliographies of recent titles in English. Longer entries often subsume discussions of specific terms. *The Oxford Dictionary* (see entry 18) and *The New Harvard Dictionary* (see entry 36) are preferable for short definitions. A particular feature of every *Oxford Companion* has been articles on individual works, including synopses of opera plots.

22. Pulver, Jeffrey. **A Dictionary of Old English Music and Musical Instruments**. New York: E. P. Dutton, 1923. 247p. illus. LC 24-758. ISBN 0-849000-42-4.

This companion to Pulver's *Biographical Dictionary of Old English Music* (see entry 108) examines the music of the Tudor and Stuart periods in England. Pulver's broad, discursive, and nontechnical style, which employs references to literary as well as musical works, gives flavor to his definitions and emphasizes the social role of music. He covers terminology of theory and performance, but is at his best with lengthy articles on musical instruments (for which he provides a small number of drawings and photographs) and dance styles of the time. Where else could one read that ladies were to dance the pavane "'with an humble countenance and downcast eyes'"?

23. Randel, Don Michael. **Harvard Concise Dictionary of Music**. Cambridge, Mass.: Belknap Press/Harvard University Press, 1978. 577p. illus. music. LC 78-5948. ISBN 0-674-37471-1; 0-674-37470-3pa.

This spinoff from the 1969 predecessor to *The New Harvard Dictionary of Music* (see entry 36) is less academically oriented than its parent and presents itself as a quick, rather than thorough, reference source. It deletes the references to other works, some foreign terms, and the country surveys, and shortens many of the longer articles contained in the 1969 *Harvard Dictionary*, but adds entries on non-Western forms and instruments along with brief biographical data on over two thousand composers.

24. Riemann, Hugo. **Riemann Musik Lexikon**. 12. völlig neuarbeitete Aufl. in drei Bänden. Herausgegeben von Wilibald Gurlitt. Mainz, West Germany: B. Schott's Söhne, 1959-75. 5v. music. LC 59-1689.

Personenteil A-K. ISBN 3-7957-0010-8; 3-7957-0011-6(leather).

Personenteil L-Z. ISBN 3-7957-0020-5; 3-7957-0021-3(leather).

Sachteil. Begonnen von Wilibald Gurlitt. Fortgeführt und herausgegeben von Hans Heinrich Eggebrecht. ISBN 3-7957-0030-2; 3-7957-0031-0(leather).

Ergänzungsband, Personenteil A-K. Begonnen von Wilibald Gurlitt. Fortgeführt und herausgegeben von Hans Heinrich Eggebrecht. ISBN 3-7957-0012-4; 3-7957-0013-2(leather).

Ergänzungsband, Personenteil L-Z. Begonnen von Wilibald Gurlitt. Fortgeführt und herausgegeben von Hans Heinrich Eggebrecht. ISBN 3-7957-0022-1; 3-7957-0023-X(leather).

First published in 1882 as the *Musik-Lexikon*, and published in successive editions with Alfred Einstein as editor, *Riemann* now stands as one of the most venerable and important reference works for music. The twelfth edition first appeared in three volumes – the first two (*Personenteil*) contain biographical entries and the other (*Sachteil*) contains subject entries. Two supplementary volumes (*Ergänzungsband*) update the biographical material. Together, the five volumes provide wide coverage of not only European music, but also of jazz and popular music (see "shimmy," for instance), and of non-Western music.

In its selection of composers, performers, and writers, its authoritative establishments of birth and death dates, its informed and concise portrayals of lives and evaluations of contributions, and its work lists and bibliographical references, the biographical section is similar to *Baker's* (see entry 80), which in fact refers to *Riemann* as a resource. The supplementary volumes signal updates to the original entries with a " + " sign, and add numerous entries for modern North American, Latin American, and European composers and performers. The *Sachteil* is a one-volume encyclopedia of music, covering terms, instruments, and national musics, and including bibliographical references. An extended article lists "Denkmäler" (editions and monuments of music) published in Europe and the United States, indexing these by composer in a manner similar to that of Heyer (see entry 417). In situating itself between the single and multivolume types of reference works, *Riemann* is able to provide both conciseness and depth of treatment.

25. Thompson, Oscar, ed.-in-chief. **The International Cyclopedia of Music and Musicians.** 11th ed. Bruce Bohle, ed. New York: Dodd, Mead, 1985. 2609p. music. LC 84-13736. ISBN 0-396-08412-5.

First published in 1938, the *Cyclopedia* is the only comprehensive reference work in the area of music having American origins. It is particularly strong in biographical entries, rivalling *Baker's* (see entry 80) and *The New Grove* (see entry 20) in the unearthing of obscure deceased European musicians. Yet it virtually ignores figures in American jazz, folk, and popular music – not until the eleventh edition was Scott Joplin included. Oriented more toward history and culture than to musicology, it features entries for individual works, non-English terms, universities, associations, and concert halls. Notated examples are few. Most entries are short and quite specific, with up to a dozen per page. Survey articles (such as "Song," "Troubadour Music," or "Oriental Music") and those on major composers extend to several pages, display prominently the subject and author's name, and include work lists or bibliographies. The eleventh edition adds to the unchanged text of the tenth edition an "Addenda" section which includes new entries and updated data for earlier entries (obituaries and additions to work lists and bibliographies, for instance). Asterisks added to updated entries in the tenth edition text refer to the addenda section; those in the addenda, to the earlier text.

26. Westrup, J. A. and F. L. Harrison. **The New College Encyclopedia of Music.** rev. ed. By Conrad Wilson. Introduction by André Previn. New York: W. W. Norton, 1981. 608p. illus. music. LC 81-11344. ISBN 0-393-00074-5pa.

The encyclopedia manages to be clear and concise without being elementary, and is indeed appropriate for college readers who do not need the breadth or technicality of other works. Published in Britain as *Collins Encyclopedia of Music* (rev. ed. London: Chancellor, 1984), it gives entries for composers and performers, works, and terms, some of which include references to books and articles in English. Notated examples and illustrations such as drawings of instruments are plentiful. Biographical articles give the years, not dates, of birth and death, and, for major composers, include selected work lists. Entries for works generally appear in their English form with a cross-reference (but not consistently) from the foreign form. Entries for operas give plot summaries. A pronunciation key in the front matter covers a selection of names and terms unfamiliar to the English-speaking reader.

3

Dictionaries of Terms and Word Lists

There are few reference works of music which are general in scope yet confine themselves to the definition of terms. Baker's *Dictionary of Musical Terms* (see entry 27) established the pattern for dictionaries of music in the English language. *The New Harvard Dictionary* (see entry 36) continues in this tradition, but with more extended definitions and the inclusion of non-Western and computer terminology. Other dictionaries included here focus on a specialized terminology. Multilingual dictionaries are never quite satisfactory, but two which have fewer problems than others have been included (see entries 34 and 41). Coover's *Music Lexicography* (see entry 399) is a valuable source for specialized and retrospective works.

27. Baker, Theodore. **A Dictionary of Musical Terms Containing Upwards of 9,000 English, French, German, Italian, Latin, and Greek Words and Phrases ... With a Supplement Containing an English-Italian Vocabulary for Composers**. New York: n.p., 1923; repr., New York: AMS Press, 1970. vi, 257p. music. LC 78-9166. ISBN 0-404-00468-7.

Baker's *Dictionary of Musical Terms* has not been revised for over sixty years, yet since the first edition appeared in 1895, it has been one of the most useful factual and terminological guides. It has none of the longer articles found in *The New Harvard Dictionary of Music* (see entry 36); all entries are short and specific. Tables of grace notes and notational signs, and lists of time and key signatures in four languages are examples of its concise presentation of essentials. Users should be aware of alternate spellings (barytone rather than baritone, for instance) which were current when the dictionary was written, and of an "Appendix of Additions and Corrections."

28. Carter, Henry Holland. **A Dictionary of Middle English Musical Terms**. Edited by George B. Gerhard. Bloomington, Ind.: Indiana University Press, 1961; repr., New York: Kraus International, 1968. xv, 655p. bibliog. (Indiana University Humanities Series, No. 45). ISBN 0-527-15150-5.

The dictionary extracts terms of musical theory, performance, materials, and forms based on the author's perusal of what the introduction claims is "essentially everything published in Middle English." It certainly is a thorough piece of work. The entry for each word indicates its part of speech, gives variant spellings, indicates briefly its etymology, defines the word, gives from one to a dozen or more examples of usage for that definition, and cites a source in the bibliography for each example.

29. Davidson, James Robert. **A Dictionary of Protestant Church Music**. Metuchen, N.J.: Scarecrow, 1975. xvi, 349p. index. LC 74-30101. ISBN 0-8108-0788-2.

In its selection of vocabulary, which draws heavily from Latin and German, and in its mention of numerous pre-Reformation composers, the dictionary shows the difficulty of extracting the uniquely Protestant threads from the church music of Europe and America. Its emphasis is historical rather than theoretical. In addition to musical terminology ("Descant"), it includes liturgical terms ("Deutsche Messe"), and bibliographical terms ("Psalters"). Each entry gives an etymology of the term, a brief definition, often a short historical explanation, and one or more references to sources in German or English. The entries overlap greatly with those in *The New Harvard Dictionary* (see entry 36) and *The New Grove* (see entry 20); thus, the dictionary's advantages rest in its focus and in its citations, many of which are unique.

30. Fink, Robert, and Robert Ricci. **The Language of Twentieth Century Music: A Dictionary of Terms**. New York: Schirmer Books, 1975. viii, 125p. music. bibliog. LC 74-13308. ISBN 0-02-870600-5.

This dictionary reminds one of the advancing age of the twentieth century. Terms such as "microtonalism," "twelve-tone technique," and "Schenkerian analysis," which once heralded new ways of defining music, are now part of history. Conversely, the dictionary dates itself as a product of the 1970s in its omission of "minimalism" and "performance art" and in its dismissal of "new music" as a term which "became popular during the 1920s and is somewhat obsolete today." As a work of its time it succeeds in appropriately selecting and clearly defining terms which are either unique to twentieth-century music or have taken on new meanings. Terms cover composition, performance, instrumentation, notation, and technology in concert, film, rock, and jazz musics. An appendix groups terms within twenty-two categories and serves as a conceptual cross-reference list.

31. Gold, Robert S. **Jazz Talk**. Indianapolis, Ind.: Bobbs-Merrill, 1975; repr., New York: Da Capo Press, 1982. xii, 322p. bibliog. (Roots of Jazz Series). LC 82-1468. ISBN 0-306-76155-6.

Jazz Talk is the successor to Gold's *A Jazz Lexicon* (Alfred A. Knopf, 1964). It continues as a lexicon as well as a dictionary through its examples of usage along with definitions and etymologies for words which originated with jazz musicians and writers about jazz. It includes terms referring to styles and techniques of jazz (such as "stride," "fours [trade]," "head," and "comp"), to nicknames for prominent jazz musicians (such as "Lady," "Hawk," and "Bird"), and to aspects of the lives of jazz musicians in the United States (such as "ofay," "jive," and "stash"). Gold takes quotations illustrating usage from reference works, other books, periodicals (all listed in the bibliography), and from song titles and lyrics, and album titles and liner notes. This portrayal of the development of an argot out of a lifestyle demonstrates, as does the *Oxford English Dictionary*, how etymology illustrates history.

32. Irwin, Stevens. **Dictionary of Pipe Organ Stops**. 2d ed. New York: Schirmer Books; London: Collier Macmillan, 1983. xx, 422p. illus. bibliog. LC 82-25545. ISBN 0-02-871150-5.

Irwin addresses the dictionary to students, performers, and listeners, all of whom will find it of some use, although performers may find some of the introductory material too rudimentary. A list of definitions of basic terms (such as "free reed" or "division") precedes the main dictionary, which lists stops by name, discusses the sound quality and the construction of the pipe, suggests uses for the stop and combinations with others, and gives examples of pitches the stop produces. Drawings, photographs, and tables abound and help to clarify complicated structural details and to compare stops. Eleven appendixes cover, among other topics, mechanical controls and mixtures of stops.

33. Krolick, Bettye. **Dictionary of Braille Music Signs**. Washington, D.C.: National Library Service for the Blind and Physically Handicapped, Library of Congress, 1979. xviii, 199p. music. bibliog. index. LC 78-21301. ISBN 0-8444-0277-X. SuDoc LC 19.2:B 73/10. (Also produced in braille for the Library of Congress, National Library Service for the Blind and Physically Handicapped, by Volunteer Services for the Blind, 1979. 2v.).

Designed as an aid to braille music readers, the dictionary defines approximately five hundred musical signs and literary abbreviations. It includes signs currently in use and others that date to the Cologne Braille Congress of 1888. The table of contents lists the sixty-three braille characters in standard braille order, and the dictionary itself groups signs composed of more than one character with the initial character. Each entry gives one or more definitions for each sign. Background material surveys formats for braille music, and gives a brief introduction to braille music. The dictionary's arrangement precludes its use as a transcription tool – given a definition, there is no way to locate the equivalent sign.

34. Leuchtmann, Horst, ed. **Wörterbuch Musik; Dictionary of Terms in Music, Englisch-Deutsch/Deutsch-Englisch, English-German/German-English**. 3d ed. New York: K. G. Saur, 1981. xv, 560p. ISBN 3-598-10338-7.

This is the most extensive and thorough of the multilingual dictionaries in music. It includes more than strictly technical terms, and covers both British and American usage. Instructions appear in both German and English, although the introduction advises, "since the *Dictionary* is intended for specialist use a basic knowledge of the two languages is presupposed." Supplementary matter includes illustrations of instruments showing terminology for different parts, a list of equivalent titles of compositions in both languages, and, for some reason, diagrams of change-ringing patterns.

35. Levarie, Siegmund, and Ernst Levy. **Musical Morphology: A Discourse and a Dictionary**. Kent, Ohio: Kent State University Press, 1983. 344p. LC 82-21274. ISBN 0-87338-286-2.

Philosophical analysis blends with musicology in this approach to the concepts rather than the specific terminology of music. Following an opening discourse on the general forms that define the parameters of a piece of music, the body of the work gives extended definitions for terms as familiar as "dance music" and "fugue" and as abstract as "clearness-unclearness" and "end." The authors ground their speculations in musical analyses, notated examples, and citations to a variety of works in the bibliography. They bring wit, clarity, and insight to this overview of the relationships between listener, performer, and composer.

36. Randel, Don Michael, ed. **The New Harvard Dictionary of Music**. Cambridge, Mass.: Belknap Press/Harvard University Press, 1986. xxi, 942p. illus. music. LC 86-4780. ISBN 0-674-61525-5.

The New Harvard Dictionary follows the lead of other "new" reference works (such as *The New Grove*, entry 20 and *The New Oxford Companion*, entry 21) which have broadened the scope of previous editions to encompass non-Western and popular forms of music. However, while most entries have been rewritten, it "carries on the tradition," as the preface maintains, of the *Harvard Dictionary of Music* edited by Willi Apel (1st ed. 1944), a work which falls neatly between the extreme concision of *The Oxford Dictionary of Music* (see entry 18) and the broad discursions of *The New Oxford Companion*. The most immediately apparent difference in content between *The New Harvard Dictionary* and the others is its omission of entries for composers and other individuals. Entries include musical forms, instruments, terms, dances, individual works with distinctive titles, countries, regions of the world, ethnic groups, and periods in the history of Western music. Far more than a "dictionary" which briefly defines terms, this is a broad-based reference work which adjusts the length of its entries to the topic at hand. For example, "Fork fingering" is allotted one sentence; "Opera" occupies seven pages. Most entries are signed by members of a team of scholarly contributors, and many include bibliographies. Musical examples are not plentiful, but are put to good use. Illustrations consist of line drawings of instruments. There are cross-references from variant forms of entry and from references within the text, particularly in the case of general surveys, such as "Musicology," which serve as guides to related entries. The preface maintains that this is a work for "laymen, students, performers, composers, scholars, and teachers." A clear style and the continuation of an established approach ensure that this "new" edition will continue as a standard resource.

37. Reid, Cornelius L. **A Dictionary of Vocal Terminology**. New York: Joseph Patelson Music House, 1983. xxi, 457p. illus. bibliog. index. LC 81-86074. ISBN 0-915282-07-0.

Reid offers a scientific and pedagogical approach to singing in an attempt to "strike a balance between aesthetics and natural functioning." Attractive typography and a large format, which allows space in the outer margin for cross-references and citations, encourage browsing, which, in the absence of detailed indexing, is a useful approach to the discursive style of the definitions. Entries include musical terminology ("Bel Canto"), physiological terminology ("Stylopharyngeal Muscles"), colloquialisms ("Necktie Tenor"), and in some cases exist only as soapboxes for the author's opinions ("Mental Concept"). Illustrations include musical examples and cutaways or skeletal views of the throat and chest. An introductory index of terms lists the entries, an index of names covers those mentioned or cited in the text, and a bibliography lists books and articles on singing technique and physiology.

38. Rèpertoire international de littérature musicale/Internationales Repertorium der Musikliteratur/International Repertory of Music Literature. **RILM English-Language Thesaurus: Subject Headings for RILM Index, Vol. XI-** . rev. ed. New York: RILM Abstracts, 1983. xiii, 51p.

Useful not only for those performing online searches of the RILM database, but also for anyone consulting *RILM Abstracts* (see entry 327), the thesaurus is, as noted in the introduction, "a 'treasury' of English words that have musical meaning or that can be used in a music-related context." It displays the subject headings used in constructing *RILM Abstracts*, and relates them, in a manner similar to *Library of Congress Subject Headings* (10th ed. Library of Congress, 1986), with "see," "sa," "x," and "xx" references. For those unfamiliar with this system, the introduction gives remarkably clear instructions.

39. Risatti, Howard. **New Music Vocabulary: A Guide to Notational Signs for Contemporary Music**. Urbana, Ill.: University of Illinois Press, 1975. 219p. illus. music. bibliog. index. LC 73-81565. ISBN 0-252-00406-X.

This guide standardizes some of the idiosyncratic notational signs which contemporary composers have invented, ranging from those specifying microtones and irregular rhythms to seldom used actions such as "slam the lid then lift it quickly" (referring to a piano). Chapters logically organize the symbols and their definitions. The first chapter gives general notational material, the next four give symbols for particular instruments, and the last gives symbols for voice. Each symbol cites as its source one or more of several hundred scores on the "List of Composers Cited," which includes works by Boulez, Stockhausen, and Carter, as well as by the author himself. A well-constructed index lists names of instruments and specific terms.

40. Seagrave, Barbara Garvey, and Joel Berman. **The A.S.T.A. Dictionary of Bowing Terms for String Instruments**. Urbana, Ill.: American String Teachers Association, 1968. 53p. ISBN 0-318-18109-6.

The dictionary identifies the language of each term and explains the technique to which it refers using, when appropriate, notated illustrative examples. Definitions mention historical variations from current practice and cite contemporary references. Definitions of phrases appear beneath the key word of the phrase. In the entry for "arco," for instance, over a dozen specific usages appear such as "alzare l'____" and "con molto ____." The dictionary includes line drawings of the frog and the head of a bow.

41. **Terminorum Musicae Index Septem Linguis Redactus: Polyglot Dictionary of Musical Terms: English, German, French, Italian, Spanish, Hungarian, Russian**. Horst Leuchtmann, redacteur-en-chef. Budapest, Hungary, Akadémai Kiadó; Kassel, West Germany: Bärenreiter-Verlag, 1978. 798p. illus. LC 78-369482. ISBN 963-05-1276-9; 3-7618-0553-5.

This dictionary attempts to standardize usage of musical terms. Beneath the German form of each term it lists equivalents in the six other languages, indicates the gender in relevant languages, and differentiates between British and American forms when necessary. Non-German terms either refer to the German entry, or give a brief multilingual definition when no equivalent exists. Separate sections list Russian terms in the Cyrillic alphabet, and show examples of notation and pictures of instruments to illustrate specific terms.

42. Tinctoris, Johannes. **Dictionary of Musical Terms: An English Translation of "Terminorum Musicae Diffinitorium" Together with the Latin Text**. Translated and annotated by Carl Parrish. New York: Free Press, 1963; repr., New York: Da Capo Press, 1978. xi, 108p. (Da Capo Press Music Reprint Series). LC 77-26753. ISBN 0-306-77560-3.

One of the first printed books on music, the dictionary dates to the late fifteenth century. This edition gives the Latin text on the left-hand pages and its English translation on the right. The derivation of many English words from Latin roots preserves, in a crude manner, an alphabetical order. The translator's notes help focus Tinctoris's sometimes ambiguous definitions which nevertheless provide a contemporary outline of Renaissance conceptions of music.

4

Specialized Information Sources and Digests

This is a potpourri of encyclopedias, dictionaries, handbooks, and digests. Each provides specialized information about a particular area of music, such as musical instruments, opera, or twentieth-century music. All were published within the last twenty years with the exception of two titles. *Cobbett's Cyclopedic Survey of Chamber Music* (see entry 45) and Julian's *Dictionary of Hymnology* (see entry 55), classics whose scope is unmatched, are frequently consulted.

43. Berger, Melvin. **Guide to Chamber Music**. New York: Dodd, Mead, 1985. xix, 470p. discog. LC 85-1469. ISBN 0-396-08385-4.

Here is an introduction for listeners to 231 individual works from the standard chamber music repertoire. Arranged by composer, it gives a brief biography and a movement-by-movement discussion of each work. Discussions of most works note the circumstances of their composition and of their first performance. Berger demands little knowledge of music on the part of his readers—he writes of mood, color, and instrumentation, uses no musical examples, and pauses to explain, for instance, the distinction between 3/4 and 6/8 meter. A short glossary defines such terms as "rondo" or "scherzo." A discography suggests one sample recording for each work.

44. Berkowitz, Freda Pastor. **Popular Titles and Subtitles of Musical Compositions**. 2d ed. Metuchen, N.J.: Scarecrow, 1975. viii, 209p. bibliog. index. LC 75-4751. ISBN 0-8108-0806-4.

Bruckner, Mahler, and Schubert have all composed symphonies nicknamed "Tragic"; this work identifies each, along with seven hundred other compositions commonly known by such nicknames. A user can locate a nickname in the alphabetical listing to find the original title of the work and a short anecdotal summary of the origin of the nickname, or use the index to locate works by a certain composer. Although the introduction maintains that nicknames "will be listed in English, as well as in the original language," this practice is inconsistent—for example, works identified as "La Chasse" are not the same as those identified as "The Hunt."

45. Cobbett, Walter Willson, ed. **Cobbett's Cyclopedic Survey of Chamber Music**. 2d ed. Supplementary material edited by Colin Mason. New York: Oxford University Press, 1963. 3v. music. bibliog. index. LC 64-1302. ISBN 0-19-318306-4.

Edited by a self-professed "amateur" who was a successful businessman and ardent patron of music, the cyclopedia is an examination, written in an expansive style, of chamber music compositions and terminology, excluding solo pieces. Entries for composers give detailed and at times extended analyses of individual works and passages, and include notated examples and work lists of chamber pieces. Other entries cover instruments, societies, national characteristics, and broad topics such as "colour in chamber music." Contributors to the first two volumes, originally published in 1929, include some of the premier authorities of the time, such as Eric Blom and Percy Scholes. Volume 2 includes an appendix of additions and corrections, a supplement giving names and dates of several hundred lesser-known composers, a general bibliography, a contents list of nonbiographical entries, and a list of contributors. Marginal asterisks and daggers in the first two volumes refer to the third, which updates the first edition with essays by Colin Mason, Nicolas Slonimsky, and I. I. Martinov on European, British, Russian, and American chamber music, and gives additions to the bibliography and additions and corrections to dates.

46. Diagram Group. **Musical Instruments of the World: An Illustrated Encyclopedia**. n.p.: Paddington Press – Two Continents Publishing Group, 1976. 320p. illus. index. LC 76-21722. ISBN 0-8467-0134-0.

The Diagram Group's distinctive style mingles illustrative text with drawings of orchestral, folk, non-Western, and ancient instruments, grouped according to the Hornbostel-Sachs organization of instruments. Hundreds of illustrations show exteriors, performance positions, and close-up or interior details. An inset box gives the pitch range of each orchestral instrument, a selection of works featuring the instrument, a diagram showing its position in the orchestra, and a notated example of several bars of music. These detailed illustrations can provide a visual complement to the more thorough texts in *The New Grove Dictionary of Musical Instruments* (see entry 66). *The Scribner Guide to Orchestral Instruments* (Scribner's, 1983) offers, in the same style, a more specialized and condensed version of this work.

47. **Dictionary of Contemporary Music**. John Vinton, ed. New York: E. P. Dutton, 1974. xiv, 834p. bibliog. LC 73-78096. ISBN 0-525-09125-4.

The dictionary's signed and authoritative entries intelligibly explain compositional techniques which have become conventions. Its scope is "concert music in the Western tradition," but its chronological boundaries are loose enough to encompass the late nineteenth century. Though composers included generally have been born after 1880 or at least were alive in 1930, even Mahler, who died in 1911, rates a substantial entry. Entries are of four types: those for individual composers, by far the largest category, which give interpretive overviews of the individual's contribution to contemporary music; extended entries on technical subjects, such as "12-Tone Techniques"; surveys of twentieth-century composing activity in individual countries; and a small number of definitions of new terms or terms with new meanings. Composer entries include lists of principal works and writings; many of these and other entries include bibliographies. This remains the most substantial encyclopedic overview of music of the twentieth century.

48. Downes, Edward. **The Guide to Symphonic Music**. New York: Walker, 1981. xxvii, 1058p. illus. music. index. LC 81-7442. ISBN 0-8027-7177-7pa.

The present volume is a reprint of *The New York Philharmonic Guide to the Symphony*, published by Walker in 1976. Reading Downes's vivid and spirited tours through symphonic works is almost as much fun as listening to the performances themselves. He derived most of these several hundred introductions to symphonies, concertos, overtures, and other works for full orchestra from his program notes written over the years for the New York Philharmonic. The selection includes crowd pleasers such as the nine symphonies of Beethoven together with twentieth-century compositions still shunned by many audiences such as works by Varèse. Arranged in alphabetical order by composer, these introductions give a historical background and highlight significant features of each movement. They often employ quotations from the composer, reviews of first performances, or musical examples. The index covers names and works discussed in the essays as well as the featured works.

49. Ewen, David. **The New Encyclopedia of the Opera**. New York: Hill and Wang, 1971. viii, 759p. LC 71-148237. ISBN 0-8090-7262-9.

This is still the most comprehensive, historically oriented general encyclopedia of opera, and is particularly strong for its entries on individual works (giving details of first performances and substantial plot summaries), and unique in its entries for individual characters and passages. Entries for composers and performers give dates and places of birth and death along with the interpretive biographies which distinguish Ewen's works. Other kinds of entries include surveys (such as "opéra-comique") and individual companies (such as "Metropolitan Opera"). *The Concise Oxford Dictionary of Opera* (see entry 74) covers more specific terminology.

50. Freeman, John W. **The Metropolitan Opera Stories of the Great Operas**. New York: The Metropolitan Opera Guild; New York: W. W. Norton, 1984. xxxii, 547p. illus. LC 84-8030. ISBN 0-393-01888-1.

For operagoers who simply want to understand the events on stage, this is a shorter and less demanding alternative to *Kobbé's Complete Opera Book* (see entry 58). The selection covers the standard repertory and adds a few recent operas which *Kobbé's* does not include. An alphabetical arrangement by composer of the 150 operas and a secondary table of contents listing opera titles in both the original language and in English translation makes consultation easy. A short biography and a black-and-white portrait introduce each composer. Entries for individual operas identify the librettist, give the theater and date of world and U.S. premieres and the date of the Metropolitan Opera premiere, list the characters, and run through the plot of the opera with little reference to the music.

51. Green, Stanley. **Encyclopaedia of the Musical Film**. New York: Oxford University Press, 1981. 344p. bibliog. discog. LC 81-735. ISBN 0-19-502958-5.

Although Green intends this as a companion to the *Encyclopedia of the Musical Theatre* (see entry 52), its scope, since virtually all movies employ music, is narrower. He bases his definition of "musical" film on the number of musical selections, the manner of presentation, the contributions of leading members of the cast, and the subject matter of the film. Thus the encyclopedia excludes composers such as Nino Rota or John Williams who are known for their film music but did not compose for musicals. Given this restriction, the work is a fine resource about a genre which had its heyday in the 1930s and 1940s. Entries cover performers, lyricists, composers, songs, and movies. The entries for movies list credits, cast, songs, and give spirited critical summaries.

52. Green, Stanley. **Encyclopedia of the Musical Theatre: An Updated Reference Guide to over 2000 Performers, Writers, Directors, Productions and Songs of the Musical Stage, Both in New York and London**. New York: Da Capo Press, 1980. vi, 492p. illus. bibliog. discog. LC 79-27168. ISBN 0-306-80113-2.

Green's encyclopedia (which was originally published by Dodd, Mead in 1976 as *Encyclopaedia of the Musical Theatre*) gives a sober and factual, but anecdotal account of popular productions in New York and London during the twentieth century. Entries for people (actors, composers, lyricists, librettists, directors, choreographers, and producers) give dates and places of birth and death, briefly trace professional careers, and list major performances. Those for productions list the composer, lyricist, and song titles; theater, dates, number of performances, credits, and cast in London and New York; and background notes on the plot and performances. Well-known songs have their own entries. Following the body of the encyclopedia are a list of winners of awards and prizes, a list of productions which ran for over one thousand performances, a bibliography of librettos and general works, and a discography of recordings by the original cast, performers, or composer. The updated edition adds to the original text illustrations of Broadway productions and several pages of addenda.

53. Griffiths, Paul. **The Thames and Hudson Encyclopaedia of 20th-Century Music**. London: Thames and Hudson, 1986. 207p. bibliog. index. LC 85-51468. ISBN 0-500-23449-3.

Griffiths, a former editor of *The New Grove* (see entry 20), provides here a reliable but brief survey of persons and terminology. Short biographies, including selected work lists and bibliographic references, comprise nearly half the entries. Other entries cover performers, institutions, instruments, terms of theory and performance, and individual works. A subject index in the front matter organizes entries by country and broad topic, and a chronology at the end enumerates important first performances by year. Griffiths's concise entries for composers contrast sharply with the extended and more fully documented entries in the *Dictionary of Contemporary Music* (see entry 47). The encyclopedia covers more terminology than the dictionary, but is not as thorough as *The New Harvard Dictionary* (see entry 36), and includes virtually no musical examples.

54. Jablonski, Edward. **The Encyclopedia of American Music**. Garden City, N.Y.: Doubleday, 1981. xii, 629p. discog. index. LC 77-16925. ISBN 0-385-08088-3.

The popular orientation of the encyclopedia may make it useful for some readers, but the lack of bibliographical references will make it unsatisfactory for others, and the format will be frustrating to all. It is divided into seven chronological parts. Each opens with a summary history of the period, then gives individual entries for composers, organizations, works, publications, and terms. The index lists only personal names, so entries such as "Bay Psalm Book" and "Blue Note" are as good as lost unless the user can guess the appropriate chronological area to consult. The discography is a narrative tour through labels specializing in Americana.

55. Julian, John, ed. **A Dictionary of Hymnology, Setting Forth the Origin and History of Christian Hymns of All Ages and Nations**. rev. ed. with new supp. London: John Murray, 1907; repr., Grand Rapids, Mich.: Kregel Publications, 1985. (2v.). xviii, 1768p. index. LC 83-8373. ISBN 0-8254-2960-6.

Eighty years old and still unsurpassed, this most recent of the reprintings of Julian's dictionary shows a continuing demand for this primary resource for the history of hymnology. Collected in the second edition are the original text of the first edition (1892), with its own indexes to first lines of hymns and to authors and translators; two appendixes, which add entries and correct earlier entries; a new supplement, which adds more entries; and collective indexes to the appendixes and supplement. All sections are rich with historical, biographical, and bibliographical detail. Entries are given in one alphabet within each of the four sections. Entries for significant hymns locate sources and note the history, author, and use of the hymn. Entries for authors of hymns give biographies and lists of works. Other entries include national surveys and histories (entered under the adjectival form of a country's name – "French," not "France"), denominational surveys of churches in Europe and North America, and other geographical and historical surveys. Indexes to first lines of hymns in specialized collections can be found in articles entitled "Breviaries"; "Hymnarium"; "Latin, Translations from the"; "Notker Balbulus"; and "Sequences." Taken together, the four sections treat almost twenty-five thousand hymns, and a multitude of topics.

56. Kallmann, Helmut, Gilles Potvin, and Kenneth Winters, eds. **Encyclopedia of Music in Canada**. Toronto: University of Toronto Press, 1981. xxix, 1076p. illus. bibliog. discog. index. LC 82-116808. ISBN 0-8020-5509-5.

Socially, ethnographically, geographically, and historically, the encyclopedia examines Canada's musical life. Its 3,162 entries cover topics in Canadian concert, jazz, popular, and indigenous folk music and omit general terms unless they have specific Canadian references. Individuals (composers, performers, and others) comprise the majority of entries. Others include associations, corporations, schools and universities, and foreign countries (detailing the activities there of Canadian musicians). Entries for subjects (such as "ethnomusicology," "piano building," "ladies colleges and convent schools," and even "winter," "lakes," and "mountains") discuss their Canadian aspects or significance in Canadian music. Most entries are signed and many include bibliographies; those for individuals often include work lists or discographies. Few are shorter than several paragraphs in length and many extend to several pages. Broad headings (such as "education") included alphabetically in the text serve as "reader's guides" (as the introduction defines them), giving multiple references to more specific articles. The detailed index specifically omits subjects which have their own headings.

57. Kinkle, Roger D. **The Complete Encyclopedia of Popular Music and Jazz 1900-1950**. New Rochelle, N.Y.: Arlington House, 1974. 4v. discog. index. LC 74-7109. ISBN 0-87000-229-5.

Kinkle's multifaceted work encompasses the birth and development of jazz, the blossoming of the Broadway theater, the invention of sound movies, and most of the years of 78rpm record production. Volume 1 lists, by year, Broadway musicals (by title, with opening date, number of performances, and credits), popular songs (by title, with composer and lyricist), movie musicals from 1927 (by title, with credits), and representative recordings from 1909 (by artist, with catalog number and title). Volumes 2 and 3 contain 2,006 short biographies of performers, composers, lyricists, and radio personalities who attained prominence between 1900 and 1950. These include dates and places of birth and selected lists of recordings, songs, or movies. The biographies continue, for those living, into the early 1970s. The appendixes in volume 4 give winners of *down beat* and *Metronome* polls, winners and nominees of Academy Awards to 1972, and chronological and numerical lists of principal record label issues. Indexes list names, musicals, and songs.

58. Kobbé, Gustave. **Kobbé's Complete Opera Book**. 10th ed. Edited and revised by the Earl of Harewood. London: Bodley Head, 1987. xvii, 1404p. illus. music. index. ISBN 0-370-31017-9.

The Complete Opera Book was first published in 1919, not long after the death of Gustave Kobbé. Subsequent editors, including the Earl of Harewood, founder of the magazine *Opera* (see entry 640), have doubled Kobbé's text with the addition of material covering the late nineteenth and twentieth centuries. *Kobbé's* is a history of operas, rather than of opera such as is Grout's *A Short History of Opera* (see entry 119). In detailed, signed essays (by Kobbé, Harewood, and the other editors) it treats in chronological order more than three hundred works. These essays begin with short introductions in abbreviated form which name the composer, librettist and source, give the theater, date, and performers of the premiere and subsequent revivals, then give a list of characters and their vocal parts. The summaries which follow do much more than flatly relate the story. They reflect with vigor and commitment the drama of each opera, relate the plot to the music both in the text and through the use of musical examples, and offer evaluative and historical commentary spiced with personal anecdotes.

59. Limbacher, James L., comp. and ed. **Film Music: From Violins to Video**. Metuchen, N.J.: Scarecrow, 1974. 835p. bibliog. discog. index. LC 73-16153. ISBN 0-8108-0651-7.

60. Limbacher, James L. **Keeping Score: Film Music, 1972-1979**. Metuchen, N.J.: Scarecrow, 1981. ix, 510p. bibliog. discog. LC 80-26474. ISBN 0-8108-1390-4.

Film Music and its successor, *Keeping Score*, rapidly established themselves as standards in an area which had previously lacked such reference sources. *Film Music* opens with a selection of several dozen pieces originally written by critics and composers for film magazines. These survey the history and technique of film music. Occupying by far the greater part of the book is a reference section in four parts: "Film Titles and Dates," "Films and Their Composers," "Composers and Their Films," and "Recorded Musical Scores (A Discography)." *Keeping Score* updates these reference sections. Since the bibliographies in both total only thirty-five entries, those needing further information will need to turn to Wescott's *Comprehensive Bibliography of Music for Film and Television* (see entry 255).

61. Lubbock, Mark. **The Complete Book of Light Opera**. With an American section by David Ewen. London: Putnam, 1962. xviii, 953p. illus. music. index.

The preface identifies the present volume as a companion to *Kobbé's* (see entry 58), but in antithetical terms; this is a guide "limited to the lightest of Light Opera...." *Die Fledermaus* is probably the only work the two have in common. These "'Musicals' which the traveller is likely to encounter" are organized by their cities of first performance – Paris, Vienna, Berlin, London, and, by David Ewen, New York. Within each city works are treated chronologically, beginning with the mid-nineteenth century salad days of light opera to the 1960 opening in New York of *Bye Bye Birdie*. Entries identify the composer and librettist, the date and place of the first performance, the characters, and summarize the plot. Lubbock's summaries tend to be much more spirited than Ewen's, and to include musical examples, which Ewen strictly avoids. An appendix lists London productions of American musicals. Well-chosen black-and-white photographs and illustrations contribute humor and personality.

62. Marcuse, Sibyl. **Musical Instruments: A Comprehensive Dictionary**. corr. ed. New York: W. W. Norton, 1975. xii, 602p. LC 74-30050. ISBN 0-393-00758-8pa.

Inspired by Curt Sach's *Real-Lexikon der Musikinstrumente* (Hildesheim, Germany: G. Olms, 1913; repr., New York: Dover, 1964), the dictionary includes current and historical Western instruments and a selection of hundreds of non-Western instruments. Virtually all entries are names of specific instruments; some, such as "string," cover structural details. Most entries extend to several lines and give an abbreviated etymology of the instrument's name, a history, a physical description, and a citation to entries in a bibliography of some two hundred items. Longer entries discuss generic forms such as "flute," or historically prominent instruments such as "piano."

63. Meeker, David. **Jazz in the Movies**. New York: Da Capo Press, 1982. new, enl. ed. unpaged. illus. index. (Roots of Jazz Series). LC 81-17364. ISBN 0-306-76147-5.

The primary strength of this work (first published in 1977) is its surprisingly large scope of some 3,724 films. The preface does not make clear whether the emphasis is on films about jazz or films which employ jazz – and the inclusion of the television series *Lassie* makes one wonder whether there are any criteria for inclusion at all. But the films one would expect to find in such a compilation are here, including Malle's *Ascenseur pour l'échafaud* (music by Miles Davis), a documentary on the Newport Jazz Festival, and, of course, Al Jolson's *The Jazz Singer*. Films are arranged alphabetically with cross-references from variant or foreign-language titles. Entries give the country of origin, date, duration, and a short summary which includes the names of musicians associated with the film. These names are gathered in the index.

64. Michaelides, Solon. **The Music of Ancient Greece: An Encyclopedia**. London: Faber and Faber, in association with Faber Music, 1978. xvi, 365p. illus. music. index. LC 78-308507. ISBN 0-571-10021-X.

In his preface, Michaelides calls this "a comprehensive work embracing as many aspects and elements of Greek musical life as possible." The encyclopedia covers musical terminology, instruments, dances, and the names of theorists, composers, philosophers, and poets of ancient Greece. Entries appear alphabetically in transliterated form, followed by their equivalent in Greek letters and the pronunciation in modern Greek. Concepts are difficult to approach unless one knows the appropriate term in Greek. For example, to find a discussion of notation, one must consult "parasemantike." Entries give short definitions of terms and note important contributions of persons by employing quotations from classical literature (in Greek, with English translations). The index offers little to readers of English – it lists terms in the Greek alphabet. The article, "Remains of Greek Music" enumerates, in a longer entry, the few extant fragments.

65. **The New Grove Dictionary of American Music.** H. Wiley Hitchcock and Stanley Sadie, eds. New York: Grove's Dictionaries of Music; London: Macmillan, 1986. 4v. illus. music. bibliog. discog. LC 86-404. ISBN 0-943818-36-2; 0-333-37879-2.

The New Grove Dictionary of Music and Musicians (see entry 20) and *The New Grove Dictionary of Musical Instruments* (see entry 66) gave to the music of the world the same importance that previous encyclopedias had given to the corpus of European music. Following in spirit a 1920 American supplement to the second edition of *Grove's Dictionary*, *The New Grove Dictionary of American Music* (*American Grove*) gives the same importance to the music of the United States. The editors state in the preface that, in comparison to its Grove predecessors, it is "based on a different cultural model, of a more pluralistic character than that of Europe, and without the same foundation in ecclesiastical, aristocratic, and state patronage." *The New Grove* provided the basis for only a small percentage of the entries – most of the material is completely new. The editors have decided to equate "America" specifically with the United States, and while they cast a wide net over both expatriates and immigrants, their firm boundaries exclude even near neighbors such as Canada's Glenn Gould.

Easily the largest group of entries are those devoted to individuals. These include Bo Diddley, Jimmy Dorsey, Igor Stravinsky, Andrew Carnegie, Emily Dickinson, Iggy Pop, Donal Henahan, and four members of the Seeger family (with a cross-reference to Ruth Crawford) – a group whose members may not all be musicians, but who have all in some way influenced American music. These biographical entries follow the same format as do those in *The New Grove*, discussing first the life, then the work of the subject. All but the most brief include bibliographies of works about the subject. Biographies of rock and jazz musicians include selected discographies; those of composers of written music generally include comprehensive work lists. The *American Grove* has rescued from oblivion many nineteenth-century performers and will undoubtedly outlive the fame of many of the plethora of rock musicians it includes.

Entries for groups – performers of rock, jazz, and chamber music, schools, organizations, and businesses – are also plentiful. Definitions of terms are few, limited to those with specifically American origin or significance, such as "blue note." Articles on cities cover the musical life, history, and performing groups associated with them ("New York" alone extends to twenty-three pages). Major survey articles cover genres or otherwise broad topics; these include "Libraries and Collections," "Periodicals," "Jazz," "European-American Music," "Indians, American," "Instruments," "Gospel Music," "Orchestral Music," "Opera," "Popular Music," "Bands," and "Notation."

Illustrations consist of black-and-white photographs. These are not plentiful, but are well-reproduced and appropriate. A list of nearly one thousand contributors at the end of volume 4 lists, contrary (thankfully so) to the practice of *The New Grove*, the entries written by each. The *American Grove* is as influential in its legitimization of culturally diverse music as is *The New Grove*, and is an equally important resource.

66. **The New Grove Dictionary of Musical Instruments**. Stanley Sadie, ed. London: Macmillan; New York: Grove's Dictionaries of Music, 1984. 3v. illus. music. bibliog. LC 84-9062. ISBN 0-333-37878-4; 0-943818-05-2.

No other work approaches *Grove*'s authority, detail, and breadth in portraying the history, construction, and use of instruments. Derived from the *New Grove Dictionary of Music and Musicians* (see entry 20), it adapts or expands many of the original entries, substantially adds to the bibliographies appended to most entries, and adds entries for thousands of instruments which formerly had been subsumed within larger topics. Most of the new entries represent some ten thousand non-Western instruments; many of these, such as "gamelan" and "koto" are substantial articles. Of course, traditional Western instruments also are featured – the "violin" article, for instance, extends to over thirty-five pages with a bibliography of several pages. Entries also cover electronic and computer instruments, instrument makers, and terms relevant to technique, performance practice, and instrument construction, such as "temperament" and "improvisation." Hundreds of black-and-white photographs and line drawings illustrate details of construction and performance practice. Though it has no overall index, cross-references from variant names of instruments, cross-references within articles, and references from entries on families of instruments to specific entries conceptually unite the dictionary.

67. Nulman, Macy. **Concise Encyclopedia of Jewish Music**. New York: McGraw-Hill, 1975. xii, 276p. illus. music. LC 74-5053. ISBN 0-07-047546-6.

The encyclopedia restricts itself to traditional forms of Jewish music – one should not expect to find entries on Schoenberg or Stern. Within this scope, its field is rich with history, covering both liturgical and secular music. Some five hundred entries cover composers and performers, genres, biblical and postbiblical instruments, terms specific to Jewish music, and common musical terms as they relate to Jewish music. Most entries, concise as they are (from one to three per page), cite both contemporary and biblical sources. A chronology lists "Highlights in the History of Jewish Music."

68. Orrey, Leslie, ed. **The Encyclopedia of Opera**. Gilbert Chase, advisory ed. New York: Scribner's, 1976. 376p. illus. LC 75-46101. ISBN 0-684-13630-9.

The encyclopedia gives entries for composers, conductors, singers, operas, cities, and theaters. All are short and strictly factual; though they are signed, there is little to distinguish one from the next. The work is particularly good, however, for the well-reproduced, numerous black-and-white and color photographs of performances, sets, costumes, and opera houses. *The Concise Oxford Dictionary of Opera* (see entry 74), despite its title, offers more extensive discussion of major composers and a wider selection of terminology.

69. Osborne, Charles. **The Dictionary of the Opera**. New York: Simon & Schuster, 1983. 382p. illus. LC 83-4752. ISBN 0-671-49218-7.

Its foreword describes the dictionary as "not a working tool for scholars but a reference book for the opera enthusiast." It offers fewer entries than *The Concise Oxford Dictionary of Opera* (see entry 74), and is similar in form, scope, and quantity of illustrations (though only in black-and-white) to *The New Encyclopedia of the Opera* (see entry 49). Entries for individuals (including composers, singers, conductors, producers, designers, and librettists) give dates and places of birth and death, and short interpretive biographies. Entries for operas give the circumstances of first productions and plot summaries. A separate section gives photographs and short histories of leading opera houses worldwide.

70. Pareles, Jon, and Patricia Romanowski. **The Rolling Stone Encyclopedia of Rock & Roll**. New York: Rolling Stone Press/Summit Books, 1983. xiii, 615p. illus. discog. LC 83-4791. ISBN 0-671-43457-8; 0-671-44071-3pa.

Rock music reference books come and go with the frequency of rock stars; here is one that should be around for a few more years. Pareles, a music critic for the *New York Times*, has organized from ten contributors a series of even-handed biographies of individual and group performers, promoters, and others, including influential country and western and jazz musicians. Each leads off with a discography of albums (giving the date and title) and then recounts the career and life of the group or individual. The attention paid to poststardom activities can answer many "What ever happened to ..." questions. Subject entries include "Festivals," "Girl Groups," and "Death Rock." Grouped listings of Grammy award winners appear alphabetically by name throughout the text.

71. Pitou, Spire. **The Paris Opéra: An Encyclopedia of Operas, Ballets, Composers, and Performers**. Westport, Conn.: Greenwood Press, 1983- .

Genesis and Glory, 1671-1715. 1983. xii, 364p. bibliog. index. LC 82-21140. ISBN 0-313-21420-4.

Rococo and Romantic, 1715-1815. 1985. xviii, 619p. bibliog. index. LC 82-21140. ISBN 0-313-24394-8.

Pitou's preface announces his intention of providing, in four volumes, "an account of the entire period of French opera and ballet from 1671 onward" and an examination of "every extant work produced at the Opéra" from its 1671 opening to the 1980s. A 130-page introduction in the first volume gives a history of the opera. The encyclopedia itself consists of entries for ballets, operas, dancers, singers, composers, librettists, and choreographers. Its primary value is in the rescuing of the obscure, for Pitou's informal entries for well-known composers and operas offer little over other sources such as *The New Grove* (see entry 20) or *Kobbé's Complete Opera Book* (see entry 58). Most entries cite items in a bibliography of English- and French-language sources which suspiciously excludes the *Annals of Opera* (see entry 124) and *The Concise Oxford Dictionary of Opera* (see entry 74). The first volume gives a list of leading female and male singers and dancers from 1971 to 1982. Both volumes include chronological listings of the repertory during the period covered.

72. Rachlin, Harvey. **The Encyclopedia of the Music Business**. New York: Harper & Row, 1981. xix, 524p. illus. LC 81-47235. ISBN 0-06-014913-2.

Rachlin's pragmatic view sees "classical," "rock," and "jazz" as separate but equal commodities. The encyclopedia's vocabulary draws from the areas of recording, broadcasting, employment, marketing, and copyright law as they relate to music. Definitions are detailed, clear, and not overly technical. Although there is no index, cross-references within the text and from alternate entries, and a table of contents which lists the page numbers of each entry provide ample access. Appendixes display sample copyright forms and list recent winners of Academy Awards, Grammys, and gold and platinum records.

73. Roche, Jerome, and Elizabeth Roche. **A Dictionary of Early Music: From the Troubadours to Monteverdi**. New York: Oxford University Press, 1981. 208p. illus. music. LC 81-82688. ISBN 0-19-520255-4.

This concise source of information on the music of the Middle Ages, Renaissance, and Early Baroque period features short and factual entries. Names of composers predominate (about seven hundred entries); these entries give birth and death dates, sketches of lives, discussion of major works, and cite published editions of works. The remaining entries cover instruments and technical terms ("mensural notation," "rhythmic modes"). Line drawings of instruments and notated examples accompany the text.

74. Rosenthal, Harold, and John Warrack. **The Concise Oxford Dictionary of Opera**. 2d ed. New York: Oxford University Press, 1979. 561p. bibliog. LC 79-318553. ISBN 0-19-311318-X.

The foreword's claim to "conciseness rather than completeness" accurately, but modestly, expresses the broad range and short, but full, content of the entries. Those for persons include singers, composers, conductors, and writers, giving dates and places of birth and death, factual details, interpretive comments ("a clear resonant voice and excellent diction"), and occasionally bibliographical references. Entries for operas give the composer and librettist, the dramatic or literary source, dates of first performance and the first in Britain and in the United States, and plot synopses. Other entries include authors whose works have inspired operas, country and city surveys, festivals, theaters, organizations, and production and singing terms ("mad scene," "coup de glotte").

75. Shaw, Arnold. **Dictionary of American Pop/Rock**. New York: Schirmer Books; London: Collier Macmillan, 1982. vii, 440p. index. LC 82-50382. ISBN 0-02-872350-3; 0-02-872360-0pa.

The dictionary pulls together terms and names loosely associated with the history and development of rock. These include technological devices, slang terms, dance steps, organizations, awards, disc jockeys, and musicians. A former music publishing company executive, Shaw has an intimate knowledge of the business aspects of popular music, which enables him to split hairs on such closely associated terms as "Rock," "Rock 'n' Roll," "Crusading Rock," and "Teenage Rock." He includes musical terms relevant to rock, such as "seventh chord," but why does he bother with a two-sentence definition of "serial technique"? Useful lists in the alphabetical body of the text give influential recording studios, drug-related fatalities of twenty-five rock musicians ("The Drug Scene"), and lists of Grammy winners under each category.

76. Shemel, Sidney, and M. William Krasilovsky. **This Business of Music**. 5th ed., rev. and enl. New York: Billboard Publications, 1985. xxvi, 646p. index. LC 85-1293. ISBN 0-8230-7754-3.

This thorough guide explains the economic and legal aspects of music in the United States—advertising, copyright, performance rights, publishing, recording, entering into contracts, trademarks, taxes, and many other topics. Its thirty-eight chapters and many more chapter sections allow information to be quickly located either in the table of contents or the index. Following the text are excerpts from relevant laws and regulations, and reproductions of several dozen license and agreement forms. Although these concerns implicitly address the popular music industry, they pertain to any kind of performance or composition.

77. Stiller, Andrew. **Handbook of Instrumentation**. Illustrations by James Stamos. Berkeley, Calif.: University of California Press, 1985. xx, 533p. music. bibliog. index. LC 82-20184. ISBN 0-520-04423-1.

This "guide to the potentials and limitations of every instrument currently in use for the performance of classical and popular music in North America" invites use as an encyclopedia by means of its sequential presentation of instruments. Part 1 covers modern instruments as used in twentieth-century practice; part 2 covers early instruments in modern reconstructions. Both give examples of music. The author notes the range, actual pitch, and availability of each instrument, then gives a thorough discussion of its physical characteristics, normal and unconventional manners of performance, and idiosyncratic forms of notation. The outstanding design of the volume features a large format text and many notated examples, fingering diagrams, and drawings of instruments.

5

Biographical Compilations

Baker's (see entry 80) is the only current biographical reference work in music which attempts to be geographically and chronologically comprehensive. Yet, despite its quantity of entries, it cannot include every subject whose biography a researcher will want to consult. There is a need for specialized sources, and this chapter has tried to provide an ample selection. With the exception of Fétis (see entry 97) and *Unvergängliche Stimmen* (see entry 105), all are in English. Some of the comprehensive encyclopedias in chapter 2 are important biographical sources which offer extended evaluations of composers and important bibliographical material. The "Annual Index of Music Necrology" in *Notes* (see entry 639) updates (or terminates) entries in these sources. The indexes and bibliographies listed in chapter 13 locate other sources of information about individuals.

78. American Society of Composers, Authors, and Publishers. **ASCAP Biographical Dictionary**. 4th ed. Compiled for the Society by Jaques Cattell Press. New York: R. R. Bowker, 1980. xii, 589p. LC 80-65351. ISBN 0-8352-1283-1.

Since not all American composers are members of ASCAP, and not all ASCAP members are listed here, this compilation represents a limited world; nevertheless, it profiles over eight thousand individuals, including many songwriters in a variety of genres. From 1914 until the founding of BMI in 1939, ASCAP represented the majority of American composers, making this a good source for most names during that period. Entries give brief, factual biographical information for both living and deceased composers, but devote most of the space to an enumeration of compositions. A list of publisher members (with no other information) concludes the volume. The selectivity of the dictionary and its heavy emphasis on songwriters allow for little overlap of entries with *Contemporary American Composers* (see entry 79).

79. Anderson, E. Ruth. **Contemporary American Composers: A Biographical Dictionary**. 2d ed. Boston: G. K. Hall, 1982. v, 578p. LC 81-7047. ISBN 0-8161-8223-X.

The several thousand composers listed here are either citizens of the United States or have spent substantial time in this country. All were born since 1870 and have achieved some minimal prominence. Composers of primarily pedagogical, jazz (with a few exceptions), popular, rock, or folk pieces are excluded. Questionnaires formed the basis for many of the entries; information in others was culled from concert announcements, publishers' lists, and recordings. The brevity of biographical information for each composer and of each one's selected list of works reflects the sources used. Addresses, when available for living composers, follow the entries – but users should remember how rapidly outdated addresses can become. *Contemporary American Composers* won the annual award given by the Music Library Association for the best book-length bibliography. The *ASCAP Biographical Dictionary* (see entry 78) has complementary information.

80. Baker, Theodore. **Baker's Biographical Dictionary of Musicians**. 7th ed. Revised by Nicolas Slonimsky. New York: Schirmer Books, 1984. xlii, 2577p. bibliog. LC 84-5595. ISBN 0-02-870270-0.

First published in 1900, *Baker's* has become music's standard biographical dictionary and one of the most useful and fascinating of all reference works. Slonimsky's prefaces to this edition and to the sixth edition, both of which appear here, are witty tales of biographical verification which exemplify his reputation for accuracy. The seventh edition updates the sixth not only with death dates for the recently deceased, but with the addition of dozens of current popular performers and the revision of major articles (for example, Beethoven and Bach). In all, it includes nearly thirteen thousand entries for composers, performers, publishers, and others from all historical periods and all parts of the world. Most entries are short, but those for major composers extend to several pages. Entries include citations to other biographical sources and lists of compositions or written works. Slonimsky is adept at using anecdotes to portray a subject's personality, compositional characteristics, or performing style. He makes no attempt to hide his opinions and often distills cogent and wry evaluations into introductory epithets for his subjects: Berlioz was "a great French composer," Caruso "a celebrated Italian tenor," Gershwin "an immensely gifted American composer." The entertaining style and abundance of not only biographical but historical and musicological information give *Baker's* primary importance in the literature.

81. Boalch, Donald H. **Makers of the Harpsichord and Clavichord, 1440-1840**. 2d ed. Oxford, England: Clarendon Press, 1974. xxi, 225p. illus. bibliog. LC 74-180634. ISBN 0-19-816123-9.

The earliest forms of the harpsichord originated circa 1440; interest in the instrument waned in the nineteenth century as the piano became more popular. This work is a guide to the works of over one thousand makers during the time of the harpsichord's original popularity. Though the only record of the work of many is a single surviving instrument, Boalch has compiled an amazing amount of information from the instruments themselves and from the catalogs and books listed in an extensive bibliography. Entries tell of makers' inventions and the kinds of instruments they produced, often quoting patents, letters, and other contemporary documents, and describe surviving instruments, noting their present locations. Supplementary material includes a geographical and chronological conspectus of makers; lists of major musical instrument collections, surviving English virginals, three-manual harpsichords, and London apprentices from 1622 to 1758; and an English-French-German-Italian glossary of technical terms. Black-and-white photographs show details of instruments and complement the work's effective and attractive design.

82. Butterworth, Neil. **A Dictionary of American Composers**. New York: Garland, 1984. xi, 523p. (Garland Reference Library of the Humanities, Vol. 296). LC 81-43331. ISBN 0-8240-9311-9.

The author's introduction expresses the hope that "this dictionary may bring to the notice of musicians on the east side of the Atlantic a new repertory of works worthy to stand beside the long tradition of European music." It includes living and deceased composers who are American by birth or who have emigrated to the United States. Though the selection excludes composers of light music, jazz, and songs, it shows a skewed perception of American music by including Stephen Foster and Lalo Schifrin and excluding Scott Joplin and Duke Ellington. Entries give places and dates of birth and death, a few sentences about the subject's life, and a generally plodding account of his or her compositions. Virtually all of the entries appear in *Baker's* (see entry 80) in more cogent form. This volume may be useful for data on some twentieth-century names and for descriptive comments on individual compositions. An appendix lists prominent teachers in Europe and America and their prominent pupils.

83. Chilton, John. **Who's Who of Jazz: Storyville to Swing Street**. 4th ed. New York: Da Capo Press, 1985. 375p. illus. (Roots of Jazz Series). LC 84-20062. ISBN 0-306-76271-4; 0-306-80243-0pa.

Two restrictions characterize Chilton's work: he includes only musicians born or raised in the United States, and more importantly, only those born before 1920. This means that the approximately one thousand musicians included are either deceased or over sixty-five. Dizzy Gillespie (born 1917) is in; Charlie Parker (born 1920), who with Gillespie was a highlight of New York's Fifty-second Street in the 1940s, is out. Entries range from several lines to a page or more in length, and cite book-length biographies and film appearances, but not recordings. Chilton is exceptionally thorough, within his criteria, in documenting the lives of these early jazz musicians, many of whom Feather's *Encyclopedia of Jazz* (see entry 94) omits.

84. Claghorn, Charles Eugene. **Biographical Dictionary of American Music**. West Nyack, N.Y.: Parker Publishing, 1973. 491p. LC 73-5534. ISBN 0-13076331-4.

Claghorn gives brief sketches of the lives of some fifty-two hundred composers, songwriters, and performers from the seventeenth century to the present who were born or spent a substantial amount of time in the United States. Sketches state the years, but not dates, of birth and death, and highlight subjects' careers through factual information. "The purpose of this book is to be all-inclusive," Claghorn maintains. He does succeed in memorializing obscure and forgotten musicians in two distinct groups—nineteenth-century songwriters and hymnists, and rock groups prominent at the time of the book's publication (few other works list the members of "Ultimate Spinach"). This is a source of last resort.

85. Claghorn, Charles Eugene. **Women Composers and Hymnists: A Concise Biographical Dictionary**. Metuchen, N.J.: Scarecrow, 1984. 272p. bibliog. index. LC 83-20429. ISBN 0-8108-1680-6.

Though this volume includes women from the twelfth century to the present from a variety of denominations and countries, the majority of biographees are nineteenth-century Protestants from English-speaking countries. Claghorn used obituaries, church records, and letters to give life to 155 composers and six hundred hymnists not likely to be found in other reference works. Entries range from a few sentences to a page in length. A brief index subdivides the composers by nationality. A twenty-six-item bibliography lists denominational hymnals. Some entries cite works in which the subject's hymns have been published, but few enumerate titles of works.

86. Cohen, Aaron I. **International Encyclopedia of Women Composers**. New York: R. R. Bowker, 1981. xviii, 597p. bibliog. index. LC 81-12233. ISBN 0-8352-1288-2.

Entries cover several thousand women from all parts of the world, from both the present and the past, and exclude only contemporary popular songwriters. Entries and *see* references from pseudonyms and maiden names all appear in one alphabetical sequence. Biographies provide facts about each composer's professional life and range in length from several words to several hundred words. A list of compositions, subdivided by category and sometimes including publishing information or date of first performance, follows each. Some entries include a list of the composer's publications. All entries cite one or more sources in a bibliography of some several hundred items. Photographs of some composers appear in a collection following the biographical entries. An appendix lists names by country and century. This is the only convenient source of information for most women composers.

87. **Contemporary Canadian Composers**. Edited by Keith MacMillan and John Beckwith. Toronto: Oxford University Press, 1975. xxiv, 248p. illus. bibliog. LC 76-351189. ISBN 0-19-540244-8.

Staff members of the Canadian Music Centre prepared these quite detailed portraits of 144 composers living in Canada who have produced all or most of their work since 1920. One can find little information about them elsewhere. These biographies give birth data and factual details of each one's education, professional positions, and compositions, along with well-informed analyses of style and of individual works. A list of compositions detailing instrumentation, publisher, date of composition or publication, and occasion of first performance accompanies each entry. Many entries include a bibliography of articles about the composer and of written works by the composer.

88. Ewen, David. **American Composers: A Biographical Dictionary**. New York: G. P. Putnam's Sons, 1982. 793p. illus. bibliog. index. LC 81-7362. ISBN 0-399-12626-0.

Ewen's substantial (one-half to three pages) biographies mix personal and professional information in an attempt to give a rounded portrait of each of three hundred composers from the eighteenth century's William Billings to the present. Essays open with a short, impressionistic description of the composer's work, trace his or her life chronologically, and conclude with a summary quotation from the subject, the source of which Ewen never provides. A list of principal works and a bibliography listing material about the subject concludes each entry. An appendix indexes titles of musical works by composer. Some overlap exists with Ewen's other works, but this volume offers an appropriate selection.

89. Ewen, David. **American Songwriters**. New York: H. W. Wilson, 1987. xi, 489p. bibliog. index. LC 86-24654. ISBN 0-8242-0744-0.

This, the final work of Ewen's prolific career as a writer of musical biographies, is a "replacement," as he explains, for his *Popular American Composers from Revolutionary Times to the Present: A Biographical and Critical Guide* (H. W. Wilson, 1962) and its *First Supplement* (H. W. Wilson, 1972). It contains 146 biographies of composers and lyricists from the nineteenth and (primarily) twentieth centuries who have achieved "a durable place in the history of the American popular song through sustained creative achievement over an extended period of time; those whose most memorable numbers have become standards." Ewen's idiosyncratic selection includes some who are more memorable than others – compare, for instance, Carly Simon with Eubie Blake or Irving Berlin. The biographies follow Ewen's standard formula: a picture of the subject, an introductory evaluation, a narrative of several pages which balances life and work, and biographical references to histories, reference works, and popular periodicals. An index lists some fifty-six hundred compositions. This is a well-rounded work which, though it cannot supplant Kinkle's *Complete Encyclopedia of Popular Music and Jazz* (see entry 57), has a life of its own.

90. Ewen, David. **Great Composers, 1300-1900: A Biographical and Critical Guide**. New York: H. W. Wilson, 1966. 429p. illus. LC 65-24585. ISBN 0-8242-0018-7.

91. Ewen, David. **Composers since 1900: A Biographical and Critical Guide**. New York: H. W. Wilson, 1969. vi, 639p. illus. bibliog. LC 72-102368. ISBN 0-8242-0400-X.

92. Ewen, David. **Composers since 1900: A Biographical and Critical Guide. First Supplement**. New York: H. W. Wilson, 1981. v, 328p. illus. bibliog. LC 81-14785. ISBN 0-8242-0664-9.

These three volumes form a set. Each of the first two provides portraits of about two hundred composers. The supplement offers forty-seven new biographies and updates material on 172 entries in the previous volumes. Biographies range in length from one to several pages. Ewen mixes personal tidbits with impressionistic descriptions of works, and employs quotes from a variety of sources and from his own familiarity with contemporary composers to flesh out biographical facts. A picture of the composer, a pronunciation guide to difficult names, a list of major works, and a short list of biographical sources accompany each essay. The nontechnical style combined with a variety of information that is not otherwise easy to locate make these portraits uniquely personal and enjoyable.

93. Ewen, David. **Musicians since 1900: Performers in Concert and Opera**. New York: H. W. Wilson, 1978. 974p. illus. LC 78-12727. ISBN 0-8242-0565-0.

The 432 subjects of this volume all made their major contributions in the twentieth century. Ewen's mixture of a variety of personal biographical detail with critics' commentary on performances, intertwining subjects' lives with their art, is particularly appropriate to prominent performers. Essays of one to two pages in length include a picture, a pronunciation guide for some names, and a brief list of references. The classified list following the biographies shows the selection to be particularly heavy in singers and conductors, with a good selection of pianists and string players and virtually no other instrumentalists.

94. Feather, Leonard. **The Encyclopedia of Jazz**. Completely rev., enl., and brought up to date. New York: Horizon Press, 1960; repr., New York: Da Capo Press, 1984. 527p. illus. bibliog. discog. LC 83-26164. ISBN 0-306-80214-7pa.

95. Feather, Leonard. **The Encyclopedia of Jazz in the Sixties**. Foreword by John Lewis. New York: Horizon Press, 1966; repr., New York: Da Capo Press, 1986. 312p. illus. bibliog. discog. LC 85-31125. ISBN 0-306-80263-5pa.

96. Feather, Leonard, and Ira Gitler. **The Encyclopedia of Jazz in the Seventies**. Introduction by Quincy Jones. New York: Horizon Press, 1976; repr., New York: Da Capo Press, 1987. 393p. illus. bibliog. discog. LC 87-517. ISBN 0-306-80290-2pa.

These three volumes provide biographies of some two thousand jazz musicians through the middle 1970s. The second two update previous information and provide new entries. Feather and Gitler write with a flair rarely found in reference books, seasoning entries with evaluative commentary and quotations from other sources. Entries range from several sentences to a full page in length and highlight performances and recordings. Most entries include short discographies. Each volume supplements the biographies with a variety of material: a bibliography of jazz books, a list of recommended LPs, results of critics' and readers' polls, black-and-white photographs, a birthday chronology, or a directory of jazz education opportunities.

97. Fétis, F. J. **Biographie universelle des musiciens et bibliographie générale de la musique**. 2me. ed. Paris: Librairie de Firmin-Didot et Cie, 1875-78; repr., Brussels: Culture et Civilisation, 1972. 8v. music. LC 72-373582.

Supplément et complément. Publiés sous la direction de M. Arthur Pougin. 1878-80; repr., Brussels: Culture et Civilisation, 1972. 2v. music.

First published in 1835-44, this biographical dictionary was a landmark in its international scope. It includes composers, performers, instrument makers, and writers on music since ancient times. Musicians from the late eighteenth and early nineteenth centuries are especially well-represented, with ample space allotted to many. Entries includes lists of compositions and bibliographies.

98. Gilder, Eric. **The Dictionary of Composers and Their Music: A Listener's Companion**. new, rev. ed. New York: Holt, Rinehart and Winston, 1985. 592p. LC 86-140019. ISBN 0-03-007177-1.

Gilder addresses his work "not only to the academic student, but also to the vast numbers of interested laymen." In this spirit, this dictionary of the lives and works of 426 composers from Machaut to those still living avoids musicological speculation, and focuses on dates. Entries give short factual biographies including places and dates of birth and death, and chronological listings of works. The dates ascribed to works vaguely refer to "when the music is first mentioned." Often Gilder opts, unhelpfully, to group compositions of a similar nature. For example, he gives dates for twelve compositions by Domenico Scarlatti, but simply mentions "over 550 single-movement harpsichord sonatas." A mass chronology from 1300 to 1984 runs together the dates of compositions and the dates of births and deaths of composers.

99. Greene, David Mason. **Greene's Biographical Encyclopedia of Composers**. Garden City, N.Y.: Doubleday, 1985. xl, 1348p. index. LC 79-6863. ISBN 0-385-14278-1.

Greene depicts the lives of 2,433 composers whose work "has been reasonably available on records in the United States." Entries run from half a page to several pages in length in a chronological arrangement (by date of birth), which necessitates consulting an alphabetical list to locate the entry number for a specific name. The first entry is Limenios of second-century B. C. Greece; several entries later the twelfth-century troubadours begin a tour of the Western tradition which ends with William Hugh Albright, born in 1944. Greene's informal style emphasizes "subjects as human beings rather than as music machines." This is a source for biographical fact, not musicological comment or citations to other works. It is important for the sheer quantity of entries and for the substantial detail it brings to the lives of many composers whom even *Baker's* (see entry 80) discusses briefly or ignores.

100. Harris, Sheldon. **Blues Who's Who: A Biographical Dictionary of Blues Singers.** New Rochelle, N.Y.: Arlington House, 1979; repr., New York: Da Capo Press, 1981. 775p. illus. bibliog. index. LC 81-7873. ISBN 0-306-80155-8pa.

The author gathered material for this thorough and unique survey from interviews and both published and unpublished sources during his years as a volunteer with the Institute of Jazz Studies. He portrays 571 blues singers (many of whom are also instrumentalists) who worked between 1900 and 1977. Entries focus on facts: birth and death dates, performances, appearances, recording dates (but not discographical information), and compositions. Quotations from other sources give personality to the sometimes dry detail. Nicknames and stage names refer the reader to proper names: for instance, "Blind Blake" leads to an entry for "Phelps, Arthur." A bibliography lists general sources the author consulted. Extensive indexes list films, radio and television programs, theatrical presentations in which the singers participated, song names, and places mentioned in the text.

101. Helander, Brock. **The Rock Who's Who: A Biographical Dictionary and Critical Discography Including Rhythm-and-Blues, Soul, Rockabilly, Folk, Country, Easy Listening, Punk, and New Wave**. New York: Schirmer Books, 1982. xiv, 686p. bibliog. discog. LC 82-80804. ISBN 0-02-871250-1.

At its best, this collection of group and individual biographies gives concise and balanced sketches of major rock figures from the 1950s to the 1980s. It occasionally suffers from its author's opinions and preferences, however, and devotes pages to minor figures and omits prominent groups such as the Police. Nevertheless it is the best single volume source of biographical information in this area. Thorough discographies of each artist's or group's LPs organize the complicated recording history of some, and include manufacturer's serial number, date, and gold or platinum record designations. A bibliography lists books and articles about artists and groups, those written by rock musicians, and a reasonable selection of books about rock music.

102. Holmes, John L. **Conductors on Record**. Westport, Conn.: Greenwood Press, 1982. xv, 734p. discog. LC 80-28578. ISBN 0-313-22990-2.

Holmes's biographies of some fifteen hundred conductors who have recorded on either LP or 78rpm records give substance to the names we see on record labels and jackets. He covers many conductors omitted by *Baker's* (see entry 80), amplifies information in many of *Baker's* biographies, and includes details of his subjects' recording activities which *Baker's* rarely mentions. Entries range in length from a paragraph to several pages. Each devotes about half its space to biographical information and half to its subject's recordings (albeit selectively and without discographical data) in a mix of historical fact and reasoned opinion and evaluation. Users should remember that this is a work about conductors; hence biographies of instrumentalists such as Pinchas Zuckerman and composers such as Darius Milhaud (whom Holmes passes off as having "no particular reputation as a conductor") focus primarily on their work as conductors.

103. **International Who's Who in Music and Musicians' Directory**. 10th ed. Cambridge, England: International Who's Who in Music, 1985. 1178p. ISBN 0-8103-0424-4.

The tenth edition includes some eight thousand living composers, performers, critics, musicologists, teachers, and others involved in music from around the world. Entries, in a uniform format, give birth date and place, main field of interest, education, and details of the subject's professional career such as titles of compositions or publications, teaching or performing positions, honors, or memberships. Most entries include an address. Appendixes list addresses, by country, for orchestras, musical organizations, sponsors of major competitions and awards, music libraries and conservatories, and "Masters of the King's/Queen's Musick." This is a standard biographical work for musicians, but the number of well-known names it traditionally and inexplicably omits (Isaac Stern, for instance) is astounding. It is useful primarily for information about the second tier of working professionals who may not be included in other more selective works.

104. Jalovec, Karel. **Encyclopedia of Violin-Makers**. Translated by J. B. Kozak. Edited by Patrick Hanks. London: Paul Hamlyn, 1968. 2v. illus. music. bibliog. LC 68-84433.

No instrument in the history of European music can compare with the violin in its longevity, consistency, and prominence. Originally published as *Enzyklopädie des Geigenbaues* (Leiden, Netherlands: E. J. Brill, 1965), the encyclopedia covers perhaps ten thousand makers, dating at least to the thirteenth century, of violin family instruments, bows, guitars, and lutes. Entries give short biographical information, a description or reproduction of the maker's label, and comments on the physical and acoustical characteristics of surviving instruments, of which the author seems to have examined thousands. The encyclopedia features a seventy-four-page alphabetical survey of stringed instruments of the world, hundreds of photographs of violins, and a bibliography of books in several languages on the history of the violin.

105. Kutsch, K. J., and Leo Riemens. **Unvergängliche Stimmen: Sängerlexikon**. Bern, Switzerland: Francke Verlag, 1982. 782p. LC 83-113596. ISBN 3-7720-1555-7.

The "immortal voices" to whom the title refers are singers who have transcended the bounds of mortality by being recorded. The second edition greatly expands the first (1962) to include biographical entries for over three thousand singers who have been recorded in any fashion from wax cylinders to modern digital techniques. Entries are short and factual, giving dates and places of birth and death, biographical and professional details, and lists of labels on which the singers have recorded. The *Sängerlexikon* includes many names not mentioned in *Baker's* (see entry 80) or *The New Grove* (see entry 20). A translation of the first edition, expanded and annotated by Harry Earl Jones, appeared under the title *A Concise Biographical Dictionary of Singers from the Beginning of Recorded Sound to the Present* (Chilton Book Company, 1969).

106. Lyle, Wilson. **A Dictionary of Pianists**. New York: Schirmer Books, 1984. 343p. illus. LC 85-8841. ISBN 0-02-919250-1.

This biographical dictionary covers some four thousand pianists and composers for the piano from the instrument's invention in the eighteenth century to the present. Its entries for composers focus on their piano performance or compositions for piano; thus, while it devotes three columns to Beethoven, it barely mentions symphonic or other works which do not feature the piano. Entries range from several lines to several columns in length. The dictionary includes many names not found in *Baker's* (see entry 80), but gives such sketchy information for some that their inclusion is of little use. An appendix gives an extensive list of "Winners of International Piano Competitions and Medalists of Conservatories and Schools."

107. Nite, Norm N. **Rock On: The Illustrated History of Rock 'n Roll**. New York: Harper & Row. 3v. LC 83-48371.

Volume 1: The Solid Gold Years. 1982. xii, 722p. illus. discog. index. ISBN 0-06-181642-6.

Volume 2: The Years of Change, 1964-1978. 1984. xvii, 749p. illus. discog. index. ISBN 0-06-181643-4.

Volume 3: The Video Revolution 1978-Present. With Charles Crespo. 1985. xviii, 444p. illus. discog. index. ISBN 0-06-181644-2.

These volumes have become the standard reference works for biographies of rock performers, and are the only places to locate information on those who have produced a hit single and then dropped out of sight. Nite gives chatty sketches of hundreds of individuals and groups, and usually includes a modicum of biographical facts. Discographies accompanying entries list only 45rpm releases; *The Rock Who's Who* (see entry 101), though it includes far fewer individuals and groups, lists albums. Each volume covers musicians active in the given period of time; some musicians with relatively lengthy careers, such as Elvis Presley, appear in more than one volume. Each volume includes an index of song titles.

108. Pulver, Jeffrey. **A Biographical Dictionary of Old English Music**. London: Kegan Paul, Trench, Trubner; New York: E. P. Dutton, 1927; repr., New York: Da Capo Press, 1973. xix, 537p. index. LC 69-16666. ISBN 0-306-71103-6.

Despite Pulver's claim that he is not writing history, his lives of composers, performers, and writers on music in the five-hundred-year-period ending with Purcell's death in 1695 take this work beyond the strict bounds of a biographical dictionary. His discursive style mingles birth and death dates, bibliographical references, and quotations from letters and contemporary accounts in sharp contrast with Slonimsky's voracious gathering of vital statistics in *Baker's* (see entry 80). An index thoroughly covers names and subjects mentioned throughout the text. Biographies of persons of historical stature (such as Byrd, Dowland, and Purcell) appropriately extend to several pages. Though *The New Grove* (see entry 20) has updated and developed most of Pulver's biographies, the work stands as a standard biographical source. The reprint contains an introduction and a bibliography of the writings of Jeffrey Pulver by Gilbert Blount.

109. Rich, Maria F., ed. **Who's Who in Opera: An International Biographical Directory of Singers, Conductors, Directors, Designers, and Administrators, Also Including Profiles of 101 Opera Companies**. New York: Arno Press, 1976. xxi, 684p. LC 75-7963. ISBN 0-405-06652-X.

The 2,350 individuals included were active in the early 1970s in one or more of a selection of 144 opera companies in thirty-three countries. The brief entry for each generally gives place and date of birth, educational background, and circumstances of the subject's debut. Lists of companies with which the biographee has worked, and pieces which he or she has staged or performed major roles in occupy the bulk of the entries. These listings give no dates. The profiles of companies also derive from questionnaires and concisely give the company's history, affiliation, recent (from the early 1970s) repertoire, and statistics on performances, budgets, and personnel.

110. Southern, Eileen. **Biographical Dictionary of Afro-American and African Musicians**. Westport, Conn.: Greenwood Press, 1982. xv, 478p. bibliog. index. (Greenwood Encyclopedia of Black Music). LC 81-2586. ISBN 0-313-21339-9; ISSN 0272-0264.

The title gives an erroneous impression – virtually all entries are for Americans. This caveat aside, the collection provides unique coverage for over fifteen hundred musicians, living and deceased. Criteria for entrants include standards for significant achievement and recognition. Exceptions are made, however, for all musicians born before the 1863 Emancipation Proclamation and for many women, due to the dearth of available information in other sources. Entries extend to more than five hundred words, and bibliographical references are appended to each. Appendixes list entries by period and place of birth and by musical occupation. The index lists all entries and names mentioned within entries.

111. Stambler, Irwin, and Grelun Landon. **The Encyclopedia of Folk, Country, and Western Music**. 2d ed. New York: St. Martin's Press, 1984. xviii, 902p. illus. bibliog. LC 82-5702. ISBN 0-312-24818-0.

The encyclopedia demonstrates that the terms folk, country, and western are now misnomers for what has become a highly commercial genre of American popular music. Detailed biographies of a diverse range of performers concentrate on commercial successes while including a handful of those who perform traditional music. The authors write with authority (their bibliography lists over two hundred items) and an appreciative flair which mingles personal and professional details in well-constructed sketches. The lack of cross-references from group names to individuals may trouble users unfamiliar with the territory. The volume includes lists of winners of recording and composing awards from the Country Music Hall of Fame and other organizations. The first edition from 1969, containing entries for those whose faded popularity has precluded their inclusion in this second edition, remains useful.

112. **Who's Who in American Music: Classical**. 2d ed. Edited by Jaques Cattell Press. New York: R. R. Bowker, 1985. xiii, 783p. index. biennial. LC 84-642464. ISBN 0-8352-2074-5; ISSN 0737-9137.

Each of the 9,038 entries for living composers, performers, educators, librarians, and others gives abbreviated biographical data in a standard format: professional classification, birth data, study and training, compositions, recorded performances, roles, positions, teaching, honors and awards, writings, memberships, research interests, publications, manager or representative's name, and mailing address. A geographic index lists entries by state and city, and a professional classification index lists entrants by fields of activity (such as "violin," "librarian," or "mezzo-soprano") with which they have identified themselves. This is a good source for brief, factual information, particularly for those not sufficiently prominent to have been included in *Baker's* (see entry 80). As in the first edition, virtually all entrants are U.S. citizens, but the criteria for selection are sufficiently broad to include Vladimir Ashkenazy (born in the USSR, citizen of Iceland, resident of the United Kingdom) and other international performers.

6

Histories and Chronologies

In the compilation of knowledge about the past, and sometimes, in the quantity of bibliographic references gathered, general histories can be considered as reference works. This chapter includes some of the more prominent general one-volume histories and multivolume historical series which have been published in the last forty years. Other histories in this chapter focus on a particular aspect of music history, such as opera or jazz. Chronologies included in this chapter offer a more factual and less interpretive format (although, as Slonimsky's *Music since 1900*, entry 136, demonstrates, the accumulation of facts can also be interpretive). *The New Grove* (see entry 20) and *MGG* (see entry 19) contain extended historical articles.

113. Abraham, Gerald. **The Concise Oxford History of Music**. New York: Oxford University Press, 1979. 968p. music. bibliog. index. LC 79-40540. ISBN 0-19-311319-8.

This is not a condensation of *The New Oxford History of Music* (see entry 127), but a completely independent work. Abraham's emphasis is on the "continuum" of Western music, although he does make several excursions into non-Western influences. He avoids lengthy discussions of major figures, and prefers to make stylistic connections between specific works which exemplify historical tendencies. Abraham's history is more disperse than Grout's (see entry 120), but its detailed index allows a reader to locate commentary on particular works, a process which is difficult in Grout. Supplementary bibliographical essays corresponding to the chapters were contributed by well-known scholars and include historical and critical works and editions of music.

114. Bordman, Gerald. **American Musical Theatre: A Chronicle**. New York: Oxford University Press, 1978. viii, 749p. index. LC 77-18748. ISBN 0-19-502356-0.

Divided into eleven "Acts" and "Intermissions," this season-by-season account records not only Broadway productions but prominent shows from off-Broadway, Chicago, Boston, and Philadelphia as well. A survey of the relatively bleak theater scene in America in the eighteenth and early nineteenth centuries leads into the chronological record beginning in 1866. Rather than simply enumerating facts, Bordman employs a lively and familiar narrative which yet methodically manages to include, for each musical, its opening date, a history of its run, a summary of the plot, and a partial list of performers. A musical can be located easily by skimming through the five to ten pages accorded to each season or by consulting the index, which lists not only shows but literary sources, songs, and people. An appendix lists works of prominent lyricists and composers.

115. Bradley, Carol June, comp. **Music Collections in American Libraries: A Chronology**. Detroit: Information Coordinators, 1981. xiii, 249p. bibliog. index. (Detroit Studies in Music Bibliography, No. 46). LC 81-2907. ISBN 0-89990-002-X.

The chronology begins in 1731 with the founding of the Library Company of Philadelphia. It traces the foundings of music libraries and the consolidations of diverse collections in public, academic, and special libraries. Each entry gives the name of the library, the address, a minichronology of significant dates at that particular library, a list of special collections, and a list of publications of and about the library. The index includes names of individual libraries.

116. Burbank, Richard. **Twentieth Century Music**. Introduction by Nicolas Slonimsky. New York: Facts on File, 1984. xxi, 485p. illus. bibliog. index. LC 80-25040. ISBN 0-87196-464-3.

This chronology of music from 1900 to 1979 arranges by date the events of each year within five categories: opera; dance; instrumental and vocal music; births, deaths, and debuts; and related events. Most of the entries in the first three categories record first performances. In addition to the date, entries give the location, the performers, and historical or descriptive notes. The next section identifies births and debuts and gives summary obituaries for the deceased. The last section includes developments in recording, broadcasting, and instrumentation; establishment of organizations and concert halls; significant publications; and political events related to music. Many entries duplicate those in *Music since 1900* (see entry 136), but *Twentieth Century Music* differs in its inclusion of dance, its exclusion of jazz and popular music, and in its index, which lists works individually, though at the expense of adequate subdivisions beneath the composer's name.

117. Chase, Gilbert. **America's Music: From the Pilgrims to the Present**. rev. 2d ed. New York: McGraw-Hill, 1966; repr., Westport, Conn.: Greenwood Press, 1981. xxi, 759p. music. bibliog. index. LC 80-28027. ISBN 0-313-22391-2.

With vigor, humor, and commitment, Chase's history ranges from the *Bay Psalm Book* of 1640 to Moravian Church music, Methodist camp meetings, black spirituals, musical theater, ragtime, jazz, and blues, and gives due attention to the American tradition of composed music in exemplars such as Edward MacDowell, Charles Ives, and Virgil Thomson. This second edition deletes from the first edition (1955) the chapter, "Indian Tribal Music," in favor of an update on music in the 1960s. Despite a nod to the musical theater, Chase tacitly omits the more commercial forms of music such as popular songs and rock—neither Frank Sinatra nor Elvis Presley rates even a mention. Nevertheless, Chase gives continuity to a pastiche of musics which does not lend itself easily to a strictly linear history. The thirty-page bibliography notes general sources and those specific to each chapter.

118. Gangwere, Blanche. **Music History from the Late Roman through the Gothic Periods, 313-1425: A Documented Chronology**. Westport, Conn.: Greenwood Press, 1986. xiii, 247p. illus. bibliog. discog. index. (Music Reference Collection, No. 6). LC 85-21934. ISBN 0-313-24764-1; ISSN 0736-7740.

The preface explains that 313 was the date of the Edict of Milan, which allowed the unhampered development of the Roman Catholic church and its subsequent vast influence on Western music. By 1425, polyphonic music was well-developed. The author promises to carry on with further volumes to the twentieth century. This is not a chronology in the normal sense of the term but a series of chronologically and topically arranged references to other works. A subject index partially eases the strain of using this system. About half the work consists of appendixes addressing Greek music, ecclesiastical modes, and forms of notation. The dot-matrix printing used is inadequate to this material, impeding a reader.

119. Grout, Donald Jay. **A Short History of Opera**. 2d ed. New York: Columbia University Press, 1965. xviii, 852p. music. bibliog. index. LC 64-11043. ISBN 0-231-02422-3.

A sophisticated and engaging style and a thorough treatment with plentiful references to musical examples and to other works make this the premiere comprehensive history of opera. Grout begins with the lyrical theater of the Greeks, moves quickly through medieval music and the predecessors of opera, then beginning with Monteverdi's *Orfeo* devotes an individual section to each century from the seventeenth to the twentieth. Grout observes that "an opera is not only a drama but also a type of musical composition" (p. 2); his approach is through historical musicology which examines works within sketched out social and artistic circumstances rather than through the relation of a string of plot summaries or the lives of singers and stories of productions. Supplementing the text are a book-length, 184-page bibliography which enumerates thousands of works in most European languages pertaining to opera, an index to modern editions of operas composed before 1800, and an index to names, works, and subjects discussed in the text.

120. Grout, Donald Jay, with Claude V. Palisca. **A History of Western Music**. 3d ed. New York: W. W. Norton, 1980. xii, 849p. music. glossary. bibliog. index. LC 80-12224. ISBN 0-393-95136-7.

Except for some material added to the chapter covering the twentieth century, some added entries in the bibliography, and the removal of some extraordinarily unattractive illustrations of composers, Grout has changed little since the first edition of 1960. He presumes "an elementary knowledge of musical terms and of harmony" but avoids overly technical approaches, preferring to frame the lives and works of major composers within their historical settings. The substantial bibliography parallels the chapters in its organization. It lists and evaluates histories, works of criticism, and editions of music. A glossary covers basic terminology, and a short chronology covers events in music, other arts, science, and politics. A "shorter edition" was published by Norton in 1981.

121. Hamm, Charles. **Music in the New World**. New York: W. W. Norton, 1983. xiv, 722p. illus. music. bibliog. discog. index. LC 82-6481. ISBN 0-393-95193-6.

Hamm's rationales for a new history of music (since Gilbert Chase's classic *America's Music* of 1966, entry 117) include the availability of a profusion of recent printed and recorded resources and the present "stylistic plateau" (introduction) of American music. He begins with the music of native Americans (which Chase's second edition omits) and takes the history through Cecil Taylor, Philip Glass, and the B-52s. The text does not lack for musical examples, but the thrust of the work is historical and social rather than analytical. The discography is as substantial as the bibliography. References to recorded music use as sources New World Records' *Recorded Anthology of American Music* and the Library of Congress's *Folk Music in America*.

122. Johnson, H. Earle. **First Performances in America to 1900: Works with Orchestra**. Detroit: Information Coordinators for the College Music Society, 1979. xxiv, 446p. illus. bibliog. index. (Bibliographies in American Music, No. 4). LC 75-23554. ISBN 0-911772-94-4.

Through this record of first performances of 1,140 works by over two hundred composers, Johnson shows that the trickle of European musical culture to the United States in the late eighteenth century grew into a wave in the late nineteenth century. The arrangement is alphabetical by composer, with each composer's works listed by form. Entries give the place of performance, the date, and the names of the orchestra, the conductor, and the soloists. Extracts from programs and contemporary reviews show the local pride in first performances and the growing sophistication of reviewers (the *New York Times* reviewer "would prefer death to a repetition of this production" of Mozart's *Sinfonia Concertante*). Appendixes identify the often anonymous reviewers of prominent newspapers of the period; list by city the dates of construction of major concert halls; index by form the works included; and give a short bibliography.

123. Láng, Paul Henry. **Music in Western Civilization**. New York: W. W. Norton, 1941. xvi, 1107p. illus. bibliog. index. LC 41-9128. ISBN 0-393-09428-6.

Láng's history remains important for its portrayal of music within broad historical themes. More than a history of music alone, it integrates the development of music with that of literature, art, philosophy, and society. Since his perspective is historical rather than analytical, Láng offers no musical examples. Three maps show the distribution of Flemish composers, Italian composers, and members of the Viennese school throughout Europe during the influential period of each. Black-and-white plates portray performers of music in exemplary works of art chosen from all periods of Western history. Láng's approach and elegant style complement the more "musical" histories in the Norton History of Music series (see entry 128).

124. Loewenberg, Alfred. **Annals of Opera, 1597-1940, Compiled from the Original Sources**. 3d ed., rev. and corr. Introduction by Edward J. Dent. Totowa, N.J.: Rowman and Littlefield, 1978. xxvp., 1756 columns. index. LC 79-105243. ISBN 0-87471-851-1.

First published in 1943, the *Annals of Opera* has been a precursor to all contemporary reference works of opera, and in its third edition remains one of the most important resources in the field. Loewenberg used scores, librettos, playbills, newspapers, periodicals, and other "original sources" to compile what the preface calls "a skeleton history of opera": a chronological account of first performances. Each entry lists the composer, the title in its original form (with translations from languages other than French, German, or Italian), the date and place of the first performance, the librettist, the literary source, the number of acts, a list of succeeding performances and translations, and historical or bibliographical notes pertaining to the work. Three separate indexes list operas, composers, and librettists or writers (such as Shakespeare) who inspired texts. A general index covers names, towns, and subjects mentioned in the entries. An asterisk before an entry indicates a related entry in a forthcoming supplementary volume.

125. Marcuse, Sibyl. **A Survey of Musical Instruments**. New York: Harper & Row, 1975. xii, 863p. illus. bibliog. index. LC 72-9135. ISBN 0-06-012776-7.

This volume demonstrates the historical development of modern forms of pre-electronic instruments. Its emphasis is on European instruments, but it examines as precursors and variants a selection of those from other parts of the world. The text differs from the dictionary arrangement of many other comprehensive works on instruments by grouping instruments into four sections – idiophones, membranophones, chordophones, and aerophones – according to the manner in which they produce sound. Within these categories and further subdivisions, Marcuse examines in detail the evolution of physical structures of individual instruments. She includes material on performance or composition only as it specifically influences structure. A glossary defines terms relating to instruments in general or to specific mechanisms. A list of almost three hundred "works referred to" testifies to the authority of this survey. Indexes cover names of individuals and of instruments.

126. Mattfeld, Julius. **Variety Music Cavalcade, 1620-1969: A Chronology of Vocal and Instrumental Music Popular in the United States**. 3d ed. Introduction by Abel Green. Englewood Cliffs, N.J.: Prentice-Hall, 1971. xx, 766p. index. LC 70-29240. ISBN 0-13-940718-9.

This account selectively lists "hymns, secular and social songs, choral compositions, and instrumental or orchestral works" for the period before 1800 and for each following year. The word *popular* in the subtitle is a reminder not to expect to find works here by Virgil Thomson or Aaron Copland. Annotations for works listed give the names of composers and lyricists, the publisher and the date of publication or copyright, and occasionally brief notes on the work. With each annual listing appears an idiosyncratic account of contemporaneous political, cultural, and musical events. The volumes of *Popular Music* (see entry 461) give more extensive listings, but for a more limited period of time.

127. **The New Oxford History of Music**. New York: Oxford University Press, 1954- .

Volume 1: Ancient and Oriental Music. Egon Wellesz, ed. 1957. xxiii, 530p. illus. music, bibliog. index. LC 57-4332. ISBN 0-19-316301-2.

Volume 2: Early Medieval Music up to 1300. Dom Anselm Hughes, ed. 1954; rev., 1967. xviii, 434p. illus. music. bibliog. index. LC 54-14955. ISBN 0-19-316302-0.

Volume 3: Ars Nova and the Renaissance, 1300-1540. Dom Anselm Hughes and Gerald Abraham, eds. 1960; repr. with corr., 1986. xix, 563p. illus. music. bibliog. index. LC 63-603. ISBN 0-19-316303-9.

Volume 4: The Age of Humanism, 1540-1630. Gerald Abraham, ed. 1968. xxv, 978p. illus. music. bibliog. index. LC 68-31926. ISBN 0-19-316304-7.

Volume 5: Opera and Church Music, 1630-1750. Anthony Lewis and Nigel Fortune, eds. 1975; repr. with corr., 1986. xxi, 871p. illus. music. bibliog. index. LC 76-370093. ISBN 0-19-316305-5.

Volume 6: Concert Music (1630-1750). Gerald Abraham, ed. 1986. xx, 786p. illus. music. bibliog. index. LC 85-2950. ISBN 0-19-316306-3.

Volume 7: The Age of Enlightenment, 1745-1790. Egon Wellesz and Frederick Sternfeld, eds. 1973. xx, 724p. illus. music. bibliog. index. LC 74-164312. ISBN 0-19-316307-1.

Volume 8: The Age of Beethoven, 1790-1830. Gerald Abraham, ed. 1982. xix, 747p. illus. music. bibliog. index. LC 82-6413. ISBN 0-19-316308-X.

Volume 9: Romanticism, 1830-1890. Forthcoming.

Volume 10: The Modern Age, 1890-1960. Martin Cooper, ed. 1974. xix, 764p. illus. music. bibliog. index. LC 74-182275. ISBN 0-19-316310-1.

The *New Oxford* succeeds the original *Oxford History of Music* (2d ed. London: Oxford University Press, 1929-38; repr., New York: Cooper Square Publishers, 1973). Within an overall time frame, each volume in the series presents an average of a dozen chapters or essays which focus on individual forms, countries, or periods. The editors and other European and American scholars contributed the essays, which manage to retain individual style and opinions yet avoid overly technical analyses. Although the *New Oxford* certainly highlights individual composers and works, it is strictly a musical history, and includes biographical details only as they are important to circumstances of composition. All essays include citations to other works and many musical examples. Because of the extended style of the essays, the *New Oxford* cannot be thought of strictly as a reference work. Nevertheless, its authority, its broadly encompassing perspective, and its extensive bibliographies accompanying each essay (but found at the end of each volume), which list pertinent editions of music along with books and articles, make it a primary resource. An index in each volume lists terms, composers, and beneath composers' names, specific works treated in that volume.

128. **[Norton History of Music]**. New York: W. W. Norton, 1940-66.

Sachs, Curt. **The Rise of Music in the Ancient World, East and West**. 1943. 324p. illus. music. index. LC 43-16820.

Reese, Gustave. **Music in the Middle Ages: With an Introduction on the Music of Ancient Times**. 1940. xvii, 502p. illus. music. bibliog. discog. index. LC 41-557. ISBN 0-393-09750-1.

Reese, Gustave. **Music in the Renaissance**. rev. ed. (1st ed. 1954). 1959. xvii, 1022p. illus. music. bibliog. index. LC 59-12879. ISBN 0-393-09530-4.

Bukofzer, Manfred F. **Music in the Baroque Era, from Monteverdi to Bach**. 1947. xv, 489p. illus. music. bibliog. index. LC 47-12355. ISBN 0-393-09745-5.

Einstein, Alfred. **Music in the Romantic Era**. 1947. xii, 371p. illus. index. LC 47-3745. ISBN 0-393-09733-1.

Austin, William W. **Music in the 20th Century, from Debussy through Stravinsky**. 1966. xx, 708p. illus. music. bibliog. index. LC 65-18776. ISBN 0-393-09704-8.

While not identified by the publisher as a series, these histories were written, and are commonly considered, as such. The authors include some of the most prominent musicologists of the twentieth century. In contrast to the collective efforts of the contributors to *The New Oxford History of Music* (see entry 127), each volume is the work of one author. As a result, each is highly individual, and reflects an idiosyncratic approach. Sachs devotes as much space to the music of East Asia, India, and the Islamic cultures as to the music of our linear ancestors, the Greeks and Romans. Reese has made "a conscious effort ... to interweave" the *Renaissance* volume with his *Middle Ages* volume and with Bukofzer's *Baroque*. Einstein employs no musical examples, on the theory that "the major – and many of the minor – works of the Romantic era ... are alive, known, and accessible to everyone." Austin finds the major innovations of music of the twentieth century not only in Schoenberg, Bartók, and Stravinsky, but in jazz as well. The volumes by Austin, Bukofzer, and Reese include extensive bibliographies.

129. **Prentice-Hall History of Music Series**. H. Wiley Hitchcock, ed. Englewood Cliffs, N.J.: Prentice-Hall, 1973-81.

Seay, Albert. **Music in the Medieval World**. 2d ed. 1975. ix, 182p. illus. music. bibliog. index. LC 74-23185. ISBN 0-13-608133-9; 0-13-608125-8pa.

Brown, Howard Mayer. **Music in the Renaissance**. 1976. xiv. 384p. music. bibliog. index. LC 75-28352. ISBN 0-13-608505-9; 0-13-608497-4pa.

Palisca, Claude V. **Baroque Music**. 2d ed. 1981. xiv, 300p. music. bibliog. index. LC 79-22140. ISBN 0-13-055954-7; 0-13-055947-4pa.

Pauly, Reinhard G. **Music in the Classic Period**. 2d ed. 1973. xvi, 206p. music. bibliog. index. LC 72-4151. ISBN 0-13-607648-3; 0-13-607630-0pa.

Longyear, Rey M. **Nineteenth-Century Romanticism in Music**. 2d ed. 1973. xiv, 239p. music. bibliog. index. LC 72-3962. ISBN 0-13-622670-1; 0-13-622647-7pa.

Salzman, Eric. **Twentieth-Century Music: An Introduction**. 2d ed. 1974. xiii, 242p. music. bibliog. index. LC 73-17211. ISBN 0-13-935015-2; 0-13-935007-1pa.

Nettl, Bruno. **Folk and Traditional Music of the Western Continents**. 2d ed. With chapters on Latin America by Gérard Béhague. 1973. xiii, 258p. illus. music. bibliog. discog. LC 72-10010. ISBN 0-13-322941-6; 0-13-322933-5pa.

Malm, William P. **Music Cultures of the Pacific, the Near East, and Asia**. 2d ed. 1977. xv, 236p. illus. music. bibliog. discog. index. LC 76-44027. ISBN 0-13-608000-6; 0-13-607994-6pa.

Hitchcock, H. Wiley. **Music in the United States: A Historical Introduction**. 2d ed. 1974. xvii, 286p. illus. music. bibliog. index. LC 73-19751. ISBN 0-13-608398-6; 0-13-608380-3pa.

Béhague, Gérard. **Music in Latin America: An Introduction**. 1979. xiv, 369p. illus. music. bibliog. index. LC 78-17264. ISBN 0-13-608919-4; 0-13-608901-1pa.

Wade, Bonnie C. **Music in India: The Classical Traditions**. 1979. xix, 252p. illus. music. bibliog. discog. index. LC 80-068. ISBN 0-13-607036-1; 0-13-607028-0pa.

These fine, concise histories and ethnomusicological studies meet a certain definition of reference work in their condensation of considerations, trends, and facts into measurable terms. Addressed to "students and informed amateurs of music" (foreword to recent editions), each stands on its own, yet the series forms a chronological and almost geographical whole. The authors are all recognized authorities in their fields and good writers who discuss their topics clearly. All volumes employ plentiful musical examples and have detailed indexes. Bibliographies take the form of short essays at the ends of chapters.

130. **Schirmer History of Music**. Léonie Rosenstiel, general ed. New York: Schirmer Books; London: Collier Macmillan, 1982. xviii, 974p. illus. music. bibliog. index. LC 81-51061. ISBN 0-02-872190-X.

A joint effort by seven contributors, *Schirmer* runs against the grain of the one-person monolithic history of music. But what it loses in personal style it gains in a sophisticated design which employs numerous illustrations and musical examples, making it more than a treatise. In its view of the history of music as the history of a performing art, it subsumes examinations of the great composers within broad discussions of form and style. As a history, its most unique feature is the separation from the linear history of Western music of the indigenous music of the New World into a final chapter. The brevity of this section, however, offers no competition to Chase's *America's Music* (see entry 117). Each of the forty chapters (divided into parts authored by each of the seven contributors) follows a similar format which concludes with a summary, notes, and a bibliography. The index is effective in its choice of specific topics and the highlighting of musical examples.

131. Schuller, Gunther. **Early Jazz: Its Roots and Musical Development**. New York: Oxford University Press, 1968. xii, 401p. music. discog. index. (History of Jazz, Vol. 1). LC 68-17610. ISBN 0-19-500097-8.

When Schuller finally completes the promised volume 2 of the *History of Jazz*, the two volumes will be the most comprehensive general history of the topic. Until then, readers must content themselves with a musically astute analysis of "the first flowering period of jazz" which came to full bloom with the Ellington band in the early 1930s. "The book is directed particularly to the 'classically' trained musician or composer," Schuller explains in the preface, "who may never have concerned himself with jazz and who cannot respond to the in-group jargon and glossy enthusiasm of most writing on jazz." An examination of the musical elements – rhythm, form, harmony, melody, timbre, and improvisation – which have been integral to jazz since its beginnings opens the work. Schuller's analyses are based on recordings, from which he supplies numerous transcriptions, of Louis Armstrong, Jelly Roll Morton, Duke Ellington, and other early innovators. His interest is music, not personality; when he turns from analysis to history, it is to note the circumstances of a recording session, not to rehash the difficulties of life on the road. However, the glossary's mixture of slang such as "gig" with more customarily musical terms such as "glissando" reflects both the musical and social vocabulary of jazz. A selected discography lists LP reissues of important early 78rpm recordings.

132. Seltsam, William H., comp. **Metropolitan Opera Annals: A Chronicle of Artists and Performances**. Introduction by Edward Johnson. New York: H. W. Wilson in association with the Metropolitan Opera Guild, 1947. xvi, 751p. illus. index. LC 47-11435.

133. Seltsam, William H., comp. **Metropolitan Opera Annals: A Chronicle of Artists and Performances. First Supplement: 1947-1957**. Foreword by Rudolph Bing. New York: H. W. Wilson in association with the Metropolitan Opera Guild, 1957. xiii, 115p. illus. index. LC 47-11435.

134. Seltsam, William H., comp. **Metropolitan Opera Annals: A Chronicle of Artists and Performances. Second Supplement: 1957-1966**. Foreword by Francis Robinson. New York: H. W. Wilson in association with the Metropolitan Opera Guild, 1968. ix, 126p. illus. index. LC 47-11435.

135. Peltz, Mary Ellis, and Gerald Fitzgerald. **Metropolitan Opera Annals. Third Supplement: 1966-1976**. Clifton, N.J.: James T. White for the Metropolitan Opera Guild, 1978. xi, 208p. illus. index. LC 47-11435. ISBN 0-88371-022-6.

This set covers a period which has seen the Metropolitan Opera performing in two different houses and, beginning in 1967, in the parks of New York. All four volumes present a chronological list of performances by the resident company, listing the opera title and the personnel for each day. The third supplement adds designers, directors, and choreographers to the listings of singers and conductors. Included with each year's account of performances is a sampling of the year's reviews. Supplement 2 includes a list of debuts from 1883 to 1966, and supplement 3 records, for the years 1966 to 1976, the years in which individual operas were staged and the number of performances for each, updating the listing in Irving Kolodin's *The Metropolitan Opera, 1883-1966: A Candid History* (Alfred A. Knopf, 1966). Indexes list operas and individuals.

136. Slonimsky, Nicolas. **Music since 1900**. 4th ed. New York: Scribner's, 1971. xvii, 1595p. index. LC 70-114929. ISBN 0-684-10550-0.

137. Slonimsky, Nicolas. **Supplement to Music since 1900**. New York: Scribner's, 1986. viii, 390p. index. LC 85-27627. ISBN 0-684-18438-9.

These volumes represent a massive attic stuffed with the achievements of composition and performance and the minutiae of anecdote. The parent volume consists primarily of a chronology of musical events from the publication of the collected works of Berlioz on 1 January 1900 to the manifestation of the harmony of the spheres in the first step on the moon on 20 July 1969. Entries relate first performances, births, deaths, establishments of orchestras, political developments (especially in Germany and the Soviet Union) related to music and musicians, debuts, publications of books and music, inventions of instruments, governmental decrees, and annual programs from concerts given by the International Society for Contemporary Music. Slonimsky provides summaries of many instrumental works and operas in his loquacious and florid style, and amplifies many with quotes from contemporary reviews and letters. Texts in a "Letters and Documents" section sample those which reflect the political and social role of modern music, including an official Soviet statement on "formalistic" music and letters from Charles Ives. A "Dictionary of Terms" uses established words and Slonimsky's neologisms (such as "pandiatonicism") as themes for essays on modern musical concepts. The supplement, published nearly fifty years after the 1937 first edition, extends the chronology to 1985, adds to or corrects entries for the period 1900 to 1969, and includes official statements on music from the Peoples' Republic of China and the text of a U.S. Army report on sabotaging the Soviets with music.

138. Southern, Eileen. **The Music of Black Americans: A History**. 2d ed. New York: W. W. Norton, 1983. xx, 602p. illus. music. bibliog. discog. index. LC 82-25960. ISBN 0-393-95279-7pa.

Southern's history (1st ed. 1971) is an important supplement to more general histories such as Chase's *America's Music* (see entry 117) or even Austin's *Music in the 20th Century* in the Norton series (see entry 128), which devote substantial, but summary attention to black American music. Jazz occupies a position among Southern's many other topics which examine the derivation of American music from African music, rural folk music in the South, music at camp meetings and in the church, and twentieth-century composers and operatic performers. The text is rich with factual information and well-supplemented with illustrations and musical examples. The bibliography is a good source both for general works and for works on specific musicians.

139. Tirro, Frank. **Jazz: A History**. New York: W. W. Norton, 1977. xvii, 457p. illus. music. bibliog. discog. index. LC 77-22623. ISBN 0-393-09078-7.

Tirro identifies his work as "an introduction to the principal movements, schools, performers, and peripheral aspects of American jazz from its origins to the present" (preface). He traces the beginnings of jazz from African music to its development within a framework of musical styles in nineteenth-century America, then surveys jazz styles and innovators from ragtime through the 1970s. Recorded examples are keyed to the *Smithsonian Collection of Classic Jazz*. Musical examples appear in the text and in a separate section of transcriptions of exemplary solos. The plentiful footnotes, general bibliography, and chapter bibliographies offer good surveys of the literature. Supplementary material following the text includes a discography of selected LP recordings, a "Synoptic Table" which links developments in jazz, other arts, and historical developments, and a glossary.

7

Collections, Quotations, Sources, and Documents

"Learning music by reading about it is like making love by mail" (attributed to Isaac Stern in *A Dictionary of Musical Quotations*, p. 55, entry 142). However, mail is sometimes a tempting prelude or necessary substitute, and, in either case, valuable. So are these anthologies which compile the words of composers, performers, theoreticians, critics, and others. Like a bibliography, an anthology can create a whole greater than the sum of its parts. The *Lexicon of Musical Invective* (see entry 148), for example, reveals not only a history of scathing reviews but a critical tendency to oppose the new. *Readings in Black American Music* (see entry 149) creates a cohesive history out of disparate, but carefully arranged, sources.

Strunk's *Source Readings in Music History* (see entry 150) was the forerunner for many of these. More recent compilations such as Rowen's (see entry 146), Weiss's (see entry 151), and MacClintock's (see entry 144) overlap surprisingly little with it and with each other.

140. Baker, David N., Lida M. Belt, and Herman C. Hudson. **The Black Composer Speaks**. A Project of the Afro-American Arts Institute, Indiana University. Metuchen, N.J.: Scarecrow, 1978. v, 506p. illus. bibliog. index. LC 77-24146. ISBN 0-8108-1045-X.

This collection of interviews with prominent black composers from several idioms includes Thomas Jefferson Anderson, David Nathaniel Baker, Noel Da Costa, Talib Rasul Hakim, Herbie Hancock, Ulysses Kay, Undine Smith Moore, Oliver Nelson, Coleridge-Taylor Perkinson, George Russell, Archie Shepp, Hale Smith, Howard Swenson, George Walker, and Olly Wilson. Most of the composers are enjoyably voluble in their discussions of their own works, influences, uses of specific elements of composition, and black music. With each interview appears a photograph of the composer, a short biography, an annotated list of compositions, and a bibliography of writings by and about the composer. Appendixes give addresses of publishers and recording companies, and list composers' works by form.

141. Chase, Gilbert, ed. **The American Composer Speaks: A Historical Anthology, 1770-1965**. n.p.: Louisiana State University Press, 1966. x, 318p. index. LC 66-11661. ISBN 0-8071-0347-0.

"The American composer has been a victim of silence," Chase states in the foreword; this collection of thirty writings examines the character of American music and the place of the composer in American life. From William Billings in the eighteenth century to Earle Brown, born in 1926, the collection spans almost two hundred years, and includes Gottschalk's reflections on the development of music in America, the practical considerations of Virgil Thomson's "How Composers Eat," and the examination of indigenous forms in Gunther Schuller's essay on jazz. Chase assumes the role of advocate in his introductory survey and in his short biographies which preface each piece. The bibliography lists works on American music and individual composers, and enumerates the sources for the present work.

142. Crofton, Ian, and Donald Fraser. **A Dictionary of Musical Quotations**. New York: Schirmer Books, 1985. xii, 191p. index. LC 85-5051. ISBN 0-02-906530-5.

Some of the dictionary's selections are candidates for the *Lexicon of Musical Invective* (see entry 148): " 'Wagner's art is diseased,' " said Nietzsche; others are telling: " 'All the wrong notes are *right*,' " Charles Ives emphasized. The dictionary arranges over three thousand quotations into about a hundred apt subject categories, and identifies each quotation by its author and source. An author index lists all authors or speakers of quotations, and a subject index lists musical terms, persons, works, and keywords, gives a citation to the text, and quotes the context of the term. Most of those quoted are living or historical musicians, but the dictionary includes a sprinkling of literary and contemporary pop figures and provides a spectrum of opinion on instruments, styles, and composers.

143. Gagne, Cole, and Tracy Caras. **Soundpieces: Interviews with American Composers**. Introduction by Nicolas Slonimsky. Introduction by Gilbert Chase. Gene Bagnato, photographs. Metuchen, N.J.: Scarecrow, 1982. xviii, 418p. illus. index. LC 81-13520. ISBN 0-8108-1474-9.

This collection developed from radio interviews conducted by the authors. Interviewed are Robert Ashley, Milton Babbit, Henry Bryant, John Cage, Elliott Carter, Aaron Copland, George Crumb, Mario Davidovsky, Charles Dodge, Jacob Druckman, Morton Feldman, Ross Lee Finney, Lukas Foss, Philip Glass, Lejaren Hiller, Ben Johnston, Barbara Kolb, Conlon Nancarrow, Steve Reich, Roger Reynolds, George Rochberg, Roger Sessions, Ralph Shapey, and Charles Wuorinen. The authors' questions display a thorough knowledge of each subject's work which helps to elicit extended and revelatory answers. A photograph, a short biography, and a chronological list of works accompany each interview.

144. MacClintock, Carol, trans. and ed. **Readings in the History of Music in Performance**. Bloomington, Ind.: Indiana University Press, 1979. xii, 432p. music. LC 78-9511. ISBN 0-253-14495-7; 0-253-20285-Xpa.

The author's intent in compiling these sixty-six selections from nearly as many writers is to demonstrate "how music was to be performed and what the accepted conventions and actual practices were in former times." The selection includes excerpts from literary works such as Boccaccio's *Decameron*; treatises such as Couperin's *L'Art de toucher le Clavecin*; letters such as those of Mozart to his father; and critical articles such as those of Berlioz. MacClintock provides a brief, informed introduction to each selection, cites her original source, and reproduces, in many cases, musical examples from the original. The arrangement is broadly chronological, with further subdivisions by topic which serve to compare individual writers' approaches to similar questions (such as "Opera: Pro and Con" in the eighteenth and nineteenth centuries).

145. Neuls-Bates, Carol, ed. **Women in Music: An Anthology of Source Readings from the Middle Ages to the Present**. New York: Harper & Row, 1982. xvi, 351p. illus. bibliog. index. LC 81-48045. ISBN 0-06-014992-2; 0-06-090032-3pa.

Increasing attention is being paid to the heretofore largely invisible historical participation of women in musical activities. This anthology offers a selection of fifty readings which exemplify important contributions of female composers, performers, patrons, and educators, or which comment on the role of women in musical society. The editor briefly introduces each selection, and cites its published source. All readings are originally in English or have been translated. The selections encompass accounts of medieval convent life, selections from the journals of eighteenth-century traveler Charles Burney, letters between Clara and Robert Schumann, an article by Aaron Copland on Nadia Boulanger, and a closing interview with Nancy Van de Vate, founder of the International League of Women Composers.

146. Rowen, Ruth Halle. **Music through Sources and Documents**. Englewood Cliffs, N.J.: Prentice-Hall, 1979. xiv, 386p. bibliog. index. LC 78-2268. ISBN 0-13-608331-5.

This selection and translation of over two hundred excerpts from ancient writings, treatises, letters, journals, and books dating from the Bible to the twentieth century overlaps little with Strunk's collection (see entry 150). The arrangement is chronological, but chapters further identify significant themes within each period (for instance, "Classical Sense of Balance and Form"). Extensive supplementary material includes footnotes and introductions which explain points and cite related sources, a detailed index, and appendixes which relate numerical and harmonic intervals.

147. Shapiro, Nat, comp. and ed. **An Encyclopedia of Quotations about Music**. Garden City, N.Y.: Doubleday, 1978; repr., New York: Da Capo Press, 1981. xii, 418p. index. LC 76-56333. ISBN 0-306-80138-8.

Shapiro's broad scope encompasses both quotations about music itself and those which use music as imagery. He groups over two thousand quotations within forty-four thematic chapters with whimsical titles such as "The Food of Love" or "Sing Me a Song with Social Significance." His fancy brings such creative assortments as "Music of the Spheres," which collects quotations about music as an expression of the universe, and tosses in Fats Waller's "One never knows, do one," which could refer to music or just about anything. Though Shapiro's headings are neither as specific nor plentiful as those in *A Dictionary of Musical Quotations* (see entry 142), the indexes to names and sources and to keywords and phrases allow a reader to find a specific quotation easily.

148. Slonimsky, Nicolas. **Lexicon of Musical Invective: Critical Assaults on Composers since Beethoven's Time**. 2d ed. New York: Coleman-Ross, 1965. 325p. index. LC 65-26270. ISBN 0-295-78579-9pa.

Slonimsky's "schimpflexicon," or dictionary of insults, quotes excerpts of contemporary and retrospective reviews and commentary on forty-three composers of the nineteenth and twentieth centuries whom we now accept as the bedrock of our received tradition. His point is to demonstrate the "non-acceptance of the unfamiliar" – to show the prejudiced and conservative critical opposition which innovative techniques have had to face. Following the quotations, an "Invecticon" indexes reviewers' deprecatory words and phrases from "aberration" applied to Prokofiev, Stravinsky, and Wagner, through "masochistic aural flagellation" applied to Mahler, to "zoo (spring fever in)" applied to Stravinsky. The index covers references to names of composers and critics, and titles of works. The second edition has added a short unindexed supplement to the text of the first.

149. Southern, Eileen, comp. and ed. **Readings in Black American Music**. 2d ed. New York: W. W. Norton, 1983. xii, 338p. music. index. LC 83-4192. ISBN 0-393-95280-0pa.

The second edition (1st ed., 1971) of this selection of forty-one documentary sources is a companion to the author's *Music of Black Americans: A History* (see entry 138). The collection opens with reports on African musicians from seventeenth-century English explorers and missionaries. Other sources, including advertisements for slaves (those noted, either as runaways or commodities, for their musical talent), journals, sheet music, autobiographies, introductions to collections of music, histories, and essays trace the development of black American music to the early 1980s. Selections include works by Frederick Douglass, W. E. B. DuBois, Dizzy Gillespie, and Amiri Baraka. The editor provides each with a succinct historical introduction, and notes the original source.

150. Strunk, W. Oliver. **Source Readings in Music History: From Classical Antiquity through the Romantic Era**. New York: W. W. Norton, 1950. xxi, 919p. music. index. LC 50-10992. ISBN 0-393-09742-0. (Repr. in 5 vols., 1965).

Antiquity and the Middle Ages. xiv, 192p. index. LC 66-489. ISBN 0-393-09680-7pa.

The Renaissance. xiv, 175p. index. LC 66-489. ISBN 0-393-09681-5pa.

The Baroque Era. xiv, 218p. index. LC 66-489. ISBN 0-393-09682-3pa.

The Classical Era. xiv, 170p. index. LC 66-489. ISBN 0-393-09683-1pa.

The Romantic Era. xiv, 167p. index. LC 66-489. ISBN 0-393-09684-Xpa.

Strunk's intention is "to make conveniently accessible to the teacher or student of the history of music those things which he must eventually read." The original nine-hundred-page volume and its substantially identical five-volume version gather eighty-seven excerpts of musical writings from nearly as many philosophers, composers, and litterateurs of the Western world, beginning with Plato and continuing with, among others, Augustine, Tinctoris, Byrd, Monteverdi, Fux, Rousseau, and culminating with Wagner. The selection represents an equally broad range of approaches, including history, theory, criticism, and aesthetics. All excerpts appear either in their original English or in translation, and cite an original source. Strunk provides a short introduction to each excerpt, giving a brief biography of the writer, setting the work in its context, and explaining its significance. His helpful footnotes elaborate and explain specific points.

151. Weiss, Piero, and Richard Taruskin. **Music in the Western World: A History in Documents**. New York: Schirmer Books; London: Collier Macmillan, 1984. xiv, 556p. illus. index. LC 83-16171. ISBN 0-02-872910-2; 0-02-872900-5pa.

The preface to this lively and mutlifaceted collection of over 155 musical writings acknowledges as its precursor Strunk's similar collection (see entry 150), but justifies the present work as more suitable for students with no previous knowledge of music. It includes works which discuss the role and evaluation of music rather than its attributes; it complements, rather than substitutes for, Strunk. All works appear in chronological order in either the original English or in translation. The compilers cite each source and introduce each piece in a concise and lucid manner. The opening selection is Ovid's story of Orpheus, whose music charmed the underworld. The closing selection pairs Milton Babbitt's "The Composer as Specialist" (which for years was identified by the belligerent title "Who Cares If You Listen") with a rebuttal by George Rochberg. A glossary aids the unsophisticated reader.

8

Directories

Directories are always geographically oriented. They locate services, individuals, and collections. They go out of date more quickly than other reference works, as addresses change more often than definitions. Therefore, a number of the directories listed here are published annually or biennially, or at least updated in a regular fashion.

This chapter emphasizes directories that cover the United States and Canada, but includes some which are international in scope and important to North American researchers. Other more specialized directories can be found under the names of organizations in chapter 21.

152. **Billboard's International Buyer's Guide of the Music-Record-Tape Industry**. New York: Billboard Publications, 1958- . annual. LC 85-643924. ISSN 0067-8600pa.

The *Buyer's Guide* demonstrates the crass commercialism of the recording industry. The first few pages give U.S. industry statistics for sales of recorded music by age, race, sex, and geographical region. The bulk of the directory gives names, addresses, and telephone numbers for U.S. recording companies, compact disc manufacturers, wholesalers, associations, licensing organizations, pressing plants, jukebox manufacturers, and other parts of the industry, listed either alphabetically or geographically within categories. An international section lists similar information under the names of individual countries. Advertisements abound for hi-tech goods most people could not even imagine.

153. **British Music Yearbook**. London: Rhinegold Publishing, 1972- . annual. index. LC 75-649724. ISSN 0306-5928.

In its quantity of detail and functional design, this is a model directory. Formerly entitled *The Music Yearbook*, it includes England, Scotland, Wales, and Northern Ireland. Introducing each issue is a narrative and enumerative survey of events of the past year, which includes lists of live and broadcast first performances, new books, and new records. Directory sections give addresses for government offices and societies, including concert organizations and halls; professional services; performers, including orchestras, ensembles, individuals, and composers; trade services, including instrument manufacturers, publishers, and retailers; educational institutions, libraries, and museums; and larger places of worship which offer music training or performances. As with many British directories, most geographical listings begin with London, then list other cities alphabetically. Indexes cover subjects and the numerous, but tasteful, advertisers.

154. Brody, Elaine, and Claire Brook. **The Music Guide to Austria and Germany**. New York: Dodd, Mead, 1975. xvi, 271p. index. LC 75-30822. ISBN 0-396-07217-8.

155. Brody, Elaine, and Claire Brook. **The Music Guide to Belgium, Luxembourg, Holland, and Switzerland**. New York: Dodd, Mead, 1977. xvi, 156p. index. LC 77-6446. ISBN 0-396-07437-5.

156. Brody, Elaine, and Claire Brook. **The Music Guide to Great Britain: England, Scotland, Wales, Ireland**. New York: Dodd, Mead, 1975. xv, 240p. index. LC 75-30809. ISBN 0-396-06955-X.

157. Brody, Elaine, and Claire Brook. **The Music Guide to Italy**. New York: Dodd, Mead, 1978. xvii, 233p. index. LC 78-6846. ISBN 0-396-07436-7.

Though dated as directories (for instance, what is now the British Library appears as the British Museum), these guides still provide valid portraits of musical activity in some of Europe's major cities. Entries for individual cities and for countries give data, as appropriate, on opera houses and concert halls, libraries and museums, conservatories and schools, musical landmarks (that is, houses and graves), musical organizations, businesses oriented to music, and other details. The authors amplify directory-type facts with historical and practical notes for the traveler. An index in each volume lists individual entries.

158. **Career Guide for Young American Singers from the United States and Canada**. 5th ed. New York: Central Opera Service, 1985. iv, 79p. index. (*Central Opera Service Bulletin*, Vol. 25, No. 4). ISSN 0008-9508.

Though directed at American singers, the guide does not restrict itself to American opportunities. Individual sections list grants to singers; regional, national, and international competitions in the United States and Canada; foreign competitions open to U.S. and Canadian singers; opera and musical theater companies in the United States and Canada, giving apprentice and educational programs, and audition and hiring policies; institutes for advanced training (nondegree); apprentice programs in fields other than singing; and educational institutions with major opera workshops. Each section lists entries geographically. Entries give an address, sometimes a telephone number, and a short description of the program. An index covers names of programs and institutions.

159. Craven, Robert R., ed. **Symphony Orchestras of the United States: Selected Profiles**. Westport, Conn.: Greenwood Press, 1986. xxiii, 521p. bibliog. index. LC 85-7637. ISBN 0-313-24072-8.

These 126 profiles show how orchestras are culturally and financially drawn from their home cities. Each recounts, in a space of several pages, the orchestra's origin, its succession of music directors and concert halls, and its financial highs and lows; summarizes its current budgetary status and programs; and, in a few cases, attempts to describe the elusive quality of the orchestra's sound. Oddly, few mention first performances of compositions or appearances by prominent soloists. A list of contributors shows that most of the authors of these profiles – generally faculty members at universities or writers on music – live near the orchestras about which they write. Appended to each profile are notes on the orchestra's recordings, a chronological list of music directors, a bibliography, and an address and telephone number.

160. **Directory of Music Faculties in Colleges and Universities, U.S. and Canada**. Boulder, Colo.: College Music Society, 1970/71- . biennial. index. LC 75-644786. ISSN 0098-664Xpa.

The directory (formerly *Directory of Music Faculties in American Colleges and Universities*) lists over twenty-five thousand faculty members in over fifteen hundred institutions in an unattractive but legible computer printout format. It does not limit entries to members of the society. The major part, the directory of institutions, lists schools alphabetically by province or state, then by city, and then by name. Each entry gives the institutions's name and address, the degrees it offers, and a list of the faculty members giving academic rank, highest degree earned, and a code (explained in a separate table) indicating area of specialization. Indexes include a list of faculty specializations, an alphabetical list of all faculty members, a list of graduate degrees, and an alphabetical list of institutions.

161. Farrell, Susan Caust. **Directory of Contemporary American Musical Instrument Makers**. Columbia, Mo.: University of Missouri Press, 1981. xii, 216p. bibliog. index. LC 80-24924. ISBN 0-8262-0322-1.

The directory's value, now that it is several years old, is primarily to establish the existence and location of over twenty-five hundred firms and individuals, and to act as a finding guide for those still in existence. It includes firms as small as Frank Hubbard and as large as Selmer, along with what are undoubtedly a large number of amateurs. Makers appear alphabetically. In a uniform format, entries give the address, the firm's starting date, the number of employees, and the types and numbers of instruments produced. Indexes list makers by instrument and by state. Appendixes list schools of instrument making, professional societies and groups, and books about instrument making.

162. Hewlett, Walter B., and Eleanor Selfridge-Field. **Directory of Computer Assisted Research in Musicology, 1986**. Menlo Park, Calif.: Center for Computer Assisted Research in the Humanities, 1986. 86p. music. bibliog. LC 86-646620. ISBN 0-936943-01-7.

This edition expands the 1985 directory by means of an updated survey taken in the winter of 1986. It enumerates over one hundred computerized projects dating from 1980 to the present covering a diverse range of approaches—bibliographies and indexes, editions of text and music, and methods of analysis. Entries give the title and scope of the project, persons associated with it, the location, the hardware and software, and publications describing or resulting from the project. An address list covers individuals and institutions. Opening the directory is a survey article on printing music by computer which includes twenty-four examples of music produced by various hardware, software, and printers. A news section notes forthcoming events, courses of study, and dissertations in progress in the area of computer applications to music.

163. **International Music and Opera Guide**. London: The Tantivy Press; New York: New York Zoetrope, 1976- . annual. illus. LC 86-25643. ISBN 0-900730-08-0(1985 ed.).

The guide is an odd combination of yearbook and directory. Each issue surveys performances and personalities in individual countries throughout Europe and in the United States, Japan, and Australia. Country sketches include a brief directory of the major orchestras and opera companies but list no more than a handful of each. Other features include profiles of performers and composers; record, performance, and book reviews; and lists of music shops, schools, and magazines. The guide distinguishes itself by lively writing, using the opinions of its individual contributors to highlight the year's performance events.

164. Jenkins, Jean, ed. **International Directory of Musical Instrument Collections**. Buren, Netherlands: Frits Knuf for the International Council of Museums (ICOM), 1977. ix, 166p. LC 78-319779.

The directory covers collections in ninety-one countries. It omits Canada and the United States, covered by *A Survey of Musical Instrument Collections in the United States and Canada* (see entry 177), but an "Addenda" section adds several entries to that listing. Entries appear alphabetically by country, then by city, and give the name of the institution, address, and telephone number, opening hours, a brief description of the collection, and a list of publications of the collection.

165. Krummel, D. W., Jean Geil, Doris J. Dyen, and Deane L. Root. **Resources of American Music History: A Directory of Source Materials from Colonial Times to World War II**. Urbana, Ill.: University of Illinois Press, 1981. 463p. bibliog. index. (Music in American Life). LC 80-14873. ISBN 0-252-00828-6.

Amid witty accounts of the authors' efforts to coax information from reluctant collectors and from overburdened libraries, the introduction distinguishes between "American music" and "music in America." This volume concerns itself with the latter, specifically the United States. The source materials are primarily nonbook materials—sheet music, songbooks, and other printed music; manuscript music; programs; catalogs; organizational papers of performing groups and institutions; personal papers; pictures; and sound recordings, including oral history tapes. There are 1,689 entries, grouped geographically, which describe the holdings of libraries, historical societies, associations, and private collectors in different states, U.S. territories, Canada, and other countries. Supplementary lists appended to each section briefly list other collections. The index lists names of collections, names of persons, and subjects of collections.

166. **Music Directory Canada**. Toronto: CM Books, 1982- . annual. LC 84-646941. ISBN 0-9691272-0-0; ISSN 0820-0416.

Over three dozen sections list a variety of music-oriented businesses and organizations from acoustic consultants to video production houses. Most sections list entries alphabetically; recording studios and radio stations appear geographically. At a minimum, entries give a name, address, and telephone number, and most include short descriptive notes. The 1983 edition fails to include the Victoria Symphony. The directory brings together a wide range of listings, but spreads itself too thin to be adequately detailed.

167. **Music Industry Directory**. 7th ed. Chicago: Marquis Who's Who, 1983. 678p. index. LC 83-645913. ISBN 0-8379-5602-1; ISSN 0740-476X.

Formerly *Musician's Guide*, the directory claims "comprehensive coverage of the music industry." Its scope is certainly wider than that of *Musical America* (see entry 168)—it includes, for instance, locals of the American Federation of Musicians, record companies, and music libraries, but it lacks the clear and concise organization and international perspective of the latter. Except for the international listings of festivals and competitions, the directory restricts listings to the United States and Canada. There are seven sections: organizations and councils; competitions, grants, and awards; education (colleges, conservatories, and schools); resources (libraries, periodicals, and music book publishers); performance (orchestras, opera companies, and festivals); profession (critics, volunteer lawyers, agents, and managers); trade and industry (record companies and producers, music publishers). Sections organize entries geographically and include indexes. A general index covers topics, but gives little more information than the table of contents.

168. **Musical America: International Directory of the Performing Arts**. New York: ABC Leisure Magazines, 1968/69- . annual. illus. index. LC 83-713. ISSN 0735-7788pa.

Musical America's listings vie for space with full-page advertisements for performing artists. Its alphabetical and categorical indexing of these advertisements testifies to their importance for readers. A guide to the business of classical music which evolved out of *Musical America* (see entry 629), it gives names, addresses, and abbreviated bits of information for orchestras, opera companies, choral groups, dance companies, performing arts series, festivals, arts administration degree programs, music schools and departments, contests, foundations, awards, publishers of music, music organizations, state arts agencies, artists' managers, music magazines, and newspapers' music critics. A separate section consists of less extensive international listings of these items. Each issue features a "Musician of the Year" award and newsy reports on people and performances.

169. National Association of Schools of Music. **Directory**. Reston, Va.: National Association of Schools of Music, 1950- . annual. index. LC 73-647227. ISSN 0547-4175.

Since the National Association of Schools of Music is an accrediting body, its directory lists accredited schools, including colleges, universities, and independent schools. It includes schools accredited by the Joint Commission on Dance and Theatre Accreditation. Institutions appear alphabetically by name. Each entry gives the address, the year of the institution's first membership in the association, a one-line description, the name of the director, and a listing of degrees granted. Degrees pending accreditation appear in italics. Indexes list members by state and executives of member institutions.

170. **Opera/Musical Theatre Companies and Workshops in the United States and Canada**. New York: Central Opera Service, 1979- . annual.

Within countries (including a section for Puerto Rico), entries appear alphabetically by state or province, then by city, then by the organization's name. Each entry gives a code (explained in the front matter) indicating the organization's characteristics or financial size, its address, telephone number, director's name, the theater in which it performs, its capacity, and its stage dimensions.

171. Penney, Barbara, comp. and ed. **Music in British Libraries: A Directory of Resources**. 3d ed. London: Library Association, 1981. index. LC 81-212170. ISBN 0-85365-981-8.

A reorganization of local governments and the resulting change of local names prompted this third edition. It covers not only public, but college and university, cathedral, Schools Council, and private libraries. Entries appear in alphabetical order by name of the local government authority, institution, or individual. In uniform format, each gives the address and telephone number, name of the library director or music librarian, number of service points, number of staff, hours, regulations for use, "stock" (size of the collection), availability of recordings, publications, special or restricted services, and special collections. Appendixes list public libraries issuing vocal sets or orchestral parts, records or tapes. Indexes cover place and library names, featured composers or types of music, and names of special collections.

172. Rabin, Carol Price. **Music Festivals in America**. rev. and enl. Stockbridge, Mass.: Berkshire Traveller Press, 1983. 286p. illus. bibliog. index. LC 86-152158. ISBN 0-912944-74-9pa.

173. Rabin, Carol Price. **Music Festivals in Europe and Britain, Including Israel, Russia, Turkey and Japan**. rev. and enl. Stockbridge, Mass.: Berkshire Traveller Press, 1984. 191p. illus. bibliog. index. LC 79-55709. ISBN 0-912944-81-1pa.

The author has attended nearly all of the more than two hundred festivals she profiles in both volumes. Her familiarity and enthusiasm give a flavor to each which is not only informative but inviting. Each guide devotes a page or two to each festival, giving its location, approximate date, history, a selection of recent performers and outstanding performances, and addresses and telephone numbers for tickets and accommodations. The *America* guide organizes entries by type of music (classical, opera, jazz, pops, folk, and bluegrass) and by state or country (including Canada and Bermuda). The *Europe* guide organizes entries by country. Both include indexes to festival names, and also brief reading lists (of little use) about music and travel.

174. Répertoire international des sources musicales/Internationales Quellenlexikon der Musik/International Inventory of Musical Sources. **Directory of Music Research Libraries**. Rita Benton, general ed. (RISM Series C).

Volume I: Canada; United States. 2d rev. ed. Kassel, West Germany: Bärenreiter-Verlag, 1983. 282p. illus. bibliog. index. LC 83-70846. ISBN 3-7618-0684-1.

Part II: Thirteen European Countries. prelim. ed. Iowa City, Iowa: University of Iowa, 1970. xviii, 235p. illus. bibliog. index.

Part III: Spain, France, Italy, Portugal. prelim. ed. Iowa City, Iowa: University of Iowa, 1972. xviii, 342p. illus. bibliog. index. LC 72-81016.

Volume IV: Australia, Israel, Japan, New Zealand. Kassel, West Germany: Bärenreiter-Verlag, 1979. xvi, 177p. illus. bibliog. index. ISBN 3-7618-0558-6.

Volume V: Czechoslovakia, Hungary, Poland, Yugoslavia. Lilian Pruett, ed. Kassel, West Germany: Bärenreiter-Verlag, 1985. 267p. illus. bibliog. index. LC 83-70846. ISBN 3-7618-0740-6.

Volume VI: Bulgaria, Greece, Romania, USSR. Lilian Pruett, ed. Forthcoming.

Volume VII: South America, Central America, Mexico and the Caribbean. Malena Kuss, ed. Forthcoming.

Originally intended as a finding guide to the pre-1800 manuscripts and publications listed in series A and B of RISM (see entries in the index to the present volume), this series has transcended its original scope. With the revision of volume 1, all volumes list collections of material from any period or genre in libraries, churches, archives, and museums. The change of scope of the series and the varying abilities of compilers to gather material from surveys by mail and personal visits results in an imbalanced presentation of individual countries (compare, for instance, the numbers of pages relative to the countries covered in part 2 and volume 5). Nevertheless, the series offers a breadth of information unavailable elsewhere. Each volume groups entries by country; within countries, entries appear alphabetically by city. Entries give each institution's name and its RISM siglum; address and telephone number; photocopying facilities; a description of catalogs and, briefly, of the collection; opening hours; and lists of special collections and descriptive publications. Each country section includes a map, a bibliography of works about the country's libraries and music, and in all but part 3, a summary of copyright law and deposit, and in all but parts 2 and 3, a list of public holidays. Indexes to each country cover names of institutions, special collections, and donors' names; those in volumes 1, 4, and 5 include subjects, composers' names, and types of compositions. Supplementary information occasionally appears in *Fontes Artis Musicae* (see entry 595).

175. Sedgwick, Don, ed. **Directory of Musical Canada**. rev. ed. Agincourt, Ont.: GLC Publishers, 1981. vii, 363p. bibliog. discog. LC 81-116928. ISBN 0-88874-086-7.

A statement from the publisher promises a new edition every three years (though none exists as of 1986). Individual sections give government agencies and other organizations; performing ensembles; educational institutions; music libraries; churches which hold performances; summer music festivals and educational opportunities; competitions; grants and awards; broadcasters and agents; publishers, instrument manufacturers and repairers, and recording companies; an unidentified group of names of presumably prominent musicians in "Creative Canada"; music magazines; a flimsy bibliography about Canadian music, and a discography of recordings of Canadian compositions and performers. The level of detail varies greatly from the names and occupations of "Creative Canada" to names, addresses, and telephone numbers in other sections to isolated entries with fuller detail.

176. **Songwriter's Market**. Cincinnati, Ohio: Writer's Digest Books, 1979- . annual. index. LC 78-648269. ISSN 0161-5971.

For those seeking to sell a first song or to locate the address of a music publisher or producer, *Songwriter's Market* is invaluable, if blatantly commercial. It lists organizations in seven major "markets": music publishers, record companies, record producers, advertising agencies, audiovisual firms, managers and booking agents, and play producers and publishers. Each of these listings gives names, an address, a telephone number, and a summary of what the organization looks for and how one should approach it. Other sections list contests and awards, associations and nonprofit organizations, publications of interest, and workshops. For the neophyte there is plenty of advice on songwriting and making contacts.

177. **A Survey of Musical Instrument Collections in the United States and Canada**. Conducted by a Committee of the Music Library Association: William Lichtenwanger (chairman and comp.), Dale Higbee, Cynthia Adams Hoover, and Phillip T. Young. n.p.: Music Library Association, 1974. xi, 137p. index. LC 74-75582. ISBN 0-914954-00-8.

Derived from a mail survey followed up with telephone calls, letters, and visits, the survey lists 572 collections ranging in size from the private collector with "many old saxophones" to the American Museum of Natural History's thousands of instruments from around the world. The entry for each collection gives its name, address, and telephone number; the name of a contact person; a description of the collection in one to several sentences; cataloging details; and an indication of its availability to the public. Within countries, entries appear alphabetically by state or province, then by city, and then name. Indexes list names of persons, institutions, and collections; of instruments and classes of instruments; and cultural, geographical, and historical origins.

178. Thorin, Suzanne E., comp. and ed. **International Directory of Braille Music Collections**. Washington, D.C.: National Library Service for the Blind and Physically Handicapped, Library of Congress, 1984. 41p. index. LC 84-600111. ISBN 0-8444-0437-3. SuDoc LC 19.11:In 8.

The directory developed out of a 1981 survey by the service. Entries, in large type, portray fifty-three braille music collections in twenty-seven countries. Each entry describes the collection's size, languages, types of material, usage, lending policies (including international lending), funding sources, and production and transcription of braille music. Minor inconsistencies result from the use of questionnaires: for instance, though England's National Library for the Blind claims that the Royal National Institute for the Blind produces braille, the institute maintains it does not. The index lists organizations by title, and producers, lenders, or sellers of braille music.

Part 2
GENERAL BIBLIOGRAPHICAL SOURCES

9

Catalogs of Music Library Collections

This chapter presents a highly select but representative listing of catalogs from some of the most important music libraries. More than merely records of individual collections, these are versatile tools whose uses include verifying titles or personal names, reviewing the works of a composer, or, if the catalog includes writings about music, locating citations on a specific topic. G. K. Hall and K. G. Saur publish catalogs of a number of other music libraries. Duckles (see entry 5) gives an extensive international list of such catalogs.

179. BBC Music Library. **Chamber Music Catalogue: Chamber Music, Violin and Keyboard, Cello and Keyboard, Various.** London: British Broadcasting Corporation, 1965. various paging. bibliog. index. LC 66-34513.

180. BBC Music Library. **Choral and Opera Catalogue**. London: British Broadcasting Corporation, 1967. 2v. bibliog. LC 67-94103.

181. BBC Music Library. **Orchestral Catalogue**. Sheila Compton, ed. London: British Broadcasting Corporation, 1982. 4v. ISBN 0-563-12478-4.

182. BBC Music Library. **Piano and Organ Catalogue**. London: British Broadcasting Corporation, 1965. 2v. bibliog. LC 66-38412.

183. BBC Music Library. **Song Catalogue**. London: British Broadcasting Corporation, 1966. 4v. bibliog. LC 66-5067.

The introductions to the first four catalogs speculate that the BBC Library "is probably the largest library of (mostly) performing editions that has ever existed." Certainly, the five catalogs taken together are one of the most comprehensive listings of music. While their emphasis is on concert music, they include representative folk and popular works: the *Song Catalogue*, for instance, includes Kern as well as Schubert, and entries in the *Piano and Organ Catalogue* range from Liszt to Fats Waller.

The *Song Catalogue* includes mostly solo songs with keyboard accompaniment. Volumes 1 and 2 are arranged by composer; volumes 3 and 4 by title. Appendixes list popular song annuals, anthologies of folk, national, and patriotic songs (by country), songs with obbligati, and duets. The *Choral and Opera Catalogue* lists works for three or more voices. These are organized by composer in volume 1, and by title in volume 2. The *Piano and Organ Catalogue* lists piano solos and arrangements by composer, with appendixes listing piano duets, piano trios, works for two pianos, works for one hand, and organ solos. The *Chamber Music Catalogue* is divided into four sections: works for three or more instruments, keyboard and violin, keyboard and cello, and other combinations and solos. A classified index organizes these by form. The *Orchestral Catalogue* lists by composer works for ten or more players. Appendixes list carols, fanfares, hymns (by first line and title), and national and patriotic airs. Bibliographic information in all is minimal and generally limited to composer, title, and publisher. All volumes include lists of publishers and addresses. As the BBC Library is not open to the public, these catalogues serve as verification, not location tools.

184. Boston Public Library. **Dictionary Catalog of the Music Collection**. Boston: G. K. Hall, 1972. 20v. LC 72-182384. ISBN 0-8161-0956-7.

First Supplement. Boston: G. K. Hall, 1977. 4v. LC 72-182384. ISBN 0-8161-1014-X.

The catalog includes rare and specialized works from the Allen A. Brown Collection as well as other titles from the music collections of the library. Volumes consist of photographic reproductions of catalog cards. Authors, composers, titles, and subjects are arranged in one alphabet (and in a separate alphabet in the supplement). Recordings and sheet music are not included.

185. **The Catalogue of Printed Music in the British Library to 1980**. London: K. G. Saur, 1981-85. 62v. LC 81-151651. ISBN 0-86291-300-4.

The British Library contains one of the world's largest collections of printed music. Its catalog is one of the most extensive single lists of music, and supercedes the *Catalogue of Printed Music Published between 1487 and 1800 Now in the British Museum* and its supplements (London, 1912-40) and other previously published catalogs. The new catalog lists works under the names of composers, compilers of collections, corporate authors or societies, or headings derived from titles of anonymous works. "Preferential headings" such as "Hymns," "Madrigals," or "Marches" group works without distinctive titles. Cross-references from such items as names of arrangers, first words of distinctive titles of vocal works, corporate bodies, and related compositions make reference to main entries. Each entry gives a work's title, place of publication, date, and size or pagination. A classified system organizes the massive entries for works of prominent composers; these entries also list thematic catalogs. Titles of Russian works appear in the Cyrillic alphabet, but names of composers are transliterated. The catalog complements the more abbreviated lists of works in *The New Grove* (see entry 20), *Baker's* (see entry 80), and *MGG* (see entry 19).

186. Eda Kuhn Loeb Music Library. **Card Catalog of the Harvard University Music Library to 1985**. New York: K. G. Saur, 1985. 224 microfiches. ISBN 3-598-40150-7.

Most other published library catalogs represent the holdings of publicly supported collections. Harvard's Eda Kuhn Loeb Library, which ranks in size with the largest of these, brings together materials formerly held by the Widener and Lamont libraries and the Harvard Department of Music, and microforms and rare books from the Isham Memorial Library. The catalog consists of reproductions of cards from the main catalog and the shelflist. The 275,000 alphabetically arranged cards from the main catalog represent entries for authors, titles, and subjects for books, music, periodicals, and microforms. The ninety thousand cards from the shelflist are arranged according to a unique subject classification scheme which is described in a booklet accompanying the microfiche catalog. Saur's use of a microfiche format for a project such as this signals the demise of the publishing of massive multivolume book catalogs described in other entries in this chapter.

187. **The Edwin A. Fleisher Collection of Orchestral Music in the Free Library of Philadelphia: A Cumulative Catalog, 1929-1977**. Boston: G. K. Hall, 1979. xix, 956p. music. index. LC 78-245557. ISBN 0-8161-7942-5.

In 1929 the Free Library of Philadelphia acquired the sizable collection of orchestral music which Fleisher had gathered. Since 1937, the Fleisher Collection has functioned as a lending library for music to orchestras throughout the world (in fact, the introduction to the catalog gives instructions for borrowing). At the time of this compilation, the collection contained some thirteen thousand works. Compositions are arranged by composer, or, in the case of anonymous works, by editor or transcriber. Incipits are provided for most eighteenth-century works not identified by a thematic catalog number. Entries list movements, instrumentation, imprint (if published), pagination, and a variety of background information including date of composition, first performance, and dedication. The index provides access to works for ensembles other than the standard orchestra, selected types of works, works requiring one or more solo or featured instruments, and works requiring voices. The breadth of the Fleisher collection makes its catalog a primary source for bibliographic information on orchestral music.

188. New York Public Library. The Research Libraries. **Dictionary Catalog of the Music Collection**. 2d ed. Boston: G. K. Hall, 1982. 45v. LC 82-218268. ISBN 0-8161-1387-4.

The catalog represents an array of works dating from the thirteenth to the twentieth centuries in one of the world's largest music collections. It incorporates and adds entries to the first edition (1964) and its supplements (1964-71). The text consists of reproductions of 698,935 catalog cards – some printed, some typed, and many handwritten in clear script – listing books, pamphlets, scores, librettos, periodicals, articles, individual chapters of books, and individual numbers of series. Entries include authors, composers, and arrangers; organizations; works, if they have distinct titles; subtitles; and subjects. The *Bibliographic Guide to Music* (see entry 311) provides an annual update.

10

Miscellaneous Bibliographical Series

This chapter enumerates items in five series: *Bibliographies in American Music*, *Detroit Studies in Music Bibliography*, the *MLA Index and Bibliography Series*, George Hill's *Music Indexes and Bibliographies*, and the *Thematic Catalog Series*. Items included in these take a variety of forms, such as subject bibliographies of music literature, indexes to articles in periodicals, thematic catalogs, and indexes to collected works. Although some of the individual items included are beyond the scope of this guide, these series represent important recent bibliographical scholarship in music. Annotations for some titles within series make reference to a full citation under an entry number in another chapter.

189. **Bibliographies in American Music**. No. 1- . Detroit: Information Coordinators for the College Music Society, 1974- .

A preface in number 1 introduces the series: "Now in an era when the interest of American music faculties turns more and more toward the study and transmission of our own cultural heritage, it seems entirely appropriate that the Society should begin to provide primary source material in the form of these bibliographies."

190. No. 1: Schwarz, Charles. **George Gershwin: A Selective Bibliography and Discography**. 1974. 118p. LC 74-75913. ISBN 0-911772-59-6.

The bibliography lists, by author, 654 items consisting of books, articles, and citations to standard reference works. There is no subject access to the list. The discography lists LP and "key" 78rpm recordings.

191. No. 2: Nathan, Hans. **William Billings: Data and Documents**. 1976. 69p. illus. bibliog. LC 75-33593. ISBN 0-911772-67-7.

The volume is attractively designed and includes a good selection of reproductions of Billings's music and of contemporary documents. A biography of Billings prefaces the bibliography, which lists and annotates original publications of his works, and lists sixty-six books and articles about Billings.

192. No. 3: Anderson, Donna K. **Charles T. Griffes: An Annotated Bibliography-Discography**. 1977. 225p. index. LC 75-23552. ISBN 0-911772-87-1.

The bibliography concentrates on reviews of performances (including first performances) and of recordings, and includes a number of fairly obscure program notes and brief notices among more substantial articles. Other sections include a chronology of published works, a discography, a list of first performances, and an index of performers.

193. No. 4: Johnson, H. Earle. **First Performances in America to 1900: Works with Orchestra**. 1979. xxiv, 446p. illus. bibliog. index. LC 75-23554. ISBN 0-911772-94-4.

See entry 122.

194. No. 5: Lowens, Irving. **Haydn in America**. With a section on Haydn manuscripts in America by Otto Albrecht. 1979. x, 134p. illus. bibliog. LC 79-92140. ISBN 0-911772-99-5.

This tribute was inspired by the festival and conference in Washington, D.C., in 1975 devoted to Haydn. It is a study of the reception Haydn's music received in the United States during his lifetime. Lowens opens with a general survey, then lists published music and gives a chronology of performances in the United States at the time. There is an inventory of Haydn's manuscripts in several locations in the country. Albrecht briefly surveys other manuscripts in the United States.

195. No. 6: Cipolla, Wilma Reid. **A Catalog of the Works of Arthur William Foote, 1853-1937**. 1980. xxi, 193p. illus. discog. index. LC 79-92139. ISBN 0-89990-000-3.

Compositions are arranged by form. Entries give instrumentation, parts, date of composition, location of the manuscript, publisher, source of vocal text, dedication, and circumstances of first performance. Also included are literary works by Foote and secondary literature about Foote.

196. No. 7: Doyle, John G. **Louis Moreau Gottschalk, 1829-1869: A Bibliographical Study and Catalog of Works**. 1982. x, 386p. illus. discog. index. LC 75-24917. ISBN 0-89990-015-1.

The bibliography is exhaustive, and, in its citations to reference works in which Gottschalk may only be mentioned, too thorough. A separate section lists newspaper coverage of Gottschalk in North and South America. Other sections include an annotated list of collections of Gottschalk material, a list of manuscripts and their locations, an annotated catalog of works, and lists of modern editions and recordings.

197. No. 8: Heintze, James R. **American Music Studies: A Classified Bibliography of Master's Theses**. 1984. xxv, 312p. index. LC 84-9103. ISBN 0-89990-021-6.

See entry 403.

198. No. 9: Phemister, William. **A Bibliography of American Piano Concertos**. 1985. xviii, 323p. bibliog. LC 85-19746. ISBN 0-89990-026-7.

Phemister's research has yielded a total of 1,123 concertos by 801 composers. Works are arranged by composer. Data accompanying each citation not only describe each work by title, movements, publisher, date of composition, duration, and orchestration, but also identify its reception by listing a first performance, recordings, and excerpts from reviews. Phemister is careful to document his sources from a list of catalogs, biographical compilations, or a letter from the composer.

199. No. 10: Warner, Thomas E. **Periodical Literature on Music in America, 1620-1920: A Classified Bibliography with Annotations**. Forthcoming (1987).

200. No. 11: Brookhart, Edward. **Music in American Higher Education: An Annotated Bibliography**. Forthcoming (1987).

* * *

201. **Detroit Studies in Music Bibliography**. No. 1- . Detroit: Information Coordinators, 1961- . ISSN 0070-3885.

This series is as well-established as Information Coordinators' most renowned publication, *The Music Index* (see entry 324). It includes bibliographies of music and of music literature, discographies, thematic catalogs, and directories. Some titles in the series have rapidly faded into obscurity, and some, such as Dorothy Stahl's *Discography of Solo Song* and its supplements (Nos. 24, 34, and 52) and Wescott's *Comprehensive Bibliography of Music for Film and Television* (No. 54) are outstanding and unique resources whose value will not rapidly diminish. The series features notable works in American music, such as Bradley's *Music Collections in American Libraries* (No. 46), but also includes works which address music on a worldwide basis, such as *Reference Materials in Ethnomusicology* (No. 1).

202. No. 1: Nettl, Bruno. **Reference Materials in Ethnomusicology: A Bibliographic Essay**. 2d ed., rev. 1967. xv, 40p. LC 68-481. ISBN 0-911772-21-9pa.

See entry 11.

203. No. 2: Poladian, Sirvart, comp. **Sir Arthur Sullivan: An Index to the Texts of His Vocal Works**. 1961. xviii, 91p. LC 62-3339. ISBN 0-911772-22-7pa.

The index lists titles, first lines, refrains, and sections of Sullivan's operettas and other larger vocal works, as well as single songs, hymns, and anthems.

204. No. 3: MacArdle, Donald W. **An Index to Beethoven's Conversation Books**. 1962. xiii, 46p. LC 63-1071. ISBN 0-911772-23-5pa.

Beethoven's deafness forced him to converse with friends in writing. This index covers topics discussed in Beethoven's published conversation books.

205. No. 4: Mixter, Keith E. **General Bibliography for Music Research**. 1962. 38p. LC 63-1385. ISBN 0-911772-24-3pa.

This has been superseded by a second edition, No. 33.

206. No. 5: Mattfeld, Julius. **A Handbook of American Operatic Premieres, 1731-1962**. 1963. 142p. index. LC 64-55003. ISBN 0-911772-25-1pa.

Operas are listed by title, giving dates and locations of first performances. An index lists composers.

207. No. 6: Coover, James, and Richard Colvig. **Medieval and Renaissance Music on Long-Playing Records**. 1964. xii, 122p. index. LC 65-916. ISBN 0-911772-26-Xpa.

This volume covers LPs to 1960, and a bound-in supplement covers 1960-61. No. 26, covering 1962-71, greatly supplements No. 6.

208. No. 7: Mangler, Joyce Ellen. **Rhode Island Music and Musicians, 1733-1850**. 1965. xix, 90p. bibliog. index. LC 65-8473. ISBN 0-911772-27-8pa.

This is essentially a biographical dictionary arranged by name, with professional and chronological indexes.

209. No. 8: Blum, Fred. **Jean Sibelius: An International Bibliography on the Occasion of the Centennial Celebrations, 1965**. 1965. xxi, 114p. index. LC 66-3288. ISBN 0-911772-28-6pa.

This thorough compilation, published in the year of the one hundredth anniversary of the birth of Sibelius, cites and annotates nearly fifteen hundred books, dissertations, and articles.

210. No. 9: Hartley, Kenneth R. **Bibliography of Theses and Dissertations in Sacred Music**. 1966. viii, 127p. index. LC 67-5647. ISBN 0-911772-29-4pa.

Arranged by institution and author, the bibliography covers current and retrospective works. There is a crude subject index.

211. No. 10: Fruchtman, Caroline S. **Checklist of Vocal Chamber Works by Benedetto Marcello**. 1967. xvi, 37p. bibliog. LC 67-6772. ISBN 0-911772-30-8pa.

Works are listed by form and located in one of sixteen European libraries.

212. No. 11: Warner, Thomas E. **An Annotated Bibliography of Woodwind Instruction Books, 1600-1830**. 1967. xvi, 138p. index. LC 68-482. ISBN 0-911772-31-6pa.

Works are arranged in chronological order, with indexes to authors, instruments, and publishers, engravers, and printers.

213. No. 12: Hansell, Sven Hostrup. **Works for Solo Voice of Johann Adolph Hasse (1699-1783)**. 1968. viii, 110p. music. LC 68-6461. ISBN 0-911772-32-4pa.

This thematic catalog includes incipits, and lists a library location for each work.

214. No. 13: Stahl, Dorothy A. **A Selected Discography of Solo Song**. 1968. xi, 90p. index. LC 79-5370. ISBN 0-911772-33-2pa.

This has been superseded by No. 24.

215. No. 14: Epstein, Dena J. **Music Publishing in Chicago before 1871: The Firm of Root & Cady, 1858-1871**. 1969. x, 243p. bibliog. index. LC 78-4713. ISBN 0-911772-36-7pa.

This is a history of the firm and a checklist, with indexes, of its published music.

216. No. 15: Spiess, Lincoln, and Thomas Stanford. **Introduction to Certain Mexican Musical Archives**. 1969. 1v. (various paging). illus. music. bibliog. LC 73-12866. ISBN 0-911772-37-5pa.

Manuscript holdings of ten archives are indexed by composer.

217. No. 16: Weichlein, William J. **A Checklist of American Music Periodicals, 1850-1900**. 1970. 103p. index. LC 74-15083. ISBN 0-911772-38-3pa.

The checklist lists titles alphabetically, giving beginning and ending dates, publisher, place of publication, names of personnel, and locations of publication, and title changes.

218. No. 17: Roberts, Kenneth. **A Checklist of Twentieth-Century Choral Music for Male Voices**. 1970. 32p. LC 70-18364. ISBN 0-911772-39-1pa.

Arranged by composer, the checklist indicates a source for each piece.

219. No. 18: De Smet, Robin. **Published Music for the Viola da Gamba and Other Viols**. 1971. 105p. bibliog. index. LC 75-151302. ISBN 0-911772-40-5pa.

This list organizes compositions by instrumental combinations and gives a publisher for each piece.

220. No. 19: Lee, Douglas A. **The Works of Christoph Nichelmann: A Thematic Index**. 1971. 100p. music. LC 71-151301. ISBN 0-911772-41-3pa.

The index includes thematic incipits, and cites sources for manuscripts and published works.

221. No. 20: Gillespie, James E., Jr. **The Reed Trio: An Annotated Bibliography of Original Published Works**. 1971. 84p. LC 74-174729. ISBN 0-911772-42-1pa.

The bibliography lists, by composer, currently available works for oboe, clarinet, and bassoon.

222. No. 21: Parkinson, John A. **An Index to the Vocal Works of Thomas Augustine Arne & Michael Arne**. 1972. 82p. LC 78-175175. ISBN 0-911772-45-6pa.

The index lists titles of works by these eighteenth-century English composers and their locations in eighteenth-century collections. Thomas Augustine Arne is best remembered for his composition "Rule Britannia."

223. No. 22: Krummel, Donald W. **Bibliotheca Bolduaniana: A Renaissance Music Bibliography**. 1972. 191p. illus. index. LC 71-175176. ISBN 0-911772-46-4pa.

This is a reproduction and a catalog of the 1,299 titles of musical works from the *Bibliotheca philosophica* of the seventeenth-century Pomeranian pastor Paulus Bolduanus.

224. No. 23: Krohn, Ernst C. **Music Publishing in the Middle Western States before the Civil War**. 1972. 44p. LC 70-175173. ISBN 0-911772-47-2pa.

This is a study of publishers in St. Louis, Cincinnati, Louisville, Detroit, Cleveland, and Chicago.

225. No. 24: Stahl, Dorothy. **A Selected Discography of Solo Song: A Cumulation through 1971**. 1972. 137p. index. LC 79-90432. ISBN 0-911772-35-9; 0-89990-009-7pa.

See entry 535.

226. No. 25: Iotti, Oscar R. Based on the work by Alexander Feinland. **Violin and Violincello in Duo without Accompaniment**. 1972. 73p. LC 77-187707. ISBN 0-911772-48-0pa.

This is a list of works, by composer, for the duo.

227. No. 26: Coover, James B., and Richard Colvig. **Medieval and Renaissance Music on Long-Playing Records: Supplement, 1962-1971**. 1973. 258p. index. LC 65-916. ISBN 0-911772-44-8.

Like the original volume (No. 6), this volume lists anthologies by title and indexes them by composer and performer.

228. No. 27: Marks, Paul F. **Bibliography of Literature Concerning Yemenite-Jewish Music**. 1973. 50p. discog. LC 72-90431. ISBN 0-911772-57-Xpa.

The bibliography deals with both the Jewish tradition within the Islamic culture of Yemen, and the Yemenite Jewish community in Israel.

229. No. 28: Gillespie, James E., Jr. **Solos for Unaccompanied Clarinet: An Annotated Bibliography of Published Works**. 1973. 79p. discog. LC 73-87277. ISBN 0-911772-58-8.

The bibliography lists, by composer, works which are currently available, and provides substantial annotations.

230. No. 29: Abravanel, Claude. **Claude Debussy: A Bibliography**. 1974. 214p. index. LC 72-90430. ISBN 0-911772-49-9.

This thorough bibliography lists 854 works by, and primarily about, Debussy. Entries are organized by topic into categories representing aspects of Debussy's life and work.

231. No. 30: Sollinger, Charles. **String Class Publications in the United States, 1851-1951**. 1974. 71p. LC 73-87276. ISBN 0-911772-61-8.

This annotated bibliography of publications for string instruction classes includes a historical introduction to string music education.

232. No. 31: Kenneson, Claude. **Bibliography of Cello Ensemble Music**. 1974. 59p. LC 73-79444. ISBN 0-911772-60-X.

The bibliography includes works which are both in-print and out-of-print.

233. No. 32: Tischler, Alice. **Karel Boleslav Jirak: A Catalog of His Works**. 1975. 85p. index. LC 74-33792. ISBN 0-911772-75-8.

The catalog indicates the publisher or, in the case of unpublished works, a library location, and notes a first performance and other data.

234. No. 33: Mixter, Keith E. **General Bibliography for Music Research**. 2d ed. 1975. 135p. LC 72-174731. ISBN 0-911772-75-8.

See entry 10.

235. No. 34: Stahl, Dorothy. **A Selected Discography of Solo Song: Supplement, 1971-1974**. 1976. 99p. index. LC 76-12132. ISBN 0-911772-80-4.

See entry 535.

236. No. 35: Taylor, Thomas F. **Thematic Catalog of the Works of Jeremiah Clarke**. 1977. 134p. music. bibliog. index. LC 75-23551. ISBN 0-911772-84-7.

The catalog organizes works by form, and includes thematic incipits.

237. No. 36: Frisbie, Charlotte J. **Music and Dance Research of Southwestern United States Indians: Past Trends, Present Activities, and Suggestions for Future Research**. 1977. 109p. illus. LC 77-74663. ISBN 0-911772-86-3.

This bibliographic essay examines written research from the 1880s to the present, and suggests future topics for research. An appendix lists recordings of native American music.

238. No. 37: McGowan, Richard A. **Italian Baroque Solo Sonatas for the Recorder and the Flute**. 1978. 70p. index. LC 77-92345. ISBN 0-911772-90-1.

Two separate sections list eighteenth-century editions and manuscripts, and modern editions.

239. No. 38: Weaver, Robert Lamar, and Norma Wright Weaver. **A Chronology of Music in the Florentine Theater, 1590-1750: Operas, Prologues, Finales, Intermezzos, and Plays with Incidental Music**. 1978. 421p. illus. bibliog. index. LC 77-74664. ISBN 0-911772-83-9.

The title accurately identifies this as a chronology of *music*, not productions. While it notes dates of performances and members of casts, it identifies the music and text, discusses their origins, and cites a source for the music in either a European or American library. A substantial introduction discusses the theaters and academies of the time.

240. No. 39: Brown, A. Peter. **Carlo d'Ordonez, 1734-1786: A Thematic Catalog**. 1978. 234p. illus. bibliog. index. LC 78-61024. ISBN 0-911772-89-8.

Citations to works are arranged by form; each includes a thematic incipit, and locates the item in a library collection. The catalog is notable for its attempts to identify copyists, and includes numerous illustrations of the styles of selected copyists and of watermarks.

241. No. 40: Lyons, David B. **Lute, Vihuela, Guitar to 1800: A Bibliography**. 1978. 214p. index. LC 78-63602. ISBN 0-911772-93-6.

The bibliography lists modern works dealing with the predecessors to the guitar and other related instruments, composers of works for these instruments, and editions of music during the period 1500 to 1800. Works cited are in English and other languages, and include books, chapters, articles, and dissertations. The selection is good, but the arrangement is confusing. *Guitar and Vihuela: An Annotated Bibliography* (see entry 349) offers a much more efficient arrangement of similar material.

242. No. 41: Kimmey, John A., Jr. **The Arnold Schoenberg-Hans Nachod Collection**. 1979. 230p. illus. bibliog. index. LC 78-70020. ISBN 0-911772-88-X.

Most of the volume consists of photographic reproductions of correspondence and music exchanged between Schoenberg and Nachod, his cousin. A prefatory section gives physical descriptions and transcriptions of written correspondence.

243. No. 42: Williams, Michael D. **Music for Viola**. 1979. 362p. bibliog. LC 78-70022. ISBN 0-911772-95-2.

Works are listed by instrumental form, then by composer. Most, but not all, of the entries give a publisher.

244. No. 43: Cohen, Albert, and Leta E. Miller, comp. **Music in the Paris Academy of Sciences, 1666-1793: A Source Archive in Photocopy at Stanford University: An Index**. 1979. 69p. illus. index. LC 78-70025. ISBN 0-911772-96-0.

This work lists items pertaining to music from the collection of six distinct series of published proceedings, papers, and mémoires.

245. No. 44: Snow, Robert J. **The Extant Music of Rodrigo de Ceballos and Its Sources**. 1980. 155p. illus. music. LC 78-70024. ISBN 0-89990-001-1.

The work includes a discussion of the extant works, a catalog with thematic incipits, illustrations of manuscripts, and transcriptions into modern notation of four motets.

246. No. 45: Tischler, Alice, with the assistance of Carol Tomasic. **Fifteen Black American Composers: A Bibliography of Their Works**. 1981. 328p. illus. bibliog. index. LC 81-1162. ISBN 0-89990-003-8.

The bibliography lists the works of twentieth-century composers Edward Boatner, Margaret Bonds, Edgar Clark, Arthur Cunningham, William Dawson, Roger Dickerson, James Furman, Adolphus Hailstork, Robert Harris, Wendell Logan, Carman Moore, Dorothy Moore, John Price, Noah Ryder, and Frederick Tills. In addition, it provides a photograph and short biographical sketch of each composer.

247. No. 46: Bradley, Carol June, comp. **Music Collections in American Libraries: A Chronology**. 1981. xiii, 249p. bibliog. index. LC 81-2907. ISBN 0-89990-002-X.

See entry 115.

248. No. 47: Coover, James B. **Musical Instrument Collections: Catalogs and Cognate Literature**. 1981. 464p. index. LC 81-19901. ISBN 0-89990-013-5.

The catalogs included represent hundreds of collections from around the world; in sequential order appear catalogs from Tiflis (USSR), Tilburg (Netherlands), Tokyo (Japan), and Toledo (Ohio). The first section lists, by city, catalogs of institutional collections and expositions. The second lists private collections by owner's name. In addition, Coover has included citations to articles and books which describe the collections, and guides, descriptions, and reports relevant to the collections. An index lists names of individuals and museums; a subject index would have been helpful in locating collections devoted to a specialty.

249. No. 48: Roman, Zoltan. **Anton von Webern: An Annotated Bibliography**. 1983. 219p. index. LC 82-23344. ISBN 0-89990-015-1.

This includes 859 works from Europe, the United States, and Japan, arranged by author. Reviews and "journalistic" materials are excluded. Indexes list persons and subjects.

250. No. 49: Temperley, Nicholas, and Charles G. Manns. **Fuging Tunes in the Eighteenth Century**. 1983. xi, 493p. index. LC 83-10782. ISBN 0-89990-017-8.

According to the substantial "Historical Introduction," fuging tunes originated in England and Scotland in the early eighteenth century and were later brought to the colonies. Using a numerical scheme to represent the melody of each tune, this work indexes tunes from several hundred printed sources. Other indexes cover texts, tune names, and compilers, composers, and other persons.

251. No. 50: Frasier, Jane. **Women Composers: A Discography**. 1983. viii, 300p. bibliog. index. LC 83-22563. ISBN 0-89990-018-6.

See entry 505.

252. No. 51: Kratzenstein, Marilou, and Jerald Hamilton. **Four Centuries of Organ Music, from the Robertsbridge Codex through the Baroque Era: An Annotated Discography**. 1984. ix, 300p. bibliog. index. LC 84-546. ISBN 0-89990-020-8.

See entry 518.

253. No. 52: Stahl, Dorothy. **A Selected Discography of Solo Song: Supplement, 1975-1982.** 1984. 236p. LC 84-19794. ISBN 0-89990-923-2.

See entry 535.

254. No. 53: Greene, Richard D. **Index to Composer Bibliographies**. 1985. x, 76p. index. LC 85-18202. ISBN 0-89990-025-9.

See entry 389.

255. No. 54: Wescott, Steven D., comp. **A Comprehensive Bibliography of Music for Film and Television**. 1985. xxi, 432p. index. LC 85-27184. ISBN 0-89990-027-5.

Wescott justly identifies this weighty enumeration of 6,340 sources in eighteen languages from twenty-eight countries as "a compendium of all the basic materials, resources, and references which inform the study of music as it has collaborated in the

100-year development of film and television." A detailed classification scheme organizes the citations. Section 1 covers the history of film and television music, listing surveys first and organizing the rest within chronological divisions. Section 2 lists works dealing with 114 composers. Section 3 collects works on the aesthetics of silent and sound films. Section 4 lists "special topics" such as the performance of music on film and television, animated sound, and musical graphics. Section 5 lists reference sources. In all sections, Wescott underlines entry numbers to identify works of exceptional importance. Access to subjects is available not only by means of the classification scheme, but in numerous cross-references, and, to a limited extent, in the index (although this is primarily a list of authors and personal names). No other similar work approaches the breadth of this excellent bibliography.

256. No. 55: Murray, Sterling E. **Anthologies of Music: An Annotated Index**. 1987. xxiii, 178p. index. LC 86-27735. ISBN 0-89990-031-3.

Murray indexes compositions contained in thirty-three anthologies published between 1931 and 1984 "that are likely to be readily accessible in most college and university libraries" (introduction). He expands greatly upon the coverage of Hilton's *Index to Early Music in Selected Anthologies* (see entry 294). All anthologies chosen for indexing are arranged historically and include complete movements or compositions. The chronological coverage of compositions is broad, dating from works of the first century A.D. to works of living composers. Following a section of anonymous works, the arrangement is by composer. Each entry gives the title of the composition, date, location in one or more anthologies, and, in abbreviated form, other information, such as the presence of a text translation or of nontraditional clefs. The index lists works by genre.

* * *

257. **MLA Index and Bibliography Series**. No. 1- . [place varies]: Music Library Association, 1963- . ISSN 0094-6478.

The initial volumes in the series, for the most part, were indexes to collected works (hence the original name of the series, *MLA Index Series*). Bibliographies such as numbers 12, 13, 14, and 15 expanded the scope of the series. Some of these works are quite brief, and their titles are self-explanatory: a researcher clearly either needs them or not. Some are quite specific tools; number 3, now in its fourth edition, and Wenk's bibliographies of analyses are more broadly significant.

258. No. 1: Bibliography Committee of the New York Chapter of the Music Library Association, ed. **An Alphabetical Index to Claudio Monteverdi: Tutte le Opera, Nuovamente Date in Luce da G. Francesco Malipiero Asolo 1926-1942**. 1963. 17p. LC 66-41376.

The index lists titles or incipits, and gives volume and page numbers.

259. No. 2: Bibliography Committee of the New York Chapter of the Music Library Association, ed. **An Alphabetical Index to Hector Berlioz Werke: hrsg. von Charles Mahlerbe und Felix Weingartner, Leipzig und Wien, Breitkopf und Härtel, 1900-1907**. 1963. 6p. LC 66-41375.

The index lists titles of works, and titles translated into English.

260. No. 3: Baily, Dee. **A Checklist of Music Bibliographies and Indexes in Progress and Unpublished**. 4th ed. 1982. 104p. index. LC 81-22498. ISBN 0-914954-27-Xpa.

The checklist has continuously increased in size since its first edition of 1964. The latest edition includes 533 annotated projects arranged by author or sponsoring organization. Entries note the format of the work, future publisher (if any), and an address for the author or organization. The index provides subject access.

261. No. 4: Coral, Lenore. **A Concordance of the Thematic Indexes to the Instrumental Works of Antonio Vivaldi**. 2d ed. 1972. 40p. LC 73-150818.

In tabular form, the concordance coordinates catalog numbers between three catalogs. The first edition was published in 1965.

262. No. 5: Bibliography Committee of the New York Chapter of the Music Library Association, ed. **An Alphabetical Index to Tomás Luis de Victoria, Opera Omni**. 1966. 26p. LC 66-6126.

The index lists in one alphabet titles, first lines, settings, and liturgical feasts or occasions for which pieces were written.

263. No. 6: Ochs, Michael, comp. **Schumann Index, Pt. 1: An Alphabetical Index to Robert Schumann Werke**. 1967. 26p. LC 68-6428.

The index lists instrumental works by title, and vocal works by title and first line.

264. No. 7: Weichlein, William J., comp. **Schumann Index, Pt. 2: An Alphabetical Index to the Solo Songs of Robert Schumann**. 1967. 35p. LC 68-6428.

The index lists songs by title and first line from the standard edition of Schumann and several other anthologies.

265. No. 8: Rogers, Kirby. **Index to Maurice Frost's English & Scottish Psalm & Hymn Tunes**. 1967. 28p.

The index lists titles and first lines of tunes.

266. No. 9: Wolff, Arthur S. **Speculum: An Index of Musically Related Articles and Book Reviews**. 2d ed. 1981. 64p. LC 81-11302. ISBN 0-914954-26-1pa.

Speculum: A Journal of Medieval Studies is not a musicological journal, but it frequently discusses the role of music in the Middle Ages. This edition updates the 1970 edition to cover material from volume 1 (1926) to volume 54 (1979).

267. No. 10: Ochs, Michael, comp. **An Index to Das Chorwerk, Volumes 1-110**. 1970. iv, 38p. bibliog. index. LC 70-31221.

Das Chorwerk (1929-) is a series of musical scores. The index lists works by composer and title.

268. No. 11: Whaples, Miriam K. **Bach Aria Index**. 1971. xi, 88p. index. LC 70-29717.

Citations to arias are arranged according to instrumental combinations. Indexes list first lines of arias and names of instruments.

269. No. 12: Thompson, Annie Figueroa. **An Annotated Bibliography of Writings about Music in Puerto Rico**. 1975. v, 34p. index. LC 74-30256. ISBN 0-914954-02-4pa.

The bibliography contains 304 items in both Spanish and English dating from 1844 to 1972. It enlarges greatly on the "Puerto Rico" section in Chase's *Guide to the Music of Latin America* (see entry 332), which lists twenty-one items.

270. No. 13: Wenk, Arthur, comp. **Analyses of Twentieth-Century Music: 1940-1970**. 1975. 94p. index. LC 76-375324. ISBN 0-914954-04-0pa.

271. No. 14: Wenk, Arthur, comp. **Analyses of Twentieth-Century Music: Supplement**. 2d ed. 1984. 132p. index. LC 84-2015. ISBN 0-914954-28-8pa.

272. No. 15: Wenk, Arthur, comp. **Analyses of Nineteenth-Century Music: 1940-1980**. 2d ed. 1984. 83p. index. LC 84-2017. ISBN 0-914954-29-6pa.

Numbers 13, 14 (1st ed. 1975), and 15 (1st ed. 1976) offer an excellent means of locating formal analyses of individual works and stylistic analyses of more than one work. They survey periodical articles, books, dissertations, and festschriften which have been written since 1940. All three omit biographies, accounts of performances, and discussions of manuscripts or performance practice. All list citations to analyses alphabetically by composer, and provide an index to authors.

273. No. 16: Warfield, Gerald. **Writings on Contemporary Music Notation: An Annotated Bibliography**. 1976. iii, 93p. index. LC 81-213182. ISBN 0-914954-07-5pa.

In 452 citations, this annotated bibliography provides a comprehensive survey of the literature from 1950 to 1975 on new notation, and a selective list of works from 1900 to 1950 on notation and related topics.

274. No. 17: Edwards, J. Michele. **Literature for Voices in Combination with Electronic and Tape Music: An Annotated Bibliography**. 1977. 194p. bibliog. index. LC 77-10614. ISBN 0-914954-09-1pa.

The bibliography includes four hundred works written between the late 1930s and middle 1970s which use at least three live performers who sing or speak.

275. No. 18: Dedel, Peter. **Johannes Brahms: A Guide to His Autograph in Facsimile**. 1978. 86p. illus. index. LC 77-28624. ISBN 0-914954-12-1pa.

The guide indexes musical works, arrangements, correspondence, and miscellany from over 150 sources.

276. No. 19: Williams, Michael D. **Source: Music of the Avant Garde: Annotated List of Contents and Cumulative Indices**. 1978. 52p. index. LC 78-4954. ISBN 0-914954-13-Xpa.

This work covers compositions, articles, and recordings from the eleven issues of *Source* published between 1967 and 1973.

277. No. 20: Fuld, James J., and Mary Wallace Davidson. **18th-Century American Secular Music Manuscripts: An Inventory**. 1980. xiii, 225p. bibliog. index. LC 79-92993. ISBN 0-914954-16-4pa.

See entry 416.

278. No. 21: Keller, Kate Van Winkle. **Popular Secular Music in America through 1800: A Preliminary Checklist of Manuscripts in North American Collections**. 1981. xviii, 140p. bibliog. index. LC 81-1167. ISBN 0-914954-22-9pa.

See entry 419.

279. No. 22: Hall, Alison. **Palestrina: An Index to the Casimiri, Kalmus and Haberl Editions**. 1980. xiii, 84p. index. LC 80-14756. ISBN 0-914954-18-0pa.

Works are listed by title and form.

280. No. 23: Hall, Alison. **E. H. Fellowes: An Index to the English Madrigalists and the English School of Lutenist Song Writers**. 1984. 100p. index. LC 84-3345. ISBN 0-914954-30-Xpa.

The index lists works by composer and title.

* * *

281. **Music Indexes and Bibliographies**. George R. Hill, ed. Hackensack, N.J.: Joseph Boonin, 1970-76. Nos. 1-12. Clifton, N.J.: European American Music Corporation, 1978-79. Nos. 13-15.

George R. Hill compiles a regular listing in *Notes* (see entry 639) of music publishers' catalogs, and has contributed to *Notes*, in collaboration with Joseph Boonin, a series of updates on music price indexes. Number 13 in the Music Indexes and Bibliographies series has become somewhat of a standard resource in music collections; other numbers in the series are more specialized, and many are thematic catalogs.

282. No. 1: Hill, George R., and Murray Gould, in collaboration with David Noon and others. **A Thematic Locator for Mozart's Works, as Listed in Köchel's "Chronologisch-thematisches Verzeichnis" – Sixth Edition**. 1970. vii, 76p. LC 75-021921. ISBN 0-913574-01-5.

Themes are arranged first, by intervallic size, and second, by pitch name (beginning all themes on C).

283. No. 2: Hill, George R. **A Preliminary Checklist of Research on the Classic Symphony and Concerto to the Time of Beethoven (Excluding Haydn and Mozart)**. 1970. vii, 58p. index. LC 77-023022.

The checklist includes 450 books and articles, organized by geographical area. An index lists names of composers.

284. No. 3: Surian, Elvidio. **A Checklist of Writings on 18th Century French and Italian Opera (Excluding Mozart)**. 1970. xiv, 121p. LC 70-023023.

The checklist groups fifteen hundred books and articles by broad subject categories. Separate sections list studies of individual composers and of individual cities.

285. No. 4: Boonin, Joseph M. **An Index to the Solo Songs of Robert Franz**. 1970. v, 19p. index. LC 71-021920.

This index to collections published by Ditson, Schirmer, and Peters lists songs by opus number. Indexes cover first lines, titles, and names of poets whose works were used as texts.

286. No. 5: Chusid, Martin. **A Catalog of Verdi's Operas**. 1974. xi, 201p. illus. bibliog. index. LC 74-169169. ISBN 0-913574-05-8.

Arranged by opera, the catalog describes libretti, autograph manuscripts, and published editions.

287. No. 6: Newman, Joel, and Fritz Rikko. **A Thematic Index to the Works of Salamon Rossi**. 1972. xiv, 143p. illus. music. bibliog. index. LC 73-156321.

For each entry, the index gives facsimile reproductions of the title page and other items from the first edition, location of extant copies and later editions, contents, incipits, original clefs, authors of editions, and modern editions.

288. No. 7: Kostka, Stefan M. **A Bibliography of Computer Applications in Music**. 1974. iii, 58p. LC 74-169159.

The bibliography lists 641 books and articles in English and other languages. There is no subject index.

289. No. 8: Bedford, Frances, and Robert Conant. **Twentieth-Century Harpsichord Music: A Classified Catalog**. 1974. xxi, 95p. LC 74-174993. ISBN 0-913574-08-2.

This is a source list for published and unpublished compositions. It is organized into thirty-four instrumental combinations.

290. No. 9: Ripin, Edward M. **The Instrument Catalogs of Leopoldo Franciolini**. 1974. xix, 201p. illus. index. LC 74-168317. ISBN 0-913574-09-0.

The preface identifies Franciolini (1844-1920) as an important dealer of musical instruments and a forger. This volume reproduces text and illustrations from catalogs. An appendix discusses the decision of the court in the trial of Franciolini in Florence for forgery.

291. No. 10: Mathiesen, Thomas J. **A Bibliography of Sources for the Study of Ancient Greek Music**. 1974. iv, 59p. LC 74-169157. ISBN 0-913574-10-4.

The 949 citations to books and articles, in English and other languages, are arranged by author. There is no subject index.

292. No. 11: Flanders, Peter. **A Thematic Index to the Works of Benedetto Pallavicino**. 1974. x, 85p. illus. music. index. ISBN 0-913574-11-2.

The index provides facsimile reproductions of title pages of first editions, location of extant copies and of later editions, text and musical incipits, clefs, and other detail.

293. No. 12: Hill, George R. **A Thematic Catalog of the Instrumental Music of Florian Leopold Gassman**. 1976. xix, 171p. music. LC 77-366756. ISBN 0-913574-12-0.

The catalog organizes works by type, and gives thematic incipits and a source for each work.

294. No. 13: Hilton, Ruth B. **An Index to Early Music in Selected Anthologies**. 1978. xii, 127p. LC 78-109998. ISBN 0-913574-13-9.

Hilton indexes the contents of nineteen general anthologies commonly found in music libraries. Some are not indexed by Charles (see entry 413) or Heyer (see entry 417). The first section arranges works by composer. The subject index provides access to works by form (such as "Ballades" or "Minnelieder").

295. No. 14: Saltonstall, Cecilia D., and Henry Saltonstall. **A New Catalog of Music for Small Orchestra**. 1978. xxv, 323p. LC 80-120161. ISBN 0-913574-14-7.

Over six thousand works are included. Most are currently available. The arrangement is by composer.

296. No. 15: Buff, Iva M. **A Thematic Catalog of the Sacred Works of Giacomo Carissimi**. 1979. viii, 159p. music. LC 80-142011. ISBN 0-913574-15-5.

Works are listed alphabetically by textual incipit. Entries give musical incipits and locate sources.

* * *

297. **Thematic Catalogue Series**. No. 1- . New York: Pendragon Press, 1977- .

Works in the series serve as indexes to established editions or present the works of relatively unknown composers. Individually, most would be too specialized for inclusion in the present work; but taken as a whole, they represent current research with early sources and supplement or enlarge upon established catalogs listed in Barry Brook's *Thematic Catalogues in Music* (see entry 398). They vary in quality and approach, and the design of most (except No. 13) is utilitarian rather than aesthetically pleasing. As thematic indexes, all present themes of their subjects' works either in musical notation or in a form based on Barry Brook's "Plaine and Easie Code" for notating music with typewriter symbols (*Fontes Artis Musicae* 12, no. 3 [1965]: 156-60).

298. No. 1: Paymer, Marvin E. **Giovanni Battista Pergolesi, 1710-1736: A Thematic Catalogue of the Opera Omnia, with an Appendix Listing Omitted Compositions**. 1977. xix, 99p. illus. bibliog. index. LC 77-1419. ISBN 0-918728-01-0.

This index to *Giovanni Battista Pergolesi Opera Omnia* (Rome: Gli Amici della Musica da Camera, 1941) employs Brook's "Plaine and Easie Code" for notating thematic incipits. It is organized by musical form, and includes a "Thematic Locator" which lists themes by alphabetic equivalents of notes of the scale.

299. No. 2: Benton, Rita. **Ignace Pleyel: A Thematic Catalogue of His Compositions**. 1977. xxviii, 482p. illus. music. index. LC 77-22681. ISBN 0-918728-04-5.

A winner of the annual award given by the Music Library Association for the best book-length bibliography, this is a work of stunning detail. It is arranged by musical form and includes a thematic index of incipits transposed to C.

300. No. 3: Charteris, Richard. **John Coprario: A Thematic Catalogue of His Music, with a Biographical Introduction**. 1977. x, 113p. music. LC 77-22738. ISBN 0-918728-05-3.

The biographical introduction occupies a short thirty-four pages; the rest is the catalog itself.

301. No. 4: Larsen, Jens Peter. **Three Haydn Catalogues/Drei Haydn Kataloge**. 2d facsimile ed. with a survey of Haydn's oeuvre. 1979. xlvi, 119p. illus. bibliog. LC 79-14675. ISBN 0-918728-10-X.

The introductory material, in English and German, surveys Haydn's works and editions. The remainder of the work reprints in facsimile three catalogs "dating back to Haydn's time, and, more or less, written or supervised by the composer himself" (introduction).

302. No. 5: Freeman, Robert N. **Franz Schneider (1737-1812): A Thematic Catalogue of His Works**. 1979. xxxiii, 237p. illus. music. bibliog. index. LC 79-15260. ISBN 0-918728-13-4.

Developed out of a doctoral dissertation, this is a list of works by an Austrian composer of church music. It was derived largely from manuscript sources.

303. No. 6: Schiødt, Nanna, and Sybille Reventlow. **The Danish RISM Catalogue: Music Manuscripts before 1800 in the Libraries of Denmark**. 1977. 20 microfiches.

The Danish RISM Catalogue is a byproduct of series A II of RISM (see entry 429), which will list music manuscripts from 1600 to 1800 in European libraries. It lists manuscripts in Danish libraries which are neither monophonic nor written in tablature. The catalog itself appears on microfiche in an unfriendly computerized format as a series of five sequences sorted by composer, library, genre, text incipit, and musical incipit. Bibliographic data for each entry follow a uniform format of numbered fields which can include library, composer, author, genre, title, parallel title, performer, date and size, parts, instrumentation, contents, musical incipit in abbreviated form, text incipit, bibliographical references, other related dates, language of text, provenance, binding, and shelf number. *The Danish RISM Catalogue, Manuscripts: An Introduction*, a twenty-page booklet which accompanies the microfiche, explains the mechanics of the catalog.

304. No. 7: Mongrédien, Jean. **Catalogue thématique de l'oeuvre complète du compositeur Jean-François Le Sueur (1760-1837)**. 1980. xxviii, 434p. music. LC 79-16463. ISBN 0-918728-12-6.

The biographical introduction (in French and English) identifies Le Sueur as "one of the leading figures of French musical life in his day." The catalog is divided by form and includes operas, religious works, hymns and songs of the revolution, and other works, including musical writings.

305. No. 8: Bryant, Stephan C., and Gary W. Chapman. **A Melodic Index to Haydn's Instrumental Music: A Thematic Locator for Anthony van Hoboken's Thematisch-bibliographisches Werkverzeichnis, Volumes I & III**. Foreword by Jan LaRue. 1982. xvii, 100p. LC 81-17727. ISBN 0-918728-19-3.

The first section lists incipits, in alphabetical form, in their original keys; the second lists the same incipits transposed to C.

306. No. 9: Wienandt, Elwyn A. **Johann Pezel (1639-1694): A Thematic Catalogue of His Instrumental Works**. 1983. xxxiii, 102p. illus. music. LC 82-12288. ISBN 0-918728-23-1.

The catalog lists the contents of eight seventeenth-century collections.

307. No. 10: Lee, Douglas A. **Franz Benda (1709-1786): A Thematic Catalogue of His Works**. 1984. xxii, 221p. illus. music. bibliog. LC 84-1728. ISBN 0-918728-42-8.

Organized by musical form, this catalog works from manuscript and printed sources. An appendix reproduces watermarks found in many of the manuscripts.

308. No. 11: Charteris, Richard. **Alfonso Ferrabosco the Elder (1543-1588): A Thematic Catalogue of His Music with a Biographical Calendar**. 1984. xvi, 227p. music, bibliog. index. LC 84-2833. ISBN 0-918728-44-4.

The catalog indexes scattered works in early editions and in the author's *Opera Omnia of Alfonso Ferrabosco the Elder (1543-1588)*, No. 96 in *Corpus Mensurabilis Musicae* (Neuhausen Stuttgart, 1984-).

309. No. 12: White, Chappell. **Giovanni Battista Viotti (1755-1824): A Thematic Catalogue of His Works**. 1985. xix, 175p. illus. music. LC 84-26366. ISBN 0-918728-43-6.

"Viotti was the most influential violinist of the late 18th century" (introduction). The catalog lists works in manuscripts and published editions.

310. No. 13: Tommasini, Anthony. **Virgil Thomson's Music Portraits**. Preface by Virgil Thomson. 1986. xii, 237p. illus. music. bibliog. index. LC 85-6297. ISBN 0-918728-51-7.

This, the most elegantly prepared work in the series so far, is a guide to 140 of Thomson's portraits. Thomson's preface explains that he composes his portraits in the presence of his subject, as a painter with a model. Tommasini begins the catalog with a survey of the portraits and a musical analysis of four of them. The catalog itself introduces each portrait with a photograph of the subject, a thematic incipit, a paragraph or two about the subject (often taken from Thomson himself), and a source for the music.

11

Current and Serial Indexes and Bibliographies of Music and Music Literature

Some of these works, such as the *British Catalogue of Music* (see entry 313), list only music; some, such as *RILM Abstracts* (see entry 327), list only the literature of music; two titles—*Bibliographic Guide to Music* (see entry 311) and the Library of Congress catalogs (see entries 316-17)—list both, and also include recordings. Current discographies devoted solely to recordings are found in chapter 19.

Important resources beyond the scope of this chapter are periodicals themselves, book and music reviews, and lists which regularly appear in many journals of music. The citations to journals in chapter 20 mention such features. *Notes* (see entry 639) is particularly important for the quantity of books and music it reviews, for its international coverage, and for its index to reviews of recordings.

311. **Bibliographic Guide to Music**. Boston: G. K. Hall, 1975- . annual. LC 76-643534. ISSN 0360-2753.

Items cataloged during the previous year by the New York Public Library, including books and serials pertaining to music, scores, librettos, and recordings, along with some items from the Library of Congress MARC tapes, are the basis for the guide. It supplements the New York Public Library's *Dictionary Catalog of the Music Collection* (see entry 188), and provides a comprehensive ongoing listing of music and music literature. Entries appear under author or composer, title, and Library of Congress subject headings, although only the main entry (usually the author entry) gives full bibliographic information. Computerized methods of compilation and the vast amount of material the guide includes create occasional problems such as duplicate entries for the same item, alphabetization errors, and an uncertain time lag between an item's publication date and the date of its listing, which can run from one to ten years. Yet, this is an important resource for thorough research or for verification, as it includes, eventually, bibliographic information for virtually anything an American researcher is likely to need.

312. **Bibliographie des Musikschriftums**. Frankfurt am Main, Germany: Friedrich Hofmeister, 1936-68; Mainz, West Germany: Schott, 1969- . index. LC 37-21497.

Begun in 1936, publication of this series was suspended from 1940 to 1949. Published biennially from 1950-51 to 1958-59, it has been an annual since 1960. Each volume lists between six and seven thousand articles, books, dissertations, collected works, and other writings on music from Europe and North America. The emphasis is solidly academic, excluding news magazines and most journals with a popular orientation, but including many journals from Eastern Europe not indexed by *RILM* (see entry 327), and articles from some nonmusic journals. A classified scheme of some fifty topics organizes the citations. A "Personen" section lists publications under the names of individual composers, performers, and musicologists as subjects. Indexes list subjects and keywords, authors and named persons, and titles of books. Citations appear in their original languages, and introductory material, classifications, and subject headings are in German. The notoriously late publication (about ten years behind the current year) of the *Bibliographie* and its lack of annotations make it a second choice to *RILM* for most users, but its breadth of coverage (overlapping surprisingly little with *RILM*) and multiple points of access make it valuable for researchers with even minimal facility in German.

313. **British Catalogue of Music**. London: Council of the British National Bibliography, 1957-73; London: British Library, Bibliographic Services Division, 1974- . annual, with two interim issues. index. LC 58-2570. ISSN 0068-1407. (Repr. 1957-85, New York: K. G. Saur, 1987. 10v. ISBN 0-86291-395-0).

Since its inception, this has been the most efficiently prepared and one of the most extensive ongoing listings of newly published music. Not restricted to British publications, it also includes foreign music available in Britain through a sales agent, and, since the 1982 compilation, other works acquired by the British Library Music Library. Until 1982 it included an annual listing of books about music published in Britain. A classification system, which also changed in 1982 from an alphabetical organization to one based on the numerical Dewey Decimal classification, arranges entries by instrumentation. Entries give full bibliographic information, including the name of the composer, title of the piece or collection, name of the arranger or compiler, place of publication, publisher, date of publication, physical description, informational notes, and price. A composer/title index provides access to specific works and gives abbreviated bibliographic data. A subject index lists musical forms and instrumental combinations and their corresponding classification symbols.

314. **Composium Directory of New Music**. Sedro Woolley, Wash.: Crystal Musicworks, 1971-83. 12v. LC 85-10025.

The preface to the 1982/83 volume identifies this as "a list of recent works by living composers, and includes both published and currently unpublished compositions." It arranges composer's names alphabetically, including abbreviated biographical information for each composer and a list of works which gives title, instrumentation, duration, price, publisher. An "Ensemble and Instrument Listing" organizes compositions by instrumentation. Volumes beginning in 1979 include a cumulative index to composers' names in previous volumes. *Composium* bases its listings on information submitted by composers themselves, so it is in no way a thorough record of new music. It is useful for identifying sources for some recent music, and as a biographical resource.

315. **Jazz Index: Bibliography of Jazz Literature in Periodicals and Collections**. Vols. 1-7. Frankfurt, West Germany: Norbert Ruecker, 1977-83. quarterly. LC 79-642447. ISSN 0344-5399.

Jazz Index's place of publication and its selection of titles demonstrates the strong interest jazz holds for many Europeans. It indexes not only virtually every American jazz periodical, but an equal number of European titles – a total of over eighty. Though *Jazz*

Index fails to index authors of articles, it uses form (such as "book reviews"), subject, and geographical headings, names of individuals and bands, and gives a full citation for an article under each type of heading. Headings and introductory material are in English. *Jazz Index* ventures beyond periodical literature by occasionally indexing a collection of essays or interviews, and listing "Hard-to-Get Literature" – pamphlets, privately published books, dissertations, and other materials outside of the normal publishing routes. A separate section in each issue indexes articles on blues music.

316. Library of Congress. **Library of Congress Catalog: Music and Phonorecords. A Cumulative List of Works Represented by Library of Congress Printed Cards.** Washington, D.C.: Library of Congress, 1953-72. LC 53-60012. ISSN 0041-7793. (Repr. 1953-62, Rowman and Littlefield; repr. 1963-72, J. W. Edwards).

317. Library of Congress. **Library of Congress Catalogs: Music, Books on Music, and Sound Recordings**. Washington, D.C.: Library of Congress, 1973- . semiannual, with annual cumulation. LC 74-640501. ISSN 0092-2838. SuDoc LC 30.8/6: .

The current and previous titles list scores, sheet music, librettos, musical and spoken recordings and books and periodical titles about music and musicians. Entries in *Music and Phonorecords* consisted of reproductions of typed and printed catalog cards produced by the Library of Congress. Since 1973, other cooperating North American libraries have joined with the Library of Congress to produce a union catalog representing the acquisitions of all. Entries give complete bibliographic information and often include the price of the item (at the time of cataloging). The listings appear in alphabetical order by main entry (generally the name of the author, composer, or performer of the work, or in some cases, the title). Cross-references from added entries such as variant titles and performers of recorded works refer to the main entry. The subject index covers only those works cataloged by the Library of Congress, and includes abbreviated citations.

318. Library of Congress. Copyright Office. **Catalog of Copyright Entries: Part 3, Musical Compositions**. n.s. Vols. 1-41. Washington, D.C.: U.S. Government Printing Office, 1906-46. index. LC 06-35347. SuDoc LC 3.6/3: .

319. Library of Congress. Copyright Office. **Catalog of Copyright Entries, Third Series: Part 5, Music**. Vols. 1-31. Washington, D.C.: Library of Congress, Copyright Office, 1947-77. index. LC 79-9701. ISSN 0041-7866. SuDoc LC 3.6/5: .

320. Library of Congress. Copyright Office. **Catalog of Copyright Entries, Fourth Series: Part 3, Performing Arts**. Vol. 1- . Washington, D.C.: Library of Congress, Copyright Office, 1978- . quarterly. index. LC 79-640901. ISSN 0163-7312. SuDoc LC 3.6/6: .

In its various forms, the catalog has always had the same purpose: to record works deposited with the office in order to register copyright. Although a version of the catalog existed since 1891, a separate listing of music did not appear until the new series in 1906. Since it has always included both published and unpublished works, it is very likely the most comprehensive ongoing listing of music in the United States. Entries give a bibliographic citation for each item along with its registration number. Works have generally been listed by title, except from 1973 to 1977, when they were listed by registration number. Renewal registrations have always appeared in a separate list. The index lists names of composers, arrangers, authors, and others associated with the work. Part 3 of the fourth series includes not only music, but also dramatic works, choreography, pantomimes, and certain audiovisual works. Since 1979, the catalog has been published in microfiche.

321. Maleady, Antoinette O., comp. **Record and Tape Reviews Index. 1971-74.** Metuchen, N.J.: Scarecrow, 1972-75. 4v. LC 72-3355. ISSN 0097-8256.

322. Maleady, Antoinette O., comp. **Index to Record and Tape Reviews: A Classical Music Buying Guide. 1975-82.** San Anselmo, Calif.: Chulainn Press, 1976-83. 8v. LC 72-3355. ISSN 0147-5983.

The twelve annual volumes of Maleady's indexes are still useful for locating reviews during the years of their coverage. Despite the change in title, the scope of all volumes remains essentially the same. They index more journals than does Kurtz Myers in his similar indexes for *Notes* which have been collected in his *Index to Record Reviews* (see entries 352-53). Like Myers, Maleady graphically indicates each reviewer's evaluation of a recording. Each volume lists recordings devoted to the works of one composer by the composer's name and recordings of works by more than one composer by manufacturer and number.

323. **Music Article Guide: The Nation's Only Annotated Guide to Feature Articles in American Music Periodicals Geared Exclusively to the Special Needs of School and College Music Educators.** Vol. 1- . Philadelphia: Information Services, 1966- . quarterly. LC 80-618. ISSN 0027-4240.

The subtitle says it all. The guide differentiates itself from *The Music Index* (see entry 324) by emphasizing pedagogical and practical material; excluding book, concert, and record reviews; indexing only signed articles; and briefly summarizing each article. Volume 1 listed articles from about 150 periodicals in a classified arrangement of ten categories. The guide used a variety of formats over the next few years. Volume 9 instituted the present arrangement of a list of numbered subject headings followed by integrated subject, author, and title entries. Only the subject entries give complete bibliographic information; other entries refer to the number of the subject. The guide now selectively indexes material from over two hundred periodicals per year. Each issue includes addresses and subject area classification codes in a "Directory of American Music Periodicals."

324. **The Music Index: A Subject-Author Guide to Current Music Periodical Literature.** Vol. 1- . Detroit: Information Coordinators, 1949- . monthly, with annual cumulations. LC 50-13627. ISSN 0027-4348.

The Music Index began with the ideal of being a "periodical indexing service covering all phases of music," as the introduction to the first annual claimed; it was formerly subtitled *The Key to Current Music Periodical Literature*. The first issue covered forty-one titles. Currently *The Music Index* indexes some 350 titles. Its international selection includes all music periodicals of any significance in the United States, many from Western and Eastern Europe, and representative titles from South America, Africa, and Australia. It includes program notes from major orchestras in the United States and Canada and selected articles from nonmusic periodicals. As *The Music Index* expanded its coverage, it added author entries to its subject indexing in 1957, and retrospective runs of some titles (such as *African Music* from 1954 to date in the 1968 annual). Subject headings conform to a controlled vocabulary which is published as an annual supplement to the monthly issues. Headings such as "Dating of music," "Nudity," and "Occupational diseases and hazards" exemplify the specificity of its indexing. *The Music Index* also uses form headings such as "Discographies" and "Catalogs."

The Music Index thoroughly covers reviews of published music, books, performances, and recordings, listing these by either the composer's, author's, or performer's name. An asterisk next to a review indicates a first performance. The annual cumulations give cross-references from unused subject headings, acronyms, and variant forms of personal names (most notably Russian) to the correct form. Both monthlies and annuals list addresses for publishers of indexed periodicals.

The Music Index has suffered occasionally from delayed publication, although one can expect the issue date to approximately reflect the publication date of indexed articles. Annual cumulations follow years behind publication of the monthly issues, making a thorough search a tedious task. Yet, the excellent indexing and expansive coverage make this a primary resource for any level of music research.

325. **Music Therapy Index**. Vol. 1. n.p.: National Association for Music Therapy, 1976. 224p. LC 77-640629. ISSN 0145-6164.

326. **Music Psychology Index**. Vol. 2- . n.p.: Institute for Therapeutics Research, 1978- . LC 79-644194. ISSN 0195-5802.

Music Psychology Index and its predecessor provide access not only to their titular fields of study but also to related areas of musicology, aesthetics, acoustics, physiology, education, and other fields. Though the title has changed, the philosophical approach, indexing procedure, and editorial staff have changed little through volume 3, which was published with Oryx Press. Volume 1 covers periodical literature from 1960 to 1975; volume 2 adds dissertations, expands the selection of journals, and covers 1976 and 1977; volume 3 alters slightly the choice of journals in order to put more emphasis on research, and covers 1978 to 1980. The selection of journals is worldwide. Volumes of the index integrate in one alphabetical sequence keywords from the titles of articles or dissertations with names of authors. Each entry gives a complete citation. Keyword indexing offers a means of finding articles whose titles accurately express their subjects, but uselessly includes terms (such as "home," "population," and "achievement") whose multiple or indefinite meanings lead to dead ends. But this is a relatively minor problem in a work which can save researchers hours of time otherwise spent with reference works in at least a dozen other disciplines.

327. Répertoire international de littérature musicale/Internationales Repertorium der Musikliteratur/International Repertory of Music Literature. **RILM Abstracts**. Vol. 1- . Sponsored by the International Musicological Society, the International Association of Music Libraries, and the American Council of Learned Societies. New York: RILM, 1967- . quarterly. index. LC 70-200921. ISSN 0033-6955.

RILM has changed little since its inception. It identifies itself as a source for "abstracts ... of all significant literature on music that has appeared since 1 January 1967." Each year, the first three issues list a total of about six thousand bibliographic entries arranged in a classified scheme of about eighty categories, and the fourth issue provides a cumulated subject/author index to the first three. Its scope spans books, articles, essays, reviews, dissertations, catalogs, iconographies, and just about any other type of printed material pertaining to music from worldwide sources.

Authors generally prepare their own abstracts, in English. The editors translate non-English language titles. The *RILM English-Language Thesaurus* (see entry 38) provides a standardized vocabulary for headings. A hierarchical system, which uses both general and specific headings, allows users to investigate general areas or locate specific topics. The indexes liberally use cross-references for variant forms of personal names and unused subject headings, and employ form divisions such as "obituaries" or "discographies." Two index cumulations, covering volumes 1 to 5 and 6 to 10, have appeared, both of which include cross-references from European-language terms to their English equivalents. Volume 10 included a "lacunae issue," which gathered stray citations from the period 1967 to 1976. Issues of *RILM* consistently appear five to six years after the time period they cover; nevertheless its careful preparation and wide scope make it one of the most important tools for music research.

RILM Abstracts is also available online through DIALOG. Online searching allows citations to be retrieved not only through assigned subject headings, but also through keywords in titles. Subject headings, keywords, authors, and other data elements can be combined in various ways to perform much more specific information searches than are possible in the printed form.

328. **Zeitschriftendienst Musik: Nachweis von Aufsätzen aus über 60 deutschen und ausländischen Musikzeitschriften**. Vol. 1- . Berlin: Deutscher Buchereiverband, 1966-82; Deutsches Bibliothekinstitut, 1983- . bimonthly. LC 76-649087. ISSN 0044-3824.

For English-language readers, the primary appeal of this German index to periodical literature is its ease of use and its currency. Bimonthly issues appear within several months after publication of the articles they index. Issues cumulate successively through the year; thus, the sixth issue of each year is an annual cumulation. Indexed periodicals in English include *Early Music*, *Music and Letters*, *Musical Quarterly*, *Notes*, and a number of other standard journals. Complete citations appear under alphabetical subject headings and subheadings (in German). Green pages at the end of each issue list authors and give a reference to subject headings under which their articles appear. The annual cumulation lists these headings within a topical classification, allowing an approach from a broad topic into specifics.

Part 3
BIBLIOGRAPHIES OF MUSIC LITERATURE

12

General and Subject Indexes and Bibliographies of Music Literature

This chapter includes works which list writings about music. Most focus on specific subjects which can be located in the index to this volume. The selection is balanced between older but still valuable works, such as Sendrey's *Bibliography of Jewish Music* (see entry 361), and newer compilations, which tend to be more specialized. It is relatively easy for a researcher to update an older bibliography, since the profusion of music literature since the 1950s has been accompanied by the development of good indexing in *The Music Index* (see entry 324) and *RILM Abstracts* (see entry 327).

Periodical indexes which have been published beyond the auspices of an individual journal have been included in this chapter. They are mentioned in the citations or annotations to the journals which they index.

Those sections of Répertoire international des sources musicales (RISM) which list early writings on music have been included here. Sections which list early music are covered in chapter 15.

329. Basart, Ann P. **Perspectives of New Music: An Index, 1962-1982.** Foreword by Benjamin Boretz. Berkeley, Calif.: Fallen Leaf Press, 1984. ix, 127p. LC 83-82609. ISBN 0-914913-00-Xpa.

Perspectives (see entry 648) is an important forum for the presentation and discussion of contemporary music. This index gives complete citations to 685 articles listed by author. An index to artistic works lists by form the poems, illustrations, and musical works which are such an important part of the journal. An index to subjects covers works, composers, and topics discussed in the articles. Both make reference to the author entries.

330. Basart, Ann P. **Serial Music: A Classified Bibliography of Writings on Twelve-Tone and Electronic Music.** Berkeley, Calif.: University of California Press, 1963. x, 151p. index. (University of California Bibliographic Guides). LC 61-7538.

Though dated, this is still a useful survey of historical material dealing with the development of twentieth-century music. Entries for articles, books, and parts of books are arranged in a classified system consisting of four parts—"Twelve-tone Music," "Electronic

Music," "The Viennese School (Schoenberg, Berg, Webern)," and "Other Composers Who Use Serial Techniques" – with subdivisions by subject or composer. The coverage of European journals and of articles published before *Music Index* began in 1949 is especially valuable.

331. Carl Gregor, Duke of Mecklenburg. **International Bibliography of Jazz Books.** Compiled with the assistance of Norbert Ruecker. Baden-Baden, West Germany: Verlag Valentin Koerner, 1983- . (Collection d'études musicologiques/Sammlung musikwissenschaftlicher Abhandlungen, Vol. 67). ISSN 0085-588X.

Volume 1: 1921-1949. 1983. 108p. index. LC 84-132594. ISBN 3-87320-567-Xpa.

The predecessor to this work was *International Jazz Bibliography: Jazz Books from 1919 to 1968* (Strasbourg, France: Éditions P. H. Heitz, 1969) and its various supplements. It established itself as the standard bibliography in the field. The *International Bibliography of Jazz* drops a small number of citations from the previous work to items which are beyond its scope or which have turned out to be nonexistent, but adds many entries. Each volume in the series will include works published during a specified period of time; volumes 2 through 4 covering 1950 to 1979 are forthcoming. The first volume is arranged (as presumably the others will be) by author. Entries give complete bibliographic citations and tables of contents, and make reference to the original bibliography and other sources. Volume 1 includes 389 entries and a list of unverifiable "phantom titles." Indexes list collaborators, keywords and personal names, subjects, collections and series, countries, and years of publication. Despite this seemingly extensive indexing, the access to individual items in the first volume through the keyword and subject indexes is poor. The *Jazz-Bibliographie* by Bernhard Hefele (see entry 338) is not as exacting in its bibliographical style, but it offers better subject access in its arrangement.

332. Chase, Gilbert. **A Guide to the Music of Latin America**. 2d ed., rev. and enl. A Joint Publication of the Pan American Union and the Library of Congress. Washington, D.C.: Pan American Union, General Secretariat, Organization of American States, 1962; repr., New York: AMS Press, 1972. xi, 411p. index. LC 70-181910. ISBN 0-404-08306-4.

First published in 1945 as *A Guide to Latin American Music* (Library of Congress Music Division) and updated with the addition of supplementary material to each chapter, Chase's guide is still a primary resource for the study of the music of Central and South America, the Caribbean, and the southwestern United States. Over three thousand books and articles published in the Americas and Europe cover all facets of music and musical life in precolonial, colonial, and modern times. Works are organized by country, then by subject. Chase opens each chapter with an overview of the country's music and of the most important histories, and offers short comparative and evaluative annotations for most entries. An index lists authors.

333. Cooper, B. Lee. **The Popular Music Handbook: A Resource Guide for Teachers, Librarians, and Media Specialists**. Littleton, Colo.: Libraries Unlimited, 1984. xxvi, 415p. index. LC 84-19448. ISBN 0-87287-393-5.

Presented as a set of suggestions for employing popular (rock) music in the classroom, this is also an extensive bibliography of works about rock music. The first part presents twenty-eight teaching units such as "Communication Styles" and "Economic Structure," poses issues and a teaching strategy, and suggests appropriate recordings and literary references (which go far beyond musical writings). Part 2 is a substantial bibliography of rock music which includes reference works, works dealing with individual performers, and works on related business and psychological topics. Part 3 is a compilation of discographies; part 4 is a list of suggested LP recordings. This work can be used to supplement entries in Hoffmann's *Literature of Rock* (see entries 340-41).

334. De Lerma, Dominique-René. **Bibliography of Black Music**. Westport, Conn.: Greenwood Press, 1981- . (Greenwood Encyclopedia of Black Music). LC 80-24681. ISSN 0272-0264.

Volume 1: Reference Materials. Foreword by Jessie Carney Smith. 1981. ISBN 0-313-21340-2.

Volume 2: Afro-American Idioms. Foreword by Georgia Ryder. 1981. ISBN 0-313-23144-3.

Volume 3: Geographical Studies. Foreword by Samuel A. Floyd, Jr. 1982. index. ISBN 0-313-23510-4.

Volume 4: Theory, Education, and Related Studies. Foreword by Geneva H. Southall. 1984. index. ISBN 0-313-24229-1.

In terms of coverage of the subject and coverage of the literature, de Lerma's scope is the world; but, as one would expect, the emphasis is on the United States. As of volume 4, the bibliography includes a total of 19,397 entries. Further volumes will cover individuals and black music itself and will undoubtedly add additional thousands of entries. Works included date from the early eighteenth century to the 1970s; among these are books, articles, periodicals, theses, dissertations, and entries in reference works.

Individual volumes organize entries in a scheme inspired by *RILM Abstracts* (see entry 327). Volume 1 organizes reference works by form. Of note are discographies of individual musicians, and lists, with their own indexes, of theses and dissertations and of periodical titles. Volume 2 categorizes entries by American musical forms such as "Spirituals," "Ragtime," "Concert music," and "Jazz." Volume 3 organizes works topically by country within Africa, the Caribbean, and South America, and by state within the United States. This volume includes an author index. Volume 4 collects a variety of topical loose ends such as instruments, performance practice, colleges and universities, dance, liturgy, and women's studies, and also includes an author index.

There are some relatively slight impediments for the user. The practice of repeating between and within volumes entries which could fit into more than one category minimizes the need to search for a desired topic in multiple sections. Yet, this is no substitute for a comprehensive subject index. One cannot be sure, for instance, whether to look for William Russo's *Composing for the Jazz Orchestra* in volume 2 under "Jazz," or in volume 4 under "Compositional techniques" (it appears in the latter). The lack of annotations is understandable in a work of this size, but without them, items with vague titles (such as an article entitled simply "A Noble Concert") offer no clue as to their contents.

When it is finally completed in at least six volumes, *Bibliography of Black Music* will undoubtedly be one of the most far-reaching bibliographies of music literature. In the best bibliographical tradition, de Lerma has surrounded and permeated the literature of black music.

335. Diamond, Harold J. **Music Criticism: An Annotated Guide to the Literature**. Metuchen, N.J.: Scarecrow, 1979. x, 316p. index. LC 79-22279. ISBN 0-8108-1268-1.

This is exactly what a student wishing to find criticism of a specific composition needs. Diamond has selected articles and parts of books which discuss either individual works or a composer's oeuvre within a particular musical form. His criteria are plain: "articles that deal with editorial problems, or contain a high proportion of subjective, descriptive commentary are avoided unless they have some redeeming virtue." All citations are in English and were published within the last thirty years or so. The author gives a cogent, descriptive, and evaluative annotation for each source. Each chapter covers a particular form—solo works, operas, vocal music, orchestral music, concertos, chamber music, and symphonies. Users can locate citations under a composer's name within a chapter, use the composer index to locate all citations on a particular composer, or use the composition title index for citations specific to that title.

336. Feintuch, Burt. **Kentucky Folkmusic: An Annotated Bibliography**. Lexington, Ky.: University Press of Kentucky, 1985. xvii, 105p. index. LC 85-6225. ISBN 0-8131-1556-6.

Feintuch sees Kentucky folk music as exemplary of a larger cultural entity – "whenever Americans consider folkmusic, for better or for worse, Kentucky figures in their thoughts," the introduction states. This is a list, with brief annotations, of 709 books and articles dating from the early nineteenth century to the 1980s. Feintuch maintains a sharp focus on music based on a community tradition, and leaves out the mass of material relating to country music and other commercial forms. Citations are grouped into eight subject categories; indexes to authors, subjects, and periodical titles provide more specific access.

337. Haywood, Charles. **A Bibliography of North American Folklore and Folksong**. 2d rev. ed. New York: Dover, 1961. 2v. index. LC 62-3483.

First published in 1951, Haywood's bibliography continues to be the richest overall resource for the study of North American folk music. The introduction mentions coverage of some forty thousand items, including books, articles in both popular and scholarly periodicals, pamphlets, collections of music, and recordings. Volume 1 is devoted to the people of European and African descent. Its five parts cover general sources, those pertaining to geographical regions, ethnic groups, and occupations, and miscellaneous topics (including the Shakers and white spirituals). Volume 2, devoted to native Americans and Eskimos, is arranged by geographical culture area, then by tribe. All parts are further subdivided by specific topics which separate the folklore and folk song entries. Some entries are annotated. A 130-page index lists authors, song titles, and specific subjects; a second index lists composers, arrangers, and performers.

338. Hefele, Bernhard. **Jazz-Bibliographie/Jazz-Bibliography: International Literature on Jazz, Blues, Spirituals, Gospel and Ragtime Music with a Selected List of Works on the Social and Cultural Background from the Beginning to the Present**. Munich: K. G. Saur, 1981. viii, 368p. index. LC 81-102540. ISBN 3-598-10205-4.

With publication dates on some items dating back to 1836, this bibliography attempts to provide exhaustive coverage of the literature of jazz and its predecessor forms. Some sixty-six hundred unannotated entries list books, periodicals, and many specific articles from periodicals and collected works. Entries are classified into twenty-eight subject categories. There is no subject index, but an "Index of Persons" provides access to authors and personal subjects of entries. While the introductory material is given in both English and German, roughly half the entries are from German sources – surely an unbalanced representation of the literature. The *International Bibliography of Jazz Books* (see entry 331), although more limited in its scope, offers a more balanced representation of the literature. Yet the sheer quantity of material in Hefele's bibliography (especially as listed under the names of individual musicians in the chapter entitled "Die Personen des Jazz") makes it a valuable resource.

339. Heskes, Irene. **The Resource Book of Jewish Music: A Bibliographical and Topical Guide to the Book and Journal Literature and Program Materials**. Westport, Conn.: Greenwood Press, 1985. xiv, 302p. index. (Music Reference Collection, No. 3). LC 84-22435. ISBN 0-313-23251-2; ISSN 0736-7740.

This work explores the many strains of Jewish music from ancient times to modern folk, synagogue, and concert music. It maintains a fine distinction between this topic and the extraneous topic of Jewish composers and performers. All 1,220 items cited are in

English. Considering this limitation, the breadth of sources is surprising, including reference works, books, articles, periodicals, instruction and performance materials, anthologies, and hymnals. Lengthy annotations describe works in detail to the extent of mentioning specific articles in encyclopedias and chapters in books, and listing complete contents of collected works and a number of runs of Jewish music periodicals. The author and topical indexes cover both entries and annotations. A glossary of Judaica helps those not familiar with terms such as "hora" or "niggun."

340. Hoffmann, Frank. **The Literature of Rock, 1954-1978**. Metuchen, N.J.: Scarecrow, 1981. xi, 337p. discog. index. LC 80-23459. ISBN 0-8108-1371-8.

341. Hoffmann, Frank, and B. Lee Cooper, with the assistance of Lee Ann Hoffmann. **The Literature of Rock II: 1979-1983, with Additional Material for the Period 1954-1978**. Metuchen, N.J.: Scarecrow, 1986. 2v. discog. index. LC 85-8384. ISBN 0-8108-1821-3.

The initial volume covering the period 1954-78 lists and annotates the literature of rock in seventy-two music and news magazines and sixty books. The volume covering 1979-83 actually surveys the entire period from 1954 to 1983. Over three times the length of the first volume, it cites references to 260 journals of all kinds and 558 books not included in the earlier work, but it drops the annotations. Both works employ a subject classification scheme which parallels the chronological development of rock. Its categories attend to fine distinctions (they differentiate, for example, between "Doo-wop [1954-57]" and "Neo-doo-wop [1958-]"), but in the 1979-83 volume, resort to an arcane vocabulary (see, for instance, "Oi," and "Ska/Bluebeat revival"). Within these categories, citations are arranged by subcategories or by the names of individual or group performers. Those who have spanned several genres, such as Bob Dylan, are treated in one. Both works include a list of suggested "basic" LP recordings, and an index to names and, to a very limited degree, subjects. Together, they provide easy access to references in a variety of sources to specific topics. The thorough researcher will still want to consult Paul Taylor's *Popular Music since 1955* (see entry 13) for its sophisticated and literate evaluations of the literature.

342. Horn, David. **The Literature of American Music in Books and Folk Music Collections: A Fully Annotated Bibliography**. Metuchen, N.J.: Scarecrow, 1977. xiv, 556p. index. LC 76-13160. ISBN 0-8108-0996-6.

Horn, an English librarian, preceded the relatively new journal *American Music* (see entry 562) and *The New Grove Dictionary of American Music* (see entry 65) in identifying American music as a complex collection of genres appropriate for scholarly study. While he amply scans the "cultivated tradition," his forte is coverage of indigenous American musical life and forms: blues, jazz, folk musics of ethnic and religious groups, and popular music from the Pilgrims to the twentieth century. Citations to 1,388 items, mostly in English, concentrate on recent works and exclude periodicals, yearbooks, and most scores. A thorough author and subject index complements an effective and detailed subject arrangement of entries. The careful selection of the citations and the extended and entertaining annotations make this an outstanding resource.

343. Hughes, Andrew. **Medieval Music: The Sixth Liberal Art**. rev. ed. Toronto: University of Toronto Press in association with the Centre for Medieval Studies, University of Toronto, 1980. xiii, 360p. index. (Toronto Medieval Bibliographies, No. 4). LC 79-18770. ISBN 0-8020-2358-4.

Hughes introduces music as one of the seven medieval liberal arts, having a broad intellectual significance. His excellent bibliography reflects this breadth in its interdisciplinary selection of over two thousand references to books, articles, editions of early music and musical writings, festschriften, and congress reports. Hughes's annotations are descriptive, evaluative, and comparative, yet masterfully concise. A well-organized and detailed subject classification system organizes the citations. One index covers authors, another covers names and topics from the citations and annotations. The revised edition adds to the text of the first edition (1974) a separate section containing some two hundred citations with its own indexes.

344. Iwaschkin, Roman. **Popular Music: A Reference Guide**. New York: Garland, 1986. xiii, 658p. index. LC 85-45140. ISBN 0-8240-8680-5.

This bibliography of 5,276 books, periodicals, and yearbooks (primarily in English) covers the range of American folk music, country music, rock, jazz, show tunes, and other forms. Citations give descriptive notes; about half include annotations. A complicated scheme organizes the entries into a similar format under each subject heading. Thus, although there is no subject index, a diligent researcher could eventually find *Gwreiddiau Canu Roc Cymraeg* (a history of Welsh rock) in the "Regional Histories" section of part 1, "Popular Music Generally." The index lists authors and some titles. The work's sweeping reach could prove useful in identifying obscure material, but a researcher would benefit by first consulting a more selective and evaluative work such as *Popular Music since 1955* (see entry 13) or *The Literature of Jazz* (see entry 7).

345. Jackson, Irene V., comp. **Afro-American Religious Music: A Bibliography and a Catalogue of Gospel Music**. Westport, Conn.: Greenwood Press, 1979. xiv, 210p. illus. index. LC 78-60527. ISBN 0-313-20560-4.

This work is divided into a bibliography of books, articles, theses, and dissertations, and a catalog of gospel songs which were copyrighted during the peak of gospel music's popularity between 1938 and 1965. Organized by six topical areas, the bibliography includes writings on not only music but also the black church, dance, black history, folk music, and geographical regions beyond the United States – the Caribbean, South America, and West Africa. The catalog, an attempt by the compiler to establish the sources of black gospel music, lists by composer hundreds of pieces of sheet music.

346. Krohn, Ernst C. **The History of Music: An Index to the Literature Available in a Selected Group of Musicological Publications**. St. Louis, Mo.: Baton Music, 1958. xxi, 463p. LC 59-531.

Krohn's selection of titles and of inclusive dates is idiosyncratic, as it developed out of his own card file and hence interests. He indexes articles in thirty-nine periodicals and yearbooks from Europe and the United States, beginning with some issues published in the late nineteenth century and ending in January 1952. A detailed classification scheme, which begins with ancient and non-Western music followed by a chronological listing from medieval to contemporary music, organizes the citations. The index gives names of authors and composers. Though by now most of the articles included have either been cited elsewhere or justifiably forgotten, Krohn's index is useful for verifying uncertain citations or for thorough research.

347. Kunst, Jaap. **Ethnomusicology: A Study of Its Nature, Its Problems, Methods, and Representative Personalities, to Which Is Added a Bibliography**. 3d ed., enl. The Hague: M. Nijhoff, 1959. 303p. illus. music. index. LC 59-16807. **Supplement**. 1960. 45p.

First published in 1950, this was the first, and is still the only, comprehensive bibliography in the field. The first volume lists 4,552 books and articles in most European languages, and the supplement adds some five hundred entries. Subjects include non-Western music and European folk music. Since the list is alphabetically arranged by author, users must consult the detailed indexes.

348. Lieberman, Frederic. **Chinese Music: An Annotated Bibliography**. 2d ed., rev. and enl. New York: Garland, 1979. xi, 257p. index. (Garland Reference Library of the Humanities, Vol. 75). LC 76-24755. ISBN 0-8240-9922-2.

"This bibliography attempts exhaustive coverage of publications in Western languages" (preface). Its 2,441 books, articles, theses, and reference works on not only music, but also Chinese dance and drama, show it to be indeed thorough. Annotations are given for about half the entries. In place of a subject index is the "Topic Outline and Selected Readings" which is inadequate for locating specific subjects but is probably helpful to Westerners who are unfamiliar with the terminology.

349. McCutcheon, Meredith Alice. **Guitar and Vihuela: An Annotated Bibliography**. New York: Pendragon Press, 1985. 353p. illus. index. (RILM Retrospectives, No. 3). LC 85-17437. ISBN 0-918728-28-2.

The appropriately classified arrangement, careful selection of 1,039 entries including books and periodical articles in thirteen languages dating from the sixteenth century to 1981, and the clear and descriptive annotations make this an important resource. Entries cover works on "composers, performers, theorists, music and analysis, iconography, and design and construction," but omit references to folk, jazz, and flamenco styles, and to modern instruction manuals. An appendix lists some six hundred collections of music and method books printed before 1800. Entries for modern books include citations to reviews; those for pre-nineteenth-century books give selected library locations. Chapter introductions compare and evaluate titles and suggest other reference materials beyond the scope of this work. The list of periodicals devoted to the guitar is the only flaw: it omits many longstanding and important titles found in the more comprehensive *Guitar Bibliography* (see entry 359).

350. Meadows, Eddie S. **Jazz Reference and Research Materials: A Bibliography**. New York: Garland, 1981. xii, 300p. discog. index. (Critical Studies on Black Life and Culture, Vol. 22; Garland Reference Library of the Humanities, Vol. 251). LC 80-8521. ISBN 0-8240-9463-8.

With roughly twenty-five hundred entries, the bibliography "is intended to provide a thorough survey of books, articles, and theses and dissertations written on or about specific jazz styles and jazz musicians from the turn of the century through 1978" (introduction). It emphasizes works published in the United States. The first section cites works by form within several chronological categories: "General," "Pre-Swing," "Swing," "Bop," and "Modern." The second section cites and provides knowledgeable descriptive and evaluative annotations to reference materials in parts entitled "Bibliographies-Dictionaries-Encyclopedias," "Biographies-Autobiographies," "Discographies," "Histories-Surveys," "Technical Materials," "Anthologies-Collections (Recordings)," and "Jazz Research Libraries." Both sections have indexes to authors and subjects. The distinction between the two sections is not always clear – for example, one must consult both sections to find works dealing with an individual musician. But this is a good alternative to *The Literature of Jazz: A Critical Guidė* (see entry 7).

351. Miller, Terry E. **Folk Music in America: A Reference Guide**. New York: Garland, 1986. xx, 424p. index. (Garland Reference Library of the Humanities, Vol. 496). LC 84-48014. ISBN 0-8240-8935-9.

Miller's well-considered introduction reflects on the definition of folk music (and on the book's scope), and concludes that "this collection is about the forgotten musics of America," those which are not produced with a commercial end. The guide arranges within a sensible classification scheme citations to books, scholarly articles, dissertations, and reference works. Articles in folk magazines were, for the most part, omitted. Annotations cogently describe and evaluate works. Topics covered include the music of native Americans, the Anglo-American tradition, psalmody and hymnody, shape-note singing,

Afro-American music, and music of other ethnic traditions. A good index, efficient organization, and carefully selected entries make this the finest work in this area.

352. Myers, Kurtz, comp. and ed. **Index to Record Reviews**. Based on material originally published in *Notes: The Quarterly Journal of the Music Library Association* between 1949 and 1977. Boston: G. K. Hall, 1978. 5v. index. LC 79-101459. ISBN 0-8161-0087-X.

353. Myers, Kurtz, comp. and ed. **Index to Record Reviews 1978-1983**. Based on material originally published in *Notes: The Quarterly Journal of the Music Library Association* between 1978 and 1983. Boston: G. K. Hall, 1985. xxv, 873p. LC 86-135431. ISBN 0-8161-0435-2.

Myers has been indexing reviews of LP recordings for *Notes* (see entry 639) since 1947. These volumes gather the citations to reviews into a similar format. Though admittedly selective, the index covers a major portion of the recordings of "serious" music available in the United States for the years it encompasses. Citations are organized into two sections: the first is a composer list; the second (composite recordings of works by multiple composers) is a list by manufacturer and record number. Entries give the complete contents of recordings and cite reviews. A symbol preceding the citation to each review indicates the reviewer's opinion of the quality of the performance (+, excellent; •, adequate; –, inadequate). Indexes list recordings in the composite section by composer and title of work, and in both sections by performer and by manufacturer and number.

354. Paine, Gordon. **The Choral Journal: An Index to Volumes 1-18**. Lawton, Okla.: American Choral Directors Association, 1978. xv, 170p. (Monograph No. 3). LC 79-109624.

The index lists most articles, regular columns, record reviews after 1973, and book reviews from *The Choral Journal* (see entry 582), and omits news of the association and minor features. Citations to articles and short annotations appear in chronological order within a classification scheme which includes subjects, personal names, titles of books, and composers. A general index covers authors and secondary topics.

355. Répertoire international des sources musicales/Internationales Quellenlexikon der Musik/International Inventory of Musical Sources. **Écrits imprimés concernant la musique**. Ouvrage publié sous la direction de François Lesure. Munich: G. Henle Verlag, 1971. 2v. index. (RISM Series B VI). LC 72-216060. ISBN 3-87328-010-8(vol. 1); 3-87328-011-6(vol. 2).

This is a comprehensive bibliography of works printed from 1474 to 1800 dealing with music. National groups associated with RISM contributed citations. It offers a broad selection of theoretical, historical, aesthetic, and technical writings extending to encyclopedias, periodicals, and works on theater, liturgy, and acoustics. The arrangement is by author, with anonymous works listed separately by title. Entries give author, title, place of publication, imprint, date, pagination, and locations of copies in Europe and North America. There is a chronological index and an index to printers and publishers. The introductory material appears in English, French, and German.

356. Répertoire international des sources musicales/Internationales Quellenlexikon der Musik/International Inventory of Musical Sources. **Hebrew Writings Concerning Music in Manuscripts and Printed Books from Geonic Times up to 1800**. By Israel Adler. Munich: G. Henle Verlag, 1975. lviii, 389p. bibliog. index. (RISM Series B IX 2). LC 75-330804. ISBN 3-87328-023-X.

The author emphasizes that this volume offers "a *corpus* of Hebrew writings concerning music, and not only a *catalogue* of these sources." It includes sixty-six writings in Hebrew script which date from 933 to 1800. The introduction classifies the texts by subject, literary genre, chronological period, and provenance. Entries, arranged by author, give the author's name and the title of the work in Hebrew script and transliterated into Roman letters; identify the author by dates and activities; preface the text in English with a summary and list of references to modern writings; list the locations of manuscripts and published editions; and give the text in Hebrew. Indexes cover quotations and references to other texts, and to names, subjects, and terms.

357. Répertoire international des sources musicales/Internationales Quellenlexikon der Musik/International Inventory of Musical Sources. **The Theory of Music: Descriptive Catalogue of Manuscripts**. Munich: G. Henle Verlag, 1961- . (RISM Series B III).

Volume 1: From the Carolingian Era up to 1400. Joseph Smits van Waesberghe, ed., with the collaboration of Pieter Fischer and Christian Maas. 1961. 155p. index. LC 62-5034. ISBN 3-87328-003-5.

Volume 2: From the Carolingian Era up to 1400, Italy. Pieter Fischer, ed. 1968. 148p. index. ISBN 3-87328-004-3.

Volume 3: Manuscripts from the Carolingian Era up to c.1500 in the Federal Republic of Germany (D-brd). By Michel Huglo and Christian Meyer. 1986. xxx, 232p. index. ISBN 3-87328-040-X.

This ongoing series offers an inventory and description of manuscripts containing early treatises, generally in Latin, on the theory of music. The arrangement is by library within country. Volume 1 includes Austria, Belgium, Switzerland, Denmark, France, Luxembourg, and the Netherlands. Volumes 2 and 3 are devoted to one country each. Introductory material is given in French, English, and German; the physical description of the manuscripts in English in volumes 1 and 2, and in French in volume 3; and the title and contents in the original Latin. Each volume includes an index to authors and to incipits of anonymous treatises.

358. Répertoire international des sources musicales/Internationales Quellenlexikon der Musik/International Inventory of Musical Sources. **The Theory of Music in Arabic Writings (c.900-1900): Descriptive Catalogue of Manuscripts in Libraries of Europe and the U.S.A.** By Amnon Shiloah. Munich: G. Henle Verlag, 1979. xxviii, 512p. bibliog. index. (RISM Series B X). LC 80-498379. ISBN 3-87328-031-0.

A companion to the RISM volume *Hebrew Writings Concerning Music* (see entry 356), this work describes 341 writings in Arabic, but does not give the texts, as does the previous volume. The introduction classifies these works by subject, chronological period, and provenance. The arrangement is by author, followed by anonymous writings. Entries note the dates and activities of the author; give the title in Arabic script, as transliterated into Roman letters, and as translated into English; summarize the work; give, in Arabic, the incipit (beginning) and explicit (ending) of the text; note locations of manuscripts; and list modern editions and bibliographic references. The bibliography lists library catalogs of manuscripts, works in European languages, and works in Arabic. The index covers names, subjects, and terms.

359. Schwarz, Werner, with the assistance of Monika Haringer. **Guitar Bibliography: An International Listing of Theoretical Literature on Classical Guitar from the Beginning to the Present/Gitarre-Bibliographie: Internationales Verzeichnis der theoretischen Literatur zur klassischen Guitarre von den Anfängen bis zur Gegenwart**. Munich: K. G. Saur, 1984. 257p. index. LC 84-197993. ISBN 3-598-10518-5.

This unannotated list of over forty-seven hundred items in a number of European languages intends to "give the best possible comprehensive survey on the existing theoretical literature on classical guitar and vihuela." Its wide range includes books (sometimes citing reviews), essays in collective works, journals, articles, and films, and omits only scores and instruction manuals. Publication dates range from the sixteenth century to 1983. Casting such a wide net gathers works such as Diderot's *Encyclopédie* and a filmstrip entitled *Gus Guitar and His Friends* among many more useful entries. Chapters and section headings efficiently organize entries by form and topic; biographical material on individual performers can be found in chapter 5. Textual material and section headings appear in English and German. Indexes cover authors and named persons, but not specific subjects. A more careful selection, with annotations, is *Guitar and Vihuela: An Annotated Bibliography* (see entry 349).

360. Seaton, Douglass. **The Art Song: A Research and Information Guide**. New York: Garland, 1987. xxvii, 273p. discog. index. (Music Research and Information Guides, No. 6; Garland Reference Library of the Humanities, Vol. 673). LC 86-33553. ISBN 0-8240-8554-X.

Seaton's introduction to this bibliography shows an awareness of the problems of defining art song beyond identifying it as "a solo song with keyboard accompaniment." One must consider its relation to folk song, operatic aria, and religious song, and its place in national cultures. Works listed consider forms of the art song from 1600 to the twentieth century. Included are books, articles, and dissertations in English, German, and the Romance languages. Articles directed towards a pedagogical audience have been omitted. The 970 entries are arranged alphabetically within chapters that group them by form. The chapter devoted to studies of individual composers (easily the largest) organizes entries by composer. Indexes list authors and subjects. The author's descriptive and evaluative annotations concisely indicate each work's value to a researcher.

361. Sendrey, Alfred. **Bibliography of Jewish Music**. New York: Columbia University Press, 1951; repr., New York: Kraus Reprint Company, 1969. xli, 404p. index. LC 78-316097.

Though dated, Sendrey's bibliography of over ten thousand items is still the standard resource for the subject area. It is partially updated by Irene Heskes's *Resource Book of Jewish Music* (see entry 339). Sendrey's introduction makes a sharp distinction between Jewish music and music written by Jews, and makes clear that this is a bibliography of the former. The work is divided into two parts: music literature and music. The index to names is similarly divided. Both parts are further subdivided into classified sections. Articles and books cited encompass both European and American sources. An appendix cites musical references in the Bible and in early rabbinical works.

362. Sharp, Avery T. **Choral Music Reviews Index, 1983-1985**. New York: Garland, 1986. x, 260p. index. (Garland Reference Library of the Humanities, Vol. 674). LC 86-14314. ISBN 0-8240-8553-1.

"Designed to be a useful repertoire-location tool" (introduction), the index gathers citations from sixteen English-language journals to reviews of over two thousand recently published choral pieces. Works are arranged by title within three categories – octavos, choral collections, and extended choral works. Cross-references are used from variant titles. Each review is given a separate entry. In abbreviated form, entries describe the characteristics of the work or collection, and summarize the review. Bibliographic citations to the music were taken directly from the reviews, and no attempt has been made to reconcile differing citations to the same piece. Indexes identify composers, arrangers, editors, uses or special purposes, levels of performing groups, choral and solo voicings, and accompanying instruments. The author offers no hint of whether the index will be updated, so despite the large number of reviews included, carefully detailed citations, and thorough indexing, the narrow chronological scope will soon limit the index's usefulness.

363. Skei, Allen B. **Woodwind, Brass and Percussion Instruments of the Orchestra: A Bibliographic Guide**. New York: Garland, 1985. xiii, 271p. index. (Garland Reference Library of the Humanities, Vol. 458). LC 83-49079. ISBN 0-8240-9021-7.

This gathering of citations to 1,161 books, articles, dissertations, catalogs, and historical tutors includes works not only on modern instruments but also some earlier forms, such as the cornetto and serpent. It arbitrarily excludes works on the recorder. The author states that the guide "focuses mostly on the nature and historical development of instruments." In addition, it includes bibliographies of music and discussions of performance practice. Works cited are in English, German, and French, and include quite brief annotations. Researchers will find the detailed table of contents more useful than the subject index, which suffers from the common malady of including far too many references under individual headings.

364. Skowronski, JoAnn. **Black Music in America: A Bibliography**. Metuchen, N.J.: Scarecrow, 1981. ix, 723p. index. LC 81-5609. ISBN 0-8108-1443-9.

This massive list of 14,319 books and articles from American and European sources can be recommended only for its volume, as its arrangement and omissions (despite its bulk) make it unreliable. The first section, which occupies most of the volume, is a guide, organized by name, to works about individual musicians. The selection of subjects is capricious – there are no entries for Ulysses Kay, Victoria Spivey, and Paul Robeson, for instance. References to musicians who share the same name, such as the two Billy Taylors and the two Joe Turners, "were eliminated to prevent confusion" rather than thoughtfully examined and separated. A section of "General References" includes some two thousand citations to works from 1840 to 1979. These are arranged not by author or subject, but by date of publication. With no subject indexing, this section is virtually useless. The third part of the work is a list of reference books. An author index ends the volume. *Black Music in America* could prove useful to those seeking a multitude of articles on Duke Ellington or the Jackson Five, but those involved in more sophisticated research will need to consult the *Bibliography of Black Music* (see entry 334).

365. Swanekamp, Joan, comp. **English Ayres: A Selectively Annotated Bibliography and Discography**. Westport, Conn.: Greenwood Press, 1984. viii, 141p. index. LC 83-18345. ISBN 0-313-23467-1.

The introduction identifies this work as a companion to Peter Warlock's *The English Ayre* (1926; repr., Greenwood, 1970). General materials are listed in the first chapter; each of the other twenty-seven chapters focuses on an individual composer. Chapters list literature, music, and, to a lesser extent, recordings. Entries include articles, books, and entries in standard reference works. Sections on music include both early and recent collections. Indexes list authors and titles of musical works.

366. Tjepkema, Sandra L. **A Bibliography of Computer Music: A Reference for Composers**. Iowa City, Iowa: University of Iowa Press, 1981. xvii, 276p. index. LC 81-2967. ISBN 0-87745-110-9.

The author's well-stated preface justifies the computer as a tool by comparing it to the camera: both may be used mindlessly, adeptly, or creatively. It is composers who use digital equipment rather than performers on keyboard synthesizers who will find this bibliography most useful. The 1,017 briefly annotated entries date from the years 1956 to 1979, and include books, articles, dissertations, conference reports, and user manuals. Subjects range from technical descriptions of specific procedures to philosophical discussions of aesthetic questions. A list of computer manufacturers and their models is now, not even ten years later, too dated to offer more than a historical record. The index provides the only subject and name access to the alphabetically arranged entries; unfortunately, it uses a number of vague subject headings, some of which cite up to one hundred entries.

367. Tsuge, Gen'ichi. **Japanese Music: An Annotated Bibliography**. New York: Garland, 1986. x, 161p. discog. index. (Garland Bibliographies in Ethnomusicology, No. 2; Garland Reference Library of the Humanities, Vol. 472). LC 83-49316. ISBN 0-8240-8995-2.

This is an annotated list of 881 items in Western languages (primarily English) which deal with traditional Japanese music. It is divided into three sections: "Bibliography and Discography," "Directories and Periodicals," and "Books and Articles." The latter section cites entries in reference works, a particularly useful feature for libraries that have not collected much material in this area. In addition to secondary sources, translations of lyrics and collections of music in staff notation are also mentioned. The index is categorized into several sections listing broad terms which themselves often cite one hundred or more undifferentiated items; finding specific topics is not easy.

368. Vinquist, Mary, and Neal Zaslaw. **Performance Practice: A Bibliography**. New York: W. W. Norton, 1971. 114p. index. LC 75-128038. ISBN 0-393-02148-3; 0-393-00550-Xpa.

This survey of the literature of performance practice throughout Western history cumulates two earlier bibliographies in *Current Musicology* (8 [1969] and 10 [1970]: 144-72) and adds new material; it is updated by two further bibliographies in the same journal (12 [1971]: 129-49 and 15 [1973]: 126-36). Choosing from works written in English, German, French, Italian, Spanish, and Dutch, it cites books, chapters, articles, congress reports, dissertations, and contributions to festschriften dealing with Western art music from 1100 to 1900. The alphabetical arrangement by author allows one to locate, for instance, a citation to the original printing of Tinctoris's fifteenth-century work, *De inventione et usu musicae*, a 1961 reprint, and a 1950 translation. With ample cross-references and subheadings for specific topics, the indispensible subject index serves well this list of over one thousand works.

369. Whitten, Lynn, ed. **A Classified, Annotated Bibliography of Articles Related to Choral Music in Five Major Periodicals through 1980**. Lawton, Okla.: American Choral Directors Association, 1982. xviii, 233p. index. (Monograph No. 4).

The bibliography expands upon the coverage of *The Choral Journal: An Index to Volumes 1-18* (see entry 354). It lists and annotates articles from *American Choral Review* (see entry 561) from 1958 to 1980; *Church Music* from 1966 to 1980; *Journal of the American Musicological Society* (see entry 617) from 1948 to 1980; *Music & Letters* (see entry 622) from 1920 to 1980; and *The Musical Quarterly* (see entry 631) from 1915 to 1980. The entries appear in five sections, according to their source journal; since each section has its own system of organization, users must read the prefatory material to use the listings. Trade and organizational news, continuing columns, and reviews are omitted. Indexes to authors, translators, and subjects provide a unified means of approaching the five lists.

13

Indexes and Bibliographies of Works about Individual Musicians

These works offer a means of locating biographical or critical information about composers and their compositions, performers, and, in one case, makers of wind instruments. In general, bibliographies dealing with only one musician are beyond the scope of this guide and have not been included. However, volumes within two series—*Garland Composer Resource Manuals* (see entry 381) and Greenwood's *Bio-Bibliographies in Music* (see entry 370)—are listed, since these series represent composite and outstanding current resources.

370. **Bio-Bibliographies in Music**. Donald L. Hixon and Adrienne Fried Block, series advisors. Westport, Conn.: Greenwood Press, 1984- . ISSN 0742-6968.

Each volume in the series focuses on an individual American composer of the twentieth century. Each features a short biography, a list of works, a discography, and a bibliography of reviews and critical works.

371. No. 1: Hixon, Donald L. **Thea Musgrave: A Bio-Bibliography**. 1984. x, 187p. discog. index. LC 83-22705. ISBN 0-313-23708-5.

A short biography (on which the author and subject collaborated) summarizes Musgrave's career. A list of her works is organized by genre, and gives for each piece the title, date, publisher, duration, instrumentation, premieres and other selected performances, and cites reviews listed in the bibliography section. A discography, organized by composition, also cites reviews. The annotated bibliography of works by and about Musgrave offers, in addition to articles in journals, particularly good coverage of reviews in newspapers in the United States, Scotland, and England. Appendixes give alphabetical and chronological listings of works. This volume was a winner of the Music Library Association's annual prize for the best book-length bibliography.

372. No. 2: Skowronski, JoAnn. **Aaron Copland: A Bio-Bibliography**. 1985. x, 273p. discog. index. LC 84-22417. ISBN 0-313-24091-4.

A short biography introduces Copland. A chronological list of over one hundred of his works gives the title, circumstances of the first performance, background information, and publisher. Two appendixes listing compositions by title and genre serve as indexes to this section. A discography arranges 376 entries by title of composition, and cites references to reviews. The bibliography section itself includes 1,192 references to works by and about Copland, arranged by author, with Copland's own writings preceding the others. The quantity of popular writing Copland has inspired makes the bibliography unusually unwieldy – it indiscriminately mingles newspaper articles, program notes, articles in standard reference works, books, scholarly articles, and dissertations. The index covers names, concert sites, and titles of albums, books, and compositions in the list of works, discography, and bibliography.

373. No. 3: Hennessee, Don A. **Samuel Barber: A Bio-Bibliography**. 1985. xii, 404p. discog. index. LC 84-29017. ISBN 0-313-24026-4.

"A composer with integrity," and "a neo-Romantic" are the words with which the author introduces Barber in a short opening biography. A list of works follows, which notes premieres and other selected performances, and cites reviews listed in the bibliography section. A discography organizes recorded works by the same genres, and also cites reviews. The sizable annotated bibliography of writings by and about Barber begins with general references, then gives references relating to individual works. Appendixes list compositions alphabetically and by opus number (from the list of works), and an index lists names and titles from all sections.

374. No. 4: Meckna, Michael. **Virgil Thomson: A Bio-Bibliography**. 1986. xiv, 203p. discog. index. LC 86-14229. ISBN 0-313-25010-3.

This especially well-organized work does justice to Thomson's prolific activities as a composer and writer. A short biographical sketch opens the volume. A list of works and performances is arranged by genre. Details given include date of composition, instrumentation, duration, commissions, librettist, premieres, publisher, brief reviews in the press, and references to items in the bibliographical section. A discography listing both 78rpm and LP issues is arranged by title of work. The Bibliography is divided into works by and about Thomson. This section is extremely thorough in its enumeration of reviews, articles, and books by Thomson, and citations to articles, references in books, and sections in reference books. Most entries are annotated. Appendixes provide lists of locations of manuscripts, correspondence, and other archival material, and chronological and alphabetical lists of compositions.

* * *

375. Block, Adrienne Fried, and Carol Neuls-Bates, comps. and eds. **Women in American Music: A Bibliography of Music and Literature**. Westport, Conn.: Greenwood Press, 1979. xxvii, 302p. illus. index. LC 79-7722. ISBN 0-313-21410-7.

With 5,024 entries whose publication dates range from the late eighteenth century to 1978, this is a valuable and versatile resource for the study of American music from colonial times to the present. It includes works about composers, performers, patrons, educators, and other women who were born in the United States or were immigrants active in music for ten or more years, but omits those involved in "vernacular music" since 1920. Criteria for including musical compositions are the same. Entries follow a format adopted from *RILM Abstracts* (see entry 327) – alphabetical organization by author or composer within chronological sections which are subdivided into broad subjects. Entries for music literature give publication data and pagination, note book reviews, and include thorough descriptive annotations. Entries for music give publication information, pagination, and instrumentation, and note adaptations, first performances, and recordings. Through a system of alphabetic abbreviations, entry numbers identify by form the entry within one of five categories: article, book, dissertation, musical composition, or review. Indexes cover authors and subjects of literature; composers and authors of texts and librettos of music;

and composers whose works were recorded. Index entries refer to entry numbers which include superscripts indicating the chronological and subject category, thus allowing users to differentiate between items under one index term.

376. Bull, Storm. **Index to Biographies of Contemporary Composers**. New York: Scarecrow, 1964-74. 2v. LC 64-11781. ISBN 0-8108-0065-9(vol. 1); 0-8108-0734-3(vol. 2).

In two volumes, Bull indexes over eight thousand names from roughly 177 biographical dictionaries, histories, and special issues of periodicals. Entries are short and to the point, listing the composer's name, the country with which he or she is associated (Stravinsky is listed in the United States), birth and death dates, and references to the sources. To be included, composers must either be alive, have been born in 1900 or later, or have died in 1950 or later. Corrigenda to the first volume appear at the end of volume 2. Since over half the cited sources are in languages other than English, these two volumes can locate both hard-to-find material on obscure composers and a selection of biographical perspectives on the famous.

377. Cowden, Robert H. **Concert and Opera Singers: A Bibliography of Biographical Materials**. Westport, Conn.: Greenwood Press, 1985. xviii, 278p. bibliog. index. (Music Reference Collection, No. 5). LC 85-12717. ISBN 0-313-24828-1; ISSN 0736-7740.

The largest part of this work is part 3, which lists 708 singers from the eighteenth century to the present who have been mentioned in at least three sources, including one reference work. For each singer, it notes places and dates of birth and death, and cites biographical references in ten standard music reference works, articles in nine music periodicals, individual biographies, autobiographies, and other works. The entry for Jenny Lind exemplifies the thoroughness of this section: it cites over sixty entries in at least six languages. Parts 1 and 2, which list a group of 120 collective biographies and 154 related works, are less successful: while they enumerate singers covered in these works, they are not indexed. Rather, the two indexes list authors of works included and singers covered by *The New Grove* (see entry 20). *Opera and Concert Singers: An Annotated International Bibliography* (see entry 379) takes a different approach in its annotations to book-length publications.

378. District of Columbia Historical Records Survey. **Bio-Bibliographical Index of Musicians in the United States of America since Colonial Times**. 2d ed. Washington, D.C.: Music Section, Pan American Union, 1956. xxiii, 439p. LC 57-4. (Repr., New York: AMS Press, 1972. LC 76-39375; repr., New York: Da Capo Press, 1971. LC 76-159677; repr., St. Clair Shores, Mich.: Scholarly Press, 1972. LC 76-166235).

Originally the fruit of a WPA project (1941), then expanded by the Pan American Union, this is an index to names of performers, composers, instrument makers, writers, teachers, publishers, and others in sixty-six histories, compilations, and special studies published between the late nineteenth and midtwentieth centuries. Entries give dates of birth and death, the subject's main activity and country of origin ("Belgian composer"), and page references to one or more works. An appendix lists studies of individuals. Though the publication date and selectivity of titles indexed now limits the usefulness of the index, references to such titles as *Annals of Music in Philadelphia* may offer sources of biographical information for obscure names.

379. Farkas, Andrew. **Opera and Concert Singers: An Annotated International Bibliography of Books and Pamphlets**. Foreword by Richard Bonynge. New York: Garland, 1985. xxiv, 363p. index. (Garland Reference Library of the Humanities, Vol. 466). LC 83-49310. ISBN 0-8240-9001-2.

This guide to nineteenth- and twentieth-century works by and about 796 vocalists from 1545 to the present day diligently enumerates editions and translations for a total of 1,850 entries in either twenty-eight or twenty-nine languages (the preface claims both). Part 1 lists books and pamphlets alphabetically by names of singers. Cross-references in this section refer to part 2, which lists works discussing more than one singer. Pointed, knowledgeable, and opinionated annotations often take issue with works discussed or fill in biographical detail. Farkas identifies this work as a companion to *Opera: A Research and Information Guide* (see entry 8). *Concert and Opera Singers* (see entry 377) can provide additional citations to periodical articles.

380. Floyd, Samuel A., Jr., and Marsha J. Reisser. **Black Music Biography: An Annotated Bibliography**. White Plains, N.Y.: Kraus International, 1987. xxvi, 302p. discog. index. LC 86-27827. ISBN 0-527-30158-2.

Covering 147 biographies and autobiographies dealing with eighty-seven black musicians, this is more of a survey of the literature than a comprehensive reference source. Arranged by the names of subjects, it gives not only citations but extended descriptive annotations (often employing excerpts) to each work. All subjects but Bob Marley are American. Chronologically, they date back to Blind Tom (born 1849) and include jazz artists, composers, opera singers, and pop singers. The volume includes book reviews and selected discographies of LP recordings.

381. **Garland Composer Resource Manuals**. Guy A. Marco, general ed. New York: Garland, 1981- .

This is a series of bibliographies dedicated to the work of individual composers. Projected to encompass more than one hundred composers, the series is to be published over a ten-year period. All volumes feature lists of works, bibliographies of writings (in English and other languages) about the featured composer, and illustrations of the composer and of related subjects.

382. Volume 1: Skei, Allen B. **Heinrich Schütz: A Guide to Research**. 1981. xxxi, 186p. illus. index. (Garland Reference Library of the Humanities, Vol. 272). LC 80-9028. ISBN 0-8240-9310-0.

The introduction gives a short biography and summary of scholarship on Schütz. Following is a list of works, and an annotated classified bibliography of 632 books and articles about Schütz.

383. Volume 2: Charles, Sydney Robinson. **Josquin des Pres: A Guide to Research**. 1983. xi, 235p. illus. bibliog. discog. index. (Garland Reference Library of the Humanities, Vol. 330). LC 81-48418. ISBN 0-8240-9387-9.

A short chronology pieces together known and hypothesized fragments of Josquin's life. The bibliographic structure, organized around a list of works, is complicated, but efficient. References to sources, discussions, and discographies of each work are given in abbreviated form. Full citations are listed in separate bibliographies and a discography.

384. Volume 3: Palmieri, Robert. **Sergei Vasil'evich Rachmaninoff: A Guide to Research**. 1984. xvii, 335p. illus. discog. index. (Garland Reference Library of the Humanities, Vol. 471). LC 83-49315. ISBN 0-8240-8996-0.

Rachmaninoff achieved fame as both composer and performer; therefore it is appropriate that this volume should list not only his compositions, but, in a following section, his repertoire as conductor and pianist. A discography lists recordings made by Rachmaninoff. A substantially annotated bibliography of works about Rachmaninoff lists 375 items, many of which are from Soviet sources.

385. Volume 4: Chase, Gilbert, and Andrew Budwig. **Manuel de Falla: A Bibliography and Research Guide**. 1986. xiii, 145p. illus. index. (Garland Reference Library of the Humanities, Vol. 561). LC 84-48406. ISBN 0-8240-8587-2.

Budwig developed the guide from his Ph.D. dissertation on Falla's unfinished work, *Atlántida*. A forty-page biography precedes a list of Falla's compositions. The bibliography of 385 works aims not to be comprehensive but "to offer a broad spectrum of reliable views." Three indexes cover proper names, authors, and compositions and arrangements by Falla.

386. Volume 5: Studwell, William E. **Adolphe Adam and Léo Delibes: A Guide to Research**. 1987. x, 248p. illus. index. (Garland Reference Library of the Humanities, Vol. 681). LC 86-9917. ISBN 0-8240-9011-X.

Adam and Delibes, influential composers of ballet and opera in nineteenth-century Paris, are commonly considered together as teacher and student. This guide has a separate section for each composer. Each section opens with a short biographical and historical overview. A list of musical works in each section is divided by form, and gives dates of first performance, but no publication information. The bibliography in each section cites writings of the composer and secondary works.

387. Volume 6: Miller, Mina F. **Carl Nielsen: A Guide to Research**. 1987. xvi, 245p. illus. index. (Garland Reference Library of the Humanities, Vol. 662). LC 87-6911. ISBN 0-8240-8569-8.

The Nielsen guide differs from other volumes in this series by foregoing a list of works. With the idea of making writings on this Danish composer more widely available, the bibliography of 401 entries devotes significant attention to works in Scandinavian languages in addition to those in English and European languages, and provides an extended annotation for each entry. Entries are arranged by general subject. A separate chapter lists the writings of Nielsen.

* * *

388. Greene, Frank. **Composers on Record: An Index to Biographical Information on 14,000 Composers Whose Music Has Been Recorded**. Metuchen, N.J.: Scarecrow, 1985. xxxi, 604p. LC 85-8238. ISBN 0-8108-1816-7.

Greene compiled names for the index from sixty-six discographies and record catalogs, and from the record collection of the Music Library of the University of Toronto. For each composer, he gives the years of birth and death, nationality, a biographical citation to one of over one hundred collective works in a list of references, and a citation to one or more of the sixty-six catalogs and discographies. The work certainly covers more composers than Storm Bull's *Index to Biographies of Contemporary Composers* (see entry 376). But whereas Bull cites as many biographical sources as possible, Greene generally gives only one—and in 5,497 cases, that is to *The New Grove* (see entry 20). *Composers on Record* is useful primarily as an index to discographies, and occasionally for biographies hidden in some of the more obscure sources it indexes.

389. Greene, Richard D. **Index to Composer Bibliographies**. Detroit: Information Coordinators, 1985. x, 76p. index. (Detroit Studies in Music Bibliography, No. 53). LC 85-18202. ISBN 0-89990-025-9.

This should be of some help in tracking down bibliographies of secondary sources—studies of composers—published as books, theses, or individual articles in yearbooks or periodicals. The index includes works in German and English published from the nineteenth century to the present. Since it does not include lists of references within books, it cannot by any means give a comprehensive picture of the bibliographies of any composer. Entries are arranged by composer, then by date of publication. Most are briefly annotated. The index lists authors, compilers, and editors. The unlikely appearance of entries for the Beatles, Woody Guthrie, and the Rolling Stones among more venerable composers makes one wonder about Greene's criteria for inclusion.

390. Jackson, Richard. **United States Music: Sources of Bibliography and Collective Biography**. Brooklyn, N.Y.: Institute for Studies in American Music, Department of Music, Brooklyn College of the City University of New York, 1973. vii, 80p. index. (I.S.A.M. Monographs, No. 1). LC 73-80637.

This "practical aid to students engaged in American-music studies" (introduction) is an annotated guide to ninety works in English that contain a bibliography or collective biography. Titles are divided by form into chapters: "Reference Works," "Historical Studies," "Regional Studies," and "Topical Studies." Jackson's evaluations and appropriate opinions describe accurately each title's worth. Annotations to many of the works of collective biography (which include general nonmusical compilations) include lists of names of musicians included. The index lists authors and names of subjects mentioned in annotations.

391. Langwill, Lyndesay G. **An Index of Musical Wind-Instrument Makers**. 6th ed., rev. and enl. Edinburgh, Scotland: Lyndesay G. Langwill, 1980. xix, 331p. illus. bibliog. index. LC 81-101213.

The forewords and prefaces to the various editions, all reprinted in the sixth, testify to Langwill's diligence in gathering data on historical and modern "makers of all mouth-blown wood-wind and brass instruments and, for the sake of completeness, all forms of bagpipe, whether mouth- or bellows-blown, popular or folk types." Entries, in alphabetical order by maker, give brief biographical notes in addition to references to biographies, catalogs, and other sources, and enumerate instruments held in collections worldwide. Illustrations show historic instruments and makers' marks. References in entries refer to a bibliography and list of collections. A list of towns in which makers worked is provided. The sixth edition includes lists of addenda and corrigenda to the fourth and fifth editions, each with its own bibliography, list of collections, and list of towns.

392. Meggett, Joan M. **Keyboard Music by Women Composers: A Catalog and Bibliography**. Westport, Conn.: Greenwood Press, 1981. xx, 210p. discog. LC 81-4130. ISBN 0-313-22833-7.

This work lists 290 living and deceased composers of works for piano, harpsichord, and organ. It excludes jazz, popular, and rock composers. Entries note biographical facts and flavor them with quotations from other sources. Each entry lists works in chronological order, including either the publisher and date of publication or a note that the work is in manuscript, and cites writings by the composer and biographical works about the composer. Appendixes list composers by period and country, libraries and organizations (too short a list to be useful), and a selection of recordings. The volume omits the prolific French composer Claude Arrieu (born Louise Marie Simon) and other composers for the keyboard found in the *International Encyclopedia of Women Composers* (see entry 86).

393. Skowronski, JoAnn. **Women in American Music: A Bibliography**. Metuchen, N.J.: Scarecrow, 1978. viii, 183p. index. LC 77-26611. ISBN 0-8108-1105-7.

Women active in any variety of music in the United States from 1776 to 1976 are the focus of this list of 1,305 citations to books and articles. Six chapters organize the entries; the first four group works chronologically by subject matter, and the last two list general histories and reference works. Within chapters, arrangement is alphabetical by author or title. Brief annotations supplement most citations. An index lists subjects and authors. Omissions are not hard to find – Thea Musgrave and Elizabeth Cotton have certainly been written about, but these writings will not be found here. *Women in American Music* by Block and Neuls-Bates (see entry 375) is a more thorough work.

394. Stern, Susan. **Women Composers: A Handbook**. Metuchen, N.J.: Scarecrow, 1978. viii, 191p. bibliog. LC 78-5505. ISBN 0-8108-1138-3.

The handbook indexes biographical information from some three hundred books and articles on women composers from the sixteenth to the twentieth centuries. While it specifically limits its selection to composers from "the United States, Canada, England (not all of Great Britain), Belgium, France, West Germany, Austria, the Netherlands, Switzerland, and Italy," one can find Lady John Douglas Scott, who was born and died in Spottiswoode, Berwickshire, Scotland. Entries give places and dates of birth and death, brief notes on the composers' work, and references to the list of sources. The handbook repeatedly misspells *Musical Quarterly* as *Music Quarterly*.

395. Thompson, Kenneth. **A Dictionary of Twentieth-Century Composers (1911-1971)**. New York: St. Martin's Press, 1973. 666p. bibliog. LC 78-175526.

The strength of the dictionary lies in its extensive bibliographies rather than in its brief biographies. Composers included are Bartók, Berg, Bloch, Busoni, Debussy, Delius, Elgar, Falla, Fauré, Hindemith, Holst, Honegger, Ives, Janácek, Kodály, Mahler, Martinů, Nielsen, Poulenc, Prokofiev, Puccini, Rachmaninoff, Ravel, Roussel, Satie, Schoenberg, Sibelius, Strauss, Stravinsky, Varèse, Vaughan Williams, and Webern. Comprehensive work lists give instrumentation, parts, first performances, duration, publication date, and publisher. Many entries include a bibliography of writings about the composition. General bibliographies follow each list of works.

14

Bibliographies Devoted to Specific Forms of Music Literature

Works in this chapter are devoted to listing, in comprehensive or at least broad terms, dissertations, discographies, congress reports, thematic catalogs, dictionaries, festschriften, and indexes and bibliographies. Since these are kinds of literature which other bibliographies often overlook, these works can supplement subject-oriented research. *RILM Abstracts* (see entry 327) now covers these kinds of publications on an international basis.

396. Adkins, Cecil, and Alis Dickinson. **Doctoral Dissertations in Musicology**. 7th North American ed.; 2d international ed. Philadelphia: American Musicological Society; International Musicological Society, 1984. 545p. index. LC 84-229167.

Doctoral Dissertations in Musicology, January 1983-April 1984. 1984. 23p.

Doctoral Dissertations in Musicology, May 1984-November 1985. 1986. 41p. index.

The seventh edition is the last full cumulation of this standard and reliable list of completed dissertations and work in progress at universities in the United States, Canada, Britain, West Germany, and occasional other countries. The preface to the *May 1984-November 1985* volume announces it as the first in a series of annual compilations to be cumulated every five years. As of this writing, these three volumes together provide the most complete listing of dissertations. A classification system, subdivided by periods and specific subjects, organizes the entries in each. Entries give author, title, degree, program, institution, date (if completed), University Microfilms number, and citation to *Dissertation Abstracts International*. An asterisk designates dissertations still in progress. The seventh edition cumulation includes subject and author indexes; the latest annual, only author indexes.

397. **Bibliography of Discographies**. New York: R. R. Bowker, 1977- . LC 77-22661.

Volume 1: Classical Music 1925-1975. By Michael H. Gray and Gerald D. Gibson. 1977. xi, 164p. index. ISBN 0-8352-1023-5.

Volume 2: Jazz. By Daniel Allen. 1981. xvi, 239p. index. ISBN 0-8352-1342-0.

Volume 3: Popular Music. By Michael H. Gray. 1983. ix, 205p. index. ISBN 0-8352-1683-7.

Rarely does a reference work gather, in a bibliographical sense, such an enormous amount of material to which there has been such limited access previously. Each of the volumes in the series lists several thousand discographies published as separate works, as articles, or as special features within books. The thoroughness of the scope of the volumes published thus far is exemplary; they include citations not only to works from North America and Western Europe, but to many from Eastern Europe and the USSR as well. Discographies are listed by personal names, performing groups, record labels, and subject headings which follow the Library of Congress format (with all its idiosyncracies–"Music, Polish," but "Piano Music," for instance). Volume 2 covers not only jazz, but also blues, ragtime, gospel, and rhythm and blues. Volume 3, which in certain instances overlaps with volume 2, covers pop, rock, country, hillbilly, bluegrass, motion picture, and stage show music. Indexes to each volume list compilers, editors, authors, series, and titles. Two additional volumes are forthcoming. Volume 4 will cover ethnic and folk music and volume 5 will include general discographies of music, label lists, speech, and animal sounds. The series is updated, in a limited way, by the discographies listed in the *Association for Recorded Sound Collections Journal* (see entry 571).

398. Brook, Barry S. **Thematic Catalogues in Music: An Annotated Bibliography Including Printed, Manuscript, and In-Preparation Catalogues; Related Literature and Reviews; An Essay on the Definitions, History, Functions, Historiography, and Future of the Thematic Catalogue**. Hillsdale, N.Y.: Pendragon Press under the sponsorship of the Music Library Association and *RILM Abstracts of Music Literature*, 1972. xxxvi, 347p. index. (RILM Retrospectives, No. 1). LC 72-7517. ISBN 0-918728-02-9.

Brook defines a thematic catalog as "a grouping of incipits, themes, or melodic formulas presented in any type of notation ... or code or computer input language," and proceeds to enumerate, in a lucid introduction, nine historic functions of such lists. Researchers can use thematic catalogs to identify a composition or to examine a composer's work as a whole. The bibliography contains some fifteen hundred citations to thematic catalogs; these give full bibliographic information and list reviews of recent catalogs. Catalogs of the works of individual composers appear beneath the composer's name. Collective catalogs appear beneath the name of the library or publisher whose holdings or output they represent, or under the name of the compiler. Annotations describe each work, and, for collective catalogs, list the composers included. The index gives entry numbers for references to composers, compilers, authors, subjects, genres, and titles. Brook includes (on page 43) his "Plaine and Easie Code" for notating music on a typewriter.

399. Coover, James. **Music Lexicography, Including a Study of Lacunae in Music Lexicography and a Bibliography of Music Dictionaries**. 3d ed., rev. and enl. Carlisle, Pa.: Carlisle Books, 1971. ix, 175p. index. LC 77-30104.

Coover's is the most comprehensive study and bibliography in English of dictionaries, encyclopedias, and collective biographies in music. It opens with an essay which examines the few early dictionaries of music. The bibliography itself lists 1,750 works in all European languages. An addenda brings the total to 1,801. Both are arranged by author, editor, or title. Citations note the original and reprint editions, and include supplementary bibliographical notes. Indexes list personal names, topics, and works published before 1900. This is an important source for tracing bibliographic detail and for locating reference works of this type dealing with specific or obscure topics. Additions and corrections appear in "Coover's Music Lexicography: Two Supplements" by Nyal Williams and Peggy Daub, *Notes* 30 (March 1974): 492-500.

400. Gerboth, Walter. **An Index to Musical Festschriften and Similar Publications**. New York: W. W. Norton, 1969. ix, 188p. index. LC 68-12182. ISBN 0-393-02134-3.

Since the advent of *RILM Abstracts* (see entry 327), an index such as this is no longer necessary. However, its provision of access to each of the individual works contained in these more than four hundred festschriften published before *RILM* ensures a lasting homage to their subjects. An initial list provides bibliographical details for each festschrift; a classified list follows, grouping chronologically or topically individual essays and other works. An eighth note preceding an entry signals that the work is a musical composition. The index covers authors and specific subjects of essays.

401. Gillis, Frank, and Alan P. Merriam, comp. and annot. **Ethnomusicology and Folk Music: An International Bibliography of Dissertations and Theses**. Middletown, Conn.: Wesleyan University Press for the Society for Ethnomusicology, 1966. viii, 148p. index. (Special Series in Ethnomusicology, No. 1). LC 66-23459.

Graduate research relevant to ethnomusicology has often been performed in fields other than music. This collection of 873 works written at American, German, and other universities gathers important primary research from fields throughout the humanities and social sciences. Works are arranged alphabetically by author; many are annotated. Indexes list universities and subjects.

402. Gribenski, Jean, coll. and annot. **Thèses de doctorat en langue français relatives à la musique: bibliographie commentée/French Language Dissertations in Music: An Annotated Bibliography**. New York: Pendragon Press, 1979. xxxix, 270p. index. (RILM Retrospectives, No. 2). LC 78-31600. ISBN 0-018728-09-6.

Geography and language are factors which complicate bibliographic control. Adkins (see entry 396) provides the most comprehensive coverage of dissertations in music, but until recently included only those written in the United States. Gribenski has gathered 438 dissertations written in French from Belgium, Canada, France, and Switzerland from 1883 to 1976. Categories adapted from *RILM Abstracts* (see entry 327) organize the citations. Entries give author, title, degree, university, date, pagination, special features, a citation to any published versions, and an annotation (in French). Indexes cover authors, subjects, dates, and universities. English-speaking researchers can use this work quite easily, as the introductory material and titles of dissertations appear in both English and French, and the subject index, while employing French terms, includes references from English to equivalent French terms.

403. Heintze, James R. **American Music Studies: A Classified Bibliography of Master's Theses**. Detroit: Information Coordinators for the College Music Society, 1984. xxv, 312p. index. (Bibliographies in American Music, No. 8). LC 84-9103. ISBN 0-89990-021-6.

"The master's thesis is considered a valuable source for the study of American music," proclaims the author optimistically in his introduction to this list of 2,370 works. It includes not only historically oriented theses but also those from related areas such as theater and dance, and excludes educational studies pertaining specifically to a certain area or institution. Seven broad subject headings and a number of subheadings organize the citations. Each gives the author, title, university, degree, and date of the thesis. Brief annotations clarify ambiguous titles. The author notes the source of each citation, either to an item in a list of sources or to information from a particular university.

404. Mead, Rita H. **Doctoral Dissertations in American Music: A Classified Bibliography**. Brooklyn, N.Y.: Institute for Studies in American Music, Department of Music, School of Performing Arts, Brooklyn College of the City University of New York, 1974. xiv, 155p. index. (I.S.A.M. Monographs, No. 3). LC 74-18893. ISBN 0-914678-02-7.

H. Wiley Hitchcock's foreword emphasizes that some of the most important graduate research in American music is performed beyond the confines of departments of music: "other disciplines—sociology, theater, anthropology, history, American Studies, theology, literature, education, and still others—have been almost more hospitable." The 1,226 entries, dating back to the 1890s, are arranged into categories which span these disciplines and more. Indexes to authors and subjects provide additional access.

405. Meggett, Joan M. **Music Periodical Literature: An Annotated Bibliography of Indexes and Bibliographies**. Metuchen, N.J.: Scarecrow, 1978. ix, 116p. bibliog. index. LC 77-19120. ISBN 0-8108-1109-X.

This enumeration of 335 sources which list either periodical titles or articles brings to light useful specialized and obscure works and extends, in a small way, bibliographic control previous to the inception of *The Music Index* (see entry 324) in 1949. Citations include books, serial bibliographies, journals which regularly review the periodical literature of a specific field, and articles surveying the literature of a topic or composer. Descriptive annotations give an adequate idea of the content of each work cited. Author, subject, and title indexes follow the main listing. Although this work may lead to otherwise unexpected finds, it is more useful as an overall guide to periodical literature than as a source for articles on a subject.

406. Schaal, Richard. **Verzeichnis deutschsprachiger musikwissenschaftlicher Dissertationen, 1861-1960**. Kassel, West Germany: Bärenreiter, 1963. 167p. index. LC 64-57938.

407. Schaal, Richard. **Verzeichnis deutschsprachiger musikwissenschaftlicher Dissertationen, 1961-1970, mit Ergänzungen zum Verzeichnis 1861-1960**. Kassel, West Germany: Bärenreiter, 1974. 91p. index. LC 74-346952. ISBN 3-7618-0436-9.

These two volumes provide a comprehensive retrospective list of doctoral dissertations in the German language from 1861 to 1960 and from 1961 to 1970. Arrangement in both is by author. Citations give publication information for those formally published. Both have subject indexes. German dissertations are listed annually in *Die Musikforschung* (see entry 634) and, to a limited extent, in *Doctoral Dissertations in Musicology* (see entry 396).

408. Tyrell, John, and Rosemary Wise. **A Guide to International Congress Reports in Musicology**. New York: Garland, 1979. xiii, 353p. index. LC 77-83364. ISBN 0-8240-9839-0.

Beginning with "the first congress entirely devoted to musicology for which a report was published," the guide gives complete citations to published reports and lists the author and title of each paper given. It excludes regularly published proceedings of societies, but includes some reports of national congresses of international interest and individual papers from conferences in related fields. Entries appear in chronological order by city. Four indexes cover places; titles, series, and sponsors; authors and editors; and in meticulous detail, subjects of all papers. The one drawback of this otherwise well-constructed work is its failure to indicate page numbers of individual papers.

Part 4

BIBLIOGRAPHIES OF MUSIC

15

Retrospective Indexes and Bibliographies of Music

Most of these sources concern themselves with early music composed before the nineteenth century. Eitner's *Quellen-Lexikon* (see entry 414) has been the primary bibliographical source for early European music, and Sonneck's *Bibliography of Early Secular American Music* (see entry 433) established the historical importance of its own subject matter. The specialized demands of different forms of the vast amount of material encompassed in the term "early music" has demanded equally specialized types of reference works, such as *An Index of Gregorian Chant* (see entry 411) and *The National Tune Index* (see entry 420).

409. **The British Union-Catalogue of Early Music Printed before the Year 1801: A Record of the Holdings of over One Hundred Libraries throughout the British Isles.** Edith P. Schnapper, ed. London: Butterworths, 1957. 2v. index.

Though now largely superseded by *The Catalogue of Printed Music in the British Library to 1980* (see entry 185) and by Series A I of RISM, *Einzeldrucke vor 1800* (see entry 424), the *Union-Catalogue* retains its use not only for locating music in the libraries it covers, but for verifying a small percentage of items it includes that are not in RISM. Works are arranged by composer; there are also headings for certain classes of works such as "Catches," "Dances," and "Psalms." An index lists titles of vocal works. The clear typography and cross-references have helped to make this a standard resource.

410. Brown, Howard Mayer. **Instrumental Music Printed before 1600: A Bibliography**. Cambridge, Mass.: Harvard University Press, 1965. 559p. bibliog. index. LC 65-12783.

Brown's extraordinary bibliography covers its area much more thoroughly than does RISM series B I, *Recueils Imprimés, XVIe-XVIIe Siècles* (see entry 430). It details the contents of each volume cited, gives more detailed bibliographic descriptions, and notes not only extant works, but also those known to exist, but now lost. Works are arranged chronologically. Within years, they are arranged by composer, author, or publisher. Each title page is fully transcribed. In each entry, a short description notes the number of folios, kind of notation used, special features of the work, and modern and facsimile editions. Following the description is a list of libraries which hold the edition, and a complete list of its contents. There are indexes to libraries, types of notation, performing media, names, and first lines and titles.

411. Bryden, John R., and David G. Hughes, comp. **An Index of Gregorian Chant. Volume I: Alphabetical Index. Volume II: Thematic Index**. Cambridge, Mass.: Harvard University Press, 1969. 2v. LC 71-91626. ISBN 0-674-44875-8.

The introduction explains that "the *Index* attempts to cover that portion of the chant that was in general use for a considerable period of time." The two volumes index sources which are readily accessible – modern editions, manuscripts in modern reproduction, and several special studies. Entries in both give a textual incipit, a reference to a source, and a melodic incipit in numerical form. Volume 1 indexes verses as well as main chants in one alphabetical sequence. Volume 2 lists the melodic incipits in numerical order. The index can be used not only to locate works in modern editions, but to identify texts set to a given melody and melodies used for particular texts.

412. **Census-Catalogue of Manuscript Sources of Polyphonic Music, 1400-1550**. Compiled by the University of Illinois Musicological Archives for Renaissance Manuscript Studies. Herbert Kellman, ed. (Volume I with Charles Hamm). Neuhausen-Stuttgart, West Germany: American Institute of Musicology, Hänssler-Verlag, 1979- . 4v. bibliog. index. (Renaissance Manuscript Studies, No. 1).

"This Census-Catalogue has entries for all known manuscript sources of polyphonic music in mensural notation for the period 1400-1550. Printed music and tablatures are not included." In addition, most sources copied later than 1700 and "manuscripts containing only anonymous 'primitive' polyphony" which have been included in RISM series B IV 3, 4 (see entry 425) are excluded. The catalog is organized by city, then by library. Entries include a summary list of contents, list of composers, short physical description, date and provenance, and references to bibliographical articles or books which discuss the manuscript. At the end of each volume is a bibliography of references, an index of composers, and a general index of persons, places, RISM numbers, and watermarks.

413. Charles, Sydney Robinson. **A Handbook of Music and Music Literature in Sets and Series**. New York: Free Press; London: Collier-Macmillan, 1972. 497p. index. LC 71-143502.

Now in its third edition, Heyer's *Historical Sets* (see entry 417) has established itself as the standard index to collections of music. However, Charles's handbook offers an alternative which is more selective (preferring to cite a recent edition rather than to enumerate all editions of a composer's work), more fully indexed in some ways, and which includes series of music literature. The handbook has four sections: "Sets and series containing music of several composers and sets and series containing both music and music literature"; "Sets and series devoted to one composer"; "Music literature monograph and facsimile series"; and "Music periodicals and yearbooks." The first three list individual works within series. The periodicals section does not list complete contents, but gives dates, indexing, publication history, features, and notes special issues. The index lists authors, editors, composers, titles of collections, and subjects.

414. Eitner, Robert. **Biographische-bibliographisches Quellen-Lexikon der Musiker und Musikgelehrten der christlichen Zeitrechnung bis zur Mitte des neunzehnten Jahrhunderts**. Leipzig, Germany: Breitkopf & Härtel, 1900-1904; repr., Graz, Austria: Akademische Druck- und Verlangsanstalt, 1959-60. LC 61-28852. 10v. index. (Repr. in 11 vols.).

The *Quellen-Lexikon* is one of the classics of musical bibliography. Eitner's foreword proclaims "Die Musik-Bibliographie ist die Grundlage alles historischen Wissens" (Music bibliography is the foundation of all historical scholarship). Composers from the Middle Ages to the early nineteenth century are represented. The ten volumes are arranged alphabetically by composer. Each entry gives a short biography followed by a list of printed music and manuscripts. A source, either in a printed edition, a collected edition, or a library manuscript, is given for each work. RISM series A I (see entry 424) has superseded the *Quellen-Lexikon* to a great deal, but it remains useful as a source for works lost during World War II (therefore not listed in RISM) and for its biographical data. The reprinted set was published in eleven volumes; volume 11 updates the list with a "Miscellanea Musicae Bio-Bibliographica."

415. Eitner, Robert, bearbeitet und herausgegeben von im Vereine mit Frz. Xav. Haberl, A. Lagerberg und C. F. Pohl. **Bibliographie der Musik-Sammelwerke des XVI und XVII Jahrhunderts**. Berlin: Verlag von Leo Liepmannssohn, 1877; repr., Hildesheim, West Germany: Georg Olms Verlag, 1977. ix, 964p. ISBN 0-487-00403-8.

Eitner's *Bibliographie* preceded his *Quellen-Lexikon* as a list of and index to collected editions of music published in the sixteenth and seventeenth centuries. Editions are listed in chronological order. Entries give full transcriptions of title pages, lists of contents and of composers included, and references to library collections which hold individual editions. The second two-thirds of the volume is occupied by a composer/first-line index to vocal works. RISM series B I (see entry 430) has largely superseded the *Bibliographie*, yet the latter remains useful for its detail and for its vocal index.

416. Fuld, James J., and Mary Wallace Davidson. **18th-Century American Secular Music Manuscripts: An Inventory**. Philadelphia: Music Library Association, 1980. xiii, 225p. bibliog. index. (MLA Index and Bibliography Series, No. 20). LC 79-92993. ISBN 0-914954-16-4pa; ISSN 0094-6478.

Intended as an elaboration of Sonneck's *Bibliography of Early Secular American Music* (see entry 433), the inventory offers a detailed description and itemized list of the contents of eighty-five manuscripts from twenty collections in the United States. It is more selective than Keller's checklist (see entry 419), but gives a detailed bibliographic description and a list of the contents of each item included. Thus, it offers a survey of the titles and genres of tunes which were popular in early America, some of which, such as "Sailor's Hornpipe" and "Yankee Doodle," are well known today. The inventory is geographically arranged by state, then by collection.

417. Heyer, Anna Harriet. **Historical Sets, Collected Editions, and Monuments of Music: A Guide to Their Contents**. 3d ed. Chicago: American Library Association, 1980. 2v. index. LC 80-22893. ISBN 0-8389-0288-X.

A winner of the annual award given by the Music Library Association for the best book-length bibliography, Heyer's bibliography and index details the contents of some thirteen hundred collections of music published as single volumes, multivolume sets, or ongoing series. It excludes folk music and most collections of songs. The first volume lists these collections either by composer, or, in the case of collections of works by more than one composer, by compiler or title. Each entry gives a full bibliographic citation, and lists the contents of individual volumes. The second volume is an index to the first. It lists individual works by composer, compilers, editors, and titles of collections. Of series which contain volumes of both music and music literature, Heyer generally lists only the volumes of music. Charles's *Handbook of Music and Music Literature* (see entry 413) is more selective in its choice of series, but lists all volumes in the series it includes. Since its first edition in 1957, Heyer's *Historical Sets* has become a standard and indispensable source for locating individual pieces of music.

418. Hixon, Donald L. **Music in Early America: A Bibliography of Music in Evans**. Metuchen, N.J.: Scarecrow, 1970. xv, 607p. index. LC 74-16407. ISBN 0-8108-0374-7.

Charles Evans's *American Bibliography* (1903; repr., Peter Smith, 1941) is the primary bibliography of works printed in the United States in the seventeenth and eighteenth centuries. Hixon has identified "every item containing printed musical notation, whether published in book, pamphlet, or broadside form, and whether issued separately or as part of a larger collection" (preface) in Evans and in the Readex Corporation's microprint series *Early American Imprints, 1639-1800*. He excludes periodicals, newspapers, and other serial publications. Part 1 lists items included in the microprint edition; part 2 lists those listed in Evans but (as of 1970) not reproduced in microprint due to unavailability. Entries in both sections are arranged by composer, editor, compiler, or, when none of these is identified, by title. Both sections analyze, by composer and title, the contents of collections of secular music, but not of sacred music. Part 3 gives biographical sketches of composers whose works are listed. Indexes list composers and editors, titles, and Evans's serial numbers. The full bibliographic citations, the analytics, and the emphasis placed by Hixon on composers (rather than on authors, as by Evans) make this an important bibliography in its own right.

419. Keller, Kate Van Winkle. **Popular Secular Music in America through 1800: A Preliminary Checklist of Manuscripts in North American Collections**. Philadelphia: Music Library Association, 1981. xviii, 140p. bibliog. index. (MLA Index and Bibliography Series, No. 21). LC 81-1167. ISBN 0-914954-22-9; ISSN 0094-6478.

Keller's checklist, an offshoot of her work on *The National Tune Index* (see entry 420), is a survey of seventy-seven private collections and libraries in the United States and Canada. It presents manuscripts which the introduction explains are "barometers of the popular taste." These include a copybook of Martha Washington, and a commonplace book of a long-forgotten Henry Blake which includes a journal of a march from Boston in 1776, tanner's accounts, and melodies for the fife. Collections are arranged geographically, and manuscripts are listed by collection. Each manuscript is identified by compiler, original owner, or title, and briefly described. Entries make reference to entries in *The National Tune Index* (see entry 420) and in Fuld's more selective *18th-Century American Secular Music Manuscripts* (see entry 416).

420. Keller, Kate Van Winkle, and Carolyn Rabson. **The National Tune Index**. New York: University Music Editions, 1980. 78 microfiches. bibliog.

421. Keller, Kate Van Winkle, and Carolyn Rabson. **The National Tune Index User's Guide**. New York: University Music Editions, 1980. xiv, 94p. bibliog. LC 80-54209.

The National Tune Index is a vast exploration of early Anglo-American secular tunes and their antecedents. It is derived from the National Tune Index Data Bank, which contains machine-readable information on about forty thousand tunes from over five hundred eighteenth-century sources. The microfiche index contains five separate means of approaching the tunes: a text index, which lists titles and first lines; three music indexes, which translate the melodies into numbered degrees of the scale; and a source index, which provides bibliographic information. The sources for the tunes are American imprints to 1800 of music and collections; British ballad opera libretti; British dance collections; British instructional collections of popular music; British manuscripts; Playford's *English Dancing Master*; British song collections and song sheets; and British theater works. The *User's Guide* explains it all in detail, and includes corrigenda to the microfiche.

422. Lowens, Irving. **A Bibliography of Songsters Printed in America before 1821**. Worcester, Mass.: American Antiquarian Society, 1976. xxxviii, 229p. bibliog. index. LC 75-5021. ISBN 0-912296-05-4.

Lowens's introduction traces some of the characteristics of early American songsters (the first of which was printed in 1734 by Benjamin Franklin), and offers a working definition for the purposes of the bibliography: "a collection of three or more secular poems intended to be sung ... under ordinary circumstances it would contain no musical notation." There are 542 songsters listed chronologically, then alphabetically by title.

Lowens gives a complete transcription of each title page, a detailed pagination, citations to standard bibliographies, and a list of libraries that own the work. Some entries are given for which no extant copy was located. Following the bibliography are an index of compilers, authors, proprietors, and editors, and an index of titles. Lowens's primary object here is bibliography, not musicology—he does not list contents of the songsters, but only establishes their existence.

423. Répertoire international des sources musicales/Internationales Quellenlexikon der Musik/International Inventory of Musical Sources. **Das deutsche Kirchenlied, DKL: kritische Gesamtausgabe der Melodien**. Herausgegeben von Konrad Ameln, Markus Jenny, Walther Lipphardt. Kassel, West Germany: Bärenreiter-Verlag, 1975-80. 2v. index. (RISM Series B VIII). LC 76-460284. ISBN 3-7618-0490-3(vol. 1); 3-7618-0590-X(vol. 2).

These two volumes represent an attempt to produce a "catalogue of the traceable printed sources of German hymns, of all denominations, that contain at least one melody in musical notation." Contrary to the usual practice of RISM bibliographies which include only extant items, *Das deutsche Kirchenlied* also lists items whose existence has been determined only by a bibliography or by research. Works are arranged in chronological order from 1481 to 1800, and in a list of addenda. Entries give a bibliographic description of the title page and note the place of publication, imprint, size, bibliographic references, and location, if any. There are indexes to titles, personal names, place names, printers and publishers, and DKL sigla (which identify items by category). The introduction appears in English, French, and German.

424. Répertoire international des sources musicales/Internationales Quellenlexikon der Musik/International Inventory of Musical Sources. **Einzeldrucke vor 1800**. Redaktion Karlheinz Schlager (Vols. 8 and 9 with Otto E. Albrecht; addenda, redaktion Gertraut Haberkamp und Helmut Rösing). Kassel, West Germany: Bärenreiter-Verlag, 1971-81. 9v. (RISM Series A I). LC 72-354281. ISBN 3-7618-0228-5(vol. 1); 3-7618-0241-2(vol. 2); 3-7618-0407-5(vol. 3); 3-7618-0435-0(vol. 4); 3-7618-0512-8(vol. 5); 3-7618-0551-9(vol. 6); 3-7618-0568-3(vol. 7); 3-7618-0614-0(vol. 8); 3-7618-0657-4(vol. 9). **Volume 11: Addenda and Corrigenda, A-F**. Redaktion Ilse und Jürgen Kindermann. 1986. ISBN 3-7618-0688-4.

As the largest compilation under the aegis of RISM, this is a list of over 200,000 editions of music by some eight thousand composers printed before 1800. The emphasis is on polyphonic music; it includes few songs or dances. The introduction, in English, French, and German, advises that it is "intended to comprise all individual editions of printed musical works of whatever kind, which were in circulation at any time within these three centuries under the name of a single composer." Series A includes few hymn books, psalm settings, or didactic works; collected works such as these printed during this time are the focus of the *Recueils* volumes in series B of RISM (see entries 430-31). Works are listed first by composer, then by title or date of printing. An appendix lists editions identified by their initials, and anonymous works. Some eleven hundred libraries and other collections in twenty-nine countries contributed data on their holdings for the project. As a result, each entry indicates one or more locations for each item. The *Directory of Music Research Libraries* (see entry 174) lists each of these contributors. The cutoff date of 1800 is a flexible guideline, rather than an arbitrary cutoff date, as the editors included any composer whose works appeared for the greater part before 1800. Thus, works by Haydn are included; those by Beethoven are not. Volume 10, the index, is forthcoming.

425. Répertoire international des sources musicales/Internationales Quellenlexikon der Musik/International Inventory of Musical Sources. **Handschriften mit mehrstimmiger Musik des 14., 15. und 16. Jahrhunderts**. Beschrieben und inventarisiert von Kurt von Fischer und herausgegeben in Zusammenarbeit mit Max Lütolf. Munich: G. Henle Verlag, 1972. 2v. index. (RISM Series B IV 3, 4). LC 73-202660. ISBN 3-87328-007-8(vol. 1); 3-87328-008-6(vol. 2).

These volumes continue the two previous volumes entitled *Manuscripts of Polyphonic Music* (see entries 427-28) to include three specific groups of manuscripts of music: Italian Trecento not in B IV 1, 2, and Polish and Czech sources of the fourteenth century; polyphonic music of all countries from 1400 to 1425 or 1430; and sources of organal polyphony of the fifteenth and sixteenth centuries and of choral manuscripts of the fifteenth and sixteenth centuries in which polyphonic pieces in black notation occur next to liturgically monodic ones. Works are organized by library within country. Volume 3 covers Austria, Belgium, Switzerland, Czechoslovakia, Germany, Denmark, Spain, and France; volume 4 covers Great Britain, Hungary, Italy, Iceland, the Netherlands, Portugal, Poland, Sweden, the United States, and Yugoslavia. Indexes cover textual incipits and composers. The introductory material, as with other volumes in the RISM series, appears in English, French, and German.

426. Répertoire international des sources musicales/Internationales Quellenlexikon der Musik/International Inventory of Musical Sources. **Handschriften überlieferte Lauten- und Gitarrentabulaturen des 15. bis 18. Jahrhunderts**. Beschreibender Katalog von Wolfgang Boetticher. Munich: G. Henle Verlag, 1978. 1v. (various paging). bibliog. index. (RISM Series B VII). LC 79-370353. ISBN 3-87328-012-4.

Manuscripts of music in tablature form from the fifteenth to the eighteenth century for lute, guitar, and related instruments are the subject of this bibliography. It includes solo and ensemble compositions, accompaniments for solo voice, examples in treatises, and sheets from albums. In contrast to the established form of compilation for other volumes in the RISM series in which cooperating groups in different countries contribute citations, the author of this volume has examined all items himself. The arrangement is by city and library. Entries give a detailed physical and analytical description in German (although the introductory material is also in English and French), and include bibliographical references. Indexes cover tablature categories and names of persons.

427. Répertoire international des sources musicales/Internationales Quellenlexikon der Musik/International Inventory of Musical Sources. **Manuscripts of Polyphonic Music, 11th-Early 14th Century**. Gilbert Reaney, ed. Munich: G. Henle Verlag, 1966. 876p. index. (RISM Series B IV 1). LC 67-70820. ISBN 3-87328-005-1.

428. Répertoire international des sources musicales/Internationales Quellenlexikon der Musik/International Inventory of Musical Sources. **Manuscripts of Polyphonic Music (c.1320-1400)**. Gilbert Reaney, ed. Munich: G. Henle Verlag, 1969. 427p. index. (RISM Series B IV 2). LC 67-70820. ISBN 3-87328-006-X.

Both volumes list extant manuscripts of polyphonic music by library within countries in Europe and North America. Entries give a detailed physical and analytical description of each item, often including musical and textual incipits and bibliographical references to modern editions. Indexes list composers and text incipits. Volume B IV 2 includes a supplement to the items in B IV 1.

429. Répertoire international des sources musicales/Internationales Quellenlexikon der Musik/International Inventory of Musical Sources. **Musikhandschriften 1600-1800: Datenbank-Index, Stand 1986**. Kassel, West Germany: Bärenreiter-Verlag, 1986. 2 microfiches. (RISM Series A II). ISBN 3-7618-0797-X.

As the preliminary notes to the index contain only minimal explanatory information, the article by Angelika Bierbaum, Helmut Rösing, and Joachim Schlichte entitled "RISM Series A/II Music Manuscripts 1600-1800 Database Index, 1983 Edition" (*Fontes Artis Musicae* 30 [July-September 1983]: 146-50) has been relied upon for this annotation. RISM A II is an ongoing project which locates and catalogs musical manuscripts from 1600 to 1800 in European libraries. *Musikhandschriften 1600-1800* is an index to the entries which have been input into the RISM A II database. It is projected to be successively published in cumulative editions on microfiche. Entries are arranged by composer. Individual works are listed by title or by uniform title in a standardized format. Entries briefly give the medium of performance, a citation to a standard thematic catalog, opus number, key, location of the manuscript by library siglum, and the RISM control number by which the item can be located in the database. An address to which queries regarding full information about entries can be sent is included in the introductory material to the microfiche.

430. Répertoire international des sources musicales/Internationales Quellenlexikon der Musik/International Inventory of Musical Sources. **Recueils Imprimés, XVIe-XVIIe Siècles**. Ouvrage publié sous la direction de François Lesure. Munich: G. Henle Verlag, 1960. 639p. index. (RISM Series B I). LC 60-4743. ISBN 3-87328-001-9.

431. Répertoire international des sources musicales/Internationales Quellenlexikon der Musik/International Inventory of Musical Sources. **Recueils Imprimés, XVIIIe Siècle**. Ouvrage publié sous la direction de François Lesure. Munich: G. Henle Verlag, 1964. 461p. index. (RISM Series B II). LC 65-74238. ISBN 3-87328-002-7.

These two bibliographies of printed collections of music complement the bibliography in RISM series A I (see entry 424) of printed editions of works before 1800 by individual composers. *Recueils Imprimés* lists printed collections of works by more than one composer. The first volume includes over twenty-seven hundred collections printed in the sixteenth and seventeenth centuries, and the second volume includes about eighteen hundred collections from the eighteenth century, and adds to B I collections of adaptations and arrangements of works by one composer. Volume B I is arranged chronologically. Since many entries within the scope of B II were undated, it has been arranged alphabetically by title. Indexes to both volumes cover authors, printers, and publishers; B I also has an index to titles. Introductory material appears in English, French, and German.

432. Répertoire international des sources musicales/Internationales Quellenlexikon der Musik/International Inventory of Musical Sources. **Tropen- und Sequenzenhandschriften**. Von Heinrich Husmann. Munich: G. Henle Verlag, 1964. 236p. bibliog. index. (RISM Series B V). LC 65-74239. ISBN 3-87328-009-4.

This bibliography of early liturgical music lists manuscript collections of Tropers and Graduals. Although introductory material is in English, French, and German, descriptions are in German only. Entries are arranged by country and library, and note contents, physical description, type of notation, and date. The indexes cover cities and libraries, places of origin, subjects, places, saints, and persons.

433. Sonneck, Oscar George Theodore. **A Bibliography of Early Secular American Music [18th Century]**. Revised and enlarged by William Treat Upton. n.p.: Library of Congress Music Division, 1945; repr., New York: Da Capo Press, 1964. xvi, 617p. bibliog. index. LC 64-18992. ISBN 0-306-70902-3.

Sonneck's work, first published in 1905, was a pioneering bibliography, and continues to be a standard resource for the period. The bibliography includes works, whether known to exist or only reported in an advertisement or other source, printed in America prior to the nineteenth century or written by native or naturalized Americans. Individual works and collections are listed in one sequence. Naturally, given the scope of the work, the bibliographic detail varies, but citations can include the physical description of the work, price, instrumentation, list of contents, first line (of a song), texts of related advertisements or concert programs, and parenthetical annotations by Sonneck. Upton has removed the "Articles and Essays Relating to Music" to a separate section, and has added to the original index lists of composers (with biographical detail for many), first lines, American patriotic music, opera librettos, and a geographical "Index of Publishers, Printers, and Engravers." The Da Capo edition includes a preface by Irving Lowens.

434. **The Symphony 1720-1840: A Comprehensive Collection of Full Scores in Sixty Volumes. Reference Volume: Contents of the Set and Collected Thematic Indexes.** Barry S. Brook, ed. New York: Garland, 1986. lvi, 627p. LC 85-25264. ISBN 0-8240-3860-6.

"This reference volume is designed to provide a complete table of contents of the 549 symphonic scores by 244 composers contained in the sixty volumes of *The Symphony 1720-1840* [Garland, 1981-86] and to gather in one place all the thematic indexes published in the series" (preface). Thirteen thematic indexes which were not included in the sixty volumes are also printed here. The handsomely designed large-format volume does indeed have a value beyond that of a mere index, for it summarizes the works of the major composers (except for Haydn, Mozart, and Beethoven, whose works are easily available elsewhere) and many minor composers of the period. Works are arranged by composer within sequences appropriate to each. Entries generally provide a thematic incipit, and indicate instrumentation, date of composition, references to standard catalogs, locations in selected libraries of scores and parts, modern printed scores, a source for orchestral material, and recordings.

435. Wolfe, Richard J. **Secular Music in America, 1801-1825: A Bibliography**. Introduction by Carleton Sprague Smith. New York: New York Public Library, Astor, Lenox and Tilden Foundations, 1964. 3v. index. LC 64-25006.

Wolfe extends by twenty-five years Sonneck and Upton's *Bibliography of Early Secular American Music [18th Century]* (see entry 433). Despite the omission of manuscripts, he includes roughly three times the entries in the previous work to cover the greatly increased output of the booming music industry in early nineteenth-century America. Sentimental melodies such as "Can I Again That Look Recall" and works of obviously New World origin such as "The Rapids: A Canadian Boat Song" characterize the predominantly informal songs, dances, marches, and pieces for the piano. Compositions by European composers, including Beethoven, Haydn, and Mozart appear for the most part as selections or piano reductions. The bibliography includes individual works, collections, and periodicals that published music such as *The Euterpeiad, or Musical Intelligencer.* Works are arranged by composer, or by arranger or title of anonymous pieces. Short biographies of lesser-known composers preface their works. For each entry, Wolfe gives a detailed bibliographic description, complete listing of contents, first line (of a song), and source in either a library or a collected edition. There are indexes to titles; first lines; publishers, engravers, and printers; publishers' plate and publication numbering systems; and to general names and topics. An appendix supplements entries in *A Bibliography of Early Secular American Music.*

16

Indexes and Bibliographies of Songs and Vocal Material

The works described in this chapter are sources of information for individual songs, hymns, and other kinds of short vocal pieces. Many of these works index collections or in some way point out a source for vocal music. Some, such as Kagen's *Music for the Voice* (see entry 451), evaluate works for performance. Others, such as the *Bibliography of American Hymnology* (see entry 437) or Hovland's *Musical Settings of American Poetry* (see entry 450), have a more bibliographical orientation. Vocal music currently available from publishers is listed in volumes of the Music-in-Print series (see entry 483) in chapter 17.

436. Barlow, Harold, and Sam Morgenstern. **A Dictionary of Opera and Song Themes, Including Cantatas, Oratorios, Lieder, and Art Songs**. rev. ed. New York: Crown, 1976. 547p. music. index. LC 75-30751. ISBN 0-517-52503-8.

The dictionary arranges some eight thousand vocal themes and accompanying lyrics into easily identifiable melodic quotations of several bars in length. The selection contains works from the fifteenth to the first half of the twentieth century. Themes are arranged by composer, then by work. A "Notation Index" arranges alphabetically the first six or more notes of each theme as if they were in the key of C major or C minor. Thus, one can identify an unknown theme by transposing it to C and then matching the equivalent letters of the alphabet with the list to find the entry number for that theme in the composer listing. A general index lists titles and first lines. Little, if anything, was added to the 1950 edition (published under the title *A Dictionary of Vocal Themes*).

437. **Bibliography of American Hymnology**. Compiled from the files of the Dictionary of American Hymnology. A Project of the Hymn Society of America, Inc. Leonard Ellinwood, project director and ed.; Elizabeth Lockwood, assoc. ed. New York: University Music Editions, 1983. 27 microfiches in binder. LC 83-80206.

The Dictionary of American Hymnology is, at present, a project rather than a publication. Through cooperating libraries in the United States and Canada, it is compiling an index to individual hymns. The bibliography is an offshoot of this project. Its roughly seventy-five hundred entries include 4,834 hymnals which have been indexed for the

Dictionary and others which are in the process of being indexed. The introduction does not explain what an "American" hymnal is (all seem to have been published in the United States or Canada), but maintains that the bibliography includes hymnals in all languages using the Roman alphabet except native American, Eskimo, and Hawaiian languages. On its twenty-seven microfiches are reproductions of the cards from which the staff enters citations into the Dictionary's database. These contain typed and handwritten citations in a uniform format which includes title, place of publication, publisher or printer, date, author's or editor's last name and initials, the holding library and its call number or collection name, the denomination, and other information for use by the indexing project. The arrangement is by title. Duplicate entries have been edited out. Many imprints date to the nineteenth century, and some to the eighteenth century. The introduction touts an entry for the 1640 *Bay Psalm Book*, but the entry actually represents a nineteenth-century reprint.

438. Bloom, Ken. **American Song: The Complete Musical Theatre Companion**. New York: Facts on File, 1985. 2v. index. LC 84-24728. ISBN 0-87196-961-0.

The imposing scope of *American Song* extends to some forty-two thousand songs and thirty-three hundred musical shows—"all Broadway, off-Broadway and off-off-Broadway productions from 1900 to summer 1984 are included," as well as a variety of other productions which never made it to New York. Volume 1 arranges the shows in alphabetical order, giving for each the opening date, total number of performances, composer, lyricist, other credits, source, songs (listed in alphabetical order, not by the order in which they were performed), cast, and notes and commentary in which the author gives useful background and tosses in his opinions on shows and personalities. Volume 2 consists of indexes to persons and to songs, and a chronology by year of musicals. *American Song* provides more data on more shows and songs than *Songs of the Theater* (see entry 455), but the latter has two advantages: its list of songs gives more complete information, and its index subdivides entries of prolific composers by show. This feature could ease a search for a Richard Rodgers show which the list of some one hundred undifferentiated entry numbers in *American Song* would frustrate.

439. Brunnings, Florence E. **Folk Song Index: A Comprehensive Guide to the Florence E. Brunnings Collection**. New York: Garland, 1981. lxxxi, 357p. (Garland Reference Library of the Humanities, Vol. 252). LC 80-8522. ISBN 0-8240-9462-X.

This is a title index to over fifty thousand titles of Anglo-American and other folk songs represented in over one thousand books and magazines and 695 recordings. Magazines indexed include *English Dance and Song*, *Folk Music Journal*, and virtually every issue of *Sing Out!* between 1950 and 1980. Entries are arranged alphabetically and refer by number to entries in the lists of books and of recordings. Variant titles in the main list make cross-references to standard forms of titles. The specialization and breadth of the work make it the primary resource for this kind of song.

440. Cushing, Helen Grant. **Children's Song Index: An Index to More Than 22,000 Songs in 189 Collections Comprising 222 Volumes**. New York: H. W. Wilson, 1936; repr., St. Clair Shores, Mich.: Scholarly Press, 1976. xli, 798p. (Standard Catalog Series). LC 76-39599. ISBN 0-403-07210-7.

Complementing Sears's *Song Index* (see entries 459-60), this work has selected for indexing "children's song collections which have been found most useful in libraries and to teachers of music in the elementary school" (introduction). Undoubtedly the collections have now been superseded by others, but the broad span of coverage of the index continues to make it useful in libraries which hold some of the indexed collections and as an identification guide in itself. Many of the songs (such as "Twinkle, Twinkle, Little Star") are very familiar. Entries by title (with cross-references from variant titles), subject, composer, author, and first line offer a versatile means of identifying many songs which appear in no other index.

441. De Charms, Desiree, and Paul F. Breed. **Songs in Collections: An Index**. Detroit: Information Service, 1966. xxxix, 588p. index. LC 65-27601.

This successor to Sears's *Song Index* (see entries 459-60) indexes 9,493 songs with piano accompaniment in 411 collections. The authors have attempted to include all collections of art songs and operatic arias published between 1940 and 1957, and also some collections of folk songs, Christmas carols, sacred songs, and community songs. Excluded are collections of songs by a single composer, hymnals, children's songs, and those with texts in non-Roman alphabets. The first part lists songs by composer, and anonymous songs, folk songs, carols, and sea chanteys by country or ethnic group. Entries give the first line, cite larger works of which the song is a part, note the author, and cite the collection containing the song. The index lists first lines, titles, refrains, cross-references, and authors.

442. Diehl, Katharine Smith. **Hymns and Tunes—An Index**. New York: Scarecrow, 1966. lv, 1185p. bibliog. LC 66-12743. ISBN 0-8108-0062-4.

The standard indexes to songs by Sears (see entries 459-60), de Charms and Breed (see entry 441), and Havlice (see entry 449) omit hymnals from the collections which they analyze. *Hymns and Tunes* indexes the contents of seventy-eight hymnals commonly used in Catholic, Protestant, and Jewish services in the United Kingdom and North America. All (except for a modern edition of a German hymnal first published in 1570 and still used by the Mennonites) are in English, and were published between 1876 and 1966. There are five indexes: first lines and variants; authors and first lines; tune names and variants; composers and tune names; and melodies. The latter is arranged alphabetically by letters indicating notes of the scale in an attempt to enable those with no musical knowledge to locate a tune.

443. Dox, Thurston J., comp. **American Oratorios and Cantatas: A Catalog of Works Written in the United States from Colonial Times to 1985**. Metuchen, N.J.: Scarecrow, 1986. 2v. bibliog. index. LC 85-27629. ISBN 0-8108-1861-2.

From an area which has received little bibliographical attention, this work gathers over 3,450 works by over one thousand composers. Entries are arranged in four sections: oratorios, cantatas, ensemble cantatas, and choral theater. Within sections, works are arranged by composer and title. Entries give publication information, voices and instrumentation, source of the text, duration, sections, location of the manuscript score, date and place of first performance, and, in some cases, excerpts from reviews or commentary on the piece. Indexes cover titles of works, authors of texts, and topics.

444. Espina, Noni. **Repertoire for the Solo Voice: A Fully Annotated Guide to Works for the Solo Voice Published in Modern Editions and Covering Material from the 13th Century to the Present**. Foreword by Berton Coffin. Metuchen, N.J.: Scarecrow, 1977. 2v. index. LC 76-30441. ISBN 0-8108-0943-5.

A well-conceived arrangement and a broad selection of some ten thousand works, most of which were in print at the time of publication, give this evaluative guide a thorough foundation. Most of the songs included are based on piano and voice combinations. The user is referred to the author's *Vocal Solos for Protestant Services* (third edition titled *Vocal Solos for Christian Churches*, see entry 445) for coverage of sacred songs in English. Despite the broad selection, the author villifies the avant-garde in the introduction ("not akin to the basic human nature of sound preferences"). The work is organized into sections by country of origin and three topical categories: "solo excerpts from the operas"; "florid display songs, recital vocalises, and alleluias"; and "traditional songs and spirituals." These sections are further subdivided; within these divisions, entries appear by composer. Each entry gives the title, type of voice, source of the text, range and tessitura, abbreviated evaluative comments, difficulty of accompaniment on a range from one to five, and an abbreviated reference to a printed source in one of the bibliographies accompanying each section. Indexes are to sources of texts and to composers; however, there is no index to song titles.

445. Espina, Noni. **Vocal Solos for Christian Churches: A Descriptive Reference of Solo Music for the Church Year Including a Bibliographical Supplement of Choral Works**. 3d ed. Metuchen, N.J.: Scarecrow, 1984. xiii, 241p. index. LC 84-51398. ISBN 0-8108-1730-6.

This work follows previous editions published in 1965 and 1974 entitled *Vocal Solos for Protestant Services*. If one can survive the stumbling grammar and flagrant opinions of the author's preface, one will find a well-organized list, arranged by composer, of vocal solos based on biblical and modern texts. Entries note the source of the text, range, tessitura, and type of voice; and give annotative remarks, an indication of the difficulty of the accompaniment, and a reference to a source in lists of publishers and collections. Each entry indicates occasions for which the work is suitable ("Installation for missionary service. Funerals"). Indexes list occasions, voices, titles, and composers.

446. Gooch, Bryan N. S., and David S. Thatcher. **Musical Settings of British Romantic Literature: A Catalogue**. Odean Long, ed. assistant. New York: Garland, 1982. 2v. index. (Garland Reference Library of the Humanities, Vol. 326). LC 82-2984. ISBN 0-8240-9381-X.

447. Gooch, Bryan N. S., and David S. Thatcher. **Musical Settings of Early and Mid-Victorian Literature: A Catalogue**. Odean Long, ed. assistant. New York: Garland, 1979. xxxvi, 946p. index. (Garland Reference Library of the Humanities, Vol. 149). LC 78-68274. ISBN 0-8240-9793-9.

448. Gooch, Bryan N. S., and David S. Thatcher. **Musical Settings of Late Victorian and Modern British Literature: A Catalogue**. Odean Long, ed. assistant. New York: Garland, 1976. xxiii, 1112p. index. (Garland Reference Library of the Humanities, Vol. 31). LC 72-24085. ISBN 0-8240-9981-8.

These three works provide unbroken coverage of musical settings of British literary works spanning almost two hundred years, and together cite some twenty-five thousand musical works. Entries are alphabetically arranged by author, then literary work, then composer. An original source is cited for each literary work, and a publisher or other source is noted for each musical work. Other supplementary information, such as first lines, vocal ranges, and accompaniments, is included in many entries. Each volume includes an index to composers, and the *Romantic* and *Early and Mid-Victorian* catalogs include title and first-line indexes. The breadth of the entries is surprising – chapter 1 of Dickens's *Bleak House* set to music, for instance, along with over two thousand settings of poems by Robert Burns.

449. Havlice, Patricia Pate. **Popular Song Index**. Metuchen, N.J.: Scarecrow, 1975. vi, 933p. index. LC 75-9896. ISBN 0-8108-0820-X.

First Supplement. 1978. iii, 386p. index. LC 77-25219. ISBN 0-8108-1099-9.

Second Supplement. 1984. iv, 530p. index. LC 83-7692. ISBN 0-8108-1642-3.

The basic volume indexes the contents of 301 collections published between 1940 and 1972 which contain words and music to folk songs, pop tunes, spirituals, hymns, children's songs, sea chanteys, and blues. While it covers collections published during much the same period of time as *Songs in Collections: An Index* (see entry 441), there is little overlap due to the different types of music each emphasizes. The supplements extend the coverage with more recent collections: 72 in the first, and 156 in the second. All three volumes follow the same arrangement. Collections are listed in an initial bibliography. The index itself lists titles and first lines of songs and choruses in one alphabet. First-line entries serve as cross-references to the title entries, which indicate the composer and lyricist, if known, first lines, and the collection in which the song is contained. The index lists composers and lyricists.

450. Hovland, Michael, comp. **Musical Settings of American Poetry: A Bibliography**. Westport, Conn.: Greenwood Press, 1986. xli, 531p. index. (Music Reference Collection, No. 8). LC 86-402. ISBN 0-313-22938-4; ISSN 0736-7740.

A quantitative assessment of Hovland's work – approximately fifty-eight hundred published settings by twenty-one hundred composers of twenty-four hundred titles of literary works (including some prose settings, dramatic works, and librettos) by ninety-nine American authors – can only begin to describe its scope. Arranged by poet, it includes seventeenth-century works by Anne Bradstreet, almost thirty pages of settings of poems by Emily Dickinson, almost seventy pages of settings of works by Henry Wadsworth Longfellow, and works of twentieth-century poets such as Wallace Stevens, Gary Snyder, and William Carlos Williams whose rhythmic and melodic structures demand twentieth-century settings. A date and collection are noted for each poem listed. Settings, many of which date well back into the nineteenth century, are listed beneath titles of poems. Each entry notes the composer and title (if different from the poem's title) of the composition; a publisher and date, or a reference to one or more of some 250 collections or bibliographies in which the work was located; and the form, vocal range, and accompaniment. Indexes list composers and titles of literary works.

451. Kagen, Sergius. **Music for the Voice: A Descriptive List of Concert and Teaching Material**. rev. ed. Bloomington, Ind.: Indiana University Press, 1968. xx, 780p. index. LC 68-27348.

Kagen offers a knowledgeable guide whose aim "is to provide the singer, the teacher, the coach, and the amateur in the search of suitable material with a handy guide listing as many composers of vocal solo music as seems practicable and as many examples of each composer's work as seems advisable for the purpose of giving the reader an opportunity to form a fair idea of this composer's vocal music." Works are organized within sections entitled "Songs and Airs before the Nineteenth Century," "Songs of the Nineteenth and Twentieth Centuries," "Folk Songs," and "Operatic Excerpts," and within subsections by country. Within subsections, works are listed by composer. Kagen gives a short familiar introduction to each composer's works, and in tabular form lists for each title the compass (range), tessitura, type of voice, and cogent remarks ("Very Spirited. Demands some flexibility and facile articulation"). Many entries indicate a published source for the work. Kagen includes few sacred works; a source for these is Espina's *Vocal Solos for Christian Churches* (see entry 445).

452. Laster, James, comp. **Catalogue of Choral Music Arranged in Biblical Order**. Metuchen, N.J.: Scarecrow, 1983. vii, 261p. index. LC 82-16745. ISBN 0-8108-1592-3.

The preface introduces the catalog as "an aid for the church musician and/or pastor seeking to plan unified worship services." It lists, by book, chapter, and verse, anthem settings for biblical texts in English and occasionally other languages. Each entry gives the composer's name, title of the piece, voicing, accompanying instrumentation, publisher, date of publication, and catalog number. There is no indication of availability. The index gives biblical references rather than page numbers. Users who do not know that, for instance, Isaiah precedes Jeremiah may find this confusing. The catalog can be a handy aid indeed – but since it fails to discriminate in terms of quality or character between the works it lists, it is no substitute for a familiarity with the literature.

453. Laster, James. **Catalogue of Vocal Solos and Duets Arranged in Biblical Order**. Metuchen, N.J.: Scarecrow, 1984. vii, 204p. index. LC 84-14187. ISBN 0-8108-1748-9.

With advantages and disadvantages similar to the author's *Catalogue of Choral Music Arranged in Biblical Order* (see entry 452), this work lists, in biblical sequence, works which have set biblical texts to music in the form of solos or duets. Entries give the composer's name, title of the piece, accompanying instrument, range, publisher, and date of publication. Indexes list song titles and composers.

454. Lax, Roger, and Frederick Smith. **The Great Song Thesaurus**. New York: Oxford University Press, 1984. xiv, 665p. LC 83-24927. ISBN 0-19-503222-5.

This strange amalgam of facts intends "to select, from all divisions of song literature, the 10,000 best-known popular and/or significant songs in English-speaking countries and to cross-index the pertinent data associated with each for immediate and accessible reference." Rather than noting all "pertinent data" by song in a simple arrangement, it employs a series of thematic chapters. The first arranges songs chronologically from "Summer Is Icumen In" (ca.1226) to hits of 1979. Other chapters list winners of Grammy and other awards in the United States and Britain; themes, trademarks, and signature tunes of performers, colleges, and other institutions; "Elegant Plagiarisms" – songs based on earlier works, such as "I'm Always Chasing Rainbows" (derived from a Chopin piece); and theater and broadcast productions. An alphabetical list of most of the songs from other chapters notes the year of popularity, composer, lyricist, and other facts; this is followed by an index to lyricists and composers. A keyword index allows a user who can remember only scraps such as "Lydia," "Tattoo," or "Lady" to identify "Lydia the Tattooed Lady." Other works such as Shapiro's *Popular Music, 1920-1979* (see entry 461) may be more limited in their aims, but are more coherent.

455. Lewine, Richard, and Alfred Simon. **Songs of the Theater**. New York: H. W. Wilson, 1984. ix, 897p. index. LC 84-13068. ISBN 0-8242-0706-8.

From *Robin Hood* in 1891 to *Sunday in the Park with George* in 1983, *Songs of the Theater* surveys some seventeen thousand songs and the twelve hundred musical shows in which they have been featured. The compilers have included not only "virtually every theater piece seen on Broadway," but also those off-Broadway shows which ran for fifteen or more performances or are of unusual interest, and film and television versions of these shows. A song section, which occupies most of the volume, lists songs alphabetically, and gives the composer, lyricist, show, and year of opening for each. The show section lists shows alphabetically, giving the opening date in New York, number of performances, composer, lyricist, source, and songs on opening night in order of performance. A chronology lists shows by year. A separate list covers film and television productions. An index lists composers, lyricists, and authors, subdividing these by show. *American Song* (see entry 438) includes more shows, but the full entries in the "Songs" section of *Songs of the Theater* provide more direct access to information about songs themselves.

456. Lust, Patricia, comp. **American Vocal Chamber Music, 1945-1980: An Annotated Bibliography**. Foreword by Phyllis Bryn-Julson. Westport, Conn.: Greenwood Press, 1985. xvi, 273p. music. index. (Music Reference Collection, No. 4). LC 84-25212. ISBN 0-313-24599-1; ISSN 0736-7740.

The 544 compositions featured here include "music written for one or two voices and one to fifteen instruments, but excluding pieces for voice and keyboard" (preface). These are works which other guides to more standard vocal literature, such as Espina (see entry 444) and Kagen (see entry 451), do not include. An introduction, with examples of recent forms of notation, examines some of the technical difficulties which singers of this material may have to face. Works are listed in alphabetical order by composer. Each entry notes a source for the text, titles of sections, duration, instrumentation, and occasionally a date of composition or dedication. Lust describes in an annotation the range and characteristics of the piece. Appendixes classify works by voice and instruments, by number of performers, and by type of ensemble.

457. Reed, John. **The Schubert Song Companion**. Prose translations by Norma Deane and Celia Larner. Foreword by Dame Janet Baker. Manchester, England: Manchester University Press, 1985. xii, 510p. LC 84-31065. ISBN 0-7190-1093-4.

Reed's thorough guide justifies his contention that "Schubert is to modern song what Shakespeare is to the drama" (preface). It presents the circumstances of composition and examines the relationship between text and music of each song. Songs are treated in alphabetical order by their German titles. Each entry gives a translation of the title, date of composition, author of the text, melodic and textual incipits, translation of the complete text, discussion of the song, and citations to standard works on Schubert. A second section offers a brief biographical guide to the authors whose texts Schubert employed, and beneath each lists the songs to which his or her text was set. Appendixes discuss broad topics such as the significance of Schubert's tonalities and the publication of the songs. *The Schubert Song Companion* was given the Music Library Association's annual award for the best book-length bibliography.

458. Rogal, Samuel J. **Guide to the Hymns and Tunes of American Methodism**. Westport, Conn.: Greenwood Press, 1986. xxii, 318p. bibliog. index. (Music Reference Collection, No. 7). LC 85-27114. ISBN 0-313-25123-1; ISSN 0736-7740.

The guide indexes hymns in six hymnals published between 1878 and 1966 which have been used by Methodist denominations. It enables one to trace the employment of hymns and tunes used by the developing Methodist churches, to find settings used for hymns, and to locate information about hymnodists and composers. The work is arranged alphabetically, first by hymnodist, then by first line. Each entry indicates the hymnal in which the hymn appears, the title of the tune, and the composer or arranger. Following are short biographies of hymnodists, composers, and arrangers. Indexes list first lines, composers and tune sources, and tune names.

459. Sears, Minnie Earl, ed. **Song Index: An Index to More Than 12000 Songs in 177 Song Collections Comprising 262 Volumes**. Assisted by Phyllis Crawford. New York: H. W. Wilson, 1926. xxxii, 650p. (Standard Catalog Series). LC 27-26092.

460. Sears, Minnie Earl, ed. **Song Index Supplement: An Index to More Than 7000 Songs in 104 Song Collections Comprising 124 Volumes**. Preface by Isadore Gilbert Mudge. New York: H. W. Wilson, 1934; repr., n.p.: Shoe String Press, 1966. xxxvii, 366p. LC 27-26092. (Repr. 2 vols. in 1. LC 66-25185).

The sheer quantity of material and the efficient organization of Sears's indexes make them as useful in the 1980s as they were when first published. Both follow the same selection criteria and format. The collections to be indexed were selected on the basis of surveys submitted to libraries in the United States. Works intentionally omitted include collections of the works of individual composers; hymn books; collections of folk dances, singing games, and children's songs; except for one German entry, collections not published in the United States or Britain; collections with words only; and collections without an instrumental setting. Title entries note the composer and author or identify an anonymous song with a short phrase (such as "Swedish folk song"), and indicate the collection in which the song appears. Variant titles, composers, authors, some first lines, and titles in other languages refer to the title entry. The collections are listed separately in an alphabetical list and in a subject classification scheme. *Songs in Collections* (see entry 441) indexes more recent anthologies.

461. Shapiro, Nat, and Bruce Pollock, eds. **Popular Music, 1920-1979: A Revised Cumulation**. Detroit: Gale, 1985. 3v. index. LC 85-6749. ISBN 0-8103-0847-9.

462. Pollock, Bruce. **Popular Music: Volume 9, 1980-1984**. Detroit: Gale, 1986. 336p. index. LC 64-23761. ISBN 0-8103-0848-7; ISSN 0886-442X.

463. Pollock, Bruce, ed. **Popular Music: Volume 10, 1985**. Detroit: Gale, 1986. 161p. index. LC 64-23761. ISBN 0-8103-0849-5; ISSN 0886-442X.

The 1920-79 compilation lists over eighteen thousand American popular songs, cumulating and superceding the first eight volumes of the original series. Volume 9 continues the series, and volume 10 initiates an annual series. The criteria for listing a song include popular acceptance, notable public exposure, and performance by influential artists. Sources for songs include the Library of Congress Copyright Office, the American Society of Composers, Authors, and Publishers, and Broadcast Music, Inc. Songs appear in alphabetical order within each compilation. Entries for each song give the composer and lyricist, the country of origin (if not the United States), the publisher, the copyright date, performers who introduced the song, and recordings, movies, or musicals which featured the song. Indexes list lyricists and composers, important performances in various media, Academy and Grammy awards, and publishers' addresses. The 1920-79 cumulation reprints the short essays from the first volumes which introduced the popular music of each period; volumes 9 and 10 continue these.

464. Stewart-Green, Miriam. **Women Composers: A Checklist of Works for the Solo Voice**. Boston: G. K. Hall, 1980. xxxiii, 297p. bibliog. index. (A Reference Publication in Women's Studies). LC 80-23118. ISBN 0-8161-8498-4.

This work identifies 3,746 women composers from seventy-two countries. It excludes composers of jazz and folk songs. Three sections group entries by decreasing availability of information; within sections, composers are listed alphabetically. Dates of birth and death are given when available. The first section lists from one to four works for each composer, giving a publisher or library location for each. In the second section are composers for whom the author was presumably unable to locate titles. The third section lists composers who are only believed to have composed songs. Separate lists group composers of various larger forms (such as opera) from the first three sections. The index lists all names. Since the amount of information given for individual songs is brief, the primary use of this work is its identification of women composers.

465. Studwell, William E. **Christmas Carols: A Reference Guide**. Indexes by David A. Hamilton. New York: Garland, 1985. xxxiii, 278p. index. LC 84-48240. ISBN 0-8240-8899-9.

This is a unique guide to the origins of 789 old and new carols from America and Europe. Carols are arranged in alphabetical order in the original language. Entries give the author of the lyrics and the composer, country or area of origin, date, variant titles and first lines, and a source from a bibliography of over one hundred compilations. The index collects all variant titles and first lines.

17

Bibliographies of Music and Guides to the Repertoire

Most of these works identify music which is currently available for sale or rental (and many list publishers and their addresses). The Music-in-Print series (see entry 483), which has developed over the last fifteen years, deserves special mention for the huge amount of information it gathers and for its attempt, by means of supplements and revisions to volumes and its annual supplement, to represent accurately current offerings from publishers on a worldwide basis. General bibliographies of music, such as Fuld's *Book of World-Famous Music* (see entry 474), are also included in this section. Guides to the vocal repertoire are listed in chapter 16.

466. Anderson, Paul G., comp. **Brass Ensemble Music Guide**. Evanston, Ill.: Instrumentalist Company, 1978. xiii, 259p. index.

467. Anderson, Paul G., comp. **Brass Solo and Study Material Music Guide**. Evanston, Ill.: Instrumentalist Company, 1976. x, 237p. index.

These complementary bibliographies list currently available music for brass instruments alone and in combination with other instruments. The *Solo and Study Material* volume lists works within its two groupings for each instrument. The listing of solo works includes those which are accompanied. The *Ensemble* volume is organized into categories by specific instrumental combinations. The highly abbreviated entries in both give only composer, title, and reference to a publisher, and, in the *Ensemble* volume, instrumentation. Addresses are given at the end of both volumes. Both include composer indexes. *Wind Ensemble/Band Repertoire* (see entry 490) offers a more current list of many of the same compositions in a single alphabetical sequence.

468. Arnold, Corliss Richard. **Organ Literature: A Comprehensive Survey**. 2d ed. Metuchen, N.J.: Scarecrow, 1984. 2v. illus. music. bibliog. index. LC 83-20075.

Volume I: Historical Survey. ISBN 0-8108-1662-8.

Volume II: Biographical Catalog. ISBN 0-8108-1663-6.

Arnold has updated from the 1973 edition the "Biographical Catalog" in volume 2 (the core of the work), but has not touched the "Historical Survey" in volume 1, which this edition reproduces page-for-page from the earlier edition. Volume 1 surveys organ music in Europe and North America from 1300 to 1970. The text offers little analysis; this volume is useful primarily for its chronological tables of composers, specifications of organs, and plentiful bibliographical references. Volume 2 is an alphabetical list of several thousand composers and their organ works. It includes abbreviated biographical information, and indicates a source, either a publisher or an anthology, for each work. Those familiar with Scarecrow Press's customary reproductions of typewritten copy will appreciate the more legible typeset text of volume 2. Following this catalog is a list of "German chorale titles with English translation and appropriate use," a list of "Corollary readings" which update the bibliographies in volume 1, a list of publishers and their addresses, and a general bibliography.

469. Aronowsky, S. **Performing Times of Orchestral Works**. Foreword by Percival R. Kirby. London: Ernest Benn, 1959. xxix, 802p. LC 59-4406.

This elegantly designed, large-format work makes beautiful the prosaic: it alphabetically lists composers and works, and notes average performing times (to the nearest half-minute) for each composition or movement. The author explains that he gathered his information with a stopwatch during performances as a violinist (how?), as a conductor, and as a listener in concerts in Europe and South Africa. He claims coverage of "the standard orchestral repertoire." This is a reasonable assertion, but the development of the repertoire over thirty years is evident in, for instance, his inclusion of Ives's *Symphony No. 3*, but not of *No. 4*.

470. **Band Music Guide: Alphabetical Listing of Titles and Composers of All Band Music**. 8th ed. Evanston, Ill.: Instrumentalist Company, 1982. ix, 408p. index.

This is a listing of currently available music for band. Entries are arranged by title within five sections: band titles, collections, solos and ensembles with band (this section is subdivided by featured instrument), band method books, and marching routines. The one-line-per-entry format dictates highly abbreviated entries which include only title, composer or arranger, size, level, publisher, and date. A key to publishers is given at the end. The index lists composers. *Wind Ensemble/Band Repertoire* (see entry 490) offers a more legible arrangement of similar material.

471. Barlow, Harold, and Sam Morgenstern. **A Dictionary of Musical Themes**. rev. ed. Introduction by John Erskine. New York: Crown, 1975. 642p. music. index. LC 75-15687. ISBN 0-517-52446-5.

Barlow and Morgenstern have distilled ten thousand instrumental themes into easily identifiable melodic quotations of several bars in length. Their selection emphasizes recorded works from the fifteenth to the twentieth centuries. The revisions, if any, from the 1948 edition include no works from the 1950s and 1960s, and only representative works from the twentieth century. Themes are arranged by composer, then by work. As many as twenty themes within a single work (such as Beethoven's *Symphony No. 6*) may be brought out. A "Notation Index" arranges alphabetically the first six or more notes of each theme as if they were in the key of C major or C minor. Thus, one can identify an unknown theme by transposing it to C and then matching the equivalent letters of the alphabet with the list to find the entry number for that theme in the composer listing. The index lists works by title.

472. Boston Area Music Libraries. **The Boston Composers Project: A Bibliography of Contemporary Music**. Linda I. Solow, ed.; Mary Wallace Davidson, Brenda Chasen Goldman, Geraldine E. Ostrove, assoc. eds. Cambridge, Mass.: MIT Press, 1983. xvi, 775p. index. LC 83-9922. ISBN 0-262-02198-6.

Boston's universities and conservatories have attracted and produced composers whose influence extends far beyond the banks of the Charles River. This work, which aims "to list every composition, published or unpublished, by every art music and jazz composer resident in the greater Boston area during the latter half of the 1970s" includes the works of such familiar names as Walter Piston, Gunther Schuller, David Del Tredici, Harold Shapero, and George Russell—161 composers in all. Entries for composers give short biographical data, and list works in alphabetical order, noting the date of composition, duration, medium, instrumentation, first performance, availability of the score, recordings, and the library collecting the composer's works. An appendix gives brief listings for composers who could not be contacted or who declined to be listed. Indexes cover names and titles of compositions; genres and media of performance; and composers in both sections. *The Boston Composer's Project* won the annual award given by the Music Library Association for the best book-length bibliography.

473. Daniels, David. **Orchestral Music: A Handbook**. 2d ed. Metuchen, N.J.: Scarecrow, 1982. xii, 413p. bibliog. LC 81-16678. ISBN 0-8108-1484-6.

Daniels expands the first edition (1972) with the same intent—"to provide in one handy location the sorts of information necessary to plan orchestral programs and organize rehearsals." Organized by composer and composition, the work simply gives the instrumentation, duration, and publisher for each composition. Appendixes categorize works by certain characteristics. These include choral works for a variety of orchestral sizes by duration; solo voices, by range and duration; solo instruments, by instrument and duration; orchestral works by duration and composer's nationality; and composers by nationality or ethnic group. The most unique part of the work, the appendixes, allow for bizarre as well as innovative combinations—a night of Danish, Japanese, and Rumanian music, perhaps? Or a concert of works for eight percussionists?

474. Fuld, James J. **The Book of World-Famous Music: Classical, Popular, and Folk**. 3d ed., rev. and enl. New York: Dover, 1985. xiii, 714p. illus. music. index. LC 84-21232. ISBN 0-486-24857-7.

In his "attempts to trace each of the well-known melodies back to its original printed source" (introduction), Fuld has created an absolutely unique reference work. He employs the methodology of descriptive bibliography to establish the background of hundreds of works such as (taking several entries in sequence) "God Bless America," "God Rest You Merry Gentlemen," "God Save the King," "Goldberg Variations," "Grande Valse Brillante" (Chopin), and "Greensleeves." Works are arranged by title. Each entry begins with a thematic incipit of the work, then gives a physical description of the work as first published, a short account of the circumstances of its composition, and a shorter biography of the composer. This edition reprints the text of the 1971 second edition (1st ed. 1966) and adds a supplement.

475. Fuszek, Rita M. **Piano Music in Collections: An Index**. Detroit: Information Coordinators, 1982. 895p. index. LC 78-70023. ISBN 0-89990-012-7.

The index analyzes the contents of 496 collections published since 1890 of solo piano works by 1,105 composers. Works based largely on organ music or comprised of arrangements are excluded. The first section lists works by composer, and indicates the collection in which each work appears; the second section lists the collections and their contents. Indexes list titles subdivided by composer, and editors of collections. Appendixes list editions and catalogs of composers' works.

476. Gifford, Virginia Snodgrass, comp. **Music for Oboe, Oboe d'Amore, and English Horn: A Bibliography of Materials at the Library of Congress**. Westport, Conn.: Greenwood Press, 1983. xxxvi, 431p. bibliog. index. (Music Reference Collection, No. 1). LC 83-8517. ISBN 0-313-23762-X; ISSN 0736-7740.

The author, a cataloger at the Library of Congress, compiled this bibliography by combing the shelves of the library under specific call numbers (listed at the back of the book) within the M, ML, and MT sections. She has collected 5,617 citations to books, systems, methods, studies, and, primarily, musical works. These are organized into hundreds of categories based on various combinations of one of the three instruments with other instruments. Entries list simply the composer, title, date, and classification number. Indexes cover instruments and composers.

477. Gillespie, John, and Anne Gillespie. **A Bibliography of Nineteenth-Century American Piano Music, with Location Sources and Composer Biography-Index**. Westport, Conn.: Greenwood Press, 1984. xii, 358p. bibliog. index. (Music Reference Collection, No. 2). LC 84-8993. ISBN 0-313-24097-3; ISSN 0736-7740.

Playing the piano was a popular entertainment in nineteenth-century America. From the mass of music written for the piano at that time (much of it of dubious quality), the authors have chosen "a select, practical catalog of available, published music, not a complete bibliography of all nineteenth-century American piano music." As a result of having played each of the roughly three thousand compositions, they emphasize with confidence that this selection is "representative of each composer's best efforts." Each of the five categories – solo piano; piano, one hand; piano duet; two pianos; and piano and orchestra – is arranged by composer. Entries indicate the original publisher, date, libraries which hold the edition, and anthologies which contain the work. Appendixes list publishers, libraries, and anthologies. A "Composer Biography-Index" gives short biographies and serves as an index to works in the main section.

478. Hinson, Maurice. **Guide to the Pianist's Repertoire**. 2d rev. and enl. ed. Bloomington, Ind.: Indiana University Press, 1987. xxxiii, 856p. bibliog. index. LC 85-46021. ISBN 0-253-32656-7.

The preface to the first edition (1972), reprinted here, opens with the same refrain that opens each of the author's other guides to piano music (see entries 479-81): "What is there? What is it like? Where can I get it?" *Guide to the Pianist's Repertoire* answers these queries in a review of the literature for solo piano, and of the literature for harpsichord, clavichord, and organ suitable for performance on the modern piano. All standard composers are included, and the author pays special attention to contemporary composers, especially those of the United States.

Works are arranged by composer. Entries note birth and death dates and nationality, and give a brief word on the composer's background or style. Beneath a composer's name, works are listed by opus number, title, or form. A publisher and date of a current edition is noted for each. Hinson's terse and witty commentary notes particular aspects of a piece's style, form, qualities, or pianistic problems, and suggests interpretive strategies. In the case of major composers, such as Beethoven, Hinson compares the qualities of editions and collections. Most pieces are graded as to difficulty. Many entries include bibliographic references; a general bibliography adds other references. A separate section describes anthologies and collections. Indexes list composers by country, black composers, women composers, compositions for piano and tape, compositions for prepared piano, and titles of anthologies and collections.

479. Hinson, Maurice. **Music for More Than One Piano: An Annotated Guide**. Bloomington, Ind.: Indiana University Press, 1983. xxvii, 218p. bibliog. index. LC 82-49245. ISBN 0-253-33952-9.

In the preface, Hinson observes that "most of the great composers of the last 250 years have written for the medium" of more than one piano. Here he evaluates for performance works composed, and in some cases, arranged for more than one piano, in much the same way in which he evaluates works for single piano in *Guide to the Pianist's Repertoire* (see entry 478). Arrangement is by composer. The index lists, by instrumental combination and composer, works for combinations of more than two pianos or that include other instruments.

480. Hinson, Maurice. **Music for Piano and Orchestra: An Annotated Guide**. Bloomington, Ind.: Indiana University Press, 1981. xxiii, 327p. bibliog. index. LC 80-8380. ISBN 0-253-12435-2.

This companion to *Guide to the Pianist's Repertoire* (see entry 478) follows its basic intentions and format in its selection and evaluation of works from 1700 to the present for eight or more instruments (including piano). It is organized by composer, with indexes to combinations of instruments.

481. Hinson, Maurice. **The Piano in Chamber Ensemble: An Annotated Guide**. Bloomington, Ind.: Indiana University Press, 1978. xxxiii, 570p. bibliog. index. LC 77-9862. ISBN 0-253-34493-X.

Winner of the annual award given by the Music Library Association for the best book-length bibliography, *The Piano in Chamber Ensemble* follows a format and intent similar to *Guide to the Pianist's Repertoire* (see entry 478) in its survey of compositions from 1700 to the present for up to eight instruments (including piano) which employ the piano on an equal basis with other instruments. The arrangement is by number of instruments, then by type of instrumental combination, then by composer. Indexes list works for two or more pianos and other instruments; works for piano, tape, and other instruments; and composers.

482. McGraw, Cameron. **Piano Duet Repertoire: Music Originally Written for One Piano, Four Hands**. Bloomington, Ind.: Indiana University Press, 1981. xxxix, 334p. bibliog. index. LC 80-8097. ISBN 0-253-14766-2.

In a manner similar to Hinson's *Guide to the Pianist's Repertoire* (see entry 478), McGraw's guide surveys works originally written for one piano, four hands, by nearly two thousand composers from the seventeenth to the twentieth centuries. The arrangement is by composer. Entries give birth and death dates and a word or two identifying some of the more obscure composers or commenting on a composer's work. A list of works beneath each composer's name includes key signatures, opus numbers, the original publisher and date, library locations in Europe and North America if the work is out of print, brief descriptive evaluations, and a rating of the piece's difficulty. The author's commentary is crisp and concise: one piece, for example, is a "sparkling little work with rhythmic excitement and melodic vigor."

483. **Music-in-Print Series**. Philadelphia: Musicdata. ISSN 0146-7883.

Volume 1: Sacred Choral Music in Print. 2d ed. Gary S. Eslinger and F. Mark Daugherty, eds. 1985. 2v. ads. LC 85-15368. ISBN 0-88478-017-1.

Volume 2: Choral Music in Print. Thomas R. Nardone, James H. Nye, and Mark Resnick, eds. 1974. x, 614p. ads. LC 73-87918. ISBN 0-88478-002-3; 0-88478-003-1pa.

Secular Choral Music in Print: 1982 Supplement. Nancy K. Nardone, ed. 1982. xiii, 210p. ads. LC 82-8131. ISBN 0-88478-013-9.

Volume 3: Organ Music in Print. 2d ed. Walter A. Frankel and Nancy K. Nardone, eds. 1984. xiii, 354p. ads. LC 83-26956. ISBN 0-88478-015-5.

Volume 4: Classical Vocal Music in Print. Thomas R. Nardone, ed. 1976. x, 650p. ads. LC 76-29568. ISBN 0-88478-008-2.

Classical Vocal Music in Print: 1985 Supplement. Gary S. Eslinger and F. Mark Daugherty, eds. 1986. xiii, 253p. ads. LC 86-18088. ISBN 0-88478-018-X.

Volume 5: Orchestral Music in Print. Margaret K. Farish, ed. 1979. xii, 1029p. ads. LC 79-24460. ISBN 0-88478-010-4.

Orchestral Music in Print: 1983 Supplement. Margaret K. Farish, ed. 1983. xiii, 237p. ads. LC 83-13336. ISBN 0-88478-014-7.

Volume 6: String Music in Print. 2d ed. Margaret K. Farish, ed. New York: R. R. Bowker, 1973; repr., Philadelphia: Musicdata, 1983. xiii, 237p. LC 80-18425. ISBN 0-88478-011-2.

String Music in Print: 1984 Supplement. Margaret K. Farish, ed. 1984. xiii, 269p. ads. index. LC 84-3478. ISBN 0-88478-016-3.

Music in Print Annual Supplement. annual. ads. LC 80-642167. ISSN 0192-4729.

The Music-in-Print series is an ongoing worldwide list of currently available music. It aims, within the scopes of its various series, to be comprehensive in coverage. The volume editors and production staff compile the listings from the catalogs of nearly one thousand publishers. Individual volumes are periodically supplemented by new volumes and issued in revised editions. The *Annual Supplement* updates the entire set (with the exceptions of *String Music in Print* and *Organ Music in Print*).

Main entries in all volumes are arranged by composer or by title of anonymous work. They appear in a single alphabetical list, with the exception of *String Music in Print* (first published in 1965 by R. R. Bowker), which is divided into categories by the number of stringed instruments, then by other instruments in combination, and the *Annual Supplement*, which is divided according to the volumes supplemented. All volumes employ cross-references from distinctive or popular titles of works and from variant forms of the names of composers to the entry. Individual titles in collections which contain up to six works refer to the entry for the collection; entries in larger collections are not singled out. Arrangements, excerpts, and variant titles appear within a uniform title under the main entry. Entries vary in form between volumes, but in general, for each work they give an opus or catalog number, the instrumental or vocal parts, the name of the arranger or editor, the duration, the name of each publisher, an indication of whether the item is for sale or for rental from each publisher, and the price. Each volume includes a directory of publishers and their agents in the United States.

Because information from publishers has been edited and abbreviated, and because there is of necessity a delay between publication of an item and its entry in the series, an up-to-date publisher's catalog remains the most authoritative source for current information. But for those who cannot maintain current communications with a thousand publishers and who appreciate the ease of a carefully edited, well-designed, and reasonably current compilation, the Music-in-Print series can be quite valuable.

484. **Music Library Association Catalog of Cards for Printed Music 1953-1972: A Supplement to the Library of Congress Catalogs**. Elizabeth H. Olmstead, ed. Totowa, N.J.: Rowman and Littlefield, 1974. 2v. LC 73-17184. ISBN 0-87471-474-5.

These two large volumes list about thirty thousand entries for musical works reported to the National Union Catalog of the Library of Congress but not included in the *Library of Congress Catalog: Music and Phonorecords* (see entry 316). Thus, the *Music Library Association Catalog* represents a sizable body of published music. In 1973, the new title *Library of Congress Catalogs: Music, Books on Music, and Sound Recordings* (see entry 317) began to include holdings of libraries other than the Library of Congress, eliminating the need for further supplements such as this. Entries, arranged by composer or author, appear as photographically reduced catalog cards, and vary in legibility and style. Cyrillic titles have been interfiled. Libretti have been excluded.

485. Rezits, Joseph, comp. **The Guitarist's Resource Guide: Guitar Music in Print and Books on the Art of the Guitar**. San Diego, Calif.: Pallma Music/Neil A. Kjos, Jr., 1983. 574p. index. LC 80-84548. ISBN 0-8497-7802-6.

486. Rezits, Joseph, and Gerald Deatsman. **The Pianist's Resource Guide: Piano Music in Print and Literature on the Pianist's Art, 1978-79**. San Diego, Calif.: Pallma Music/Neil A. Kjos, Jr., 1978. x, 1491p. index. LC 77-79564. ISBN 0-8497-7800-X.

These weighty bibliographies exemplify the successes and failures of works produced almost entirely by computer. Each includes perhaps fifty thousand published works for its instrument (the *Guitarist's Resource Guide* includes works for lute, mandolin, and vihuela). Main entries, listed by composer, give the title of the composition, editor, publisher's grade level, publisher, and edition number. Special interest listings organize works into categories by genre or use, such as "Christmas Music" or "Popular Music." Books are listed by author. There are indexes to titles of both works of music and books. Computer production of both volumes has resulted in a small text which lacks diacriticals and question marks, uses nonstandard alphabetization ("fingerboard" before "finger"), and does not standardize composer's names ("Sor" and "Sor, F."). These are valuable for their verification of available material, but no substitute for evaluative guides such as Hinson's *Guide to the Pianist's Repertoire* (see entry 478).

487. Voigt, John. **Jazz Music in Print and Jazz Books in Print**. 3d ed. Boston: Hornpipe Music, 1982. 195p.

Since improvisation is such a significant ingredient in jazz, it is no surprise that recordings have been a more important force than written music in the preservation and dissemination of jazz. Yet, there is a thriving market for lead sheets, piano arrangements, pedagogical works, and scores for band of "classic" jazz pieces as well as of newer compositions. This third edition of *Jazz Music in Print* covers the output of some three hundred publishers. The music is arranged by composer; each citation lists the title of the composition or the titles within a collection, the publisher, catalog number, and the price. Citations to arrangements of works include the arranger's name and the instrumentation. A separate section lists books about jazz by author. Publishers' addresses appear at the end.

488. Voxman, Himie, and Lyle Merriman, comp. **Woodwind Music Guide: Volume 1, Ensemble Music in Print**. 1982 ed. Evanston, Ill.: Instrumentalist Company, 1982. ix, 498p. index.

489. Voxman, Himie, and Lyle Merriman, comp. **Woodwind Music Guide: Solo and Study Material in Print**. 1984 ed. Evanston, Ill.: Instrumentalist Company, 1984. xi, 499p. index.

These complementary guides list current European and American sources for music for woodwinds alone and in combination with other instruments. Both guides are organized first by groups of instrumental combinations, then by composer. The highly abbreviated entries include only the composer, title, and publisher or distributor. Indexes in both volumes list composers and works. The *Solo* volume refers back to the main entry, but the index entries in the *Ensemble* volume leave one hanging with no idea about which section to consult. Keys to publishers in both give names and addresses. *Wind Ensemble/Band Repertoire* (see entry 490) overlaps somewhat in scope, and its format is much easier to handle.

490. Wallace, David, and Eugene Corporon. **Wind Ensemble/Band Repertoire**. Greeley, Colo.: University of Northern Colorado School of Music, 1984. 1v. (various paging).

The authors make no clear distinction between a wind ensemble and a band, but include and mingle works with various instrumentation suitable for high school, college, university, community, and professional groups. They have included works available from 342 publishers and 166 composers; addresses for all are given in the introductory material. The authors' criteria for including works specify that they be difficult to locate or that they have come to be accepted as part of the standard repertoire. Works are organized by composer within three sections – "Wind Ensemble/Band," "Instrumental Solo and Wind Ensemble/Band," and "Voice and Wind Ensemble/Band." Each entry gives the instrumentation and a reference to a source in the publisher or composer list.

491. Zaimont, Judith Lang, and Karen Famera. **Contemporary Concert Music by Women: A Directory of the Composers and Their Works**. A Project of the International League of Women Composers. Westport, Conn.: Greenwood Press, 1981. x, 355p. discog. index. LC 80-39572. ISBN 0-313-22921-X.

The first half is a biographical dictionary of sorts, covering seventy-two living composers and a handful of performers. The second half is a list of these composers' works. The compilers solicited material for the book through an advertisement in the newsletter of the league. Hence, the book includes only the works of league members, and trivia and overly congratulatory verbiage clutter many biographical entries. Entries in the list of works, arranged by genre and instrumentation, give the composer, title of the work, date of composition, performance time, relative level of difficulty, and availability through the composer or otherwise.

Part 5
DISCOGRAPHIES

18

Specialized and Subject Discographies

There are essentially three ways to list recordings: by performer (with or without detailing recording sessions), by composer, or by disc. Titles in this section employ all three. While discographies of concert music generally list recordings by composer, the relative importance of the performer to the composer in popular music makes a listing by performer more appropriate. Discographies are critically important to research in jazz, since so much of the music is improvised and exists only on record.

This section includes works in several categories: older works such as *The Gramophone Shop Encyclopedia* (see entry 506) which retain their value as enumerations or evaluations of early recordings; more recent works such as Leder's *Women in Jazz* (see entry 520) which compile material in a new way to illustrate a point; current evaluations of available recordings; and works such as Sears's *V-Discs* (see entry 533) or Rust's *Jazz Records 1897-1942* (see entry 531) which verify the existence of obscure recordings.

Price lists of used recordings and collecting guides are beyond the scope of the present work and have not been included. Neither have discographies dealing with individual composers or performers been included; the *Bibliography of Discographies* (see entry 397) is a primary source for locating these, whether they have been published individually or as supplements to articles or books.

492. **American Music before 1865 in Print and on Records: A Biblio-Discography**. Preface by H. Wiley Hitchcock. Brooklyn, N.Y.: Institute for Studies in American Music, Department of Music, School of Performing Arts, Brooklyn College of the City University of New York, 1976. ix, 113p. index. (I.S.A.M. Monographs, No. 6). LC 76-23559. ISBN 0-914678-05-1.

Conceived as a project appropriate for the Bicentennial year of 1976, this is a record of the music of the country's first native and immigrant composers. The first part lists 199 printed works in three sections: music in performance editions, music in facsimile reprints, and music in books. Most of the editions represented were published in the 1950s, 1960s, and 1970s. Entries are arranged by composer, or in the case of collections, by title, and list individual compositions included in collections. The compilers have favored historically accurate sources, and thus have omitted modern adaptations and most folk music unless it is explicitly based on pre-1865 sources. The second part lists 543 recorded works by the name of the composer and the title, or simply by the title of anonymous works, giving the name of the record manufacturer and serial number of the LP disc. The index lists composers, compilers, and titles from both parts. James R. Heintze has published two supplements to the discography in *Notes* (34 [March 1978]: 571-80; 37 [September 1980]: 31-36).

493. Basart, Ann P. **The Sound of the Fortepiano: A Discography of Recordings on Early Pianos**. Foreword by Edwin M. Good. Berkeley, Calif.: Fallen Leaf Press, 1985. xiv, 472p. bibliog. index. (Fallen Leaf Reference Books in Music, No. 2). LC 85-1660. ISBN 0-914913-01-8pa.; ISSN 8755-268X.

Basart has gathered citations to LP recordings of restored original and modern copies of pianos from the eighteenth to midnineteenth centuries. Compositions on 336 record labels range from Bach to twentieth-century works. The discography offers a variety of access points. The arrangement of the main list is by composer. Entries for each composition give the title, pianist, maker and date of the piano, notes on the performance, disc number, recording date (when available), title of the album, and source of the citation (when the recording itself was unavailable). Subsidiary lists give shorter entries for pianists, individual pianos (organized by maker), and record manufacturers. Indexes list data by performance medium, performers other than pianists, titles of albums, dates of pianos, and piano collections and owners.

494. Bennett, John R., comp. **Melodiya: A Soviet Russian L.P. Discography**. Foreword by Boris Semeonoff and Anatoli Zhelezny. Westport, Conn.: Greenwood Press, 1981. xxii, 832p. index. (Discographies, No. 6). LC 81-4247. ISBN 0-313-22596-6; ISSN 0192-334X.

Like *V-Discs: A History and Discography* (see entry 533), this is a catalog of recordings which are, for the most part, unavailable to North American researchers. Hence, it is particularly valuable in simply establishing the existence of these recordings from the record industry which the foreword claims is "the largest in the world." The compiler does not indicate how complete he thinks the discography is; given that he performed his research outside of the Soviet Union (mostly in Edinburgh), omissions are likely. Melodiya (the name of the Soviet record company) recorded since 1951 performances of a major part of the Western corpus of music, along with the works of dozens of Soviet composers unknown in the West. The list is organized first by composer, then by composition. Russian titles have been translated into English. Entries give the names of performers and the serial numbers of recordings. An appendix lists prominent performers, and an index covers all performers.

495. Bruyninckx, Walter. **60 Years of Recorded Jazz, 1917-1977**. Mechelen, Belgium: the author, n.d. approx. 11,000p. index. LC 84-217039.

Bruyninckx's massive typescript cumulates, to a certain extent, much of the work of the jazz discographies by Rust (see entry 531) and Jepsen (see entry 515). Yet these earlier compilations retain their value for their narrower and more easily handled scopes, their inclusion of some 78rpm records which Bruyninckx has omitted, and possibly for their greater accuracy, if the profusion of misspellings and poor grammar in Bruyninckx's introduction has an equivalent in the discographical data. The sequence and the format follow those of Rust and Jepsen: sessions are arranged first by artist, then chronologically, listing the title of the piece, matrix number, personnel, and the manufacturer and disc numbers of resulting recordings. Short biographical sketches introduce the listings of prominent jazz figures, but users can easily find this information in *The Encyclopedia of Jazz* series (see entries 94-96). One outstanding feature of Bruyninckx is his "artist index" to all musicians listed in the entries, which has no equivalent in Jepsen.

496. Clough, Francis F., and G. J. Cuming. **The World's Encyclopaedia of Recorded Music**. London: Sidgwick & Jackson in association with Decca Record Company, 1952. xvi, 890p. (Including first supplement, April 1950 to May-June 1951). index. LC 52-8431. **Second Supplement (1951-1952)**. 1953. xxii, 262p. **Third Supplement 1953-1955**. 1957. xxvi, 564p. (Repr., Westport, Conn.: Greenwood Press, 1970. 3v. LC 71-100214. ISBN 0-8371-3003-4).

The aspirations of Clough and Cuming to compile a list of "every record of permanent music issued since the advent of electrical recording up to April, 1950, throughout the world," could be realized in 1952 only with difficulty, due to the enormous number of electrical recordings made since the midtwenties. The size of the second and third supplements shows that the idea of a one-volume reference, even one whose narrow scope of "permanent music" omitted recordings of jazz, folk, popular, and dance music, was rapidly becoming impossible. The three volumes are similar in format (although the significance of abbreviated symbols changes throughout all three; users should consult the introductory material), listing recordings by composer and title of individual work. The entries list performers, record manufacturer, and disc number, along with an impressive amount of detail regarding the precise contents of each disc. Separate sections in all volumes list anthologies. Virtually all the entries in the first volume are for 78rpm discs; the supplements add increasing numbers of 45rpm and LP discs. The second and third supplements include errata to previous volumes, and the third includes a section listing prerecorded tapes. No other work offers such extensive coverage of the recordings of this period; *WERM* does not deserve its lowly acronym.

497. Cohen, Aaron I. **International Discography of Women Composers**. Westport, Conn.: Greenwood Press, 1984. xx, 254p. index. (Discographies, No. 10). LC 83-26445. ISBN 0-313-24272-0; ISSN 0192-334X.

The epigraph, quoted from Sir Thomas Beecham, should alone justify this work: "There are no women composers, never have been and possibly never will be." This list of recorded works by 468 composers covering a span of five hundred years proves him wrong. The scope of the discography is broad, and finds room for Carla Bley and even credits Wendy Carlos with the "Switched-On Bach" she recorded while still known as Walter Carlos. Each composer's entry lists titles of recorded works, the performers of each piece, and the label and catalog number of the LP or EP on which each piece appears. Entries indicate those names that appear in the author's *International Encyclopedia of Women Composers* (see entry 86). Appendixes include a list of composers by country, a list of featured instruments and musical forms, a title index, and a table of names of key signatures in twenty-one languages. Several pages of late entries follow the text. *Women Composers: A Discography* (see entry 505) is a comparable work.

498. Cohn, Arthur. **Recorded Classical Music: A Critical Guide to Compositions and Performances**. New York: Schirmer Books; London: Collier Macmillan, 1981. xii, 2164p. index. LC 80-5224. ISBN 0-02-870640-4.

There is value in an unabashedly opinionated reference work when that opinion is informed and substantiated. Cohn, former librarian, record company executive, and reviewer for the *American Record Guide* (see entry 565), offers here a mammoth compilation of evaluations of thousands of LPs that serves listeners as a guide not only to recordings but to the recorded compositions themselves. His pithy and familiar annotations never fail to illuminate the compositions, the performers, and the recordings. Cohn organizes the works by composer, and discusses individual works rather than complete records. He generally highlights one or perhaps two recorded versions of a piece, but often mentions others in his comments. The index, which lists recordings by manufacturer and disc number and gives the page number for the discussion of each piece, allows readers to locate comments on each work contained in composite albums. Cohn's scope extends from pre-Baroque to the latest twentieth-century compositions; in fact, his coverage of the twentieth century is much more thorough than that of *The Complete Penguin Stereo*

Record and Cassette Guide (see entry 507), which fails to even mention, for instance, Ives's *Symphony No. 4*. The *Penguin*, on the other hand, offers more recorded versions of each piece from which to choose.

499. Creighton, James. **Discopaedia of the Violin, 1889-1971**. Foreword by Yehudi Menuhin. Toronto: University of Toronto Press, 1974. xvi, 987p. index. LC 79-185708. ISBN 0-8020-1810-6.

Covering eighty-three years of recordings of "serious" music by nearly seventeen hundred violinists, the *Discopaedia* is a monumental achievement in its breadth, detail, and clear presentation. It covers recordings issued on hundreds of record labels in a number of formats: LP, 78 and 45rpm, and occasionally 16⅔rpm and cylinder. The main part of the discography lists recorded works under the names of individual violinists. Works listed include sonatas, concertos, recital pieces, and orchestral and other pieces for instrumental combinations which feature the violin. Within each list of violinist's recordings, works are listed by composer's name. Entries give the title and popular title, if any; scoring or arrangement; accompanying performers; matrix number, if known; and manufacturer and disc number. An index of composers lists, by composer, individual works and violinists who recorded them. Thus, the *Discopaedia* is useful both as a guide to violinists' recordings and as a survey of recorded works. An index of popular titles lists those which are "best known." Important to the full identification of the recordings is the list of manufacturers which gives the format of each numbered series of each manufacturer. Finally, a summary alphabetical list gives the names of violinists and their birth and death dates.

500. Croucher, Trevor, comp. **Early Music Discography, from Plainsong to the Sons of Bach**. Phoenix, Ariz.: Oryx Press, 1981. 2v. index. LC 81-16794. ISBN 0-89774-018-1.

Here is an extremely well-organized and legible listing and description of 3,164 LP recordings which were, at the time of publication, available in the United Kingdom as domestic products or imports. Volume 1, the record index, lists these recordings within a classification system organized basically by chronological period—Plainsong, Ars Antiqua, Ars Nova, Early Renaissance, Late Renaissance, Early Baroque, Late Baroque, and a few special issues. The Late Baroque category comprises half the recordings. Within each of these, further categories appropriate to each period organize the listings. Obviously the compiler had to make some arbitrary decisions for the classification of anthologies spanning periods. Entries for LPs list the title, the works performed, the performers, and the record label and serial number, with variant issues indicated for the United States and European countries. The indexes in volume 2 list composers and individual works, plainsong, anonymous works, and performers, and key these to entry numbers in volume 1.

501. Fagan, Ted, and William R. Moran, comp. **The Encyclopedic Discography of Victor Recordings, Pre-Matrix Series: The Consolidated Talking Machine Company, Eldridge R. Johnson, and the Victor Talking Machine Company, 12 January 1900 to 23 April 1903**. Westport, Conn.: Greenwood Press, 1983. lxix, 393p. illus. index. LC 82-9343. ISBN 0-313-23003-X.

This is certainly a specialized work, but is "the first of a series" (introduction) of discographies tracing the path of the pioneering Victor Company through corporate transformations into RCA Records. Included is a special appendix, "The Victor Talking Machine Company," by B. L. Aldridge: a pamphlet (reproduced here in facsimile) written in 1964 relating the history of the company. The discography itself lists, by pre-matrix number, recordings made until Victor changed its numbering system in 1903. A supplemental chronological listing and artist and title indexes allow access into the numbering system. "Sousa's Band," "Metropolitan Orchestra," and "Victor Grand Concert Band" are among the more prolific groups that were recorded.

502. **The Federal Cylinder Project: A Guide to Field Cylinder Collections in Federal Agencies**. Washington, D.C.: American Folklife Center, Library of Congress, 1984- . bibliog. index. (Studies in American Folklife, No. 3). LC 82-600289. SuDoc LC 39.8:C 99.

Volume 1: Introduction and Inventory. viii, 102p. S/N 030-000-00153-2.

Volume 2: Northeastern Indian Catalog; Southeastern Indian Catalog. xii, 419p. S/N 030-000-00167-2.

Volume 8: Early Anthologies. xii, 84p. S/N 030-000-00154-1.

Alan Jabbour, director of the American Folklife Center, introduces the intentions of the Federal Cylinder Project: "to organize, catalog, duplicate for preservation, and ultimately disseminate the contents of those old cylinders." The "old cylinders" of which he speaks, the precursors of disc recordings and magnetic tape, were an important tool of ethnographic field recording from 1890 to the early 1940s. The thousands of wax cylinders to be listed in this catalog represent ethnic music from around the world, including recordings of native American groups in connection with research performed by the Bureau of American Ethnology; Hawaiian and Polynesian music; Jamaican folk music; the earliest recordings of Javanese Gamelan music; Anglo-American folk songs, including those collected by John Lomax; French-American and French-Canadian music; the Hornbostel "Demonstration Collection"; and Danish and English folk songs and Polynesian music recorded by Percy Grainger. The "Inventory" in volume 1 lists the collections by the collector's name, giving the number of cylinders and the number of those recorded onto modern media; serial numbers for the cylinders; their contents; the sponsoring organization; the date and place of recording, and the provenance. Other volumes detail the contents of each cylinder. Volumes 3 through 7 are forthcoming. The recordings being made available through the Library of Congress represent fifty years of the collecting of critically important primary materials for ethnomusicological research.

503. Fellers, Frederick P., comp. **The Metropolitan Opera on Record: A Discography of the Commercial Recordings**. Westport, Conn.: Greenwood Press, 1984. xix, 101p. (Discographies, No. 9). LC 83-22587. ISBN 0-313-23952-5; ISSN 0192-334X.

From 1906 to 1972, the Metropolitan Opera made hundreds of recordings. This is a chronological listing of recording sessions which gives the date, time, location, performers, matrix numbers, works performed, and resulting recordings and reissues on 78rpm and LP records. Indexes list performers, and operas by composer. The compiler has filled out the discographical bones with helpful explanatory notes on the circumstances of many recording sessions.

504. Fellers, Frederick P., and Betty Meyers, comp. **Discographies of Commercial Recordings of the Cleveland Orchestra (1924-1977) and the Cincinnati Symphony Orchestra (1917-1977)**. Westport, Conn.: Greenwood Press, 1978. xii, 211p. bibliog. index. LC 78-3122. ISBN 0-313-20375-X.

The Cleveland Orchestra and the Cincinnati Symphony are two of the most venerable American orchestras. Their recordings include performances with George Szell during his long tenure with the Cleveland Orchestra, and guest performances by world-famous artists with both orchestras. The sixty-year span covered by this work includes 78rpm, LP, and tape recordings. Both discographies are arranged in chronological order by date of session. Entries give the composition, date of performance, conductor, soloists, matrix numbers, manufacturer, and release numbers. Both include indexes to performers and compositions.

505. Frasier, Jane. **Women Composers: A Discography**. Detroit: Information Coordinators, 1983. viii, 300p. bibliog. index. (Detroit Studies in Music Bibliography, No. 50). LC 83-22563. ISBN 0-89990-018-6.

This is a list of the recorded works of 337 women composers of classical music on about 1,030 discs. Frasier gives no indication of whether this number includes only LP recordings or other formats. The main listing groups compositions by composer, giving the manufacturer and record number for each. Three indexes follow: the first lists records by manufacturer and number, giving the name of women composers whose work is represented; the second lists composers and their works by instrumental and vocal genres; and the third lists works by title, indicating the composer. Cohen's *International Discography of Women Composers* (see entry 497) lists over one hundred more composers than *Women Composers*, yet there is little overlap between the two. An advantage of Cohen's work over Frasier's is his listing of the performer of each work.

506. **The Gramophone Shop Encyclopedia of Recorded Music**. 3d ed., rev. and enl. New York: Crown Publishers, 1948; repr., Westport, Conn.: Greenwood Press, 1970. xiii, 639p. index. LC 70-95122. ISBN 0-8371-3718-7.

This predecessor to *The World's Encyclopaedia of Recorded Music* (see entry 496) is significant as the first major list of commercial 78rpm records in the United States. The performer index in the third edition is still useful for locating early recorded performances by individuals or orchestras. The third edition purports to contain "all listings of serious music currently to be found in the catalogues of the world's record manufacturers," but drops recordings withdrawn from sale. Thus the first edition (1936, R. D. Darrell, comp.) and the second edition (1942) must be consulted for some earlier recordings. The entries are arranged by composer, then by individual work, with group entries for anonymous works and Gregorian Chant in the alphabetical sequence, and collections at the end. Entries list performers, and manufacturers and disc numbers. Short blurbs introducing the works of many composers reflect the tastes of the time – one of these notes, for instance, that Schoenberg's compositions have not achieved popularity "chiefly for their intellectual complexity and aural difficulties."

507. Greenfield, Edward, Robert Layton, and Ivan March. **The Complete Penguin Stereo Record and Cassette Guide**. Harmondsworth, England: Penguin Books, 1984. xxiii, 1387p. ISBN 0-14-046682-7pa.

508. Greenfield, Edward, Robert Layton, and Ivan March. **The Penguin Guide to Compact Discs, Cassettes and LPs**. Harmondsworth, England: Penguin Books, 1986. xxiii, 1217p. ISBN 0-14-046754-8pa.

These two volumes are the latest in a line of evaluative and selective guides by Penguin to classical recordings. The rapid growth of CD and cassette offerings justified a second guide on the heels of the *Stereo Record* guide in order to highlight these newer formats. In fact, the *Guide to Compact Discs* purports to include "all major CD issues and all the important bargain-priced chrome cassettes which seem competitive." The two volumes overlap somewhat in their selection of recordings, and their organization is identical: they list recordings by composer, and group by form those of heavily recorded composers. A section for composite recordings by several composers appears at the end of each volume.

The authors, seasoned journalists and critics, offer knowledgeable, comparative, appealing (one piece in the *Guide to Compact Discs* is "a charming Tchaikovskian trifle"), and at times extended annotations of the albums they have selected, and rate these with a system of three stars. Outstanding recordings sport a rosette, and an accolade goes to CDs of high technical quality. For some works, the authors have selected twelve or more recorded versions, all recommended, to compare. They provide catalog numbers for each format, and often note variations in British and American numbering. Cohn's *Recorded Classical Music* (see entry 498) offers similar evaluations of LPs.

509. Harrison, Max, Charles Fox, and Eric Thacker. **The Essential Jazz Records.** Westport, Conn.: Greenwood Press, 1984- . (Discographies, No. 12). ISSN 0192-334X.

Volume 1: Ragtime to Swing. 1984. bibliog. index. LC 84-7926. ISBN 0-313-24674-2.

The authors of this annotated guide to LP recordings approach their task with authority: Harrison wrote the article on jazz for *The New Grove* (see entry 20), and Fox and Thacker are jazz critics. Their introduction proclaims this "a critical guide to the entire field of recorded jazz." This first volume surveys 250 LPs, most of which are collections of earlier 78rpm recordings, from the origins of jazz in early blues and African music up to the early Charlie Parker. The projected second volume will continue to the present. Chapters organize the signed annotations in essentially chronological order by the date of the original 78rpm recordings or by the date of composition. This allows, for instance, a comparative discussion of an album of early piano rolls of Scott Joplin's rags and Joshua Rifkin's 1969 recording. While the authors are careful to provide discographical detail, the way in which they group the discussions of albums and the historical rather than analytical approach to their comments offer an informed history of jazz rather than a simple enumeration. This volume contains three indexes: to titles of albums, to musicians listed in citations or discussed in the text, and to titles of tunes. The first two are serviceable, but the index to tunes so haphazardly covers those listed on albums and discussed in the text that reference to a more reliable work such as Rust's *Jazz Records 1897-1942* (see entry 531) is necessary to compare versions by different performers of the same tune.

510. Hoffmann, Frank, comp., with the assistance of Lee Ann Hoffmann. **The Cash Box Singles Charts, 1950-1981.** Metuchen, N.J.: Scarecrow, 1983. xv, 860p. index. LC 82-19126. ISBN 0-8108-1595-8.

511. Albert, George, and Frank Hoffmann. **The Cash Box Country Singles Charts, 1958-1982.** Metuchen, N.J.: Scarecrow, 1984. x, 596p. index. LC 84-1266. ISBN 0-8108-1685-7.

512. Albert, George, and Frank Hoffmann, comp., with the assistance of Lee Ann Hoffmann. **The Cash Box Black Contemporary Singles Charts, 1960-1984.** Metuchen, N.J.: Scarecrow, 1986. xii, 704p. index. LC 85-22078. ISBN 0-8108-1853-1.

Cash Box (see entry 579) has tabulated and promoted the rise and fall of popular recordings in the United States since the 1940s. These three volumes compile the most commercially significant of its tabulations, which are based on sales and broadcast track records of 78 and 45rpm recordings. The same recording can sometimes be found in more than one compilation, depending on the way in which *Cash Box* categorized it when released. All three follow the same format. An artist index lists songs by the names of the individuals or groups who recorded them, then alphabetically by song title. Entries include the date the song first entered the charts, its label and number, its weekly numerical position on the charts, and the total number of weeks on the charts. The song title index pairs songs with their performers. Appendixes give a chronological listing of Number 1 records; records with the longest run on the charts; most chart hits per artist; most Number 1 hits per artist; most weeks at Number 1 by artist; most weeks at Number 1 by record; and record company abbreviations. This is not only industry data, but grist for the popular culture mill.

513. Hounsome, Terry. **New Rock Record.** New York: Facts on File, 1983. xi, 719p. index. LC 81-12489. ISBN 0-87196-774-X; 0-87196-770-7pa.

Covering forty thousand LPs and thirty-five thousand musicians, this is easily the most extensive analytical discography of rock recordings. A previous edition entitled *Rock Record* was published by Facts on File in 1979. The new edition is organized by the names of groups or individuals who have recorded albums. Within each entry is a list of albums in chronological order, including reissues and some EPs. These give labels and serial numbers for releases in both the United States and the United Kingdom. A list of musicians who have played with the individual or group accompanies each entry, indicating the instrument played and sometimes, through the use of a key symbol, the album on which the musician has performed. Since the musicians' names generally appear in random order, these lists can easily be frustrating when trying, for instance, to make sense of the over one hundred musicians with whom Bob Dylan has recorded. Yet, *New Rock Record* is a useful tool for identifying a group's output, and for locating, through the index, albums on which individual musicians have performed.

514. Hummel, David. **The Collector's Guide to the American Musical Theatre**. Metuchen, N.J.: Scarecrow, 1984. 2v. bibliog. index. LC 83-7520. ISBN 0-8108-1637-7.

Hummel has sought to list commercially available and private recordings on LP, 78 and 45rpm records, and on tape of "any musical presented on stage in the United States." He promises coverage of the London stage for a future day and offers as a temporary alternative introductory articles on musical theater in Britain, Australia, and Canada. Hummel's scope extends to musical comedies, musical dramas, operettas, reviews, and plays with songs or musical background, in stage presentations or resulting film or television versions. The first volume lists shows alphabetically, giving for each the composer, lyricist, original source, city, opening date, theater, number of performances, and titles of songs. The entry for each show lists recordings from the show and its revivals, noting the performers on each and giving the manufacturer and catalog number or a description of the recording. The second volume is an index to all personal names. For indexing of individual songs, one must turn to *American Song: The Complete Musical Theatre Companion* (see entry 438) or *Songs of the Theater* (see entry 455).

515. Jepsen, Jorgen Grunnet. **Jazz Records: A Discography**. [place varies], Denmark: [publisher varies], 1963-70. 8v. in 11. LC 77-374154.

Jepsen's discography continues where Rust's *Jazz Records* (see entry 531) ends – in 1942. Volumes list jazz records issued in Europe and the United States from 1942 to the years between 1962 and 1969, depending on when Jepsen completed work on that volume. This was a period of radical change for jazz and recording technology, encompassing the development of bebop and cool jazz, and the demise of the 78rpm format in favor of the EP and LP. Jepsen lists recording sessions first in alphabetical order by artist, then in chronological order, and includes the song title, matrix number, personnel, recording date, place, and manufacturer and disc numbers of the records on which the session was released. This is the standard jazz discography for the period, but it has not benefited from the repeated updating and revision that Rust has applied to his work.

516. Kinnear, Michael S., comp. **A Discography of Hindustani and Karnatic Music**. Foreword by Reis Flora. Westport, Conn.: Greenwood Press, 1985. xix, 594p. index. (Discographies, No. 17). LC 85-5584. ISBN 0-313-24479-0; ISSN 0192-334X.

Ravi Shankar's performance at the Woodstock festival and his tutelage of the Beatles helped to bring the music of the Indian subcontinent to the attention of the West. This discography of twenty-seven hundred EPs, LPs, and cassettes attests to the prolific musical culture from which his artistry developed. Recordings are organized within sections entitled "Hindustani Instrumental," "Hindustani Vocal," "Karnatic Instrumental," "Karnatic Vocal," and "Anthologies." The first four sections list artists alphabetically by first name or initial. The last lists anthologies by title. Unless one knows whether an artist is Hindustani or Karnatic – and the introduction does not explain the distinction – one must consult two sections to locate a given artist. Entries give biographical notes on the featured artist and list recordings chronologically, indicating for each the musicians; the ragas performed, their parts, and rhythm; the recording company and disc or cassette number;

and the country of origin and year of release. A glossary briefly defines Hindustani and Karnatic musical terms, and indexes list artists by raga, rhythm, instrument, and style.

517. Kondracki, Miroslaw, Marta Stankiewicz, and Frits C. Weiland. **Internationale Diskographie elektronischer Musik/International Electronic Music Discography/ Discographie internationale de la musique electronique**. Compiled in cooperation with the Institute of Sonology at Utrecht University. Mainz, West Germany: B. Schott's Söhne, 1979. 174p. index. LC 80-457166. ISBN 3-7957-0150-3.

The preface (in German, French, and English) sees the roughly two thousand pieces listed in this discography as manifestations of four trends: "musique concrète," "electronic music," "music for magnetic tape," and "tape music." Needless to say, a compilation of works dependent on such recent and continually updated technology rapidly becomes outdated; nevertheless, this discography represents some of the works which will influence future composers. John Cage has many entries, for instance. The arrangement, in reduced dot-matrix computer printout, is alphabetical by composer and work. Entries list, in addition to these two elements, the year of recording, manufacturer and disc number, institution at which the recording was produced, title of the recording, number of tracks on the disc, speed (45 or 78rpm, or LP), and method of production. The index lists composers.

518. Kratzenstein, Marilou, and Jerald Hamilton. **Four Centuries of Organ Music, from the Robertsbridge Codex through the Baroque Era: An Annotated Discography**. Detroit: Information Coordinators, 1984. ix, 300p. bibliog. index. (Detroit Studies in Music Bibliography, No. 51). LC 84-546. ISBN 0-89990-020-8.

The purpose of this discography is "to identify recordings of organ music particularly useful as illustrative material for undergraduate and graduate courses in organ literature." It lists recordings of organ works composed before 1750. Most of these are LP recordings, and most appeared between 1970 and 1980. The recordings are arranged first by chronological era—"Late Medieval," "Renaissance," and "Baroque"—then by country, then either by composer or within a section for collections. Recordings of organ music by J. S. Bach occupy a separate appendix. Entries give the performer, title of recording, manufacturer and disc number, and a list of compositions recorded therein. Indexes cover organs (geographically), performers, and composers.

519. Laster, James, comp. **A Discography of Treble Voice Recordings**. Metuchen, N.J.: Scarecrow, 1985. vii, 147p. bibliog. LC 84-22179. ISBN 0-8108-1760-8.

Laster, compiler of the *Catalogue of Choral Music Arranged in Biblical Order* (see entry 452) offers a list of commercially and privately available recordings of choral ensembles of women, girls, and boys whose voices have not yet changed. Recorded works are listed by composer, arranger, collection, or genre (such as "Gregorian Chant"), giving the title of the work, name of performing ensemble, conductor, record manufacturer, and disc number. At the end is a list of sources for privately issued recordings. The work is suspiciously skimpy—can there be only one treble voice recording of that choral staple, "Go Tell It on the Mountain"? And why include a bibliography that contains one item?

520. Leder, Jan. **Women in Jazz: A Discography of Instrumentalists, 1913-1968**. Westport, Conn.: Greenwood Press, 1985. xv, 305p. index. (Discographies, No. 19). LC 85-17657. ISBN 0-313-24790-0; ISSN 0192-334X.

This listing of recorded works by 250 women instrumentalists pointedly excludes vocalists. The author compiled names from several standard jazz discographies, and admits to difficulty in identifying the gender of some ambiguous names. Section 1 lists recording sessions alphabetically by performer and chronologically under each performer's name. Section 2 chronologically lists recordings on which two or more women perform. The index lists names of all female performers in both sections. Each entry gives the date, the city, and all personnel (male or female) at the session, and lists the title and matrix number of each cut, and the manufacturer and serial number for each record. *Women in Jazz* is useful simply for its enumeration of names of female performers as well as for its discographical information.

521. Lyons, Len. **The 101 Best Jazz Albums: A History of Jazz on Records**. New York: Morrow, 1980. 476p. illus. bibliog. index. LC 80-20392. ISBN 0-688-03720-8; 0-688-08720-5pa.

Lyons is a well-known jazz critic. His subtitle is especially telling, for he uses the 101 albums he has selected as vehicles for short essays encompassing biography, history, and comparative discography. Each of these essays includes a photograph of the album jacket, notes the label and number, and enumerates the musicians and compositions performed. Eight chapters organize the text chronologically from ragtime to free jazz. At the end of each chapter is a discography of other recommended albums which exemplify the style of the period. The volume includes plentiful photographs of jazz musicians, a bibliography listing histories of jazz, and an index to personal names, albums, and compositions mentioned in the text. Lyons's linear portrayal of jazz suffers from being too narrow and selective – for instance, he fails to mention a single recording by Django Reinhardt. *The Essential Jazz Records* (see entry 509) covers similar ground with more daring.

522. Mahwinney, Paul C. **MusicMaster: The 45rpm Record Directory: 35 Years of Recorded Music 1947 to 1982**. Allison Park, Pa.: Record-Rama, 1983. 2v. ISBN 0-910925-02-X.

Record-Rama is a record store and record locating service. The directory grew out of its card file, and consists of two massive paperback volumes. Volume 1 lists recordings by artist; volume 2 lists recordings by song title. Both give identical information about each record: an accession number, which is the same for both sides of the record; artist; song title; manufacturer and number; *MusicMaster* computer number; pressing number; a code indicating vocal, instrumental, or comedy performance; year of original issue; computer number for the verso (flip side); and descriptive information. It is all quite straightforward and easily used.

523. Oja, Carol J., ed. **American Music Recordings: A Discography of 20th-Century U.S. Composers**. A Project of the Institute for Studies in American Music for the Koussevitzky Music Foundation. Foreword by William Schuman. Brooklyn, N.Y.: Institute for Studies in American Music, Conservatory of Music, Brooklyn College of the City of New York, 1982. xxi, 368p. bibliog. index. LC 82-083008. ISBN 0-914678-19-1.

This winner of the annual award given by the Music Library Association for the best book-length bibliography portrays a rich musical heritage in works by some thirteen hundred composers born since 1870 on over thirteen thousand commercially distributed recordings. Records listed include 78, 45, and 33rpm discs available through June 1980. The compiler's concept of "American Music" encompasses works by composers born in the United States and by those who have spent a substantial part of their careers in the United States – Ernest Bloch is included, for instance, but Igor Stravinsky is not. The categorical omission of jazz, folk, and popular music necessitates the drawing of some fine lines – the discography does not list recordings of *West Side Story* or of its vocal excerpts, but includes the concert arrangement of its "Symphonic Dances."

The work is arranged first by composer (giving the years of birth and death), then by composition (giving, in most cases, the date of composition), then by individual entries for performances of compositions. Entries give the record manufacturer's name and disc number, the number of discs in the set (if more than one), and the dates of initial release and deletion from sale. Separate indexes list performing groups, conductors, vocalists and narrators, and instrumentalists. The final page lists errata to these indexes.

524. **Rigler and Deutsch Record Index**. Syracuse, N.Y.: Mi-Kal County-Matic, 1986. 6 separately numbered groups of microfiches.

Since these microfiches have no headers identifying the title and contain no introductory material, a review in *Notes* (42 [March 1986]: 535-37) was consulted to provide the title and background information. This is a union catalog and index to over 600,000 78rpm recordings in five major collections: the Belfer Audio Laboratory and Archive of Syracuse University; the Motion Picture, Broadcasting, and Recorded Sound Division of the Library of Congress; the Rodgers and Hammerstein Archives of Recorded Sound of the New York Public Library; the Stanford University Archive of Recorded Sound; and the Yale Collection of Historical Sound Recordings. To construct the index, compilers entered into computer data taken from the labels of recordings in the five collections.

The sorted data offer six indexing sequences: title, performer, composer, label and issue number, label and matrix number, and library siglum. Many rough discographical edges remain. For instance, the articles "a" and "an" were not ignored in the sorting, with a resulting huge list of songs beginning with those words. Often entries lack information which was not legible on the label of the recording. Entries for the same recording held by more than one library were not combined. These sometimes reveal discrepancies in the entries which could have been resolved with editing. Any pseudonyms on the label must appear as given in the index entries. Yet the vast scope of the project provides not only a union catalog in the library siglum section, but a valuable research tool as well in the versatile indexing to the most important discographical information about a major proportion of recorded music issued in this country.

525. Ruppli, Michael. **Atlantic Records: A Discography**. Westport, Conn.: Greenwood Press, 1979. 4v. index. (Discographies, No. 1). LC 78-75237. ISBN 0-313-21170-1; ISSN 0192-334X.

526. Ruppli, Michael. **The Chess Labels: A Discography**. Westport, Conn.: Greenwood Press, 1983. 2v. index. (Discographies, No. 7). LC 82-25148. ISBN 0-313-23471-X; ISSN 0192-334X.

527. Ruppli, Michael, with assistance from Bill Daniels. **The King Labels: A Discography**. Westport, Conn.: Greenwood Press, 1985. 2v. index. (Discographies, No. 18). LC 85-17655. ISBN 0-313-24771-4; ISSN 0192-334X.

528. Ruppli, Michael, with assistance from Bob Porter. **The Prestige Label: A Discography**. Westport, Conn.: Greenwood Press, 1980. xiii, 377p. index. (Discographies, No. 3). LC 79-8294. ISBN 0-313-22019-0; ISSN 0192-334X.

529. Ruppli, Michael, with assistance from Bob Porter. **The Savoy Label: A Discography**. Westport, Conn.: Greenwood Press, 1980. xix, 442p. illus. index. (Discographies, No. 2). LC 79-7727. ISBN 0-313-21199-X; ISSN 0192-334X.

Ruppli's prolific output of discographies is making available a wealth of detail about postwar recordings of all types of popular music. His access to the files of the record companies whose output he details gives him an advantage over other discographers who have little more than issued records with which to work. The five labels and their subsidiaries which he has covered thus far have been some of the most important recorders of American jazz, blues, rhythm and blues, gospel, and (from Atlantic Records) rock. The format of each discography varies according to the numbering procedures of each company, but in general each lists, in a reasonably clear typescript, recording sessions either in chronological order or by master number. Entries for sessions indicate the artist or group and often backup musicians, city where the recording took place, date, titles of pieces recorded, master numbers, and number of the recording or reissue. An index in each discography lists artists or groups.

530. Rust, Brian. **The American Dance Band Discography 1917-1942.** New Rochelle, N.Y.: Arlington House, 1975. 2v. index. LC 75-33689. ISBN 0-87000-248-1.

This is a companion to Rust's *Jazz Records* (see entry 531) whose two thick volumes it rivals in bulk. Rust maintains a plausible distinction between jazz and dance music; in the case of crossover artists such as Artie Shaw, entries for records appear in both works. The present title lists, by band, 78rpm records released in the United States, Canada, or Britain from the time of the first jazz recordings in 1917 to the recording ban beginning 31 July 1942 of the American Federation of Musicians. Beneath the names of bands, entries list recording sessions, giving the musicians, place, date, tunes recorded, matrix number of each piece, and the manufacturer and disc number on which each tune was released. Rust advises anyone planning to kick off his or her shoes that "all titles are fox trots unless marked otherwise," and carefully notes waltzes, rumbas, and other less conventional rhythms. The index lists the names of individual musicians within bands.

531. Rust, Brian. **Jazz Records 1897-1942.** 5th rev. and enl. ed. Chigwell, England: Storyville Publications and Company, 1982. 2v. index. ISBN 0-902391-04-6.

The successive editions (1st ed. 1965) of Rust's enormous discography of 78 rpm records have established a framework for the appreciation of and research in early jazz. His scope is broad enough to include American and British musicians and others of international stature and narrow enough to exclude blues, country and western, and dance music. The introduction defines the work as a list of "discs made in the name of jazz, or of dance music with close affiliation to jazz, as well as vocal records with jazz groups used as accompaniment, made between 1917 and 1942. Also included are important and interesting records made of ragtime." The compilation uses as closing date the 31 July 1942 ban on recording by the American Federation of Musicians.

Individual recording sessions form the basis for organization. Sessions are listed by the individual or group credited on the record label (with some standardization of minor variations or of obvious pseudonyms). Thus, performances by Stephane Grappelli together with Django Reinhardt appear under each of their names and also under the "Quintette of the Hot Club of France," depending on the initial credit on the record label. Entries for sessions indicate musicians, city, date, matrix number, title of each tune, the "take" (symbols indicate first, second, and so forth), and the record labels and numbers on which each tune appeared. Two indexes covering musicians and titles of tunes, and a list of additions and corrections appear at the end of the second volume. Rust's work has been a model for other discographies. His form of entry, which focuses on individual sessions, is particularly appropriate to the identification of jazz recordings which modern LP reissues often gather together on one disc.

532. Sanders, Alan, comp. **Walter Legge: A Discography.** Foreword by Elisabeth Legge-Schwartzkopf. Westport, Conn.: Greenwood Press, 1984. xx, 452p. index. (Discographies, No. 11). LC 84-8991. ISBN 0-313-24441-3; ISSN 0192-334X.

From the 1930s to the 1970s, Legge was a prolific producer of records in his native Britain and throughout Europe. He worked with Sir Thomas Beecham, formed the Philharmonia Orchestra, married soprano Elisabeth Schwartzkopf, and attracted many artists of international fame to the studios of EMI in London. Though little relates these performers to each other, their collective prominence lends a significance to this discography of the hundreds of recordings Legge produced. The arrangement is chronological. A short narrative introduces the listings for each year. Within each year, entries list recordings by composer and work, noting the performers, matrix number, and manufacturer and recording number. Indexes list works and names of recording artists.

533. Sears, Richard S. **V-Discs: A History and Discography**. Prepared under the auspices of the Association for Recorded Sound Collections. Westport, Conn.: Greenwood Press, 1980. xciii, 1166p. illus. index. (Association for Recorded Sound Collections Discographic Series; Discographies, No. 5). LC 80-1022. ISBN 0-313-22207-X; ISSN 0192-334X.

Between 1943 and 1949, the U.S. War Department (later the Defense Department) recorded and distributed to troops more than eight million V-Discs. These were 78rpm recordings by volunteer musicians whose number included Glenn Miller, Bing Crosby, Duke Ellington, Count Basie, the NBC Symphony Orchestra conducted by Arturo Toscanini, the CBS Symphony conducted by Fritz Reiner, the Boston Symphony Orchestra conducted by Serge Koussevitzky, and many other musicians of international fame. Few of the V-Discs have been commercially released, and very little has been published about them—for instance, *The New Grove Dictionary of American Music* (see entry 65) has no entry for that heading. Sears provides a sixty-page introduction to the V-Disc project which includes pertinent photographs and letters. The discography occupies most of the volume and lists recording sessions by artists and groups. Entries give the date of the session, location, text of any spoken introduction, disc numbers, names of featured musicians, mastering date, notes on Armed Forces Radio Service transcriptions of the recording, and EP or LP releases. Appendixes list recordings by number in three sections: EP or LP discs; Army V-Discs; and Navy V-Discs.

534. Sheridan, Chris. **Count Basie: A Bio-Discography**. Westport, Conn.: Greenwood Press, 1986. xxvi, 1350p. illus. bibliog. index. (Discographies, No. 22). LC 86-9916. ISBN 0-313-24935-0; ISSN 0192-334X.

Sheridan has gathered and arranged in chronological order an enormous amount of discographical data on one of the most prolific artists in jazz. The work covers some one thousand recorded performances from 1929 to 1984, including commercial recordings, electrical transcriptions primarily for the Armed Forces Radio Service, films, radio and television broadcasts, and recordings on location. An informal narrative interspersed throughout the discography locates sessions within the events in Basie's life and travels. Details for each session give the date, location, musicians, and tunes, and note for each tune the master number, duration, soloists, and the resulting records by label and number. Appendixes include a list of recordings on EP, LP, CD, or tape, with reference to recording sessions in the main text; a day-by-day itinerary of the band covering nearly fifty years; and a bibliography of books and articles dealing with Basie and the history of jazz. Indexes list film and video appearances, names and subjects in the narrative, arrangers, musicians, and tune titles.

535. Stahl, Dorothy. **A Selected Discography of Solo Song: A Cumulation through 1971**. Detroit: Information Coordinators, 1972. 137p. index. (Detroit Studies in Music Bibliography, No. 24). LC 79-90432. ISBN 0-911772-35-9; 0-89990-009-7pa.

Supplement, 1971-1974. 1976. 99p. index. (Detroit Studies in Music Bibliography, No. 34). LC 76-12132. ISBN 0-911772-80-4.

Supplement, 1975-1982. 1984. 236p. (Detroit Studies in Music Bibliography, No. 52). LC 84-19794. ISBN 0-89990-923-2.

The intent of this continuing listing of LP releases, as stated in the preface to each volume, is "to make accessible to teachers and students vocal works on recordings that can be easily procured." The scope of successive supplements continues to broaden: the first covered the releases of thirty-four record manufacturers, the second covered those of thirty-eight, and the most recent covered releases of fifty-five, both domestic and foreign. The three volumes follow an identical format. The first section lists songs by composer and title (the ubiquitous "Anonymous" fails to make an appearance—no folk songs are to be found here), giving the vocalist and the title and number of the LP. The second section lists, by composer or, in the case of collections, by manufacturer and disc number, the recordings analyzed in the first section. The third section is an index to song titles and first lines. The failure to include recording dates in any of the three volumes is most inconvenient in the case of the *Cumulation through 1971*, which lists many examples of the rerecording of the same work by the same singer, but offers no way of determining the chronological sequence.

536. **Studies in Jazz**. Dan Morgenstern and William Weinberg, general ed. Metuchen, N.J.: Scarecrow and the Institute of Jazz Studies, Rutgers University, 1982- .

The series includes thorough and highly detailed discographies of important figures in jazz.

537. No. 1: Berger, Morroe, Edward Berger, and James Patrick. **Benny Carter: A Life in American Music**. 1982. 2v. illus. music. bibliog. discog. index. LC 82-10634. ISBN 0-8108-1580-X.

Volume 1 traces Carter's career not by relating tales of one-night stands but by using his music as a focal point for a musicological and historical survey of jazz which, through liberal bibliographical references, serves also as a survey of its literature. Volume 2 consists primarily of a discography which is subdivided by Carter's often exclusive roles as either instrumentalist or arranger and composer. The instrumentalist half is arranged in conventionally chronological order by session. The arranger and composer half is arranged alphabetically by tune. Both sections include appropriate indexes. The extensive bibliography provides complete citations to the references in the text.

538. No. 2: Laubich, Arnold, and Ray Spencer. **Art Tatum: A Guide to His Recorded Music**. 1982. xxviii, 330p. bibliog. index. LC 82-10752. ISBN 0-8108-1582-6.

This discography is notable not only for its thorough coverage of Tatum's work but also for the attention it pays to recordings issued outside the United States. It is organized chronologically by recording session. A "Compilation of Issued Discs" organizes releases by label. There are indexes to titles of tunes and musicians, and lists of recorded imitations in Tatum's style, films in which he appeared, published compositions or transcriptions, and piano rolls of Tatum's music.

539. No. 3: Doran, James M. **Erroll Garner: The Most Happy Piano**. 1985. xv, 481p. illus. bibliog. index. LC 84-17886. ISBN 0-8108-1745-4.

This laudatory record of Garner's life and music opens with a collection of over forty transcribed interviews with family members and acquaintances. Their value is anecdotal rather than evaluative. The discography, which occupies two-thirds of the book, lists each of Garner's recording sessions, detailing the date and musicians of each, and enumerating the compositions that were recorded and the records on which each was issued. Following is a list of unissued sessions. A "Compilation of Issued Discs" organizes releases by label. Song title and artist indexes, a filmography, and a general index make details easy to locate.

540. No. 4: Brown, Scott E. **James P. Johnson: A Case of Mistaken Identity**. Discography by Robert Hilbert. 1986. viii, 500p. illus. bibliog. index. LC 86-3830. ISBN 0-8108-1887-6.

Like other works in the series, this is a combination of biography and discography. The biography includes appendixes listing stage productions to which Johnson contributed and a list of his compositions. The discography covering the years 1917 to 1950 is organized by session, and gives for each entry the date and place, musicians, matrix number, compositions performed, and recordings on which each take was issued.

* * *

541. Tudor, Dean. **Popular Music: An Annotated Guide to Recordings**. Littleton, Colo.: Libraries Unlimited, 1983. xxii, 647p. bibliog. index. LC 83-18749. ISBN 0-87287-395-1.

Popular Music combines and updates material from four earlier works compiled by Dean Tudor and Nancy Tudor and published by Libraries Unlimited in 1979: *Black Music*, *Contemporary Popular Music*, *Grass Roots Music*, and *Jazz*. Here Tudor surveys sixty-two hundred LP recordings in six sections: black music, folk music, jazz music, mainstream music (including vocalists, big bands, and musical theater and film), popular religious music, and rock music. Each of these sections is subdivided into specific genres. An asterisk indicates a recording of particular importance. Tudor's annotations range in style from curt to verbose, from superficial to meaty, from flippant to earnest. In fact, his opinionated evaluations sometimes obscure otherwise useful summaries of an album's contents. The breadth of his selection, however, compensates for his lack of subtlety and serves a need for a comprehensive overview of a goodly portion of the "American Music" which has been "discovered" in the last few years. A fifteen-page bibliography and an index to all performing artists enhances the value of this as a solid reference work.

542. Warren, Richard, Jr., comp. **Charles E. Ives: Discography**. New Haven, Conn.: Historical Sound Recordings, Yale University Library, 1972. xii, 124p. index. (Historical Sound Recordings Publication Series, No. 1). LC 72-190226. ISBN 0-317-40565-9.

At the time of this compilation, Warren was curator of historical sound recordings at Yale. He bases the discography on the Ives Collection at Yale, which holds all but one of the items mentioned. Entries are arranged by title of work, giving the Kirkpatrick catalog number for each and cross-references to variant titles. Beneath each title is a list of recordings in chronological order, indicating the performers, place and date, the label and serial number, and sometimes matrix number of any commercial recording which resulted from the performance. The main section lists 560 recorded pieces, and a supplementary section lists forty-three pieces. Added lists enumerate documentary broadcasts of discussions of Ives and recorded comments about Ives at Yale by those who were familiar with him. An index lists the performers on all recordings.

19

Current and Serial Discographies

The titles in this section represent the major current discographies in the United States, France, Great Britain, and West Germany, along with several other ongoing compilations. All, except the *IJS Jazz Register* (see entry 551), *The Green Compact Disc Catalog* (see entry 550), MUSICAT (see entry 554), and *Phonolog* (see entry 555) include LPs, cassettes, and CDs. Although there is a healthy international trade in recordings, multinational recording companies distribute recordings under different labels in different countries, and many smaller labels never cross international boundaries. Thus for current discographical research, several of these lists may be necessary. For retrospective research, the major national discographies may not offer the detail of more specialized works, but they provide the most complete overall listing of available recordings within a country at a certain point in time.

543. **Bielefelder Katalog Jazz**. Vols. 1-18. Bielefeld, West Germany: Bielefelder Verlagsanstalt, 1963-80; Vols. 19-21. Karlsruhe, West Germany: G. Braun, 1980-83; Vol. 22- . Stuttgart, West Germany: Vereinigte Motor-Verlage, 1984- . annual. LC 84-640595. ISSN 0171-9505.

544. **Bielefelder Katalog Klassik**. Vols. 8-28, No. 1. Bielefeld, West Germany: Bielefelder Verlagsanstalt, 1960-80; Vol. 28, No. 2-Vol. 31. Karlsruhe, West Germany: G. Braun, 1980-83; Vol. 32- . Stuttgart, West Germany: Vereinigte Motor-Verlage, 1984- . semiannual. LC 83-640928. ISSN 0721-7153.

Continuing *Die Langspielplatte*, the *Bielefelder Katalog Klassik* is the West German equivalent of the classical parts of the Schwann series (see entries 557-59) from the United States; it lists recordings currently available within the country. The first section of this catalog lists, in an easily legible format, classical recordings, by composer and composition. Following is a short listing, by author, of recorded works of literature. The second section lists records by manufacturer and disc or tape number, giving the complete contents of each record.

The jazz catalog has no equivalent in the United States. It contains three sections: a title index to each composition on each album; an artist index to groups and individual performers on each album; and a label index, which lists recordings by manufacturer and disc or tape number, and within each entry, details the date of recording, and lists each composition and each performer. Thus the *Bielefelder Katalog Jazz* offers more than just a list of recordings available in West Germany, and can serve as an index to the contents of jazz albums.

545. **Billboard's Music Yearbook**. Joel Whitburn, comp. Menomonee Falls, Wisc.: Record Research, 1983- . annual.

Whitburn's name is associated with a number of works compiling data from the charts of *Billboard* (see entry 573) which track the popularity of newly released recordings. This recently begun series will serve to exemplify Whitburn's work. Originally titled *Joel Whitburn's Music Yearbook*, it lists all recordings which debuted on *Billboard*'s charts during the year. Singles and albums are categorized by the markets to which they appeal, such as pop, country, or black. Entries, arranged by artist, give the song or album title, manufacturer and serial number, and the initial date of appearance, peak position, and number of weeks on the charts.

546. **Diapason catalogue general classique**. Paris: Diapason, 1964- . annual. ads. LC 77-647796. ISSN 0498-9105.

This is another national variation on the Schwann series (see entries 557-59). *Diapason* lists LP records, CDs, and cassettes currently available in France. It is organized by composer and work, with a section for collections. An index lists performers. *Diapason* has its own distinct features, aside from its large format: a list of works with distinctive titles which enables a user to identify the composer; and the inclusion of references to reviews in the magazine *Diapason*.

547. **Gramophone Classical Catalogue**. Vol. 1- . Harrow, England: General Gramophone Publications, 1953- . quarterly. LC 76-640055. ISSN 0309-4367.

548. **Gramophone Compact Disc Guide and Catalogue**. Vol. 1- . Harrow, England: General Gramophone Publications, 1984- . annual. LC 86-658041. ISSN 0267-2162.

549. **Gramophone Popular Catalogue: The Pop Cat**. Vol. 1- . Harrow, England: General Gramophone Publications, 1955- . quarterly. LC 76-640050. ISSN 0309-4359.

Like the Schwann catalogs in the United States (see entries 557-59), the Gramophone catalogs provide an ongoing listing of currently available recordings; in this case, however, they list those available in the United Kingdom. The *Classical Catalogue* (title varies) lists LPs and tapes, and *The Pop Cat* includes CDs. The arrangement of the *Classical Catalogue*, by composer and work, with an index to performers, is similar to that of the classical sections of the Schwann catalogs. *The Pop Cat* lists, by performer, light, popular, dance, jazz, folk, film, and show music. It differs from Schwann in its omission of recording dates and by its inclusion, within the entry for each album, of all pieces performed. The *Compact Disc Guide* follows these formats. A star symbol in any of the three catalogs indicates that the entry is a new release.

550. **The Green Compact Disc Catalog**. Vol. 1- . Peterborough, N.H.: WGE Publishing, 1985- . bimonthly. ads. LC 84-641718. ISSN 8756-3851.

This competitor to the *Schwann Compact Disc Catalog* (see entry 559) offers similar but more abbreviated listings of currently available CDs, offering an appeal more to the audiophile at home than to the record merchant. It includes short reviews, editorials, and comments from readers by means of a "reader CD rating card" included in each issue with which readers can vote for their favorites. Over a dozen categories organize the entries. Entries for classical recordings are organized by composer; all others by performer.

551. **IJS Jazz Register**. Newark, N.J.: Institute of Jazz Studies, Rutgers University, 1979- . quarterly. microfiche. index. LC 85-14524. ISSN 0889-8723.

The register of the Institute of Jazz Studies provides cataloging and indexing for two groups of jazz recordings: 78rpm records which predate electrical recording processes of the mid-1920s; and recent LP recordings. The latter group includes reissues from the 1960s, 1970s, and 1980s; airchecks; broadcast performances; recordings on obscure labels; rare and unique recordings in the IJS collection; and tapes onto which these in the last group have been recorded. Each new quarterly issue supersedes the previous issue.

The main register lists in an arbitrary sequence analytical entries for individual tracks (except for some recent LPs) and entries for each LP itself. Entries give the title of the LP or tune; performer; name of the label and number of the disc; a physical description of the disc; individual performers; duration of the tune or the album; a list of the contents of albums; subject headings; and additional detail including references to Rust's *Jazz Records* (see entry 531). Indexes list individual performers and groups with which they played; performers and the titles of selections they played; performing groups; titles of tracks and albums; composers; and label names and issue numbers. From 1978 to 1983, the institute input these cataloging records into the OCLC (Online Computer Library Center) database, and it has input records since 1983 into the RLIN (Research Libraries Information Network) database. One can only wish that such thorough indexing were available for a greater number of recordings.

552. Library of Congress. Copyright Office. **Catalog of Copyright Entries, Third Series: Part 14, Sound Recordings**. Vols. 28-31. Washington, D.C.: Library of Congress, Copyright Office, 1974-77. LC 06-35347. ISSN 0094-3592. SuDoc LC 3.6/5: .

553. Library of Congress. Copyright Office. **Catalog of Copyright Entries, Fourth Series: Part 7, Sound Recordings**. Vol. 1- . Washington, D.C.: Library of Congress, Copyright Office, 1978- . semiannual. LC 79-640905. ISSN 0163-7355. SuDoc LC 3.6/6: .

The catalog records works deposited with the office in order to register copyright. Although it was begun in 1891, a separate listing of recordings did not appear until 1974. Entries give a bibliographic citation for each item along with its registration number. The third series provided an index to names and titles, followed by the main list in registration number sequence. The fourth series arranges recordings by title, and the index lists names associated with each recording. Renewal registrations appear in a separate list. Since 1979, the catalog has been published in microfiche.

554. **MUSICAT**. Woodbridge, Ont.: Esson and Tucker, 1986- . quarterly.

MUSICAT is an information service for recorded music. It supplies subscribers with diskettes containing access programs and discographic data for LP and CD recordings. The system presently contains data for about six thousand recordings. Literature accompanying a demonstration program maintains that the company catalogs "all new releases." Subscribers can also enter their own bibliographic records onto the system. A set of sample diskettes contained works by Schubert, Mozart, Vivaldi, and W. C. Handy. Discographic records include composer, title and variant titles, instrumentation, key signature, opus and catalog numbers, date of composition, publisher, first performance, performers, record manufacturer, and label number, in addition to other detail. Users locate data by means of a series of menu-driven procedures which prompt for search terms and offer "true" or "false" options.

555. **Phonolog Reporter**. San Diego, Calif.: Trade Service Publications, 1948- . weekly. looseleaf. LC 81-406. ISSN 0279-6562.

Phonolog is first a sales tool for record stores and incidentally a valuable tool in libraries as an index to currently available 45rpm and LP recordings, CDs, and cassette tapes. It consists of a tray of looseleaf pages at least a foot thick. The first three-quarters are biege and cover popular records; the second are blue and cover classical records. The popular section begins with a list of titles of individual tunes on singles and on albums, and gives the record numbers. The next part of the popular section lists popular artists and their albums and singles. The third lists popular albums alphabetically by title, giving the contents of each album. The first part of the classical section lists titles of works, performers, and the recordings on which they appear. Names of individual composers further subdivide generic titles such as "Concerto." The second part is a composer index to the list of titles. Finally, the last part of the classical section lists performers, works, and recordings. The most important aspect of *Phonolog* is its title indexing.

556. **Records in Review**. Vols. 1-26. Great Barrington, Mass.: publisher varies, 1955-81. annual, index. LC 55-10600. ISSN 0073-2095.

Readers have long depended on the reviews in *High Fidelity* (see entry 601) both to announce and to evaluate new LP recordings. Until its demise, *Records in Review* compiled these reviews annually from monthly issues of the previous year, and reprinted them with little alteration. Each volume arranges the reviews by composer, and groups collections in a separate section. An index in each volume lists all performers.

557. **Schwann (Super Schwann)**. Vol. 38- . Boston: Schwann Publications, 1986- . quarterly. ads. LC 86-25856. ISSN 0742-7239.

558. **Schwann Artist Issue**. Vol. 1- . Boston: Schwann Publications, 1975- . annual. ads. LC 76-645816. ISSN 0582-1487.

559. **Schwann Compact Disc Catalog**. Vol. 1- . Boston: Schwann Publications, 1985- . monthly. ads. index. LC 86-645087. ISSN 0893-0430.

Schwann changes its format almost with the change of seasons. Earlier titles were *Schwann Record and Tape Guide* and *Schwann Long-Playing Record Catalog* (Vols. 1-37, 1948-85). This bibliographic information can only claim to represent the catalogs as of early 1987. The function of the Schwann catalogs remains the same, however: to list new and currently available recordings in the United States.

The CD catalog lists in three sections newly released CDs, newly released LPs and cassette tapes, and all CDs released to date. These sections list recordings within categories: classical (organized by composer and individual work); electronic; collections; musicals, movies, and TV shows; popular; popular collections; jazz; jazz anthologies; spoken and miscellaneous; and international pop and folk. An index covers performers on recordings in the classical section of the main CD list. The *Super Schwann* organizes all currently available recordings in all formats within the same categories as the CD catalog. The *Artist Issue* lists currently available classical recordings within categories by type of performer: orchestras and chamber ensembles; conductors; instrumental soloists; choral groups; operatic groups; and vocalists. Entries in all catalogs of the Schwann series give the manufacturer and disc or tape number, and a variety of other details such as birth and death dates of composers, and dates of recording for jazz and popular recordings.

Since Schwann drops from its lists recordings withdrawn from sale, back issues remain valuable for retrospective research. The best source for the most current Schwann catalogs is often a record store, which demands the most recent listings, rather than a library, which most likely will follow at a more leisurely pace in its acquisitions and cataloging procedures.

Part 6
SUPPLEMENTAL SOURCES

20

Current Periodicals

This chapter includes the major scholarly journals in English and a selection of those from Europe. All are currently published as of early 1987. Prominent magazines which one might find on a newsstand are also included. Publications of organizations and societies which devote attention to matters about music outside of their own organizational concerns are included here; others can be found mentioned under the name of the sponsoring organization in chapter 21. Journals devoted to audio technology have been included if they also offer reviews of recordings or coverage of musical performers or performances. No journals devoted to composers are listed. Many of these are published by societies devoted to a particular composer and will be found in chapter 21. A useful, but now somewhat out-of-date, listing of these by John R. Douglas is "Publications Devoted to Individual Musicians: A Checklist" (*Bulletin of Bibliography* 33 [April-June 1976]: 135-39+). *Notes* (see entry 639) and *19th Century Music* (see entry 638) occasionally review new periodicals.

Titles appear in alphabetical order. Citations give the date and volume number of the first issue of the title, and the location and name of the present publisher. Entries note special features such as the presence of regular bibliographies, advertising, illustrative material, notated music, and reviews of recordings, books, music, or performances. The use of an editorial board ("ed. board") or similar refereeing process to select articles was noted if that information appeared on the masthead. Cumulative indexes have been noted. Annotations represent the periodicals as they have appeared over the last few years; no attempt has been made to provide complete histories.

560. **Acta Musicologica**. Vol. 1- , 1928- . Basel, Switzerland: Bärenreiter-Verlag, for the International Musicological Society. semiannual. annual index. ed. board. ads. music. LC 57-33616. ISSN 0001-6241.

The six to eight substantial, scholarly articles published in each issue of the last few years have tended to fall into four areas: historical studies of Western music from the thirteenth to the nineteenth centuries; ethnomusicological studies of non-Western musics; reviews of musicological studies in individual countries; and bibliographic surveys of research on individual composers. Other articles have reviewed or presented the activities of large-scale publishing ventures, such as *The New Grove* or the forthcoming *Music in the*

Life of Man. Most articles are in English or German. A "Commentaries" section notes future conferences or publishing activities. Volume 25 provides an index to volumes 1-25.

561. **American Choral Review**. Vol. 1- , 1958- . Philadelphia: The American Choral Foundation. quarterly. cumulated index. ads. music. reviews of performances, recordings. LC 78-421. ISSN 0002-7898.

Each issue includes several informal articles, analytical studies, and notes on performance practice of individual choral works or genres. Many issues are devoted to studies of one or several works of a single composer. Reviews of both performances and recordings of choral works, and an enumeration of recently published choral scores, appear irregularly. There is an index to volumes 1-13; indexing is also provided by Whitten's bibliography (see entry 369).

562. **American Music: A Quarterly Journal Devoted to All Aspects of American Music and Music in America**. Vol. 1- , 1983- . Champaign, Ill.: Sonneck Society and University of Illinois Press. quarterly. annual index. ed. board. ads. illus. music. reviews of books, recordings. LC 83-643978. ISSN 0734-4392.

"Our model is Oscar Sonneck," proclaimed the editor in the first issue of *American Music*, seeing in that scholar an inspiration to grant a legitimacy to the richness of American musical life. These scholarly articles offer a point of view more often historical, aesthetic, or sociological rather than analytical in approach. The selection of articles has included an account of a performance of John Cage's *HPSCHD*, a study of Kansas City jazz, an interview with Milton Babbitt, and an account of early nineteenth-century concerts in New York. Each issue features substantial book reviews and reviews of recordings of works of American composers or of historical collections of early popular music.

563. **American Music Teacher**. Official Journal of the Music Teachers National Association. Vol. 1- , 1951- . Cincinnati, Ohio: Music Teachers National Association. 6/yr. ads. illus. reviews of books, music. LC 55-34023. ISSN 0003-0112.

Similar in purpose to *Music Educators Journal* (see entry 624), *American Music Teacher* combines articles on broad musical topics with those addressed specifically to teachers. News of the association features prominently. Books reviewed are of interest to teachers; reviews of music evaluate works in pedagogical terms.

564. **The American Organist**. Vol. 13- , 1979- . New York: American Guild of Organists. monthly. annual index. ads. illus. reviews of books, music, recordings. LC 79-643327. ISSN 0164-3150.

Continuing *Music*, this is the official journal of not only the American Guild of Organists, but of the Royal Canadian College of Organists and of the Associated Pipe Organ Builders of America as well. The cover of each issue appropriately displays a striking color photograph of an organ or a console. Reflecting the interests of these several societies, *American Organist* offers articles on both organs and music. Special supplements on Handel (February 1985), Bach (March 1985), and Schütz and Scarlatti (October 1985) have examined their compositions for organ and recordings of these compositions. Interviews, news of the organizations and their members, a calendar of recitals, announcements of new organ installations, and short nontechnical articles on organ construction and mechanics appear regularly. There is an index to the years 1967-77.

565. **American Record Guide**. Vols. 1-39, 1935-72; Vol. 40- , 1976- . Millbrook, N.Y.: Salem Research. bimonthly. annual index. ads. illus. reviews of recordings. LC 42-9739. ISSN 0003-0716.

The *American Record Guide* resumed interrupted publication with its editor's promise in the first issue of volume 40 to "again endeavor to review the latest in classical recordings as accurately and impartially as possible." Currently, its regular staff contributes signed comparative and evaluative reviews of about one hundred LPs and an increasing number of CDs in each issue. Occasional columns foray into reviews of jazz, film music, or rereleased mono recordings. Regular features include "In Box," a list of recordings received during the previous two months, and a list of addresses of record distributors.

566. **The American Recorder**. Vol. 1- , 1960- . New York: American Recorder Society. quarterly. ed. board. ads. illus. music. reviews of books, music. ISSN 0003-0724.

Similar to *The Guitar Review* (see entry 599) in its attractive design and sophisticated appeal to both amateurs and professionals, this journal for players of the recorder mingles historical articles on the recorder and other early instruments and their music with technical articles on recorder construction and practical articles on sight reading and practicing. Regular features include good coverage of early music festivals, news of local society chapters, insightful reviews of books and of music for the recorder, and at least one modern or historical piece of music for the recorder.

567. **American String Teacher**. Vol. 1- , 1951- . Athens, Ga.: American String Teachers Association. quarterly. ed. board. ads. illus. reviews of books, music. LC 59-30834. ISSN 0003-1313.

A magazine for students and teachers of bowed instruments, harp, and guitar, *American String Teacher* offers news of competitions and conventions, and short informal articles on performers and performance on all types of stringed instruments. For instance, the Summer 1986 issue included articles on Swedish keyed fiddles and on Gasparo da Salo, inventor of the violin. Regular columns give special attention to each instrument. Reviews of music briefly evaluate new compositions in terms of student performance.

568. **Annual Review of Jazz Studies**. Vol. 1- , 1982- . New Brunswick, N.J.: Transaction Books. annual. ed. board. music. reviews of books. LC 82-644466. ISSN 0731-0641.

Easily the most scholarly and literate forum in the English language for the examination of jazz, the *Annual Review* (published in connection with the Institute of Jazz Studies at Rutgers University and originally titled *Journal of Jazz Studies*) brings a sophistication to the study of jazz which, except for occasional articles in *Black Perspective in Music* (see entry 575), is rarely found. Well-documented articles by prominent scholars take the form of musical analyses, discographies, interviews, and studies of the social setting of jazz. Musical examples are plentiful. A selection of articles includes a description of the *IJS Jazz Register* (see entry 551) (1 [1982]: 110-27); a study of computer-aided analysis (3 [1985]: 41-70); and an examination of bebop melodic lines (3 [1985]: 97-120). Reviews, generally written by Edward Berger and Dan Morgenstern of the institute staff, are few, but long and aggressively evaluative.

569. **Archiv für Musikwissenschaft**. Vol. 1- , 1918- . Stuttgart, West Germany: Franz Steiner Verlag Wiesbaden GmbH. quarterly. annual index. ed. board. ads. music. LC 54-41506. ISSN 0003-9292.

The several articles in each issue represent some of the most outstanding scholarship in West Germany on broad topics of the variety found in *The Musical Quarterly* (see entry 631). The emphasis is generally on the music of German composers, but a notable exception was the recent "Was ist Ragtime?" (42, no. 2 [1985]: 69-86).

570. **Asian Music**. Journal of the Society for Asian Music. Vol. 1- , 1969- . New York: Society for Asian Music. semiannual. ed. board. illus. music. reviews of books, recordings. LC 72-621878. ISSN 0004-9202.

The term "Asian music" identifies a group of musical styles as distinct as the peoples and the geography of the continent. Recent issues of *Asian Music* have reflected this diversity in topics such as the liturgical music of Jews who emigrated from Bombay to

Israel, Western music as performed in nineteenth- and twentieth-century Egypt, music of the modern Burmese Hsaing ensemble, and the instruments of Malay music. Sociology, history, musical analysis, and lyrical analysis are among its approaches. Most articles employ musical examples, line drawings, or photographs to introduce musical forms which are unfamiliar to the West. Reviews are few, but highlight materials which are too esoteric for coverage in other journals.

571. **Association for Recorded Sound Collections Journal**. Vol. 1- , 1968- . Washington, D.C.: Association for Recorded Sound Collections. 3/yr. index 1968-79. ads. bibliog. discog. reviews of books, recordings. LC 79-7391. ISSN 0004-5438.

A low-budget design and chronically late publication do not diminish the value of the journal for discographers. It features articles on record collections and historical recording techniques. Of particular interest was the "Survey of Record Collectors' Societies" (16, no. 3 [1984]: 17-36). Discographies list recordings of historical record labels or of an individual composer's works. Book and record reviews emphasize items for the specialist: discographies and histories of recording companies, and reissues of historical recordings or comparisons of performances by different artists.

572. **Audio**. Vol. 38- , 1954- . New York: CBS Magazines. monthly. ads. illus. reviews of audio equipment, recordings. LC 80-11244. ISSN 0004-752X.

Like *Stereo Review* (see entry 661), *Audio* is a magazine for people who are as interested in the electronic reproduction of music as in its substance. Its emphasis is on evaluations of audio equipment, although it does include an occasional feature on a popular musician (December 1986 featured the aging Jerry Lieber and Mike Stoller). About thirty reviews in each issue cover classical and popular CDs and LPs. A distinctive strength of *Audio* is its ability to put as much technical data into evaluative articles as other equipment reviews, yet to patiently explain otherwise obfuscating detail to readers in the "Questions" column.

573. **Billboard: The International Newsweekly of Music and Home Entertainment**. Vol. 1- , 1894- . New York: Billboard Publications. weekly, except last week in December. ads. illus. reviews of recordings. LC 64-36753. ISSN 0006-2510.

The voice of the recording industry, *Billboard* reports on and promotes the sale and broadcasting of records, CDs, and videocassettes. In short articles and colloquial jargon it covers corporate, legal, advertising, and merchandising news. *Billboard*'s albums, singles, and videos charts are important indicators of weekly sales in categories such as pop, adult contemporary, classical, and black music. The final issue of each year is a wrap-up of sales and performers. The charts, the weekly playlists from the largest and most influential top forty radio stations, and the brief promotional reviews of new recordings determine, in a significant way, what America listens to.

574. **Black Music Research Journal**. 1980- . Chicago: Center for Black Music Research, Columbia College. annual. ed. board. ads. illus. music. reviews of books, recordings. LC 83-641760. ISSN 0276-3605.

Research itself, rather than musical analysis or biography, is the primary focus of *Black Music Research Journal*. In this way it differentiates itself from *Black Perspective in Music* (see entry 575). The 1986 issue includes papers given at the National Conference on Black Music Research that addressed black music biography, the preparation of a black music dictionary, and the Jazz Oral History Project. Some articles are bibliographical in nature, such as Dominique-René de Lerma's "A Concordance of Black Music Entries in Five Encyclopedias: Bakers, Ewen, Grove, MGG, and Rich" (1981-82: 127-50). The few reviews are article-length examinations of individual works.

575. **Black Perspective in Music**. Vol. 1- , 1973- . Cambria Heights, N.Y.: Foundation for Research in the Afro-American Creative Arts. semiannual. annual index. ed. board. ads. illus. music. reviews of books, music, recordings. LC 73-642106. ISSN 0090-7790.

American music, especially jazz, features significantly in these articles whose approach ranges from a scholarly study of the use of ostinato in black improvised music to an interview with composer Undine Smith Moore. When articles cover a topic beyond the United States, it is generally to survey the music of an African or a Caribbean country. Authors are primarily historians and musicologists; a "+" symbol in the list of contributors and elsewhere in the journal indicates those who are black. Many issues feature book and record reviews, listings of new books and dissertations pertaining to black music or printed music by black composers, and notes on recent performances or events. Issue number two of each year provides obituaries. Volume 10 includes an index to volumes 1-10.

576. **British Journal of Music Education**. Vol. 1- , 1984- . Cambridge, England: Cambridge University Press. 3/yr. annual index. ed. board. illus. reviews of books, music. LC 85-642039. ISSN 0265-0517.

The stated aims of the journal are "to provide clear accounts of current issues and research in progress and particularly to strengthen professional development and improve practice within music education." Although many of its authors are Americans, the United States can offer no equal to this journal's fine, long, scholarly articles. Most of their topics have evolved out of classroom situations into reports of research or overviews relating to a variety of kinds of music education. An annual cassette tape includes recorded examples of music referred to in that volume's articles. Critical reviews examine publications of both pedagogical and general musical interest.

577. **Bulletin of the Council for Research in Music Education**. No. 1- , 1963- . Urbana, Ill.: Council for Research in Music Education. quarterly. index to Nos. 1-12 in No. 13. reviews of books, dissertations. LC 79-10478. ISSN 0010-9894.

The bulletin is a forum for reports on research, surveys of research, and discursive articles on broad questions of learning and teaching in music. The reviews of books vary considerably in quality, but the several reviews in each issue of doctoral dissertations – an unusual feature – carefully and critically examine the objectives, methodology, and results of each.

578. **Cadence: The American Review of Jazz & Blues**. Vol. 1- , 1976- . Redwood, N.Y.: Cadence Magazine. monthly. ads. illus. reviews of books, records. LC 81-640946. ISSN 0162-0973.

Interviews and record reviews – two or three of the former, and many, in a variety of formats, of the latter – are the primary editorial material of *Cadence*. Its low-budget format offers no competition to the glossy pages of *down beat* (see entry 589), but the quantity of its reviews, which cover new releases and rereleases from both major and miniscule recording companies, make it the primary resource for jazz libraries and researchers. While the reviews are critically objective, they undoubtedly help to promote *Cadence*'s sales of records by mail.

579. **Cash Box: The International Music/Coin Machine/Home Entertainment Weekly**. Vol. 1- , 1942- . New York: Cash Box. weekly. illus. LC 55-23069. ISSN 0008-7289.

Cash Box, a competitor of *Billboard* (see entry 573), is an industry journal of the popular music and video recording industry. Charts list top-selling albums, singles, compact discs, and videocassettes in various categories. Regional reporters cover people and business developments within the industry. *Music Times*, an insert, presents market statistics and playlists of prominent radio stations.

580. **Central Opera Service Bulletin**. Vol. 1- , 1959- . New York: Central Opera Service. quarterly. book reviews. LC 83-6928. ISSN 0008-9508.

The bulletin and its associated publications offer a comprehensive information service to those involved in opera production and performance in the United States and Canada. Regular columns cover news of companies and national organizations, theater renovations, appointments to positions, new editions of operas, and more. Annual features include obituaries, a calendar of the year's performances, and a statistical survey of performances and companies in the United States. Book reviews are short and descriptive.

Directories published as numbers of the bulletin include *Directory of Operas and Publishers* (18, nos. 2, 3); *Directory of American Premieres 1962-68* (11, no. 2); directories of American and foreign contemporary operas (10, no. 2; 12, no. 2; 17, no. 2; 22, no. 2); *Directory of Children's Operas and Musicals* (24, no. 4); *Directory of English Translations* (16, no. 2); *Directory of Sets and Costumes for Rent* (21, no. 2); *Career Guide for Young American Singers* (25, no. 4) (see entry 158); and *Directory of Selected Opera Films* (19, no. 2). Most of these are updated periodically.

581. **Chamber Music**. Official Publication of Chamber Music America. Vol. 1- , 1984- . New York: Chamber Music America. quarterly. ads. illus.

Reflecting the interests of professional chamber musicians, *Chamber Music* offers illustrated articles on everyday concerns such as competitions, personal finance, fundraising, and instrument theft. The authors are chamber musicians who write with humor and conviction. The "American Ensemble" column notes news of performances, festivals, programs, premieres, recordings, and achievements by members.

582. **The Choral Journal**. Official Publication of the American Choral Directors Association. Vol. 1- , 1959- . Lawton, Okla.: American Choral Directors Association. 10/yr. index to Vols. 1-18. ads. illus. music. reviews of books, music. LC 72-28530. ISSN 0009-5028.

Choral Journal keeps choral directors informed of news of the association, offers articles on the history and performance of choral music, and gives practical suggestions for the design of programs. Plentiful advertisements for music, choral wear, and educational opportunities reflect this practical orientation. Reviews of choral music in each issue evaluate recent publications in terms of aspects of performance. The special convention issue of the association appears in January. An index to volumes 1-18 was published in 1978 (see entry 354).

583. **Clavier**. Vol. 1- , 1962- . Northfield, Ill.: Instrumentalist Company. 10/yr. annual index. ed. board. ads. illus. music. reviews of music, recordings. LC 66-32665. ISSN 0009-854X.

Articles on performers and the piano teaching profession, news of conferences and awards, and questions and answers on teaching methods are some of the features which make *Clavier* an important journal for piano teachers. The occasional feature entitled "Commissioned by Clavier" presents new short works to be used with students. "New Music Reviews" evaluates recently published collections and individual works in terms of their pedagogical usefulness, and identifies their level of difficulty. Each March issue includes a directory of summer camps and keyboard workshops.

584. **College Music Symposium**. Journal of the College Music Society. Vol. 1- , 1961- . Boulder, Colo.: College Music Society. annual. ed. board. ads. music. LC 62-52900. ISSN 0069-5696.

This hefty (about two hundred pages per volume) journal offers a range of topics—analysis, history, ethnomusicology, pedagogy—which reflect the broad interests of the membership of the society in an equally broad range of styles, including reports of research and less formal "how-to" articles and opinion pieces. Some recent articles have been

"Integrating Music by Women into the Music History Sequence" (25 [1985]: 21-27); "Enumeration of Dissonance in the Masses of Palestrina" (32, no. 1 [1983]: 50-64); "From Yankee Doodle thro' to Handel's Largo: Music at the World's Columbian Exposition" (24, no. 1 [1984]: 81-96); and "Ugh! Why Pink? A Brief History of Music's Academic Color" (24, no. 2 [1984]: 149-52).

585. **Computer Music Journal**. Vol. 1- , 1977- . Cambridge, Mass.: MIT Press. quarterly. index to Vols. 1-9 in Vol. 10, nos. 1-2. ads. illus. music. reviews of books, recordings. LC 77-644286. ISSN 0148-9267.

Sophisticated design and many illustrations and photographs of music, video displays, and electronic equipment visually distinguish *Computer Music Journal* as a forum for serious research that has wide appeal. Upbeat yet authoritative articles by authors, split evenly between academic and corporate affiliation, evaluate hardware, software, and programs; offer new procedures for composition; report on conferences; and discuss the use of computers in traditional forms of analysis and notation. Letters from readers, announcements of new equipment and upcoming conferences, and evaluative reviews of books and recordings appear in every issue. Advertisers include computer equipment manufacturers and publishers of books about computer music.

586. **Contact: A Journal of Contemporary Music**. No. 1- , 1971- . York, England: Philip Martin Music Books. semiannual. ads. music. reviews of books, music, performances. LC 81-642085. ISSN 0308-5066.

Contact occupies a place between *Perspectives of New Music* (see entry 648) and *Tempo* (see entry 666) – slimmer and more focused than the former, less reserved than the latter. Contributors are composers, performers, and scholars, generally from Britain. Articles portray, examine, or analyze contemporary works in thorough, documented articles which make good use of musical examples. Reviews cover contemporary music festivals throughout Europe.

587. **Current Musicology**. No. 1- , 1965- . New York: Music Department, Columbia University. semiannual. ed. board. ads. music. reviews of books. LC 66-80412. ISSN 0011-3735.

The most unique and telling feature of *Current Musicology* is the reports from American and foreign universities on conferences, festivals, and activities of their graduate programs. These appear in each issue, though not regularly from each university. The several scholarly articles in each issue cover musicological interests from Josquin to salsa, although the focus is on the European tradition. Bibliographical interests, such as a description of a rare edition of music or an enumeration of works on a certain subject, feature in a significant number of articles. Most issues include book reviews and lists of new publications.

588. **The Diapason: An International Monthly Devoted to the Organ, the Harpsichord and Church Music**. Official Journal of the International Society for Organ History and Preservation. No. 10- , 1909- . Des Plaines, Ill.: Scranton Gillette Communications. monthly. ads. illus. music. reviews of books, music, recordings. LC 42-28467. ISSN 0012-2378.

A professional journal for organists in a distinctive, large format, *The Diapason* offers news of appointments, conferences, festivals, and installations of new organs. Each issue normally includes one lengthy, in-depth study of a composer or a composition, such as "An Index to the Organ Works of J. S. Bach" in modern editions (907 [June 1985]: 9-13). A calendar lists coming organ recitals. Reviews of books are long and critical; reviews of music are shorter and cover music for organ and for organ and voice.

589. **down beat: For Contemporary Musicians**. Vol. 1- , 1934- . Elmhurst, Ill.: Maher Publications. monthly. ads. illus. reviews of books, recordings. LC 63-4684. ISSN 0012-5768.

Originally the purist voice of jazz, *down beat* has loosened its criteria and now includes jazz-influenced rock within its purview. Each issue features three or four article-length profiles of musicians; these invariably include a note detailing his or her equipment and giving a selected discography. Regular critics offer knowledgeable, signed reviews and review columns of LPs and CDs, and continue to undercut their own good criticism with summary one-to-five star ratings. The blindfold test, a venerable feature, asks well-known jazz musicians to comment on recordings which are not identified to them. Transcriptions of recorded solos and reviews of live performances in New York and elsewhere are frequent features. The annual critics' and readers' polls tally votes for the most appreciated musicians in various categories.

590. **Ear: Magazine of New Music**. Vol. 1- , 1976- . New York: New Wilderness Foundation. monthly. ads. illus. reviews of performances, recordings. LC 84-7624. ISSN 0734-2128.

The large tabloid format and wild graphic design of *Ear* are inextricable from its coverage of the people and events of new and improvised music. It is published in collaboration with the Jazz Composers Orchestra Association and the New Music Distribution Service. It includes interviews, reviews of performances and recordings, legal advice for composers (such as "Read Your Contract!" in the October 1986 issue), and a calendar of performances in New York with a focus, but not a myopic one, on that city.

591. **Early Music**. Vol. 1- , 1973- . London: Oxford University Press. quarterly. annual index. ads. illus. music. reviews of books, music, recordings. LC 73-645648. ISSN 0306-1078.

Advertisements from instrument makers and abundant historical illustrations characterize this visually enticing magazine as much as does its editorial content. The first issue spelled out the intentions of *Early Music* in this way: "We want to provide a link between the finest scholarship of our day and the amateur and professional listener and performer." In this spirit, articles by scholars and performers discuss music, musical instruments, and performance until the time of Mozart. Plentiful reviews evaluate books, recordings, and editions of early music. An irregular column tells of recent sales at auction of historical manuscripts and instruments. An index to 1973-77 was published in 1980.

592. **Early Music History: Studies in Medieval and Early Modern Music**. Vol. 1- , 1981- . Cambridge, England: Cambridge University Press. annual. index to Vols. 1-3 in Vol. 3. ed. board. illus. music. reviews of books. LC 83-645056. ISSN 0261-1279.

An even newer addition to this burgeoning field than *Early Music* (see entry 591), *Early Music History* looks at music up to the early seventeenth century in two particular areas: the social circumstances of early music, including music printing, instrument making, and public performance; and early manuscript sources. Volumes are hardbound and feature reproductions and transcriptions of manuscripts. A series of articles describing, in detail, a number of new sources of English polyphony from the thirteenth to the sixteenth centuries has appeared in volumes 2, 3, and 4.

593. **Ethnomusicology**. Journal of the Society for Ethnomusicology. Vol. 1- , 1953- . Ann Arbor, Mich.: Society for Ethnomusicology. 3/yr. annual index. ed. board. illus. music. reviews of books, films, recordings. bibliog. LC 56-12963. ISSN 0014-1836.

Through the use of reportage, analysis, and discourse addressing problems of fieldwork, structure of musical expression, and the social function of music, this scholarly journal reflects ethnomusicology's diverse approaches. Topics range culturally from gamelan orchestras to Norwegian discotheques. Most articles include musical examples which employ either traditional notation or novel diagrammatic forms. In addition to its numerous reviews, the "Current Bibliography, Discography, and Filmography" in each issue makes *Ethnomusicology* an important source for ongoing work in the field. This feature enumerates, on a worldwide basis, books, articles, pamphlets, reports, government publications, dissertations, theses, films, and recordings relating in any way to the methods, interests, or results of ethnomusicology. There are indexes to volumes 1-10 and 11-20.

594. **Fanfare: The Magazine for Serious Record Collectors**. Vol. 1- , 1977- . Tenafly, N.J.: Fanfare. bimonthly. ads. reviews of recordings. LC 77-644246. ISSN 0148-9364.

No other record review approaches *Fanfare*'s extensive coverage of releases from small labels as well as from industry giants. Each issue runs a hefty 350 to 400 pages, and little of that space is occupied by advertising. Regular contributors review several hundred classical, and a sprinkling of jazz and pop, LPs, CDs, and cassettes in each issue. The reviewers have a lot to say, and their signed comments range in style from focused to rambling and from witty to flippant. The heated exchanges in the "Letters" column between readers and reviewers show that *Fanfare* has the ability to raise hackles. In addition to reviews, columnists offer group (based on composers or genres) surveys of new and older recordings, interviews with performers, and extended columns on audio equipment or film music.

595. **Fontes Artis Musicae**. Review of the International Association of Music Libraries, Archives and Documentation Centres. Vol. 1- , 1954- . Kassel, West Germany: Bärenreiter-Verlag. quarterly. annual index. ed. board. music. reviews of books. LC 62-68268. ISSN 0015-6191.

Fontes exemplifies its international outlook by publishing scholarly articles in English, German, French, and occasionally other languages. Within a broad theme of bibliographic control of music and music literature, it includes reviews of research on composers or genres; bibliographies; histories of publishers; surveys of music libraries and librarianship in individual countries; reports on large-scale publishing efforts; and book reviews of reference works or works dealing with music libraries or publishing. The first issue of each year devotes itself to reports from the annual conference of the association. An "Information" section notes upcoming meetings, new publications, and activities of association groups. "Publications à caractère bibliographique" cites recent publications of not only reference works but catalogs, studies, and new periodicals.

596. **The Galpin Society Journal**. No. 1- , 1948- . n.p.: Galpin Society. annual. ed. board. index to Nos. 1-5. ads. illus. reviews of books. LC 55-36071. ISSN 0072-0127.

Similar in many ways to the *Journal of the American Musical Instrument Society* (see entry 616), the *Galpin Society Journal* is also devoted to the history of musical instruments, but it focuses more on instruments themselves rather than on their music. It combines longer articles on makers or types of instruments with "Notes and Queries" – brief descriptions of individual historical instruments in collections.

597. **Gramophone**. Vol. 1- , 1923- . Harrow, England: General Gramophone Publications. monthly. annual index. ads. illus. reviews of books, recordings, audio equipment. LC 85-649842. ISSN 0017-310X.

Gramophone is an established and reliable survey of recordings and audio equipment in Britain. It features news and articles highlighting performers and a "New Releases" column which lists the month's LP, CD, and cassette releases in Britain. A regular staff (which includes composer John Duarte and editor of *The New Grove* Stanley Sadie) contributes some two hundred reviews of recordings in each issue. These are divided by categories labeled "Orchestral," "Chamber," "Instrumental," "Choral and Song," "Opera," and "Nights at the Round Table" – short reviews of spoken recordings, military music, and jazz. The "Audio" section offers features and reviews of new equipment. *Gramophone* gives a series of record awards each autumn.

598. **Guitar Player**. Vol. 1- , 1967- . Cupertino, Calif.: GPI Publications. monthly. ed. board. ads. illus. reviews of guitars and recordings. LC 86-7027. ISSN 0017-5463.

Like *Keyboard* (see entry 618), also published by GPI, *Guitar Player* is a magazine for rock musicians, but occasionally ventures into other areas. Well-illustrated and lively in style, feature articles portray rock guitarists and luthiers, discuss the workings of electric guitars, and examine new equipment. Each issue gives at least a nod to classical guitarists – in a recent issue, a staff writer covered a Segovia master class and interviewed Segovia himself (20 [December 1986]: 42-45). Regular columns feature well-known guitarists from a variety of backgrounds such as John Duarte, Chet Atkins, and Larry Coryell, who offer transcriptions and give advice. Recent issues have included a "soundpage" – a flexible plastic recording. *Guitar Player* sponsors an annual series of awards to winners of the readers' poll.

599. **The Guitar Review**. No. 1- , 1946- . New York: Albert Augustine. quarterly. ads. illus. music. reviews of books, music, performances. LC 55-36470. ISSN 0017-5471.

The Society for the Classic Guitar founded the *Review* as a means of promoting guitar music and performance. Each issue includes two or three pieces of music for the guitar. Articles feature performers, analyze works for the guitar, or discuss performance techniques. Reviews regularly cover books, printed music, and concerts. Makers of guitars and publishers of guitar music advertise in each issue. George Giusti and Vladimir Bobri (who served for years as editor) have provided imaginative cover art, balanced design, and illustrations for the text since 1946.

600. **Hi-Fi News and Record Review**. Vol. 16- , 1971- . Croydon, England: Link House Magazines. monthly. ads. illus. reviews of audio equipment, books, recordings. LC 82-5232. ISSN 0142-6230.

The priorities of this substantial monthly are obvious – equipment first, recordings second. Advertisements for equipment flood the editorial material. Yet the reviews of audio equipment are long and technical, and its news, articles, coverage of audio conventions, and interviews with manufacturers are cast in energetic prose. Short signed reviews of about two hundred recordings each month are divided into categories of classical and nonclassical, and noticeably adjust their style to each.

601. **High Fidelity**. Vol. 1- , 1951- . New York: ABC Leisure Magazines. monthly. ads. illus. reviews of recordings, audio equipment, video equipment. LC 82-8247. ISSN 0018-1455.

After over twenty years of supporting the inserted *Musical America* (see entry 629), *High Fidelity* is again being published on its own as of 1987. Its glossy package laden with advertising remains otherwise unchanged, leaving it now even less distinguishable from *Stereo Review* (see entry 661). Regular columnists offer advice on managing one's audio equipment. In-depth test reports of audio (and increasingly, video) equipment evaluate new entries on the market. The dependable thirty to forty short reviews of LP, CD, and cassette recordings continue to appear in each issue.

602. **High Performance Review**. Vol. 1- , 1981- . Stanford, Calif.: High Performance Review. quarterly. ads. illus. reviews of audio equipment, recordings. LC 82-645293. ISSN 0277-1357.

A relatively low-keyed newcomer to the usually high-energy world of audio reviews, *High Performance Review* has much to offer. Its advertisements are few, as opposed to the glut in *Stereo Review* (see entry 661) or *Hi-Fi News* (see entry 600). Detailed, technical reviews of audiophile equipment occupy about two-thirds of each issue. The remainder is devoted to signed reviews of about one hundred recordings and prerecorded tapes in each issue, in which classical recordings predominate.

603. **The Hymn**. A Journal of Congregational Song. Vol. 1- , 1949- . Fort Worth, Tex.: Hymn Society of America. quarterly. annual index. ed. board. ads. illus. music. LC 55-36466. ISSN 0018-8272.

"A journal of research and opinion containing practical and scholarly articles, *The Hymn* reflects diverse cultural and theological identities," states the editorial policy. The journal traces the European heritage of the hymn in Canada and the United States in articles on individual hymn-tune writers and liturgical traditions. The "Ethnic Hymnody Series" has examined tunes of the Amish (37 [October 1986]: 20-26), the Dutch Reformed (36 [July 1985]: 23-25), and even the Snake Handlers (37 [April 1986]: 30-36). New hymns and news of the society appear in most issues. The regular feature "Hymns in Periodical Literature" indexes and summarizes recent articles in other journals. There is an index to volumes 1-32.

604. **Imago Musicae: International Yearbook of Musical Iconography/Internationales Jahrbuch für Musikikonographie/Annuaire international d'iconographie musicale**. Official Organ of the International Repertory of Musical Iconography. Vol. 1- , 1984- . Basel, Switzerland: Bärenreiter-Verlag; Durham, N.C.: Duke University Press. annual. ed. board. illus. bibliog. LC 85-651927. ISSN 0255-8831.

The quality of the typography, the layout, and the plentiful black-and-white photographs of art works in this hardcover annual appropriately complement its purpose, as stated in the directions to contributors: "the publication of original musicological and art-historical articles on the representation of music in the visual arts." An international journal, it accepts contributions in several languages, but English predominates. The extended, scholarly articles deftly balance music and art. Some examples are "Hands, Music, and Meaning in Some Seventeenth-Century Dutch Paintings" (1 [1984]: 75-102); "Men, Women, and Music at Home: The Influence of Cultural Values on Musical Life in Eighteenth-Century England" (2 [1985]: 51-134); and, one of the several articles exploring non-Western art and music, "The Realm of the Senses: Images of the Court Music of Pre-Colonial Bali" (2 [1985]: 143-78). A bibliography lists recent books, articles, and exhibition catalogs in categories of "Music and Art," "Iconography," "Portrait Iconography," and "Organology."

605. **The Instrumentalist**. Vol. 1- , 1946- . Northfield, Ill.: Instrumentalist Company. monthly. annual index. ads. illus. reviews of books, music. LC 86-25852. ISSN 0020-4331.

The Instrumentalist provides band directors and teachers of instrumental music in junior high schools, high schools, and colleges with suggestions for materials and methods of teaching instrumental music, and news of programs and equipment. "New Music Reviews" evaluates recent compositions and arrangements for bands and ensembles in terms of their difficulty and applicability to teaching purposes. Particularly useful annual features include a buyer's guide to sources for instruments, uniforms, music, and services; a directory of summer camps, clinics, and workshops; a directory of music organizations; a directory of music schools; and a survey of school instrumental music budgets.

606. **Interface: Journal of New Music Research**. Vol. 1- , 1972- . Lisse, Netherlands: Swets Publishing Service. quarterly. annual index. ed. board. illus. music. LC 75-641401. ISSN 0303-3902.

Interface is a leader in promoting the theoretical aspects of contemporary music. The editorial statement identifies it as "an international journal devoted to discussion of all questions which fall into the borderline areas between music on the one hand, physical and human sciences or related technologies on the other." Most authors are European, although most articles are in English. Their backgrounds are in physics, mathematics, and acoustics as well as music; consequently they are as likely to employ mathematical equations or diagrams illustrating artificial intelligence processes as musical notation. When *Interface* addresses traditional music, it approaches it from the fringe, such as in the article entitled "Did Beethoven Use the 'Enneadecaphonic' Theory?" (14, no. 1-2 [1985]: 1-9). This is not a journal for the timid.

607. **International Review of the Aesthetics and Sociology of Music**. Vol. 1- , 1970- . Zagreb, Yugoslavia: Institute for Musicology, Zagreb Academy of Music. semiannual. ed. board. music. ISSN 0351-5796.

Though published in Yugoslavia, the *International Review* addresses a worldwide audience of scholars. Articles appear in English, German, and French, with summaries in Serbo-Croatian and, when articles are in German or French, in English. The approach uniquely combines studies on the theory of music criticism, the reception of music by audiences, and philosophical approaches to musics of the world. The authors are musicologists and social scientists from Eastern and Western Europe and North America. Book reviews evaluate works in a similar sphere.

608. **Jazz Journal International**. Vol. 1- , 1977- . London: Jazz Journal. monthly. ads. illus. reviews of books, recordings. LC 77-643205. ISSN 0140-2285.

From a British perspective, *Jazz Journal International* offers news of jazz personalities and performances. Three to four feature articles in each issue portray musicians (generally Americans). Foreign correspondents report on festivals and clubs in Europe and North America. Each issue includes at least a dozen record reviews; these thankfully avoid the numerical rating system of *down beat* (see entry 589), and give detailed listings of musicians on each track, but the reviews themselves tend to be simplistic in their evaluations. Book reviews appear sporadically.

609. **Journal of Band Research**. Vol. 1- , 1964- . Troy, Ala.: Troy State University Press for the American Bandmasters Association. semiannual. index to Vols. 1-19, Vol. 20. ed. board. illus. music. LC 81-6010. ISSN 0021-9207.

A surprising array of approaches characterizes the articles in this journal for band directors. Psychological studies of musical perception, historical studies of bands, musical analyses of individual works for band, and surveys of current instructional techniques have value to those outside the field.

610. **Journal of Church Music**. Vol. 1- , 1959- . Philadelphia: Fortress Press. monthly, except July and August. annual index. ads. illus. music. reviews of books, music, recordings. LC 66-99815. ISSN 0021-9703.

The journal offers anecdotal "how-to" articles on organizing church choral groups, programming services, and performing choral works. Although Fortress Press is a Lutheran publisher, the journal addresses a nondenominational audience. Regular features include the music and text for several anthems, with an order form for purchasing these through the journal; a list of suggested hymns for use in Sunday services in the approaching months; and short reviews of books, recordings, and music.

611. **Journal of Music Theory**. Vol. 1- , 1957- . New Haven, Conn.: Yale University. semiannual. annual index. ed. board. ads. illus. music. reviews of books. LC 66-99830. ISSN 0022-2909.

Most articles deal with the music of twentieth-century composers or modern methods of analysis and composition, although some delve into music of the nineteenth century or earlier periods. All are documented and scholarly in nature. Each issue features several extended book reviews, a list of recently published works identified only as "Books and Articles," and notifications of upcoming conferences. There is an index to volumes 7-14.

612. **Journal of Music Therapy**. Vol. 1- , 1964- . Washington, D.C.: National Association for Music Therapy. quarterly. annual index. ed. board. reviews of books. LC 76-641354. ISSN 0022-2917.

Each issue presents several reports of experimental research dealing with the effect of music on behavior or the employment of specific music therapies. Signed contributed reviews evaluate books of interest to the profession.

613. **Journal of Musicology: A Quarterly Review of Music History, Criticism, Analysis, and Performance Practice**. Vol. 1- , 1982- . St. Joseph, Minn.: Imperial Printing. quarterly. ed. board. ads. music. reviews of books. LC 82-641565. ISSN 0277-9269.

Historical and analytical studies of works from the Middle Ages to the nineteenth century and textual examinations of musical manuscripts or early editions of music predominate. Articles are long and documented. Often the lead article in an issue will address a broader topic, such as "Classical Music as Popular Music" (3 [Winter 1984]: 1-18). One or more extended book reviews or reports of conferences appear in each issue.

614. **Journal of Research in Music Education**. Vol. 1- , 1953- . Reston, Va.: Music Educators National Conference. quarterly. annual index. ed. board. music. LC 54-43754. ISSN 0022-4294.

The journal is a scholarly cousin to *Music Educators Journal* (see entry 624). Each issue offers several reports of historical or experimental research on the teaching of music appreciation, instrumental or vocal performance, or ear training to all age levels. The "Forum" features editorial or historical pieces which summarize or offer suggestions for research. "Research Resources" lists recent tables of contents from related journals. The volume 32, number 4 issue (Winter 1984) offers three retrospectives on the founding and content of the journal. There is an index to volumes 1-10 in volume 10.

615. **Journal of the American Musical Instrument Society**. Vol. 1- , 1974- . Vermillion, S.D.: American Musical Instrument Society. annual. ed. board. ads. illus. reviews of books. LC 76-643009. ISSN 0362-3300.

The annual journal offers long and documented articles on instrument construction and design, performance practice, and instrument makers throughout Western history and in non-Western cultures. *The Galpin Society Journal* (see entry 596) covers the same material in a slightly different way. Drawings and black-and-white photographs are plentiful. The international listing of recent books and dissertations in the field is valuable for its specificity – other ongoing bibliographies in music have a much broader scope. Each year, the journal announces in a short testimonial the current winner of the society's Curt Sachs Award.

616. **Journal of the American Musicological Society**. Vol. 1- , 1948- . Philadelphia: American Musicological Society. 3/yr. cumulated index. ed. board. ads. music. reviews of books. LC 50-12713. ISSN 0003-0139.

As did Lowell Mason, an American whose European journals were featured in an article entitled "Lowell Mason on European Church Music and Transatlantic Cultural Identification: A Reconsideration" in the Summer 1985 issue, these articles from American musicologists look to Europe for their subject matter. The approach favors the historical and textual rather than the analytical; in all cases, the contributions are solid and scholarly, yet written for a wide audience. The several book reviews in each issue are long, thorough, and sometimes contentious. "Communications" in the form of letters to the editor often are requests for information on a research topic; these and the list of "Publications

Received," and in fact, the general tenor of the articles, all offer an overview of current American musicology. A cumulated index covers the years 1948 to 1980 (see entry 369).

617. **Journal of the Royal Musical Association**. Vol. 112- , 1987- . Oxford, England: Oxford University Press for the Royal Musical Association. semiannual. ed. board. ads. illus. music. reviews of books. ISSN 0269-0403.

The journal continues the long-running and well-respected *Proceedings of the Royal Musical Association*. Scholarly articles represent research in historical musicology, textual studies, theory, and other areas. Book reviews are lengthy. A unique feature is the listing, with brief abstracts, of papers read at recent conferences in Britain.

618. **Keyboard**. Vol. 1- , 1975- . Cupertino, Calif.: GPI Publications. monthly. ed. board. ads. illus. reviews of books, equipment, recordings. LC 81-649762. ISSN 0730-0158.

Musical hi-tech has no stronger advocate than *Keyboard*, formerly *Contemporary Keyboard*. Its lush, full-page advertisements for synthesizers, drum machines, and MIDI processing units speak to readers more strongly than its editorial content which purports to address a wide audience of jazz, rock, and classical appreciators. Among the advertisements, one can actually find a substantial amount of energetic writing which has featured Keith Jarrett, Igor Kipnis, Wendy Carlos, and other performers on piano, harpsichord, or electronic equipment (although the emphasis is strongly on the latter). Reports and evaluations of new equipment appear as regular and special features, and a half-dozen columnists give advice on keyboard performance topics ranging from Ives piano sonatas to the employment of chromatic passing chords. Issues since 1986 have included a "Soundpage"—a recording on flexible plastic of a featured performer.

619. **Living Blues: A Journal of the Black American Blues Tradition**. Vol. 1- , 1970- . University, Miss.: Center for the Study of Southern Culture, University of Mississippi. bimonthly. ads. illus. reviews of books, recordings. LC 72-620160. ISSN 0024-5232.

For *Living Blues*, blues is not merely a historical tradition, but a vigorous genre which follows a traditional style. Correspondents from cities throughout the world cover performances for the "Living Bluesletter" column. Blues-oriented radio stations in the United States and Canada regularly contribute to its composite playlist. Interviews, obituaries, classified advertisements, and plentiful reviews of recordings offer a panorama of contemporary blues. The annual "Blues Radio Guide" is a state-by-state directory of radio programs.

620. **Medical Problems of Performing Artists**. Vol. 1- , 1986- . Philadelphia: Hanley & Belfus. quarterly. ed. board. ads. illus. reviews of books. LC 85-6290. ISSN 0885-1158.

Though published by a medical publisher for medical practitioners, the growing awareness of the unique problems suffered by performers gives this journal an important place in music libraries. At least half the articles in each issue deal specifically with musicians or vocalists. Most authors are physicians whose specialties range from psychiatry to ophthalmology to neurology; others are musicians. Most articles are scholarly in nature, and cite as references works from the medical literature. Recent articles have included "A Psychoanalytic View of Performance Anxiety" (1 [June 1986]: 64-67), and "The Musician and Occupational Sound Hazards" (2 [March 1987]: 22-25).

621. **Music Analysis**. Vol. 1- , 1982- . Oxford, England: Basil Blackwell. 3/yr. ed. board. ads. music. reviews of books. LC 83-641578. ISSN 0262-5245.

A relative newcomer, *Music Analysis* reflects the increasing specialization of interests in scholarly journals. Each issue features two to four extended studies of individual works or of approaches to analysis. Volume 1, number 3 (October 1982) combined these approaches in a massive one-hundred-page semiological analysis of Varèse's brief, in comparison, *Density 21.5*. Reviews are few, but equally thorough. Issue number 3 of each volume includes an "Article Guide" – an annotated listing of recent articles on analytical writings.

622. **Music & Letters**. A Quarterly Publication. Vol. 1- , 1920- . Oxford, England: Oxford University Press. quarterly. annual index. ed. board. ads. music. reviews of books, music. LC 63-24794. ISSN 0027-4224.

George Bernard Shaw's article on Sir Edward Elgar in the first issue of *Music & Letters* provided a fitting opening to this now well-established scholarly exploration of libretti, musical manuscripts, historical writings about music, and the history of music. The plentiful reviews are a notable feature; each issue includes several dozen substantial reviews of books and perhaps half that number of reviews of music and of historical editions of music. There is an index to volumes 1-40, and a cumulated index is included in Whitten's bibliography (see entry 369).

623. **Music & Musicians**. Vol. 1- , 1981- . Croydon, England: Brevet Publishing. monthly. ads. illus. reviews of books, music, performances, recordings. LC 83-644296. ISSN 0027-4232.

After a short hiatus several years ago, *Music & Musicians* has emerged as a comprehensive, sophisticated magazine addressed to British music lovers but also of interest across the Atlantic. It offers news of competitions and prizes, profiles of performers and composers, and feature articles such as a series in 1986 on New Age music. Coverage of television and radio performances, of live performances, books, recordings, and even music is extensive. A "Music Guide" offers a calendar of musical performances throughout Britain.

624. **Music Educators Journal**. Vol. 1- , 1934- . Reston, Va.: Music Educators National Conference. monthly, except June, July, August. annual index. ed. board. ads. illus. reviews of books, software. LC 82-3107. ISSN 0027-4321.

News of new technology and of activities of the conference, practical advice on teaching techniques, and advertisements for instruments are the features of this upbeat and well-illustrated magazine for teachers of music from the elementary to the college level. A selection of recent articles shows its scope: Lewis Porter writing on women jazz musicians (September 1984: 42-52; October 1984: 42-51); using Suzuki methods in choral teaching (May 1985: 43-45); planning an elementary school musical (October 1986: 23-27); and an entire issue devoted to the employment of computers in music education (December 1986). Book reviews and software reviews examine subjects in surprising depth. Each April issue runs advertisements for summer study programs.

625. **Music Perception**. Vol. 1- , 1983- . Berkeley, Calif.: University of California Press. quarterly. ed. board. ads. music. reviews of books. LC 84-644031. ISSN 0730-7829.

The composition of the editorial board, which includes members of university departments of physics, psychology, music, and speech, exemplifies the strikingly interdisciplinary quality of *Music Perception*. The information for authors asks for "original theoretical and empirical papers, methodological articles and critical reviews concerning the study of music ... from a broad range of disciplines, including music theory, psychology, psychophysics, linguistics, neurology, neurophysiology, ethology, artificial intelligence, computer technology, and physical and architectural acoustics." Articles investigating these areas include "Representation of Phrase Structure in the Perception of Music" (3 [Winter 1985]: 191-220) and "Messiaen's Synaesthesia: The Correspondence between Color and Sound Structure in His Music" (4 [Fall 1986]: 41-68). The clear and attractive design and layout reflect the usual standards of the University of California Press.

626. **The Music Review**. Vol. 1- , 1940- . Cambridge, England: Heffers Printers. quarterly. ed. board. music. reviews of books, music, periodicals. LC 56-29749. ISSN 0027-4445.

The articles in the May 1985 issue illustrate this literate journal's interdisciplinary nature: "An Index to the Songs in *The London Magazine* (1732-1783)"; "On the Structural Integrity of Beethoven's Ninth Symphony"; and "Philip Heseltine (Peter Warlock): A Psychological Study." The book reviews are equally interdisciplinary, and cover recent publications in depth. Reviews of music favor recent compositions with an occasional nod to a new edition of Handel or Vivaldi. Reviews of periodicals are an unusual feature; these are not the critical evaluations one would expect, but informal notes on recent articles from several journals. Guy Marco authored a retrospective examination of the first twenty-five years of *Music Review* (26 [August 1965]: 236-46).

627. **Music Theory Spectrum**. The Journal of the Society for Music Theory. Vol. 1- , 1979- . Bloomington, Ind.: Society for Music Theory. annual. ed. board. music. reviews of books. LC 79-644237. ISSN 0195-6167.

The opening editorial in volume 1 stresses the breadth of the field of music theory, "encompassing historical studies, contributions to pedagogy and reflections upon the discipline itself, analyses of a wide variety, refinements or innovations in analytic methods, and more speculative statements about musical logic, meaning, and effect." The six to ten articles in each issue have employed these approaches and more, as shown in the extensive "Studies of Time and Music: A Bibliography" (7 [1985]: 72-106).

628. **Musica Disciplina: A Yearbook of the History of Music**. Vol. 1- , 1946- . Neuhausen-Stuttgart, West Germany: American Institute of Musicology; Hänssler-Verlag. annual. illus. music. LC 86-10259. ISSN 0077-2461.

The institute publishes several series of editions of medieval and Renaissance music and musical writings. A retrospective honoring Armen Carapetyan, editor for almost forty years, boasts that *Musica Disciplina* is "famous for its descriptions and catalogues of the great repertories of fifteenth- and sixteenth-century polyphony" (37 [1983]: 9). Long scholarly articles in English focus on this period and occasionally on the Baroque period. The first volume was published as *Journal of Renaissance and Baroque Music*.

629. **Musical America: The Journal of Classical Music**. Vol. 107- , 1987- . New York: ABC Consumer Magazines. bimonthly. ads. illus. reviews of books, recordings. LC 87-21331. ISSN 0735-777X.

After over twenty years as an insert to *High Fidelity* (see entry 601), *Musical America* emerged in 1987 to continue as it had since 1898. It stuffily proclaims itself a journal, but its newsy articles and glossy pages address the same concert-going public as *Opus* (see entry 644) and *Ovation* (see entry 646). The first issue of 1987 covers competitions in China, the Soviet Union, and the Orkney Islands, and offers short reviews of performances throughout the United States. *Musical America* shares reviewers with *High Fidelity*. Its reviews of recordings are similarly short and informed.

630. **The Musical Mainstream**. Vol. 1- , 1977- . Washington, D.C.: National Library Service for the Blind and Physically Handicapped, Library of Congress. bimonthly. LC 76-640164. ISSN 0364-7501. SuDoc LC 19.12: .

The Musical Mainstream is a lively collection of articles reprinted from such journals as *Ovation* (see entry 646), *Opera News* (see entry 642), and *Keyboard* (see entry 618), selected to appeal to music aficionados among the visually handicapped. Avoiding highly specialized material, it presents news, history, commentary, and interviews. Recent articles include a profile of Nicolas Slonimsky, a history of the pedal piano in America, and an opinion piece on bad conductors. In each issue, a feature article highlights a program or publication of the service, and in most issues a list identifies additions in braille, print, or recorded form to the library's collections. *The Musical Mainstream* itself appears in large-print, braille, and cassette formats.

631. **The Musical Quarterly**. Vol. 1- , 1915- . New York: Macmillan. quarterly. annual index. ed. board. ads. music. reviews of books. LC 16-24484. ISSN 0027-4631.

From its first issue in 1915 (then edited by Oscar Sonneck), *The Musical Quarterly* has been the outstanding forum for "high-level generalist writing on music," as the most recent editor, Eric Salzman, writes in his editorial opening to volume 71 (1985). He sees the past and future role of the quarterly as "the voice of a large community ... of writers, critics, and thinking musicians – as well as a large, intelligent, and musical public." Recent articles show it to be not only generalist, but interdisciplinary as well. These link music with psychology: "The Development of Cognition in Music" (70 [Spring 1984]: 218-33); philosophy: "Phenomenology as a Tool for Musical Analysis" (70 [Summer 1984]: 355-73); literary criticism: "In Defense of Musical Analysis" (71, no. 1 [1985]: 38-51); and even landscape architecture: "On 'looking over a ha-ha' " (71, no. 1 [1985]: 27-37). Several reviews per issue critically examine a selection of important recent works, and the quarterly book list surveys North American and European works. The journal was published for years by Schirmer, but Macmillan, the former parent company of Schirmer, now publishes it directly under its own name. There is an index covering 1915-59 and a cumulated index is included in Whitten's bibliography (see entry 369).

632. **The Musical Times**. Vol. 1- , 1844- . London: Novello and Company. monthly. ads. illus. music. reviews of books, music, recordings. LC 54-525. ISSN 0027-4666.

Throughout its long history, *The Musical Times* has astutely reviewed the London music scene, giving an occasional glance to the rest of the world. Its polished journalistic style complemented by ample photographs and illustrations appeals to the musical literati. Articles cover historical topics of broad interest, for example, a study of London taverns as concert halls (127 [July 1986]: 382-85); works currently in performance in London; or contemporary composers and performers. Reviews of books, recordings, music, and performances in London and elsewhere appear in each issue, as does a "London Music Diary" for the coming month. A regular section devoted to church and organ music offers its own features and reviews. Advertising for books, music, employment, education, concerts, prizes, services, and instruments reflects the wide readership.

633. **Musician**. No. 1- , 1977- . Gloucester, Mass.: Amordian Press. monthly. ads. illus. reviews of recordings. LC 82-644166. ISSN 0733-5253.

Musician, formerly *Musical America*, will reward rock fans, consumers of rock music equipment, and those who fancy themselves as rock musicians with a hip and energetic image similar to a rock song – short, seemingly intimate, and not too demanding. Articles take the form of interviews and profiles of rock musicians, or of evaluations and promotions of high-tech guitars and synthesizers, in a fast-talking, plentifully illustrated style. *Musician* gave extended and thoughtful coverage to the congressional hearings on sexually explicit lyrics in rock music (86 [December 1985]: 50-62).

634. **Die Musikforschung**. Herausgegeben von der Gesellschaft für Musikforschung. Vol. 1- , 1948- . Kassel, West Germany: Bärenreiter-Verlag. quarterly. annual index. music. reviews of books. LC 51-28227. ISSN 0027-4801.

The official journal of the major musicological society in West Germany, *Die Musikforschung* offers extended scholarly articles and shorter contributions, reports on musicological conventions, and some two dozen book reviews in each issue. Articles are in German, and the perspective and reporting show a preference for, but does not limit itself to, Germany. Issue number 3 (July-September) of each year includes an annual list of lectures given at West German institutes of higher education.

635. **The NATS Journal**. The Official Publication of the National Association of Teachers of Singing. Vol. 42- , 1985- . Jacksonville, Fla.: National Association of Teachers of Singing. bimonthly, except July/August. annual index. ed. board. ads. illus. music. reviews of books, music, recordings. LC 86-647306. ISSN 0884-8106.

A magazine for teachers and student singers, *The NATS Journal* (formerly *NATS Bulletin*) examines teaching methods, physical aspects of singing, historical singers, performance, and music. Several articles in each issue have a scholarly orientation, and others take the form of less formal regular columns, news of association conferences and workshops, and short reviews.

636. **NZ: Neue Zeitschrift für Musik**. Jahrgang 140- , 1979- . Mainz, West Germany: Musikverlag B. Schott's Söhne. monthly. annual index. ads. illus. reviews of books, recordings. LC 82-20138. ISSN 0170-8791.

A notice beneath the title proudly proclaims "gegründet 1834 von Robert Schumann," celebrating the famous founder of *Neue Zeitschrift für Musik* and over 150 years of nearly continuous publication. But for the years 1975 to 1978, when it was merged as *Melos/NZ*, the title has changed little. Now a sophisticated, lively, and literate German-language journal, its closest parallel in the English language is *The Musical Times* (see entry 632). Profiles of contemporary performers and composers, and historical articles and reviews of opera performances predominate. Each issue features several dozen record reviews and several book reviews.

637. **The New Records**. Vol. 1- , 1933- . Flourtown, Pa.: New Records Division, H. Royer Smith. monthly. ads. reviews of recordings. LC 47-43236. ISSN 0028-6559.

Calling itself "the oldest continuously published magazine devoted primarily to Classical Recordings in America," *The New Records* is published by a record shop. It reviews about one hundred LPs and CDs per issue. These reviews are knowledgeable and critical, but (perhaps because the publisher wants to sell records) are almost unfailingly positive.

638. **19th Century Music**. Vol. 1- , 1977- . Berkeley, Calif.: University of California Press. 3/yr. annual index. ed. board. ads. illus. music. reviews of books. LC 77-644140. ISSN 0148-2076.

"A blend of analysis, criticism, history, and source work" are the words with which the editors recently described *19th Century Music* (9 [Summer 1985]: 80). Scholarly articles explore the music and the intellectual and social settings of composition and performance in the nineteenth century. Lengthy book reviews appear in most issues. Two notable features are "Rehearings"—fresh analyses of well-known nineteenth-century works; and "Comment and Chronicle"—notes on publications and events in a witty style similar to that of *The New Yorker*'s "The Talk of the Town."

639. **Notes**. The Quarterly Journal of the Music Library Association. Nos. 1-15, 1934-42. Vol. 1- , 1943- . Canton, Mass.: Music Library Association. quarterly. annual index. ads. illus. music. reviews of books, music, periodicals. LC 43-45299. ISSN 0027-4380.

Notes initiated a new series when it changed from mimeographed to typeset text. By 1948 it had adopted a format which has changed little since then. An enumeration of the regular bibliographic features of *Notes* will show its importance to librarians and researchers. In each issue are about sixteen reviews of books and two dozen reviews of music; lists of recently published books, music publishers' catalogs, and music; and indexes to reviews of recordings. Reviews of new music periodicals appear semiannually. Appearing annually are an overview of price indexes of music; an index to reviews of audio equipment; an "Index to Music Necrology"; indexes to subjects of articles, titles of articles, reviewed books and compositions, and authors, composers, editors, reviewers, and translators; and an index to record manufacturers' numbers in the "Index to Record Reviews." "Notes for NOTES," a regular column, announces prizes, library acquisitions, publications, exhibitions, and conferences. Two to three articles per issue mediate between the scholarly and the practical. These have included a descriptive checklist of Stravinsky's manuscripts (40 [June 1984]: 719-50); a glossary of German musical terms useful in music libraries (42 [September 1985]: 29-35); and an overview of education for music librarianship (40 [March 1984]: 510-28). D. W. Krummel has examined *Notes* in two retrospective articles (41 [September 1984]: 7-25 and 21 [September 1964]: 56-82). As a voice for music librarians, it offers a microcosm of a library in the form of a journal: a reliable, scholarly, and vigorous bibliographic and informational resource.

640. **Opera**. Vol. 1- , 1950- . London: Opera. monthly. annual index. ads. illus. reviews of books, performances. LC 55-36490. ISSN 0030-3526.

Founded by the Earl of Harewood, editor of *Kobbé's Complete Opera Book* (see entry 58), and edited for thirty-three years by Harold Rosenthal, coauthor of *The Concise Oxford Dictionary of Opera* (see entry 74), *Opera* has established itself as the most thorough ongoing record and review of opera performances worldwide (albeit with a strong interest in Britain). Feature articles on historical and current performances and an occasional numbered series portraying opera personalities open each issue. "Our Critics Abroad" keep their discerning eyes on performances throughout Britain, Europe, and North America. A special autumn issue reviews the summer's festivals. "Coming Events" notes performances, festivals, and BBC broadcasts, and provides an opera calendar for "home" and "abroad."

641. **Opera Canada**. Vol. 1- , 1960- . Toronto: Foundation for Coast to Coast Opera Publication. quarterly. ads. illus. reviews of books, performances, recordings. LC 83-311310. ISSN 0030-3577.

A recent (27 [Winter 1986]: 3) editorial takes pride in noting that "now, already well-known in the fields of science, medicine, sports and education, Canada is beginning to be applauded for its place in the world of opera as well." Comparable in spirit and format to *Opera News* (see entry 642), *Opera Canada* examines performers, productions, and opera companies. Its emphasis, although not its exclusive attention, is on Canada. The "Roundup" offers short reviews of performances in Canada and elsewhere, and a calendar lists performances worldwide.

642. **Opera News**. Vol. 1- , 1936- . New York: Metropolitan Opera Guild. monthly, May-November; biweekly, December-April. annual index. ads. illus. reviews of books, performances. LC 80-159. ISSN 0030-3607.

The October 1986 issue celebrates the fiftieth anniversary of *Opera News*. The magazine still devotes much of its space to coverage of the Metropolitan Opera, but emerges occasionally to examine opera throughout the United States and Europe and on film. Illustrations feature heavily in the substantial articles on performers, productions, music, audio equipment, and even art and food, written by staff writers, critics, and composers. Regular departments include a calendar of upcoming performances, obituaries, and reviews of recordings and performances. The colorful format features many advertisements for books, recordings, and audio equipment. There is an index to 1936-81.

643. **The Opera Quarterly**. Vol. 1- , 1983- . Chapel Hill, N.C.: University of North Carolina Press. quarterly. ed. board. ads. illus. music. reviews of books, recordings, video recordings. LC 83-644370. ISSN 0736-0053.

The quarterly's writers are journalists and scholars who write substantial and well-researched articles with wide appeal. Recent articles have covered the television production of opera (3, no. 1 [Spring 1985]: 1-18), the early years of Maria Callas (3, no. 2 [Summer 1985]: 6-13), and the first production of Mussorgsky's *Boris* (4, no. 2 [Summer 1986]: 75-92). The sober design and spare black-and-white illustrations contrast with the more extravagant *Opera News* (see entry 642), but the regular "Quarterly Quiz" lightens the tone with games or puzzles for opera aficionados. Complementing the plentiful reviews are lists of recordings, videotapes, and books received.

644. **Opus: The Classical Music Magazine**. Vol. 1- , 1984- . Harrisburg, Pa.: Historical Times. bimonthly. ads. illus. reviews of books, recordings, audio and video equipment. LC 86-641375. ISSN 8750-488X.

The previous subtitle of *Opus* (*The Magazine of Recorded Classics*) more clearly expresses its scope than does the present one—this is a review of recordings, not of live performances. It can boast among its reviewers music historian Paul Henry Lang, harpsichordist Igor Kipnis, critic and radio personality Tim Page, and librarian and editor of *Notes* (see entry 639) Susan Thiemann Sommer. They compare and evaluate several dozen recordings each month. Feature articles survey recordings of an individual conductor or composer. Most issues include an article on audio equipment. Regular departments list recent recordings or offer a forum for contributors' views on books, video or audio equipment.

645. **The Organ Yearbook: A Journal for the Players and Historians of Keyboard Instruments**. Vol. 1- , 1970- . Buren, Netherlands: Frits Knuf. annual. ads. illus. music. reviews of books, music, recordings. LC 73-641132. ISSN 0078-6098.

Despite the location of its publisher, this is an English-language publication with an English editor. It contrasts sharply with the more newsy and illustrated magazines for organists such as *The American Organist* (see entry 564) or *The Diapason* (see entry 588) in its restriction to scholarly articles. Topics encompass profiles of historical organ builders, descriptive and technical studies of organs, harpsichords, and clavichords, and musical analyses of works for the organ. Reviews are plentiful, at seventy or more per volume, and show a clarity and directness for which only one reviewer—the editor—is responsible.

646. **Ovation: America's Classical Music Monthly**. Vol. 1- , 1980- . New York: Classical Music Publications. monthly. ads. illus. reviews of audio equipment, books, recordings. LC 80-648764. ISSN 0196-433X.

A magazine for listeners, similar in many ways to *Opus* (see entry 644), *Ovation*'s appeal is in its well-illustrated and easily read profiles of star performers such as Yehudi Menuhin or Kathleen Battle. Regional editions carry a program guide from a local classical radio station: in New York, this is WQXR; in Philadelphia, WFLN. Some two dozen signed, evaluative reviews each month of LPs and CDs and tests of new audio equipment are comparable to those in *Stereo Review* (see entry 661).

647. **Periodica Musica**. Publication of the Rèpertoire international de la presse musicale. Vol. 1- , 1983- . Vancouver, B.C.: Centre for Studies in Nineteenth-Century Music/Centre international de recherche sur la presse musicale and Department of Music of the University of British Columbia. annual. ed. board. LC 84-39007. ISSN 0822-7594.

"A Note from the Editors" speaks of this slim (twenty to thirty pages) annual as "an opportunity for scholars, archivists and librarians to disseminate information concerning nineteenth-century periodical literature dealing with music and musical life." Issues have included a checklist of nineteenth-century Russian periodicals (2 [1984]: 14-16; 4 [1986]: 6-11); a research report on music in popular magazines (4 [1986]: 18-20); and notes on the activities of the RIPM, which operates under the auspices of the International Musicological Society (Basel, Switzerland) and the International Association of Music Libraries, Archives and Documentation Centres (College Park, Md.).

648. **Perspectives of New Music**. Vol. 1- , 1962- . Seattle, Wash.: Perspectives of New Music. semiannual. index to 1962-82. ed. board. ads. illus. music. reviews of books, music. LC 66-89176. ISSN 0031-6016.

For over twenty years, *Perspectives* has celebrated the composition, performance, and analysis of contemporary music. Each hefty issue (usually containing three to four hundred pages) is a gold mine of articles, graphics, and music. Writers are composers, theorists, and sometimes poets or artists whose contributions include scholarly analyses of twentieth-century works, essays on approaches to composition or performance, reports of festivals, interviews with composers, opinion pieces on broad issues concerning contemporary music, reviews of books, music, and cassettes, and original illustrations or musical works. Cassette tapes featuring performances of contemporary music accompany some issues. Ann Basart has compiled a cumulative index to the years 1962-82 (see entry 329).

649. **The Piano Quarterly**. No. 1- , 1952- . Wilmington, Vt.: Piano Quarterly. quarterly. index to 1952-84, 1984. ed. board. ads. illus. music. reviews of books, music, recordings. LC 80-11137. ISSN 0031-9554.

Humor and opinion spice the pages of *The Piano Quarterly* and subtly differentiate it from the more earnest *Clavier* (see entry 583). Interviews, articles on historical pianists and on performance practice, and reports on competitions address an audience of pianists as well as teachers. Recent articles include a comparison of recent Scarlatti editions (131 [Fall 1985]: 54-57); a report on the use of the chemical Inderal to combat stage fright (134 [Summer 1986]: 30-35); and a study of Haydn's ornamentation (135 [Fall 1986]: 38-48). Reviews of new music focus on pedagogical applications and feature reproductions of the first page of each work reviewed.

650. **Popular Music**. Vol. 1- , 1981- . Cambridge, England: Cambridge University Press. 3/yr. ed. board. illus. music. reviews of books. bibliog. LC 82-645331. ISSN 0261-1430.

What is popular music? The preface to the first volume emphasizes a commercial quality – "popular music is typical of societies with a relatively highly developed division of labour and a clear distinction between producers and consumers, in which cultural products are created largely by professionals, sold in a mass market and reproduced through mass media." Articles in succeeding volumes have examined gypsy music, Jewish oriental ethnic music in Israel, and popular music in Fascist Germany, but have most often taken rock as their exemplar and have approached it with a critical lucidity unparalleled in any other source. *Popular Music* is a sympathizer, but not an apologist. Its scholarly articles employ musicological, sociological, historical, and anthropological methods in examinations of the productions, nature, and audiences of popular music. Plentiful book reviews and an annual annotated booklist offer good opportunities for keeping in touch with the field.

651. **Popular Music and Society**. Vol. 1- , 1971- . Bowling Green, Ohio: Bowling Green University Popular Press. quarterly. ed. board. reviews of books, recordings, video recordings. LC 72-627179. ISSN 0300-7766.

Bowling Green University is well known for its support of the study of popular culture. *Popular Music and Society* examines popular music, especially rock, within society as a commodity, an entertainment, and a social barometer. Articles examine lyrics more closely than music. Those who remember playing the Beatles' *White Album* (Capitol SWBO 101) backwards for its "message" will appreciate the survey entitled "Backward

Messages in Commercially Available Recordings" (10 [1985]: 2-13). Reviews are short and undemanding.

652. **Psychology of Music**. Vol. 1- , 1973- . Staffordshire, England: Society for Research in Psychology of Music and Music Education. semiannual. index to Vols. 1-10. ed. board. reviews of books. LC 74-641791. ISSN 0305-7356.

Articles present reports of research and reviews of research dealing with, in the words of the editorial policy, "increasing scientific understanding of any psychological aspect of music, including listening, performing, creating, memorising, analysing, describing, learning, teaching, applying, and social developmental and attitudinal factors." In its emphasis on children and adolescents, it overlaps with journals of the teaching of music such as *Journal of Research in Music Education* (see entry 615) and *Bulletin of the Council for Research in Music Education* (see entry 577). But it also includes adults as subjects of study – two recent articles attempted to define "The Personality Structure of the Musician" (9, no. 1 [1981]: 3-14; no. 2: 69-75).

653. **Research Chronicle**. No. 1- , 1961- . London: Royal Musical Association. annual. illus. music. reviews of books. LC 64-776. ISSN 0080-4460.

An editorial (16 [1980]: 1-3) stresses that "the primary commitment and loyalty of the *Chronicle* must be to nitty-gritty historical musicology," and explains that "the characteristics we chiefly seek are originality and thrust rather than easy accessibility." Long and extensively documented articles concentrate on historical or bibliographical studies of manuscripts, printed music, early publications, and ephemera. A "Register of Theses on Music in Britain and Ireland" appears irregularly.

654. **Revista de Música Latina Americana/Latin American Music Review**. Vol. 1- , 1980- . Austin, Tex.: University of Texas Press. semiannual. ed. board. ads. illus. music. reviews of books. LC 80-644355. ISSN 0163-0350.

Indigenous music, popular music, and transported European music as composed and performed in Latin America are the areas of interest addressed by these scholarly articles. Authors from North and South America write in English, Spanish, and Portuguese. They employ both traditional musicological and ethnomusicological approaches, and include plentiful musical examples. Book reviews are critical and thorough. A short section devoted to "communications and announcements" notes conferences, awards, and publications.

655. **Revue de musicologie**. publiée avec le concours du Centre national de la recherche scientifique. No. 1- , 1917- . Paris: Société française de musicologie. semiannual. index 1917-66; 1967-81. ed. board. ads. illus. music. reviews of books, music. LC 86-9895. ISSN 0035-1601.

This is the official journal of the major French musicological society. Recent issues have published three scholarly articles in French with summaries in English. The approach is generally historical, the topic often the music of France. "Notes et Documents" reports on musicological conferences throughout Europe.

656. **La Revue musicale**. No. 1- , 1920- . Paris: Éditions Richard-Masse. 10/yr. music. LC 21-611. ISSN 0035-3736.

Each issue is devoted to a particular theme. Often the theme is a contemporary composer, although the double number 379-80 featured papers from the international congress on Gregorian chant held in Paris in 1985. Issues devoted to composers include interviews, testimonials, analyses, and a discography or catalog of the composer's work.

657. **Rivista italiana di musicologia**. Vol. 1- , 1966- . Florence, Italy: Leo S. Olschki Editore. semiannual. annual index. ed. board. ads. illus. music. reviews of books. LC 80-1014. ISSN 0035-6867.

As the official journal of the Società Italiana di Musicologia, *Rivista* publishes scholarly articles in Italian with an emphasis on the history of Italian music. Recent issues have included one extended book review and a list of books in Italian, English, German, and French in the field of musicology received by the journal.

658. **Rolling Stone**. No. 1- , 1967- . New York: Straight Arrow. biweekly. ads. illus. reviews of recordings, video recordings. LC 73-644466. ISSN 0035-791X.

In recent years, *Rolling Stone*'s editorial scope has branched out into motion pictures, fashion, and politics, but its appeal still thrives on rock music and rock stars. Its large tabloid format laden with photographs encourages browsing, yet it does offer good reading matter – investigative reporting of liberal political issues, news of the music business, and interviews with stars and figures in the news. Record reviews cover the most prominent rock albums in a hip language which equates packaging and personality with musical content. A chronicle of touring itineraries of rock figures and a chart listing the top-selling rock recordings are regular features.

659. **Sacred Music**. Vol. 1- , 1874- . St. Paul, Minn.: Church Music Association of America. quarterly. annual index. ed. board. illus. reviews of books, music. LC 80-702. ISSN 0036-2255.

Former titles were *Caecilia* and *The Catholic Choirmaster*. Several articles in each issue examine the current and historical use of music in the Roman Catholic liturgy. The style is scholarly, and the tone is sober and sometimes noticeably devout. Signed reviews examine recent histories and collected editions of European or of Catholic music, new arrangements and compositions for organ, chorus, or other instruments, and the contents of recent issues of European Catholic music journals.

660. **Sing Out! The Folk Song Magazine**. Vol. 1- , 1950- . Easton, Pa.: Sing Out Corporation. quarterly. ed. board. ads. illus. music. reviews of books, recordings. LC 61-45751. ISSN 0037-5624.

Interviews, profiles, features on ethnic music, and plenty of songs have carried *Sing Out!* through a continually precarious financial existence. Regular contributors (whose number still includes Pete Seeger) cover news of festivals and local folk organizations, answer questions about songs, and offer tips on playing the guitar, mandolin, fiddle, or dulcimer. Book reviews and record reviews tend to be congratulatory rather than critical, but reflect a spirit of faith in the ability of the amateur and the barely professional to keep alive a rich tradition of American folk music.

661. **Stereo Review**. Vol. 1- , 1968- . Los Angeles, Calif.: CBS Magazines. monthly. ads. illus. reviews of recordings, video recordings. LC 76-828. ISSN 0039-1220.

Readers of *Stereo Review* are consumers of sophisticated audio and video equipment and of recordings. In a slick, heavily illustrated format, the magazine offers them evaluations of equipment, announcements of new equipment, and tips on the use of equipment. Advertising covers half the pages; the inclusion in each issue of a reader service card by means of which one can obtain information about the advertised equipment is an indication that readers pay attention to these. Reviews, divided into categories of popular, jazz, and classical, cover about eighty albums or CDs from major labels each month. These are short, breezy, and prone to off-the-cuff qualitative judgments.

662. **The Strad**. Vol. 1- , 1890- . London: Novello and Company. monthly. ads. illus. LC 05-2289. ISSN 0039-2049.

The Strad has become a magazine of wide musical interest, one that is not limited to its primary audience of performers and buyers of bowed string instruments. An increase in format dimensions in 1979 brought with it ample photographs. These have allowed articles on historical instruments and contemporary construction techniques to portray fully and attractively their subjects. Other articles through the years have featured performers, performance techniques, and instrument makers, and have followed sales at auction of historical instruments. Regular classified advertisements list instruments for sale and wanted, and a regular index to advertisers of accessories, schools, dealers, and instrument makers shows these ads to be of use to readers.

663. **Strings: The Magazine for Players and Makers of Bowed Instruments**. Vol. 1- , 1986- . San Anselmo, Calif.: String Letter Corporation. quarterly. ads. illus. LC 86-1437. ISSN 0888-3106.

The publisher has christened the first issue as "a thoughtful, reliable, well-written, and good-looking magazine about our music and our instruments." It is indeed good-looking, printed in a large format with tasteful black-and-white photographs. Articles examine both performance and instruments. For example, the Winter 1985 issue features an article by Yehudi Menuhin, and a regular column reports on recent sales at auction of instruments. This is a credible beginning, and offers an alternative to, but certainly does not eclipse, *The Strad* (see entry 662).

664. **Studies in Music**. No. 1- , 1967- . Nedlands, Western Australia: Department of Music, University of Western Australia. annual. ed. board. music. bibliog. LC 74-641851. ISSN 0081-8267.

This outstanding annual collection of scholarly articles, whose purpose, as the editors state, "is to report the results of musicological studies in Australia and New Zealand, sometimes in company with contributions from scholars in other countries, and to provide a forum for the discussion of all facets of musical thought," offers a quality of writing which deserves to transcend geographical limitations. Articles in number 19 (1985) exemplify an investigation of broad issues. These include "What Is Style?" (1-13); "The Philosophical Implications of the Study of Large and Apparently Homogenous Repertoires" (28-60); and "Applications of Contemporary Notation to Ethnomusicological Analysis" (114-32). Number 16 (1982) is devoted to articles on Australian-born composer Percy Grainger. Each issue includes a "Register of Theses" on music from universities in Australia and New Zealand.

665. **Symphony Magazine**. Vol. 1- , 1948- . Washington, D.C.: American Symphony Orchestra League. bimonthly. ads. illus. LC 80-644609. ISSN 0271-2687.

The official journal of the league, *Symphony Magazine* features articles of general interest, such as an interview with William Kraft (37 [December 1986]: 18-20+), and news of grants, competitions, meetings, and governmental developments affecting the membership. A directory of orchestra and business members of the league appears annually in the December issue.

666. **Tempo: A Quarterly Review of Modern Music**. No. 1- , 1939- . London: Boosey and Hawkes Music Publishers. quarterly. ads. illus. music. reviews of books, recordings, performances. LC 51-36700. ISSN 0040-2982.

Tempo's interest in "modern music" extends first to Britons—articles on Maxwell Davies, Britten, and Vaughan Williams appear in almost every issue—then to the rest of the world—Villa-Lobos, Rorem, and Bartók have all been the subjects of recent articles. Articles take the form of analyses of twentieth-century works, or of portraits, either as critical overviews or as interviews, of contemporary composers. *Tempo* overlaps little with *Perspectives of New Music* (see entry 648), whose aggressive commitment to the avant-garde contrasts with the former's more staid style and preoccupations. Yet, *Tempo* keeps an eye to the present in its reviews of first performances throughout Europe, as well as of books and recordings.

667. **The Tracker**. Journal of the Organ Historical Society. Vol. 1- , 1956- . Richmond, Va.: Organ Historical Society. quarterly. ads. illus. reviews of books, recordings. LC 76-15. ISSN 0041-0330.

The title refers to the mechanical, or "tracker," action used in organs before the development of electric or pneumatic action. This is a journal for those interested in the preservation or renovation of these instruments. Articles present well-illustrated and thoroughly documented historical studies of organs and organ makers.

668. **The World of Music/Le Monde de la musique/Die Welt der Musik**. Journal of the International Institute for Comparative Music Studies and Documentation in association with the International Music Council. Vol. 1- , 1957- . Berlin: International Institute for Comparative Music Studies and Documentation. 3/yr. ads. illus. music. reviews of books, recordings. LC 67-034327. ISSN 0043-8774.

The World of Music examines the role of music in non-Western cultures. Its combination of specialized and general studies addresses both ethnomusicologists and a broader audience of those interested in intercultural studies. All articles appear in English with French and German summaries. Each issue includes several reviews of books and recordings, reports of conferences, and news of the International Music Council.

669. **Yearbook for Traditional Music**. Vol. 13- , 1981- . New York: International Council for Traditional Music. annual. ed. board. music. reviews of books, recordings. LC 74-630766. ISSN 0316-6082.

The council's interests extend to just about any kind of music, be it that performed in a New York concert hall or on the streets of Cairo. Articles in the yearbook, which continues the *Yearbook of the International Folk Music Council* (Vols. 1-12, 1969-80), reflect this broad range of interests; in fact, many also could be candidates for *Ethnomusicology* (see entry 593). Each issue includes about six substantial, documented articles by scholars from North America and Europe, in either English, French, or German, and several equally substantial reviews of books in ethnomusicology and recordings of non-Western music and European folk music.

21

Associations, Research Centers, and Other Organizations

Organizations involved in music reflect its diverse aspects as a performing art, a business, a hobby, and a scholastic subject. The many organizations listed in this chapter are prominent in the United States or on an international basis.

The chapter has been divided into six sections:

Composer Societies. These are groups whose name indicates interest in an individual composer. A somewhat dated, but more extensive list is John R. Douglas's "Musician and Composer Societies: A World Directory" in *Notes* 30 (June 1974): 755-58.

Musical Instrument Societies. Most of these groups promote interest in a particular instrument, with a few devoted to the study of instruments in general.

Research Centers and Institutes. These are geographically located organizations which promote research in a specific area. They are commonly associated with an archive or library collection. No attempt has been made to enumerate music library collections, however. Volumes in the *Directory of Music Research Libraries* (see entry 174) cover collections in North America, Europe, and other parts of the world.

Service Organizations. These exist to serve performers or groups with financial or advisory assistance.

Trade and Business Associations. These are all involved in the legal or business aspects of music.

Membership Societies and Associations. No attempt was made to distinguish between professional and amateur groups. These organizations promote the common interests of their members.

Information for all entries is based on literature supplied by the organizations, or, in some cases, from a telephone call to the organization. Entries give the full name of the organization, its address as supplied on its literature, and, when available, a telephone number. Activities are enumerated in abbreviated form. Some of these lists of activities are brief, since many organizations involve themselves in little more than one major activity. Regularly appearing publications, such as newsletters or annual reports, have been listed, and selected other publications are mentioned. Cross-references from titles of publications indicate those discussed elsewhere in this guide.

Composer Societies

670. **American Beethoven Society**
c/o Ira F. Brilliant Center for Beethoven Studies
Wahlquist Library North 614
San Jose State University
One Washington Square
San Jose, CA 95192-0171
(408) 277-9243

Activities: Financially supports the Ira F. Brilliant Center. *Publication*: *The Beethoven Newsletter*, 3/yr.

671. **American Handel Society**
Department of Music
University of Maryland
College Park, MD 20742
(301) 454-5758

Activities: Provides information to scholars and compiles a computerized bibliography of writings about Handel, his music, and related subjects; compiles a Handel discography. *Publication*: *Newsletter of the American Handel Society.*

672. **American Institute for Verdi Studies**
Department of Music, New York University
268 Waverly Building
Washington Square
New York, NY 10003
(212) 598-3431

Activities: Maintains the Verdi Archive at New York University; promotes research on Verdi and encourages performances of his music. *Publication*: *AVIS Newsletter*, semiannual.

673. **Arnold Schoenberg Institute**
University Park-MC 1101
University of Southern California
Los Angeles, CA 90089-1101
(213) 743-5362

Activities: Sponsors concerts of twentieth-century music, lectures, seminars, exhibits, and conferences; maintains an archive of Schoenberg manuscripts, printed music, and other materials. *Publications*: *Journal of the Arnold Schoenberg Institute*, semiannual; newsletter.

674. **Charles Ives Society**
Institute for Studies in American Music
Conservatory of Music
Brooklyn College/CUNY
Brooklyn, NY 11210
(718) 780-5655

Activities: Supports the preparation of performing editions of the works of Charles Ives.

675. **Ernest Bloch Society**
34844 Old Stage Road
Gualala, CA 95445
(707) 884-3473

Activities: Promotes the music of Ernest Bloch; maintains a library and archive. *Publication*: Bulletin, annual.

676. **International Alban Berg Society**
Ph.D. Program in Music
City University of New York
33 West 42nd Street
New York, NY 10036
(212) 790-4554

Activities: Promotes appreciation of and research on Alban Berg. *Publication*: Newsletter.

677. **Ira F. Brilliant Center for Beethoven Studies**
Wahlquist Library North 614
San Jose State University
One Washington Square
San Jose, CA 95192-0171
(408) 277-9243

Activities: Maintains a library of Beethoven scores, books, and recordings; supports the performance of compositions by Beethoven on original instruments; sponsors the Young Pianist's Beethoven Competition. *Publication*: *The Beethoven Newsletter*, 3/yr.

678. **Kurt Weill Foundation for Music**
142 West End Avenue, Suite 1R
New York, NY 10023
(212) 873-1465

Activities: Perpetuates the legacies of Kurt Weill and Lotte Lenya; administrates Weill's copyrights; awards grants for research, performance, translation, and publication related to Weill and Lenya; assists researchers and producers through the Weill-Lenya Research Center. *Publication*: *Kurt Weill Newsletter*, semiannual.

679. **Riemenschneider Bach Institute**
Baldwin-Wallace College Conservatory of Music
Merner-Pfeiffer Hall
49 Seminary Street
Berea, OH 44017
(216) 826-2207

Activities: Serves as a research center for the study of Bach and his contemporaries; maintains a library of manuscript copies and first printings of works by Bach, Handel, C. P. E. Bach, and J. S. Bach; holds an annual Bach festival, and symposia and concerts featuring other Baroque composers. *Publication*: *Bach*, quarterly.

680. **Wagner Society of America**
P.O. Box A 3229
Chicago, IL 60690

Activities: Promotes the music of Richard Wagner; maintains a library. *Publications*: *Wagner News*; membership directory.

Musical Instrument Societies

681. **American Accordionists' Association**
P.O. Box 616
Mineola, NY 11501
(516) 746-0145

Activities: Promotes accordion performance, teaching, retailing, and manufacturing by sponsoring national contests, commissioning compositions, and standardizing notation and accordion types. *Publication*: Newsletter.

682. **American Guild of English Handbell Ringers**
601 West Riverview Avenue
Dayton, OH 45406
(513) 227-9455

Activities: Organizes national, area, and state festivals; promotes the art of English handbell ringing (English handbells are played in an upright rather than in a suspended position). *Publication*: *Overtones*, 6/yr.

683. **American Guild of Organists**
815 Second Avenue, Suite 318
New York, NY 10017
(212) 687-9188

Activities: Administers certification examinations for professional organists and choirmasters; produces educational publications and audiocassettes dealing with organ and choir performance; sponsors competitions in organ and choral composition and in organ performance; holds national and regional conventions in alternate years. *Publications*: *The Organ Yearbook*, annual; *The American Organist*, monthly (see entry 564).

684. **American Harp Society**
P.O. Box 38334
Los Angeles, CA 90038-0334
(213) 463-0716

Activities: Promotes the appreciation of the harp as a musical instrument; commissions works for the harp; presents young artist harpists in concert; sponsors competitions and awards; maintains a repository and computerized index of harp-related materials; holds an annual conference. *Publications*: *American Harp Journal*, semiannual; membership directory.

685. **American Musical Instrument Society**
c/o The Shrine to Music Museum
414 East Clark Street
Vermillion, SD 57069
(605) 677-5306

Activities: Promotes the study of the history, design, and use of musical instruments in all cultures and from all periods; holds an annual conference. *Publications*: Journal, annual (see entry 615); newsletter, 3/yr.

686. **American Recorder Society**
596 Broadway, #902
New York, NY 10012
(212) 966-1246

Activities: Encourages and supports players of the recorder; sponsors regional workshops; provides an education program for individuals and a biennial seminar for teachers.

Publications: Membership directory, annual; *The American Recorder*, quarterly (see entry 566); newsletter, 3/yr.

687. **American Viola Society**
512 Roosevelt Boulevard
Ypsilanti, MI 48197
(313) 482-6288

Activities: Facilitates communication between viola players as the national chapter of the Internationale Viola-Forschungsgesellschaft. *Publication*: Newsletter.

688. **Galpin Society**
c/o Pauline Holden
38 Eastfield Road
Western Park
Leicester LE3 6FE England
533 85 51 36

Activities: Promotes research in the history, construction, and use of musical instruments. *Publication*: *The Galpin Society Journal*, annual (see entry 596).

689. **International Clarinet Society**
c/o Norman Heim
Music Department
University of Maryland
College Park, MD 20742

Activities: Supports clarinet performance; maintains I.C.S. Research Center at the University of Maryland; encourages research on the clarinet and composition of clarinet music; holds an annual meeting. *Publication*: *The Clarinet*, quarterly.

690. **International Double Reed Society**
c/o Lowry Riggins
626 Lakeshore Drive
Monroe, LA 71203
(318) 343-5715; (318) 342-2145

Activities: Facilitates communication between performers, students, teachers, and manufacturers of double reed instruments; maintains a library of books, music, and recordings at the University of North Carolina at Greensboro; holds an annual meeting. *Publications*: *The Double Reed*, 3/yr.; journal, annual.

691. **International Horn Society**
c/o Ruth Hokanson
1213 Sweet Brier Road
Madison, WI 53705
(608) 233-6336

Activities: Exchanges information between horn players; maintains an archive at Ball State University; holds an annual horn workshop and an annual symposium. *Publications*: *The Horn Call*, semiannual; newsletter, quarterly; membership directory, annual.

692. **International Society for Organ History and Preservation**
P.O. Box 104
Harrisville, NH 03450
(603) 827-3055

Activities: Represents the interests of professional organists. *Publication*: *The Diapason*, monthly (see entry 588).

693. **International Society of Bassists**
School of Music
Northwestern University
Evanston, IL 60201
(312) 492-7228

Activities: Serves as a communications network for double bassists; promotes public interest and research in the double bass; sponsors a biennial convention. *Publication*: *International Society of Bassists*, 3/yr.

694. **International Trumpet Guild**
School of Music
Florida State University
Tallahassee, FL 32306-2098

Activities: Promotes communication between trumpet players; works to improve the artistic level of trumpet performance, teaching, and literature; maintains an archive at Western Michigan University; holds an annual conference. *Publications*: *ITG Journal*, quarterly; membership directory, biennial.

695. **Lute Society of America**
P.O. Box 1328
Lexington, VA 24450
(703) 463-5812

Activities: Promotes the study of the lute and related instruments; maintains a microfilm lending library of manuscripts and academic publications; organizes annual summer seminars on performance, history, national styles and repertoires, and lute construction. *Publications*: Journal, annual; newsletter, quarterly.

696. **National Flute Association**
c/o Myrna Brown
805 Laguna Drive
Denton, TX 76201
(817) 387-9472

Activities: Promotes music for the flute and flute teaching; sponsors annual competitions; maintains a library of flute music at the University of Arizona; holds an annual convention. *Publication*: *The Flutist Quarterly*, quarterly.

697. **North American Guild of Change Ringers**
c/o Martin Meier
P.O. Box 5760
Woodland Park, CO 80866
(303) 687-6656

Activities: Promotes change ringing (a method of playing tuned bells in sequential patterns) in towers specially designed for change ringing and on hand bells; conducts courses in the technique; arranges tours of towers in England; distributes books and films. *Publication*: *The Clapper*, quarterly.

698. **Organ Historical Society**
P.O. Box 26811
Richmond, VA 23261
(804) 353-9226

Activities: Maintains the Archives of American Organ History at Virginia Commonwealth University; maintains a master list of extant organs built prior to 1900 in the United States; organizes recitals on historic organs throughout North America; holds an annual convention. *Publications*: *The Tracker*, quarterly (see entry 667); *Organ Handbook*, annual.

699. **Percussive Arts Society**
214 West Main Street
Urbana, IL 61801
(217) 367-4098

Activities: Facilitates communication between players of percussion instruments; sponsors annual percussion composition contest and other contests; holds an annual convention. *Publications*: *Percussive Notes*, bimonthly; *Percussion News*, monthly.

700. **Society for the Preservation and Advancement of the Harmonica**
P.O. Box 865
Troy, MI 48099
(313) 647-2706

Activities: Promotes respect for the history of the harmonica and encourages its acceptance as an instrument; holds an annual convention. *Publication*: *Harmonica Happenings*, quarterly.

701. **Tubists Universal Brotherhood Association**
c/o Paul D. Ebbers
School of Music
Florida State University
Tallahassee, FL 32306

Activities: Promotes the development, literature, pedagogy, and performance of instruments in the tuba and euphonium family; maintains a library at Ball State University; holds a national conference. *Publication*: *T.U.B.A. Journal*, quarterly.

702. **Viola da Gamba Society of America**
c/o John A. Whisler
1823-D Valley Road
Champaign, IL 61820

Activities: Supports the performance of music on viols and related early stringed instruments; promotes construction of viols; maintains a collection of viols for rent; distributes music and literature. *Publications*: *VDGSA Newsletter*, quarterly; journal, annual.

703. **Viola d'Amore Society of America**
39-23 47th Street
Sunnyside, NY 11104
(718) 729-3138

Activities: Promotes the teaching and performance of music on the viola d'amore; encourages the construction of new instruments and the composition of new works; holds an annual congress. *Publication*: Newsletter, semiannual.

704. **Violin Society of America**
85-07 Abingdon Road
Kew Gardens, NY 11415
(718) 849-1373

Activities: Encompasses interests in instrument and bow construction, history of instruments, technique, performance practice, repertory, and acoustics; provides financial assistance to aspiring makers; holds a biennial competition for new instruments and bows; holds an annual convention. *Publication*: Journal.

Research Centers and Institutes

705. **American Gamelan Institute**
Box 9911
Oakland, CA 94613

Activities: Serves as a clearinghouse for composers and scholars working in the field of new music for gamelan (Indonesian percussion orchestras) and related ensembles, such as the Philippine kulintang; provides instructional programs for children and adults; distributes scores and tapes; maintains a resident ensemble, B.A.N.G. (Bay Area New Gamelan). *Publication*: *Balungan*, 3/yr.

706. **American Institute of Musicology**
Hänssler-Verlag
Bismarckstrasse 4
Postfach 1220
D-7303 Neuhausen-Stuttgart, West Germany
(07158) 177-0

Activities: Sponsors the publication of music, early writings on music, and modern studies relating to music of the medieval, Renaissance, and Baroque periods. *Publications*: Corpus Mensurabilis Musicae; Corpus Scriptorum de Musica; Renaissance Manuscript Studies; Musicological Studies and Documents; Corpus of Early Keyboard Music; *Musica Disciplina*, annual (see entry 628).

707. **Archive of Folk Culture**
Library of Congress
Washington, DC 20540
(202) 287-5510

Activities: Collects and maintains collections of recordings of traditional music, focusing on the United States but including music throughout the world; provides assistance to researchers in the library and by mail or telephone; produces recordings from its collections for sale; produces findings aids and bibliographies. *Publications*: Reference Aid series; Finding Aid series.

708. **Archives of Traditional Music**
Morrison Hall
Indiana University
Bloomington, IN 47405-2501
(812) 335-8632

Activities: Maintains collection of 350,000 sound recordings of world music, other collections of jazz recordings, the Archives of the Languages of the World, and Hoagy Carmichael memorabilia. *Publication*: *Resound*, quarterly.

709. **Black Music Archives**
Morgan State University
Baltimore, MD 21239

Activities: Develops a name authority file for black musicians; compiles material for the *Bibliography of Black Music* (see entry 334); administers other indexing and cataloging projects; maintains vertical files and book collection in the Soper Library of Morgan State University. *Publication*: *Music Rap*.

710. **Center for Black Music Research**
Columbia College Chicago
600 South Michigan Avenue
Chicago, IL 60605-1996
(312) 663-9463

Activities: Maintains a research library and a computerized union catalog of holdings of materials dealing with black music in the Chicago area; holds conferences and concerts; sponsors the Black Music Repertory Ensemble. *Publications*: *Black Music Research Newsletter*, semiannual; *Black Music Research Journal*, annual (see entry 574).

711. **Center for Computer Assisted Research in the Humanities**
525 Middlefield Road, Suite 120
Menlo Park, CA 94025
(415) 322-7050

Activities: In terms of musicology, it studies the electronic representation of musical notation, the development of text transfer systems, and the formation of large musical databases, in particular the works of J. S. Bach. *Publication*: *Directory of Computer Assisted Research in Musicology* (see entry 162).

712. **Center for Music Experiment and Related Research**
Q-037, University of California, San Diego
La Jolla, CA 92093
(619) 534-4383

Activities: Explores applications of computers to all phases of music; investigates learning environments for music and sound; sponsors colloquia, seminars, and performances of new music. *Publication*: Annual report.

713. **Center for Music of the Americas**
School of Music
Florida State University
Tallahassee, FL 32306-2098
(904) 644-5786

Activities: Supports academic programs, performing ensembles, and research in traditional and contemporary musics of the Americas.

714. **Center for Music Research**
School of Music
Florida State University
Tallahassee, FL 32306-2098
(904) 644-5786

Activities: Offers courses for undergraduates leading to the Computers in Music Certificate; sponsors postdoctoral research in three areas: computers in music, music research, and music therapy. *Publication*: Report series.

715. **Centre for Studies in Nineteenth-Century Music/Centre international de recherche sur la presse musicale**
University of British Columbia
6361 Memorial Road
Vancouver, BC V6T 1W5 Canada

Activities: Cooperates with an associated center in Parma, Italy, in indexing and cataloging writings on music and musical iconography in the nineteenth century as a part of the Répertoire international de la presse musicale du dix-neuvième siècle (RIPMxix). *Publication*: *Periodica Musica*, annual (see entry 647).

716. **Council for Research in Music Education**
School of Music
1114 West Nevada Street
University of Illinois at Urbana-Champaign
Urbana, IL 61801
(217) 333-1027

Activities: Serves as a clearinghouse for information and projects in music education at the collegiate and graduate level. *Publications*: *Bulletin of the Council for Research in Music Education*, quarterly (see entry 577); *International Directory of Dissertations in Progress in Music Education*, annual.

717. **Country Music Foundation**
4 Music Square East
Nashville, TN 37203
(615) 256-1639

Activities: Operates the Country Music Hall of Fame and Museum; maintains library and media center; presents educational programs; records interviews with performers, writers, and business people in the country music industry as part of an oral history project; provides consultation and research services. *Publications*: *Journal of Country Music*, 3/yr.; newsletter.

718. **Foundation for Research in the Afro-American Creative Arts**
P.O. Box I
Cambria Heights, NY 11411

Activities: Supports the publication of a journal. *Publication*: *Black Perspective in Music*, semiannual (see entry 575).

719. **Institute for Studies in American Music**
Conservatory of Music
Brooklyn College/CUNY
Brooklyn, NY 11210
(718) 780-5655

Activities: Encourages research in all types of music in the United States; sponsors research fellowships, concerts, colloquia, and conferences; provides research assistance to inquirers. *Publications*: *I.S.A.M. Newsletter*, semiannual; I.S.A.M. Monograph series; Recent Researches in American Music series.

720. **Institute of Jazz Studies**
Bradley Hall
Rutgers University
Newark, NJ 07102
(201) 648-5595

Activities: Maintains collection of recordings, books, periodicals, clipping files, printed and manuscript music, film, and realia; provides facilities for research; conducts recorded interviews with jazz musicians through the Jazz Oral History project; sponsors concerts, conferences, and seminars; produces a radio program, "Jazz from the Archives." *Publications*: *Annual Review of Jazz Studies*, annual (see entry 568); *IJS Jazz Register*, quarterly (see entry 551).

721. **Moravian Music Foundation**
20 Cascade Avenue
Winston-Salem, NC 27107
(919) 725-0651

Activities: Maintains an archive of music manuscripts and editions of music used in early America, and a library of materials dealing with American music and hymnology; supports the performance of Moravian music; prepares editions of early American music. *Publications*: *Moravian Music Journal*, quarterly; newsletter.

722. **Shrine to Music Museum and Center for Study of the History of Musical Instruments**
USD Box 194
414 East Clark Street
University of South Dakota
Vermillion, SD 57069-2390
(605) 677-5306

Activities: Maintains several collections of musical instruments from all parts of the world; sponsors concerts played on original instruments. *Publications*: *Catalog of the Collections*; newsletter, quarterly.

Service Organizations

723. **American Choral Foundation**
c/o Association of Professional Vocal Ensembles
251 South 18th Street
Philadelphia, PA 19103
(215) 545-4444

Activities: Affiliated with the Association of Professional Vocal Ensembles and the American Choral Directors Association; provides advisory services. *Publications*: *American Choral Review*, quarterly (see entry 561); Research Memoranda series.

724. **American College of Musicians**
808 Rio Grande
P.O. Box 1807
Austin, TX 78767-1807
(512) 478-5775

Activities: Acts as the parent organization of the National Guild of Piano Teachers and the National Fraternity of Student Musicians; sponsors annual noncompetitive, evaluative piano auditions for students; sponsors annual composition and recording competitions and, in part, the International Van Cliburn Piano Competition.

725. **American Composers Alliance**
170 West 74th Street
New York, NY 10023
(212) 362-8900

Activities: As an affiliate of Broadcast Music, Inc., assists composers of concert music with collection of royalties, and with copyrights, contracts, licenses, and other legal activities; publishes facsimile editions of compositions; cooperates with Composers Recordings, Inc. in providing for the recording of contemporary compositions; gives the ACA Recording Awards and the Laurel Leaf Award for distinguished achievement in fostering and encouraging American music; cooperates with the American Composers Orchestra. *Publications*: Facsimile editions of compositions, and catalogs of these editions through American Composers Edition, Inc.

726. **American Institute of Musical Studies**
2701 Fondren Drive
Dallas, TX 75206
(214) 691-6451

Activities: Through the A.I.M.S. Graz Experience (a summer program in Graz, Austria), provides training for young singers and instrumentalists who are planning a professional career. *Publications*: *AIMS Bulletin*, annual; *Towards a Career in Europe*; *The Professional Singer's Guide to New York*.

727. **American Music Center**
250 West 54th Street, Room 300
New York, NY 10019
(212) 247-3121

Activities: Encourages the creation, performance, and recognition of American music; maintains a circulating library of music; acts as liaison between composers and performers, publishers, granting agencies, and radio stations; disseminates information on American music; serves as an advocate for creative artists. *Publications*: *AMC Newsletter*, 5/yr.; *AMC Membership Directory*; catalogs of music.

728. **American Music Scholarship Association**
1826 Carew Tower, Department 00516
Cincinnati, OH 45263
(513) 421-5342

Activities: Conducts minifestivals and evaluations for student pianists, master classes, and an annual international piano competition; prescribes a comprehensive course of study for piano teachers and students. *Publication*: *Teacher's Piano Syllabus*.

729. **American Symphony Orchestra League**
633 E Street, NW
Washington, DC 20004
(202) 628-0099

Activities: Provides management and information services to symphony orchestras of all sizes in North America; sponsors training programs for volunteers, management, and artistic personnel; provides consultants in the areas of labor relations, copyright law, accounting, and taxes; provides computerized information on financial and operational conditions of orchestras; offers the Orchestra Library Information Service which provides data on composers, compositions, editions, and more. *Publication*: *Symphony Magazine*, bimonthly (see entry 665).

730. **Canadian Music Centre/Centre de musique canadienne**
Chalmers House/Maison Chalmers
20 St. Joseph Street
Toronto, ON M4Y 1J9 Canada
(416) 961-6601

Activities: Maintains a library of scores, records, and tapes of works by Canadian composers; sells and loans scores and recordings; provides information on music in Canada; encourages the study and performance of Canadian music. *Publication*: *Acquisitions*, annual.

731. **Center for Renaissance Studies**
317 17th Avenue, SE
Minneapolis, MN 55414
(612) 379-4463

Activities: Supports Concentus Musicus in its performances of medieval and Renaissance music.

732. **Central Opera Service**
Metropolitan Opera
Lincoln Center
New York, NY 10023
(212) 799-3467

Activities: Maintains a library and operatic archive to supply information on performances, translations, and companies to its members; holds an annual conference. *Publications*: *Central Opera Service Bulletin*, quarterly (see entry 580); directories.

733. **Chamber Music America**
545 Eighth Avenue
New York, NY 10018
(212) 244-2772

Activities: Acts as an advocate and coordinates funding for chamber music; sponsors residencies; commissions works; sponsors seminars, conferences, and workshops. *Publications*: *Chamber Music*, quarterly (see entry 581); membership directory, annual; *Directory of Summer Workshops, Schools & Festivals*, biennial.

734. **Concert Artists Guild**
850 Seventh Avenue
New York, NY 10019
(212) 333-5200

Activities: Sponsors an annual international competition and organizes recital debuts in New York and other cities. *Publication*: *Guild Notes*, 3/yr.

735. **Early Music America**
65 West 95th Street
Suite 1A
New York, NY 10025
(212) 662-0600

Activities: Promotes the historically informed performance and recording of early music in the United States and Canada; sponsors the Survey of Early Music in America to provide information on performers, presenters, managers, and instrument makers; plans, by means of a new journal, to provide a forum for research and communication. *Publication*: *EMA News*, irregular.

736. **Fédération internationale des Jeunesses Musicales**
Palais des Beaux-Arts de Bruxelles
10 rue Royale
1000 Brussels, Belgium
32 2 5139774

Activities: Encourages young people to listen to and play music; operates the Jeunesses Musicales World Orchestra, the Groznjan Cultural Centre in Yugoslavia, an international competition in Belgrade, the International Documentation Centre for Musical Animation Techniques in Bydgoszcz, Poland, and other programs throughout Europe. *Publication*: *Forte*, monthly.

737. **Federation of International Music Competitions/Fédération des concours internationaux de musique**
12, rue de l'Hôtel-de-Ville
CH-1204 Geneva, Switzerland
022 21 36 20

Activities: Coordinates the activities of over sixty international music competitions; promotes prizewinners of the competitions. *Publication*: Calendar of competitions.

738. **International Federation for Choral Music**
College of Music CB 301
University of Colorado
Boulder, CO 80309-0301
(303) 492-8314

Activities: Supports choral festivals organized by seven national and international constituent organizations; promotes international exchange programs; encourages the formation of choral organizations; facilitates cooperation between organizations and dissemination of choral repertoire. *Publications*: *International Choral Bulletin*, quarterly; *World Choral Census*.

739. **International Institute for Comparative Music Studies and Documentation/Internationales Institut für vergleichende Musikstudien und Dokumentation**
Winklerstrasse 20
D-1000 Berlin 33 Federal Republic of Germany
30 826 28 53; 30 826 18 89

Activities: Promotes the musical traditions of the world other than Western art music; cooperates in the production of the UNESCO collection of traditional music; assists touring artists in Europe; organizes concerts, lectures, workshops, and an annual Festival of Traditional Music. *Publication*: *The World of Music*, 3/yr. (see entry 668).

740. **International MIDI Association**
11857 Hartsook Street
North Hollywood, CA 91607
(818) 505-8964

Activities: Promotes the Musical Instrument Digital Interface (MIDI); distributes technical information dealing with the production of music by computer; maintains a hotline for technical assistance. *Publications*: Bulletin, 11/yr.; *MIDI 1.0 Detailed Specification Document*.

741. **International Music Centre/Internationales Musikzentrum/Centre international de la musique**
Lothringerstrasse 20
A-1030 Vienna, Austria
222 72 57 95

Activities: Promotes music in television, film, radio, and recordings; organizes screenings, workshops, seminars, and competitions for music in the media; maintains an archive of music productions in media; holds a triennial congress. *Publication*: *IMZ Bulletin*, 10/yr.

742. **International Music Council/Conseil international de la musique**
1, rue Miollis
75732 Paris Cedex 15 France
1 45 68 25 50

Activities: Coordinates the activities of national music committees in sixty-five countries and of twenty international member organizations; advises UNESCO on musical matters; produces the UNESCO collection of recordings of traditional music; sponsors international and regional rostra which promote composers and performers from various regions of the world; cooperates in documentation projects including *RILM Abstracts* (see entry 327); sponsors the "Music in the Life of Man" project (a world history of music); holds a biennial general assembly. *Publication*: Newsletter.

743. **International Society for Music Education**
14 Bedford Square
London WC1B 3JG England
1 6365400

Activities: Promotes music education as an integral part of general education and community life, and as a profession; serves as an advisory body to UNESCO in the field of music education; organizes regular international conferences and seminars. *Publications*: *International Journal of Music Education*, semiannual; *ISME Year Book*, annual.

744. **Jazz Composers Orchestra Association**
500 Broadway
New York, NY 10012
(212) 925-2121

Activities: Produces recordings and distributes them through New Music Distribution Service.

745. **Music Performance Trust Funds**
1501 Broadway
New York, NY 10036
(212) 391-3950

Activities: Provides free performances of instrumental music in the United States and Canada, under agreement with the American Federation of Musicians, and financed by the recording industry.

746. **Musicians National Hot Line Association**
277 East 6100 South
Salt Lake City, UT 84107
(801) 268-2000

Activities: Serves as a national center for employment information for musicians by maintaining a computerized file of individuals and organizations. *Publication*: Newsletter.

747. **National Institute for Music Theater**
John F. Kennedy Center for the Performing Arts
Washington, DC 20566
(202) 965-2800

Activities: Provides internships, grants, and awards dedicated to supporting American opera, musical comedy, and experimental music theater; sponsors colloquia.

748. **National Jazz Service Organization**
1201 Pennsylvania Avenue, NW
Suite 720
Washington, DC 20004
(202) 393-8585

Activities: promotes jazz music; through a technical assistance program, provides consultative assistance to performers and organizations in law, development, planning, public relations, fundraising, and other areas. *Publication*: *The American Jazz Music Audience* (with the National Endowment for the Arts).

749. **National Music Council**
45 West 34th Street, Suite 1010
New York, NY 10001
(212) 265-8132

Activities: Serves as U.S. representative to the International Music Council; represents and provides services to over fifty national music organizations; initiated the Composers in the Schools project; participated in the development of the U.S. State Department's Cultural Exchange Program; sponsors the National Black Music Colloquium and Competition; presents the American Eagle Award for distinguished service to American music; holds an annual music leadership meeting. *Publication*: Newsletter.

750. **Opera America**
633 E Street, NW
Washington, DC 20004
(202) 347-9262

Activities: Promotes the performance of opera and serves opera companies in North, Central, and South America; compiles statistics on finances and performances of member companies; assists managers and staff of opera companies in planning and programming through seminars and an annual conference; supports opera education. *Publications*: *Profile*, annual; *Intercompany Announcements*, monthly; *Scenery, Costumes and Musical Materials Directory*, biennial.

751. **Young Concert Artists**
250 West 57th Street
New York, NY 10019
(212) 307-6655

Activities: Promotes the careers of young performers; holds annual international auditions; provides management services and bookings throughout the United States; holds concert series in New York and Washington, D.C.; sponsors residencies.

Trade and Business Associations

752. **American Music Conference**
c/o PRB/Needham Porter Novelli
303 East Wacker Drive
12th Floor
Chicago, IL 60601
(312) 856-8888

Activities: Represents the music industry in promoting participation in musical activities by amateurs. *Publication*: *Music USA*, annual.

753. **American Society of Composers, Authors, and Publishers**
One Lincoln Plaza
New York, NY 10023
(212) 595-3050

Activities: Licenses and collects fees from broadcasters, orchestras, and establishments, giving them performance rights for members' musical compositions; pays royalties to members; offers awards, grants, and scholarships. *Publications*: *ASCAP in Action*, irregular; *ASCAP Biographical Dictionary* (see entry 78); *ASCAP Symphonic Catalog*; *ASCAP Index of Performed Compositions*.

754. **Black Music Association**
1500 Locust Street, Suite 1905
Philadelphia, PA 19102
(215) 545-8600

Activities: Represents and promotes performers and corporations in the black music industry; through the BMA Foundation, provides educational and scholastic opportunities. *Publication*: *innerVisions*, bimonthly.

755. **Broadcast Music, Inc.**
320 West 57th Street
New York, NY 10019
(212) 586-2000

Activities: Licenses broadcast and live performance rights for musical compositions; collects fees; pays royalties to composers and publishers; cooperates with foreign licensing societies. *Publications*: *The Many Worlds of Music*; *BMI Symphonic Catalog*.

756. **Country Music Association**
P.O. Box 22299
Seven Music Circle North
Nashville, TN 37202
(615) 244-2840

Activities: Represents the country music industry as a trade organization; supplies information to members on country music broadcasting and recording personnel and on marketing techniques; presents the annual CMA Award and other awards; conducts annual elections for inductees into the Country Music Hall of Fame; organizes promotional activities. *Publication*: *CLOSE UP Magazine*, monthly.

757. **Jazz World Society**
P.O. Box 777, Times Square Station
New York, NY 10108
(201) 939-0836

Activities: Facilitates marketing and promotion by maintaining computerized lists of jazz musicians, promoters, broadcasters, journalists, and others, and by making these available. *Publications*: *Jazz World*, bimonthly; *Jazz Festivals International Directory*; *European Jazz Directory*.

758. **Music Distributors Association**
135 West 29th Street
New York, NY 10001
(212) 564-0251

Activities: Represents and acts as an advocate for wholesalers, manufacturers, and importers of musical merchandise.

759. **Music Industry Conference**
1902 Association Drive
Reston, VA 22091
(703) 860-4000

Activities: Serves as an auxiliary of the Music Educators National Conference; maintains contact between professional and commercial interests in the field of music education; holds an annual meeting. *Publication*: *Music Industry Conference Guide for Music Educators*.

760. **National Association of Music Merchants**
5140 Avenida Encinas
Carlsbad, CA 92008
(619) 438-8001

Activities: As a trade association, represents and provides business and insurance services to retailers of musical instruments; holds the annual NAMM International Music and Sound Expo; supports Friends and Music, U.S.A., which encourages involvement in music by young people. *Publications*: *Music Retailer News*; *Business Barometer.*

761. **National Council of Music Importers and Exporters**
135 West 29th Street
New York, NY 10001
(212) 564-0251

Activities: Promotes international trade interests of members and provides information to members on governmental activities and industry statistics; holds an annual meeting. *Publication*: Newsletter, 10/yr.

762. **National Music Publishers Association**
205 East 42nd Street
New York, NY 10017
(212) 370-5330

Activities: Represents the legal interests, especially in terms of copyright law, of music publishers in the United States; supports the Harry Fox Agency, which represents music publishers in connection with licensing rights to mechanical reproduction of copyrighted music. *Publication*: *NMPA Bulletin*, quarterly.

763. **New Music Distribution Service**
500 Broadway
New York, NY 10012
(212) 925-2121

Activities: Distributes records from small and independent record companies; provides promotional records to the press and to radio stations. *Publication*: Catalog.

764. **Recording Industry Association of America**
1020 19th Street, NW
Suite 200
Washington, DC 20036
(202) 775-0101

Activities: Promotes the business and legislative interests of the recording industry; investigates record and tape piracy and counterfeiting; certifies gold and plantinum awards for sales of recordings. *Publication*: *Inside RIAA*, quarterly.

765. **SESAC Inc.**
10 Columbus Circle
New York, NY 10019
(212) 586-3450

Activities: Issues licenses for performing rights to organizations and broadcasters; collects fees; distributes royalties to copyright holders.

Membership Societies and Associations

766. **Amateur Chamber Music Players**
545 Eighth Avenue
New York, NY 10018
(212) 244-2778

Activities: Encourages and facilitates the playing of chamber music by amateurs by listing members and the instruments they play in geographical directories. *Publications*: *North and Central American Directory*, biennial; *Overseas Directory*, biennial; *List of Recommended Chamber Music for Strings, Winds, and Keyboard*, irregular; newsletter, annual.

767. **American Association for Music Therapy**
66 Morris Avenue
Springfield, NJ 07081
(201) 379-1100

Activities: Approves music therapy degree programs at the bachelor's and master's levels; certifies clinicians; provides job referrals; promotes research and public awareness. *Publications*: *Music Therapy*, annual; *International Newsletter of Music Therapy*, annual; *Tuning In: The Newsletter of the AAMT*, quarterly; *AAMT Membership Directory*, annual.

768. **American Bandmasters Association**
2019 Bradford Drive
Arlington, TX 76010
(817) 261-8629

Activities: Promotes and recognizes outstanding achievement in concert band music; encourages composition for the concert band; supports a research center at University of Maryland, College Park. *Publication*: *Journal of Band Research*, semiannual (see entry 609).

769. **American Choral Directors Association**
P.O. Box 6310
Lawton, OK 73506
(405) 355-8161

Activities: Represents members from schools, colleges and universities, community and industrial organizations, churches, and professional groups; promotes performance, composition, publications, and research in choral music; sponsors festivals, clinics, workshops, and conventions on state, division, and national levels. *Publication*: *The Choral Journal*, 10/yr. (see entry 582).

770. **American Federation of Musicians of the United States and Canada**
Suite 600, Paramount Building
1501 Broadway
New York, NY 10036
(212) 869-1330

Activities: As a union of professional musicians and vocalists in the United States and Canada, negotiates contracts; enforces employer observance of wage scales, working conditions, and fringe benefits; handles collective bargaining in the recording and broadcast industries; enforces ethical standards for booking agents; provides other benefits for members. *Publication*: *International Musician*, monthly.

771. **American Guild of Musical Artists**
1841 Broadway
New York, NY 10023
(212) 265-3687

Activities: As a labor union, represents the interests of performers in opera, ballet, and concert music; negotiates contracts between performers and employers; provides benefits to performers.

772. **American Musicological Society**
201 South 34th Street
Philadelphia, PA 19104-6313
(215) 898-8698

Activities: Promotes research in music; sponsors publication of books and editions of music; awards fellowships to doctoral candidates; holds an annual conference. *Publications*: *Journal of the American Musicological Society*, 3/yr. (see entry 616); newsletter, semiannual; directory, annual; *Doctoral Dissertations in Musicology* (see entry 396).

773. **American Orff-Schulwerk Association**
P.O. Box 391089
Cleveland, OH 44139-1089
(216) 543-5366

Activities: Promotes the musical educational methods of Carl Orff and Gunild Keetman; assists in the development of training programs for Orff-Schulwerk teachers. *Publication*: *The Orff Echo*, quarterly.

774. **American Society for Jewish Music**
155 Fifth Avenue
New York, NY 10010
(212) 533-2601

Activities: Attempts to raise standards of composition and performance of Jewish music; encourages research; sponsors performances and programs; commissions new works. *Publication*: *Musica Judaica*, annual.

775. **American Society of Music Arrangers**
P.O. Box 11
Hollywood, CA 90078
(213) 871-2762

Activities: Represents the interests of arrangers and orchestrators; presents annual Golden Score Award; offers workshops and teaching clinics.

776. **American String Teachers Association**
P.O. Box 2066
Georgia University Station
Athens, GA 30612-0066
(404) 542-2741

Activities: Promotes study, performance, and research on bowed instruments, guitars, and harps; presents String Teacher of the Year and Distinguished Service awards; organizes summer workshops; holds a national convention. *Publications*: *American String Teacher*, quarterly (see entry 567); *The A.S.T.A. Dictionary of Bowing Terms for String Instruments* (see entry 40).

777. **Association for Recorded Sound Collections**
P.O. Box 2086
Fairfax, VA 22031
(703) 684-8244

Activities: Encourages the preservation of historically important recordings; promotes the exchange and dissemination of research and information about sound recordings; holds an annual conference. *Publications*: *Association for Recorded Sound Collections Journal*, 3/yr. (see entry 571); bulletin, annual; newsletter, quarterly; membership directory, biennial.

778. **Association of College, University and Community Arts Administrators**
6225 University Avenue
Madison, WI 53701-1099
(608) 233-7400

Activities: Maintains database of performing arts organizations; sponsors workshops on fundraising, marketing, and planning; provides employment referral service; holds an annual conference. *Publications*: Bulletin; membership directory; *The Professional Performing Arts: Attendance Patterns, Preferences and Motives.*

779. **Association of Concert Bands**
19 Benton Circle
Utica, NY 13501
(315) 732-2737

Activities: Promotes community concert bands; maintains a clearinghouse for information related to concert bands; holds an annual conference. *Publication*: Newsletter.

780. **Association of Independent Conservatories of Music**
11021 East Boulevard
Cleveland, OH 44106
(216) 791-9191

Activities: Explores mutual concerns of the constituent members: the Cleveland Institute of Music, the Juilliard School, Manhattan School of Music, the Mannes College of Music, New England Conservatory of Music, Peabody Conservatory of Music, Philadelphia College of the Performing Arts, and the San Francisco Conservatory of Music.

781. **Association of Professional Vocal Ensembles**
251 South 18th St.
Philadelphia, PA 19103
(215) 545-4444

Activities: Represents choral groups and individuals to government agencies, funding sources, and other performing arts organizations; provides benefits for professional singers; provides information to professional choral companies; holds an annual conference. *Publications*: *Voice*, bimonthly; membership list.

782. **Catgut Acoustical Society**
112 Essex Avenue
Montclair, NJ 07042

Activities: Supports research in musical acoustics and in design and construction of instruments in the violin family; promotes the Violin Octet (a group of violin family instruments in graduated sizes and tunings). *Publication*: *Journal of the Catgut Acoustical Society*, semiannual.

783. **Church Music Association of America**
548 Lafond Avenue
St. Paul, MN 55103
(612) 293-1710

Activities: Fosters the study of music in the history and liturgy of the Roman Catholic church. *Publication*: *Sacred Music*, quarterly (see entry 659).

784. **Clarion Music Society**
2067 Broadway, Suite 49
New York, NY 10023
(212) 769-0650

Activities: Sponsors concerts and promotes the performance of little-known Baroque music in the New York area.

785. **College Band Directors National Association**
c/o Richard L. Floyd
The University of Texas at Austin
P.O. Box 8028
Austin, TX 78713-8028
(512) 471-5883

Activities: Conducts research on the music of concert bands, marching bands, wind ensembles, and jazz bands in the college and university setting; sponsors clinics and workshops; holds regional and national conferences in alternate years. *Publications*: Report, quarterly; journal, semiannual.

786. **College Music Society**
1444 15th Street
Boulder, CO 80302
(303) 449-1611

Activities: Represents music teachers in institutions of higher education in the United States and Canada; supports research and publication in American music; holds an annual conference. *Publications*: *College Music Symposium*, annual (see entry 584); *CMS Newsletter*, 10/yr.; *Directory of Music Faculties in Colleges and Universities*, biennial (see entry 160); Bibliographies in American Music series (see entries 189-200).

787. **Comhaltas Ceoltóirí Éireann**
Belgrave Square
Monkstown, County Dublin, Ireland
01-800295

Activities: Promotes traditional Irish music, song, dance, and language; organizes festivals and classes throughout Ireland and other countries; maintains an archive of Irish music and song. *Publication*: *Treoir*, quarterly.

788. **Confederation internationale de musique electroacoustique/ International Confederation for Electroacoustic Music**
Place André-Malraux
18000 Bourges, France
(48) 20-41-87

Activities: Promotes the production of electroacoustic compositions; sponsors an international competition.

789. **Country Dance and Song Society of America**
505 Eighth Avenue, Suite 2500
New York, NY 10018-6505
(212) 594-8833

Activities: Through affiliated groups in the United States and Canada, offers regular programs of traditional English and American dance and folk music; distributes recordings and books; holds a series of summer music and dance festivals at Pinewoods Camp in Massachusetts; maintains a library of folk music and dance books, recordings, and manuscripts. *Publications*: *News*, bimonthly; *Country Dance and Song*, annual.

790. **Delta Omicron International Music Fraternity**
1352 Redwood Court
Columbus, OH 43229
(614) 888-2640

Activities: As an academic fraternity, supports projects in colleges and universities; provides scholarships to members; provides scholarships and awards for high school music students; endows seats at Lincoln Center and the John F. Kennedy Center; holds a triennial Composition Competition and Conference. *Publication*: *The Wheel of Delta Omicron.*

791. **Gay and Lesbian Association of Choruses**
4016 S.W. 57th Avenue
Portland, OR 97221
(503) 292-6442

Activities: Sponsors choral festivals; exchanges music between choruses; holds an annual conference.

792. **Guild of American Luthiers**
8222 South Park Avenue
Tacoma, WA 98408-9989
(206) 472-7853

Activities: Serves as a clearinghouse for information on the construction of stringed musical instruments; holds an annual convention and exhibition. *Publications*: *American Lutherie*, quarterly; *Data Sheets.*

793. **Hymn Society of America**
Texas Christian University
Fort Worth, TX 76129
(817) 921-7608

Activities: Serves as a clearinghouse for the study of hymns; supports the Dictionary of American Hymnology project at Oberlin College; maintains a library at Texas Christian University; distributes books and cassette tapes; holds an annual conference. *Publications*: *The Hymn*, quarterly (see entry 603); *The Stanza*, semiannual.

794. **International Association for the Study of Popular Music**
c/o John Shepherd
Department of Music
Carleton University
Ottawa, ON K1S 5B6 Canada

Activities: Supports research on popular contemporary music from all parts of the world; through the DOPMUS (Documentation of Literature on Popular Music) project, maintains database of research studies; supports compilation of material for an *Encyclopedia of Popular Music of the World. Publications*: *Review of Popular Music*; *Popular Music Perspectives.*

795. **International Association of Music Libraries, Archives and Documentation Centres**
Music Library, Hornbake 3210
University of Maryland
College Park, MD 20742
(301) 454-6903

Activities: Promotes coordination on an international level between music libraries; investigates problems of bibliographic control. *Publication*: *Fontes Artis Musicae*, quarterly (see entry 595).

796. **International Conference of Symphony and Opera Musicians**
P.O. Box 20013
Seattle, WA 98102
(206) 329-3118

Activities: Represents the economic and professional interests of symphony and opera musicians in the United States. *Publication*: *Senza Sordino*, bimonthly.

797. **International Congress on Women in Music**
P.O. Box 12164
La Crescenta, CA 91214
(818) 248-1249

Activities: Promotes the international exchange of information and creation of music of all kinds by women; maintains a library at California State University, Northridge; sponsors international meetings and regional conferences, concerts, and workshops. *Publications*: Newsletter, quarterly; journal, semiannual.

798. **International Council for Traditional Music**
Department of Music
Columbia University
New York, NY 10027
(212) 678-0332; (212) 280-5439

Activities: Studies and documents folk, popular, classical, and urban music, and dance of all countries through national committees and study groups on historical sources of folk music, analysis and systematization, musical instruments, ethnochoreology, Oceania, music archaeology, and iconography of traditional music; holds international conferences and colloquia. *Publications*: *Yearbook for Traditional Music*, annual (see entry 669); bulletin, semiannual; membership directory; *ICTM Directory of Interests and Projects*.

799. **International Federation of Musicians/Fédération internationale des musiciens/Internationale Musiker-Föderation**
Hofackerstrasse 7
8032 Zurich, Switzerland
01-55 66 11

Activities: Coordinates the activities of member organizations throughout the world; protects the rights of musicians in recording, broadcast, or public performance; advocates better working conditions for musicians. *Publication*: *FIM Bulletin*, 3/yr.

800. **International League of Women Composers**
c/o Elizabeth Hayden Pizer
P.O. Box 42
Three Mile Bay, NY 13693
(315) 649-5086

Activities: Sponsors concerts and radio programs of members' compositions; sponsors an annual composition contest. *Publications*: Newsletter, 3/yr.; *Contemporary Concert Music by Women: A Directory of the Composers and Their Works* (see entry 491).

801. **International Musicological Society/Internationale Gesellschaft für Musikwissenschaft/Société internationale de musicologie**
P.O.B. 1561
CH-4001 Basel, Switzerland

Activities: Provides a vehicle for international cooperation in musicological research; holds an international congress every five years, and occasional international symposia. *Publications*: *Acta Musicologica*, semiannual (see entry 560); *Communiqué*, irregular; cooperates in publishing *RILM Abstracts* (see entry 327).

802. **International Society for Contemporary Music/Internationale Gesellschaft für neue Musik/Société internationale pour la musique contemporaine**
Postfach 3
A-1015 Vienna, Austria
43 222 658695

Activities: Promotes contemporary music through the activities of national sections and through annual festivals (World Music Days). *Publications*: Bulletin; newsletter.

803. **League of Composers – International Society for Contemporary Music**
c/o American Music Center
250 West 54th Street, Room 300
New York, NY 10019
(212) 362-5481

Activities: Represents the United States to the International Society for Contemporary Music.

804. **Mu Phi Epsilon**
833 Laurel Avenue
Highland Park, IL 60035
(312) 940-1222

Activities: As an academic fraternity, offers membership to music minors and majors, graduate students and faculty members; offers scholarships, fellowships, grants, and awards. *Publication*: *The Triangle*, quarterly.

805. **Music Critics Association**
6201 Tuckerman Lane
Rockville, MD 20852
(301) 530-9527

Activities: Establishes and promotes standards for music criticism in the American press; maintains liaison with other musical organizations; through MCA Musical Activities, Inc., organizes institutes and workshops; holds an annual meeting. *Publication*: Newsletter, 3/yr.

806. **Music Educators National Conference**
1902 Association Drive
Reston, VA 22091
(703) 860-4000

Activities: Promotes music education at the school, college, and university level; provides financial, travel, and medical benefits for members; sponsors awards, a hall of fame, and the Tri-M Music Honor Society. *Publications*: *Music Educators Journal*, monthly except June, July, August (see entry 624); *Journal of Research in Music Education*, quarterly (see entry 614); *Soundpost*, quarterly.

807. **Music Library Association**
P.O. Box 487
Canton, MA 02021
(617) 828-8450

Activities: Provides a medium for communication between music librarians, and for discussion and research on music library practices; presents annual publication awards; provides a placement service; holds an annual conference. *Publications*: *Notes*, quarterly (see entry 639); *MLA Newsletter*, quarterly; *Music Cataloging Bulletin*, monthly; MLA Index and Bibliography series (see entries 257-80); *MLA Technical Reports*.

808. **Music Teachers National Association**
2113 Carew Tower
Cincinnati, OH 45202-2982
(513) 421-1420

Activities: Represents faculty members and private music teachers; provides teacher certification; holds auditions and composition contests for students. *Publication*: *American Music Teacher*, 6/yr. (see entry 563).

809. **National Academy of Songwriters**
6381 Hollywood Boulevard, Suite 780
Hollywood, CA 90028
(213) 463-7178; (800) 826-7287

Activities: Provides information to songwriters on business, legal, and creative affairs; maintains a library and a bookstore offering materials on songwriting; provides assistance in obtaining publicity; offers workshop and critique services. *Publication*: *SongScene*, bimonthly.

810. **National Association for Music Therapy**
505 11th Street, SE
Washington, DC 20003-2831
(202) 543-6864

Activities: Accredits programs for music therapy in colleges and universities; sets criteria and provides registration for professional music therapists; holds an annual conference. *Publications*: *Journal of Music Therapy*, quarterly (see entry 612); *Music Therapy Index* (see entry 325).

811. **National Association of College Wind and Percussion Instructors**
Fine Arts Division
Northeast Missouri State University
Kirksville, MO 63501-0828
(816) 785-4442

Activities: As an associated organization of the Music Educators National Conference, promotes music for wind and percussion instruments; sponsors composition contests and catalogs of music; maintains a library at the University of Maryland, College Park; holds an annual meeting. *Publication*: Journal, quarterly.

812. **National Association of Composers, USA**
P.O. Box 49652, Barrington Station
Los Angeles, CA 90049

Activities: Produces concerts of music by members; sponsors national contests for young performers and composers; maintains a library of scores and documents at California State University, Dominguez Hills. *Publication*: Newsletter, 3/yr.

813. **National Association of Jazz Educators**
P.O. Box 724
Manhattan, KS 66502
(913) 776-8744

Activities: As an organization associated with the Music Educators National Conference, supports jazz education at all age levels; provides scholarships and awards; provides job placement assistance. *Publications*: *Jazz Educators Journal*, quarterly; newsletter, semiannual.

814. **National Association of Professional Band Instrument Repair Technicians**
P.O. Box 51
Normal, IL 61761
(309) 452-4257

Activities: Provides standards of qualifications for instrument repairers; provides for the exchange of technical information between members; sponsors technical clinics as part of a continuing education program. *Publication*: *Techni-Com*, bimonthly.

815. **National Association of Schools of Music**
11250 Roger Bacon Drive, No. 5
Reston, VA 22090
(703) 437-0700

Activities: Operates under the approval of the Council on Postsecondary Education and the U.S. Department of Education to accredit educational programs in music at conservatories, colleges, universities, and music schools; establishes curricular standards and guidelines; holds an annual meeting. *Publications*: Handbook, biennial; directory, annual; *Proceedings of the Annual Meeting*, annual.

816. **National Association of Teachers of Singing**
2800 University Boulevard, North
J.U. Station
Jacksonville, FL 32211

Activities: Promotes educational and ethical standards for teachers of singing and students at all levels; sponsors Artist Awards; organizes regional and chapter meetings and summer workshops. *Publication*: *The NATS Journal*, bimonthly except July/August (see entry 635).

817. **National Band Association**
P.O. Box 121292
Nashville, TN 37212
(615) 329-2620

Activities: Represents band directors as an organization associated with the Music Educators National Conference; sponsors the National High School Honors Band and the National High School Honors Jazz Band; presents awards in marching, composition, and other areas. *Publications*: *The Instrumentalist*, monthly (see entry 605); *NBA Journal*, quarterly; *NBA Directory*, biennial.

818. **National Catholic Bandmasters Association**
Box 1023
Notre Dame, IN 46556
(219) 239-7136

Activities: Represents bandmasters, woodwind, brass, and percussion instructors, and others in Catholic grammar schools, high schools, and colleges; maintains a liturgical music library at the University of Notre Dame; supports the NCBA National Honors Concert and Jazz Bands, and the National Tape Festival; holds a national conference. *Publication*: Newsletter.

819. **National Federation of Music Clubs**
1336 North Delaware Street
Indianapolis, IN 46202
(317) 638-4003

Activities: Coordinates and provides awards and scholarships to students. *Publications*: *Music Clubs Magazine*, quarterly; *Junior Keynotes*, quarterly.

820. **National Fraternity of Student Musicians**
P.O. Box 1807
808 Rio Grande
Austin, TX 78767-1807
(512) 478-5775

Activities: As a division of the American College of Musicians, represents students who participate in piano playing auditions sponsored by the National Guild of Piano Teachers.

821. **National Guild of Piano Teachers**
P.O. Box 1807
808 Rio Grande
Austin, TX 78767-1807
(512) 478-5775

Activities: As a division of the American College of Musicians, establishes goals and awards for piano students; administers the annual national piano playing auditions. *Publication*: *Piano Guild Notes*, bimonthly.

822. **National Opera Association**
c/o Mary Elaine Wallace
Route 2, Box 93
Commerce, TX 75428
(214) 886-3830

Activities: Promotes the performance and composition of operas; sponsors annual voice auditions, a biennial new opera competition, and an opera production contest; maintains a score and tape library at the American Music Center; holds an annual convention. *Publications*: *Opera Journal*; newsletter; membership directory.

823. **National School Orchestra Association**
345 Maxwell Drive
Pittsburgh, PA 15236
(412) 882-6696

Activities: Promotes participation in and performance of school orchestras as an associate of the Music Educators National Conference; sponsors a job listing of available positions in orchestras; sponsors an orchestra composition contest and an orchestra award. *Publication*: *NSOA Bulletin*, quarterly.

824. **National Traditional Country Music Association**
106 Navaho
Council Bluffs, IA 51501
(712) 366-1136

Activities: Sponsors seminars and conventions dealing with acoustic traditional music; sponsors the annual Old-Time Country Music Festival in Avoca, Iowa; produces "The Living Tradition" television show and "Country Roots Today" radio show. *Publication*: *Tradition*, quarterly.

825. **North American Brass Band Association**
Campus Box 7311
Music Department
North Carolina State University
Raleigh, NC 27695
(813) 949-1022

Activities: Promotes the establishment of British-type brass bands (as opposed to marching bands and concert bands) in the United States and Canada; sponsors contests and workshops; maintains archives at North Carolina State University. *Publications*: *The Brass Band Bridge*; *The Care and Feeding of a Community British Brass Band.*

826. **Organization of American Kodály Educators**
Department of Music
University of Wisconsin-Whitewater
Whitewater, WI 53190
(414) 472-1341

Activities: Promotes the philosophy and methodology of music education of Zoltán Kodály through the use of rhythmic and tonal syllables, movement, and singing; provides publications and videotapes on the Kodály method; provides grants and loans for projects and study. *Publications*: *Kodály Envoy*, quarterly; membership directory, triennial.

827. **Phi Mu Alpha Sinfonia Fraternity**
10600 Old State Road
Evansville, IN 47711-1399
(812) 867-2433

Activities: As an academic fraternity, operates through local chapters on college campuses; sponsors new works and local musical performances. *Publications*: *The Sinfonian*, quarterly; *The Red & Black*, irregular.

828. **Pi Kappa Lambda National Music Honor Society**
School of Music
Northwestern University
Evanston, IL 60201
(312) 491-5737; (312) 251-9182

Activities: Awards academic achievement through elected membership. *Publication*: Newsletter, annual.

829. **Piano Technicians Guild**
9140 Ward Parkway
Kansas City, MO 64114
(816) 444-3500

Activities: Represents the interests of piano tuners and technicians; administers examinations to members who wish to be certified as registered technicians. *Publication*: *The Piano Technicians Journal*, monthly.

830. **Presbyterian Association of Musicians**
1000 East Morehead Street
Charlotte, NC 28204
(704) 333-9071

Activities: Provides advice and training for church musicians through consultation services and regional conferences; sets guidelines for hiring church musicians; provides job referral service; certifies Presbyterian church musicians. *Publications*: *Reformed Liturgy and Music*, quarterly; newsletter, quarterly.

831. **Sigma Alpha Iota International Music Fraternity for Women**
c/o Dorothy Whinery
4119 Rollins Avenue
Des Moines, IA 50312
(515) 255-3079

Activities: Provides transcription of music for the blind and partially sighted; supports a residence at the MacDowell Colony; supports projects in specific needy communities worldwide; provides awards and scholarships. *Publication*: *Pan Pipes*, quarterly.

832. **Society for Asian Music**
Hagop Kevorkian Center
50 Washington Square South
New York, NY 10012
(212) 666-0420

Activities: Promotes discussion between scholars on Asian music; sponsors monthly concerts at the Metropolitan Museum of Art. *Publication*: *Asian Music*, semiannual (see entry 570).

833. **Society for Ethnomusicology**
P.O. Box 2984
Ann Arbor, MI 48106
(313) 665-9400

Activities: Facilitates the discussion between scholars on the problems and results of research in ethnomusicology. *Publications*: *Ethnomusicology*, 3/yr. (see entry 593); *SEM Newsletter*.

834. **Society for General Music**
1902 Association Drive
Reston, VA 22901
(703) 860-4000

Activities: Acts as a special interest group within the Music Educators National Conference for those interested in general music education. *Publications*: *Soundings*, quarterly; *Exchange*, monthly.

835. **Society for Music Teacher Education**
1902 Association Drive
Reston, VA 22901
(703) 860-4000

Activities: Acts as a special interest group within the Music Educators National Conference for those interested in music teacher education.

836. **Society for the Preservation and Encouragement of Barber Shop Quartet Singing in America**
6315 3rd Avenue
Kenosha, WI 53140-5199
(414) 654-9111

Activities: Promotes singing in barber shop quartet style (four parts in close harmony) by men in the United States and Canada; supports the Institute of Logopedics in Wichita,

Kansas, in its work with speech handicaps; holds an annual convention and contest. *Publication*: *The Harmonizer*, bimonthly.

837. **Sonneck Society**
c/o Kate Keller
410 Fox Chapel Lane
Radnor, PA 19087
(215) 688-6989

Activities: Promotes research and education in music in American life; holds an annual meeting. *Publications*: *American Music*, quarterly (see entry 562); newsletter, 3/yr.; membership directory, annual.

838. **Suzuki Association of the Americas**
P.O. Box 354
212 Cedar Street
Muscatine, IA 52761
(319) 263-3071

Activities: Promotes the educational methods of Shin'ichi Suzuki through the teaching of violin, cello, flute, and piano. *Publication*: *American Suzuki Journal*, bimonthly.

839. **Sweet Adelines**
P.O. Box 470168
Tulsa, OK 74147
(918) 622-1444

Activities: Promotes the performance of four-part barber shop quartet vocal music by women from the United States, Canada, and other countries; provides educational programs in singing for members; holds an annual convention. *Publications*: *The Pitch Pipe*, quarterly; *Thirty Years of Harmony: Sweet Adelines, Inc., 1947-1977.*

840. **Tau Beta Sigma National Honorary Band Sorority/Kappa Kappa Psi National Honorary Band Fraternity**
122 Seretean Center
Oklahoma State University
Stillwater, OK 74078
(405) 372-2333

Activities: Sponsors the National Intercollegiate Bands Program; commissions works for band; presents the Outstanding Service to Music Award. *Publication*: *The Podium*, semiannual.

841. **Women Band Directors National Association**
344 Overlook Drive
West Lafayette, IN 47906
(317) 463-1738

Activities: Encourages and supports women band directors and their students; presents awards to members and to students; holds an annual meeting. *Publication*: *The Woman Conductor*, quarterly.

Author/Title Index

This index lists titles of works given full annotations, titles of organizations listed in chapter 21, and authors, editors, translators, compilers, series, and corporate bodies associated with the publication of the works included. Numbers cited in the index are entry numbers. The index also lists works and authors cited within annotations; these are signalled by the letter "n" following the entry number.

Subject Index

The index covers entries for all reference works, periodicals, and organizations given annotations in the guide. Numbers cited in the index are entry numbers.